OXFORD WORLD'S CLASSICS

THE GOSPELS

THE GOSPELS of Matthew, Mark, Luke, and John are regarded by Christians the world over as their most precious and sacred writings. They provide the fullest and most memorable accounts of the life and teachings of Jesus Christ, one of the most influential figures in human history. Each portrays from its own distinctive viewpoint the turbulent ministry of Jesus in Galilee and Judea, as he goes about healing the sick, performing miracles, and teaching by means of parables, and they describe in unforgettable detail the events leading up to his trial by the Roman authorities and his crucifixion outside Jerusalem. These extraordinary narratives have provided subject matter for innumerable works of art, literature, and music in Western culture. Their authorship has traditionally been ascribed to people who had known Jesus or were prominent in the early Church. Matthew and John were among the twelve disciples; Mark was an associate of the Apostle Peter; and Luke was a Greek convert who accompanied the Apostle Paul on his missionary journeys. Scholars now doubt whether these were the actual authors, but in the absence of conclusive evidence, their names continue to be attached to these famous works. This Oxford World's Classics edition presents the Gospels in the English translation known as the Authorized Version, or King James Bible, first published in 1611. It was in this form and in these words that English readers for over three centuries read and heard the Gospels. No book has shaped more profoundly the culture, religious thought, and literature of the English-speaking world.

W. R. OWENS is Professor of English Literature at The Open University. His publications include two volumes in the Clarendon Press edition of *The Miscellaneous Works of John Bunyan* (1994), and an edition of *The Pilgrim's Progress* in the Oxford World's Classics series (2003). He is co-author, with P. N. Furbank, of *The Canonisation of Daniel Defoe* (1988), *Defoe De-Attributions* (1994), *A Critical Bibliography of Daniel Defoe* (1998), and *A Political Biography of Daniel Defoe* (2006), and they are joint General Editors of *The Works of Daniel Defoe* (44 volumes, 2000–9).

OXFORD WORLD'S CLASSICS

*For over 100 years Oxford World's Classics have brought
readers closer to the world's great literature. Now with over 700
titles—from the 4,000-year-old myths of Mesopotamia to the
twentieth century's greatest novels—the series makes available
lesser-known as well as celebrated writing.*

*The pocket-sized hardbacks of the early years contained
introductions by Virginia Woolf, T. S. Eliot, Graham Greene,
and other literary figures which enriched the experience of reading.
Today the series is recognized for its fine scholarship and
reliability in texts that span world literature, drama and poetry,
religion, philosophy, and politics. Each edition includes perceptive
commentary and essential background information to meet the
changing needs of readers.*

OXFORD WORLD'S CLASSICS

The Gospels
Authorized King James Version

Edited with an Introduction and Notes by
W. R. OWENS

OXFORD
UNIVERSITY PRESS

OXFORD
UNIVERSITY PRESS

Great Clarendon Street, Oxford OX2 6DP
Oxford University Press is a department of the University of Oxford.
It furthers the University's objective of excellence in research, scholarship,
and education by publishing worldwide in

Oxford New York

Auckland Cape Town Dar es Salaam Hong Kong Karachi
Kuala Lumpur Madrid Melbourne Mexico City Nairobi
New Delhi Shanghai Taipei Toronto

With offices in

Argentina Austria Brazil Chile Czech Republic France Greece
Guatemala Hungary Italy Japan Poland Portugal Singapore
South Korea Switzerland Thailand Turkey Ukraine Vietnam

Oxford is a registered trade mark of Oxford University Press
in the UK and in certain other countries

Published in the United States
by Oxford University Press Inc., New York

First published as an Oxford World's Classics paperback 2011

British Library Cataloguing in Publication Data

Data available

Library of Congress Cataloging in Publication Data

Data available

Typeset by Glyph International, Bangalore, India
Printed in Great Britain
on acid-free paper by
Clays Ltd, St Ives plc

ISBN 978-0-19-954117-1

1 3 5 7 9 10 8 6 4 2

ACKNOWLEDGEMENTS

THE idea for this book came from Judith Luna, Commissioning Editor for Oxford World's Classics. She has been a fount of encouragement, advice, and guidance throughout its preparation and it has been a pleasure to work again with her.

Others have helped in many different ways. I thank my colleagues at The Open University in London—Jamal Hadaway, Maurice Hindle, Sophie Oxenham, Alice Whieldon, and Naoko Yamagata—whose kindness enabled me to spend more time on this project. Naoko provided expert help with queries about New Testament Greek. I am grateful to Ian Spackman for assistance with the preparation of the electronic text, and to Robert Fraser for sending me a copy of his as yet unpublished article on the Gospels and the biographer's art. A number of people commented helpfully on drafts of my editorial material. I thank particularly my sister, Shirley Herron, and also Caroline Broome, Christopher Chessun, Philip Davison, Cortland Fransella, Nick Furbank, and Peter McGeary. These friends should not be assumed to have agreed with everything I say here; shortcomings and errors are entirely my responsibility.

Most of all, I wish to acknowledge my debt to two very special women. My mother read a chapter of the Bible to me every morning before I went to school, and has never wavered in her faith, or in her love for me. I'm proud to be her son. My wife, Patti, lives out every day her commitment to the Jesus of the Gospels. Only she and I know how much I owe her for her help and encouragement. My part in this book is dedicated to her, with much love.

W. R. Owens

The Open University

CONTENTS

INTRODUCTION

JESUS CHRIST is the central figure in Western culture and must be counted as among the most important and influential figures in all human history. His birth has been taken as the supreme dividing moment of history, signified by the use of 'BC' for dates 'before Christ', and 'AD' ('anno Domini', 'in the year of our Lord') for dates after Christ.[1] He gave his name to a religion which, from humble origins in first-century Palestine, has grown over the centuries to become a global phenomenon. Something like 2 billion people now describe themselves as 'Christians'—one in three of the population of the world—and the majority of these are no longer in Europe, once the centre of Christianity, but are in Latin America (over 500 million), Africa (nearly 400 million), Asia (over 300 million), and North America (over 200 million).[2]

Yet Jesus is by no means the possession only of Christians. He is revered by members of many other religious faiths, and by people who do not profess any religion. Mahatma Gandhi drew much of his inspiration from Jesus. His first reading of the Sermon on the Mount, he said, 'went straight to my heart', and he saw similarities between the teachings of Jesus and those of Krishna in the *Bhagavad Gita*.[3] Many Jews have admired the historical Jesus, among them Albert Einstein, who was 'enthralled by the luminous figure of the Nazarene'. 'No one can read the Gospels without feeling the actual presence of Jesus,' Einstein said, 'his personality pulsates in every word.'[4] The Qur'an devotes considerable space to discussion of the life and work of Jesus, and, though Muslims do not accept his divinity, they regard him as a prophet of God and 'a sign for all people'.[5]

Most of our knowledge of Jesus comes from the narratives of his life known as the Gospels of Matthew, Mark, Luke, and John.

---

[1] Even though 'BC' and 'AD' are now generally replaced by the more neutral 'BCE' ('before the common era') and 'CE' ('common era'), the effect remains the same: the birth of Jesus Christ is the point of division.

[2] Philip Jenkins, *The Next Christendom: The Coming of Global Christianity* (rev. edn., Oxford and New York, 2007), 2.

[3] Louis Fischer, *The Life of Mahatma Gandhi* (London, 1997), 53.

[4] Max Jammer, *Einstein and Religion: Physics and Theology* (Princeton, 1999), 22.

[5] See *The Qur'an*, trans. M. A. S. Abdel Haleem (Oxford, 2005), 21:91 (p. 207).

Written in Greek, in the second half of the first century, these form the first four books of the New Testament in the Christian Bible, and are regarded by Christians as their most precious and sacred writings. Readings from them have a central place in the Communion service (also known as the Eucharist, or Mass) in which Christians commemorate the Last Supper of Jesus and his disciples before his crucifixion. For over a thousand years in the Western Catholic Church the Gospels were heard and read in a single language, that of the renowned Latin translation of the Bible made by St Jerome in the late fourth century (the 'Vulgate'). Manuscript copies of the Latin Gospels, some of them beautifully illustrated, were produced by scribes in monasteries, usually for the use of rich patrons. In the sixteenth century, however, under the impetus of the Renaissance and the Protestant Reformation, the Bible began to be translated afresh from the original languages of Hebrew and Greek into the vernacular languages of Europe, and copies became available to ordinary readers by means of the new technology of printing by movable type.

The text of the Gospels presented here is the one included in the English translation of the Bible popularly known as the Authorized Version (AV) or the King James Bible, first published in 1611. Representing the culmination of almost a century of translation activity that had begun with William Tyndale (?1494–1536), the AV gradually became established as *the* Bible in English, a position it would hold unchallenged for nearly 300 years. Its preparation— between 1604 and 1611—coincided with the production of some of Shakespeare's greatest plays, and, as with Shakespeare, many of its phrases and expressions have become part of everyday English.

So unshakably established in anglophone culture did the AV become that it was not until late in the nineteenth century that the first revision was undertaken. The 'Revised Version', as it was known, was published in 1881 (New Testament) and 1885 (Old and New Testaments). Since that time there have been many other translations of the Bible into English, some the work of individuals, others the work of teams of scholars. These have been able to incorporate significant advances in knowledge about the manuscripts on which the text of the Bible is based, and their translations are presented in a contemporary English idiom. Nevertheless, there are two overwhelming reasons for choosing to reproduce the 1611 AV text for this Oxford World's Classics edition of the Gospels. The first is aesthetic: the splendour and music and rhythms of the AV, experienced particularly when read aloud, make it one of the most beautiful and memorable works of prose in English. The second is the simple historical fact that it was in this form and in these words that English readers for three centuries read, and even more heard, the Gospels. No other book has shaped in such profound ways the culture, religious thought, and literature of the English-speaking world.

The Gospels in the First Century

The Gospels are generally agreed by scholars to have been written in the second half of the first century. The earliest was almost certainly Mark, which is usually dated to the years around 70 CE. Matthew and Luke are usually dated to around 80–90, and John is usually dated to somewhere around 95–110 CE. This means that they were not contemporaneous with the events they describe, but were composed between forty and eighty years after the crucifixion of Jesus, which took place, probably, in 30 CE. They were written in Greek (not in the language Jesus spoke, which was Aramaic, a Semitic language closely related to Hebrew, the language of the Jewish scriptures), and they were addressed to mainly Gentile Christians in urban centres like Antioch, Alexandria, Ephesus, and Rome, a readership very different from the first Jewish followers of Jesus in rural Galilee. It is important also to note that they were not the earliest Christian writings: the Apostle Paul's letters were written about 50–60 CE, well before the first Gospel, and it is clear from them that Paul knew details of Jesus's life and teachings, including the words he uttered at the Last Supper.[6]

The word 'gospel' (derived from the Old English word godspel, meaning 'good tidings') is the English translation of the Greek word evangelion (Latin evangelium), meaning 'good news', and hence the authors of the Gospels came to be known as 'the Evangelists'. The titular authors, Matthew, Mark, Luke, and John, were real people—Matthew and John were disciples of Jesus; Mark was a close associate of the Apostle Peter; and Luke was a Gentile, a Greek who accompanied Paul on some of his missionary journeys[7]—but for a variety of reasons it seems unlikely that they were the actual

---

[6] See 1 Thess. 4:14–17 and 1 Cor. 11:23–5.
[7] For more information, see the Glossary of Persons, below, pp. 265–72.

authors. The first known reference to their names in this connection is from the later part of the second century, about the year 180 CE; before that date quotations from the Gospels made no reference to authors.[8] The Gospels that subsequently came to bear these names were not the only accounts of Jesus in circulation, and it seems to have been the custom for works describing themselves as 'gospels' to be attributed to well-known figures. A good deal is now known about these other gospels, following the discovery in 1945 near the town of Nag Hammadi in Egypt of a collection of some forty ancient texts, translations into Coptic of Greek originals some of which may date back to the second century CE, with titles such as the Gospel of Thomas, the Gospel of Philip, the Gospel of Mary, and the Gospel of Judas.[9] Despite their titles, these are not narratives of the life and ministry of Jesus, but are discourses or meditations on his message. Some may include authentic material—in particular the Gospel of Thomas, a collection of sayings of Jesus—but the Church authorities eventually decided at the Council of Nicaea in 325 CE that only the Gospels of Matthew, Mark, Luke, and John should be regarded as 'canonical'—that is, accepted as sacred texts and admitted into the Christian scriptures which became known as the New Testament. As part of the process of canonization, it would have been important that these Gospels were attached to authors who were closely connected to Jesus, or who had status within the early Church.[10]

Although written by different people, at different times, and with different purposes in mind, the four Gospels have much in common. They may indeed be regarded as four accounts of a single gospel. All of them focus exclusively on the person of Jesus, and although only two include birth stories, they each present a roughly chronological narrative account of the final years of his life, including his public ministry in Galilee, the events leading up to his trial and execution in Jerusalem, and his resurrection and reappearance to his followers.

It soon becomes apparent to readers, however, that Matthew, Mark, and Luke have much more in common with each other than they do with John. Not only do they tell many of the same stories about Jesus, they often use identical wording. Ever since the eighteenth century they

---

[8] See E. P. Sanders, *The Historical Figure of Jesus* (London, 1993), 63–4.

[9] See *The Nag Hammadi Scriptures*, ed. Marvin Meyer (New York, 2007).

[10] Although the real names of the authors of the Gospels are unknown, I follow the customary practice of referring to them as Matthew, Mark, Luke, and John.

have been known as 'the Synoptic Gospels' because the material they share can be set out in three parallel columns and 'viewed together' (the literal meaning of 'synopsis'). A great deal of scholarly endeavour has been devoted to the 'synoptic problem': how to account for the similarities and the differences between Matthew, Mark, and Luke. The most widely accepted explanation is known as the 'four-source hypothesis'. According to this, when Matthew and Luke came to be written, about ten or fifteen years after Mark, they each used Mark as a source—so much so that about 90 per cent of the 661 verses in Mark also appear in Matthew, and about 50 per cent also appear in Luke. However, they are both longer than Mark, and share material that is not found in Mark (some 230 verses, including the Lord's Prayer and the Beatitudes). To explain this, it is suggested that they made use of another source, known as 'Q' (from the German word for source, *Quelle*), which is thought to have been a compilation of sayings of Jesus (though no one can be sure, because no copy of Q, if it ever existed, has come to light). Finally, there are stories about Jesus that only appear in Matthew, and some that only appear in Luke, and this is explained by their having had access to sources available only to themselves, known as 'M' and 'L'. The 'four sources' are thus Mark, Q, M, and L.[11]

When we turn to the Gospel of John, it is clear that it stands somewhat apart and that there are significant differences between it and the Synoptic Gospels. In all three Synoptic Gospels the public ministry of Jesus lasts for about a year or eighteen months at most. After his baptism by John the Baptist, he is tempted by the devil in the wilderness, goes about Galilee proclaiming the coming of the kingdom of God, performs miracles of healing and exorcism, teaches by means of parables, and is transfigured on a mountain top. Finally, he makes his way to Jerusalem, where he shares a Passover meal with his disciples. The same night he goes to the Garden of Gethsemane, where he is arrested and brought before the Jewish high court, the Sanhedrin, and is then delivered to the Roman authorities, who sentence him to be put to death by crucifixion outside the city walls.

In John, by contrast, the ministry of Jesus takes place over a period of about three years, since he mentions three Passovers and several journeys to Jerusalem. The Jesus of John is not tempted in the wilderness; he does not proclaim the kingdom of God; he performs

[11] See further Bart D. Ehrman, *The New Testament: A Historical Introduction to the Early Christian Writings* (4th edn., New York and Oxford, 2008), 92–9.

no exorcisms; he does not teach in parables; there is no mention of a transfiguration; the final meal he shares with his disciples is not a Passover meal (it takes place on the previous evening); he is not brought before the Sanhedrin. Some of the miracles in John are found in none of the other Gospels: the turning of water into wine at Cana, for example, or—most impressive of all—the raising of Lazarus from the dead, and they are presented not for their own sake, but as 'signs' that prove the supernatural 'otherness' of Jesus and manifest his glory. Finally, many of the words of Jesus recorded in John occur only in this Gospel, and take the form not of pithy aphorisms or parables, as in the Synoptic Gospels, but of lengthy metaphorical discourses. To explain these unique features, many scholars argue that John made use of sources (written or oral) not available to the earlier writers. More importantly, it seems clear that the author of John is imposing a highly developed Christian theology on to his material, with later Christian ideas being presented as if said in these very words by Jesus. John is interested less in recounting events in the life of Jesus than in explaining how that life is to be understood in theological terms.

It is important to remember that the Gospels did not get written down until a generation or so after the death of Jesus. By this time what scholars call the early 'Jesus Movement' within Judaism had begun to develop into a distinctive 'Christian' church, with missionaries like Paul spreading the new religion of faith in Jesus Christ as the Son of God among Jews and Gentiles, and establishing congregations in major cities across the Mediterranean world. The words of Jesus were preserved among these early Christian communities mainly as oral traditions. Stories about him would have been told and retold and remembered in oral and communal fashion for many years before they began to be written down in the form of 'gospels'.[12]

This brings us to the question of genre, to the *kind* of literary works the Gospels are. It seems obvious enough that they are, in some sense, biographical narratives. Equally obviously, they are very different from modern biographies. They leave out a great deal of the basic 'factual' information we would expect (telling us virtually nothing of Jesus between his early childhood and his early thirties, for example), and there is little exploration of psychological motivation and development of character. However, if the Gospels are not modern biographies, they do resemble ancient 'lives' of individuals of the

[12] See James D. G. Dunn, *A New Perspective on Jesus* (London, 2005).

kind written by classical authors such as Plutarch, Suetonius, and Tacitus.[13] As with the Gospels, these were often based mainly on oral sources, and took a highly selective approach to their subjects, one which concentrated on revealing character by reporting words and actions rather than by reflection and analysis. In the often-quoted preface to his life of Alexander the Great, Plutarch explained that he had omitted many facts about the achievements of Alexander, because he was 'not writing history but biography'. In the way that painters concentrate on the face to reveal the character of a subject, he says, so the biographer concentrates on 'those aspects which indicate a person's mind', leaving historians to recount details of 'their major exploits and battles'.[14] Similarly, in writing their 'lives' of Jesus the Evangelists select and shape their material so as to persuade their readers that it was through the person of Jesus that God was revealed to humanity.

It is unlikely that the authors of the Gospels would have regarded themselves as writing 'scripture', texts that would become part of a new 'Bible'. For the early followers of Jesus, as for Jesus himself, the 'Bible' was the Hebrew scriptures. This is not surprising, because the early Christians were almost all ethnic Jews, and for quite a long time the main converts to the new religion continued to be Jews. However, from about the middle of the first century onwards believers in Jesus began to produce their own writings. By the middle of the second century some of these, in particular the letters of the Apostle Paul, were being cited as scripture (see 2 Peter 3:15–16), and according to Justin Martyr, writing in about 155 CE, portions of 'the memoirs of the apostles [i.e. the Gospels]' as well as 'the writings of the prophets [i.e. the Hebrew scriptures]' were being read at meetings of Christians (as the followers of Jesus were now called).[15] There was as yet no fixed 'canon' of Christian writings, partly because there was as yet no single, normative form of Christianity. By the end of the second century, however, agreement on a list of authoritative texts was beginning to emerge, with the four Gospels and thirteen letters ascribed to Paul having already been accepted as canonical works.

---

[13] See Richard A. Burridge, *What Are the Gospels? A Comparison with Graeco-Roman Biography* (2nd edn., Grand Rapids, Mich., 2004).

[14] *Plutarch: Greek Lives*, trans. Robin Waterfield, intro. Philip A. Stadter (Oxford, 1998), 312.

[15] Justin Martyr, *First Apology* (c.155), quoted in Christopher Bryan, *A Preface to Mark* (Oxford, 1993), 57.

By the middle of the fourth century the process of deciding upon a Christian canon had been concluded. The first known list including all twenty-seven books making up what would become known as the 'New Testament' appears in a letter written in 367 CE by Athanasius, bishop of Alexandria, and the same twenty-seven books were approved as scripture at the Synod of Hippo in 393 CE.[16]

The Christian Bible was not restricted to the 'New Testament', however, but incorporated within it the Hebrew Bible. Known to Jews as the *Tanakh*, the Hebrew Bible is composed of three parts: *Torah* ('Law'), the five books from Genesis to Deuteronomy, traditionally ascribed to Moses; *Nevi'im* ('Prophets'), eight books including the prophecies of Isaiah, Jeremiah, and Ezekiel, the 'minor' prophets (twelve books counted as one), and historical narratives from Joshua through to 2 Kings; and *Kethuvim* ('Writings'), a collection of eleven books including psalms, proverbs, and apocalyptic writings.[17] In the Christian Bible the same collection of twenty-four books is referred to as the 'Old Testament', but rearranged into four groupings: the books of the Law (Genesis to Deuteronomy), historical books (Joshua to Esther), wisdom and poetical books (Job to Song of Solomon), and prophetic books (Isaiah to Malachi). The word 'testament' means 'covenant'. In speaking of 'Old' and 'New' testaments Christians were declaring their belief that the special covenant (or compact) that God had with Israel, by which he would protect them as his special people, and which was confirmed by the giving of the Torah (Law) to Moses on Mount Sinai (Exodus 19–20), had been replaced by a new covenant between God (in the person of Jesus) and the Christian Church. Christians regarded this as having been foretold by Jeremiah, who had prophesied that God would make a 'new covenant' with his people: 'I will forgive their iniquity, and I will remember their sin no more' (31:31–4). So, in the Gospels, Jesus speaks of the 'new testament [or covenant]', to be sealed by his own blood which had been 'shed for many for the remission of sins'—words which would become a central feature of the Christian liturgy.[18]

The Gospel writers therefore assume that their readers will be familiar with the Old Testament scriptures, and regard these as

[16] See F. F. Bruce, *The Books and the Parchments* (rev. edn., London, 1991), 103.

[17] See Marc Zvi Brettler, *How to Read the Jewish Bible* (Oxford and New York, 2007), 9–11.

[18] See Matt. 26:28; Mark 14:24; Luke 22:20; and cf. 1 Cor. 11:23–6.

essential to an understanding of the claims about Jesus made by Christians. According to the Gospel accounts, the promises of a redeemer, or Messiah, in the Old Testament had come to pass in the life and death of Jesus Christ. Reading in the synagogue a passage from Isaiah—'The Spirit of the Lord is upon me, because he hath anointed me to preach the gospel to the poor', etc.—Jesus appropriates these words to himself, telling his hearers, 'This day is this scripture fulfilled in your ears' (Luke 4:18–21). The Gospel writers are continually pointing out how events in the life of Jesus may be understood as 'fulfilling' the Old Testament, as we can see when we turn to the opening words of the Gospel chosen from the earliest times to be placed first among the four, Matthew.

The Gospel According to Matthew

Matthew opens with a genealogy of 'Jesus Christ, the son of David, the son of Abraham'. The name 'Jesus' (derived from the Greek form, 'Iesous', of the Hebrew 'Joshua' or *Yeshua*) means 'God is salvation' (v. 21). 'Christ' is the English form of the Greek noun *christos*, meaning 'anointed one', which is the equivalent of the Hebrew noun *mashiach*, rendered in English as 'Messiah', also meaning 'anointed one'. 'Christ' and 'Messiah' are thus identical in meaning, and when the Hebrew Bible was translated into Greek in the second century BCE, in the famous translation known as the Septuagint, the word *mashiach* was rendered in Greek as *christos*. Strictly speaking, therefore, 'Christ' is a title, not a name, and 'Jesus Christ' here should be understood as 'Jesus the Christ/Messiah'. Shortly after the death of Jesus, however, his followers came to use 'Christ' as a part of his name and even to refer to him simply as Christ (see, for example, 1 Thessalonians 1:1 and Galatians 1:6), so much so that their enemies began to call them 'Christians' (see Acts 11:26, 26:28; and 1 Peter 4:16).

The term 'Messiah' was an important one for Jews, though it was understood by them in different ways. Originally, in the Hebrew Bible, it was used of the king of Israel, who was known as 'the Lord's anointed'.[19] Later, however, after the Jewish monarchy was overthrown by the Babylonians in 587 BCE, it came to refer to a future deliverer of Israel. There were several schools of thought within Judaism as to what this future Messiah would be like. Some held that he would be

[19] See e.g. 1 Sam. 10:1; 2 Sam. 23:1; Isa. 45:1.

a warrior-king, a 'Son of God' who would re-establish an independent Jewish state. For others, the Messiah would be a priestly figure, through whose power the proper worship of Israel's God would be established. Yet others believed that he would be a supernatural being, known as the 'Son of Man', who would descend from the heavens to defeat the powers of evil and rule the whole earth.[20]

The point of the genealogy with which Matthew opens is to stress the credentials of Jesus as the Messiah. His lineage is traced back through David (*c.*1000 BCE), the greatest king of Israel, to the patriarch Abraham (*c.*1500 BCE), the father of the Jewish people, in this way suggesting that the history of the Jews has culminated in the birth of Jesus. The Jewishness of Jesus will in fact be a key theme in Matthew, and the focus of this Gospel will be on his relationship with Judaism. So, for example, the birth narrative here—an event-packed and suspenseful one—is designed to demonstrate that Jesus was a child of destiny, whose birth had been foretold in a whole series of Old Testament prophecies. No fewer than five are cited in the first two chapters (1:22–3, 2:5–6, 15, 17–18, 23), and there are others throughout Matthew, often introduced by the formula, 'that it might be fulfilled which was spoken by the prophet'. Jesus is born of a virgin (1:22–3) because this is what had been predicted of the Messiah by Isaiah (7:14).[21] Similarly, he is born in Bethlehem (2:5–6), and not in Nazareth where Mary and Joseph lived, because Bethlehem was the birthplace of King David, and according to the prophet Micah (5:2), the Messiah would come out of Bethlehem.

As well as these 'predictions', Matthew constantly presents events in the life of Jesus as having been 'foreshadowed' by events in the Jewish scriptures. An example of this is the threat to the life of the infant Jesus by King Herod's 'Massacre of the Innocents' (2:16). This is designed to bring to mind the story in Exodus (1:16, 22) of how Pharaoh threatened the life of the infant Moses. Indeed, Matthew frequently draws parallels between Jesus and Moses, the great deliverer of the Israelites and the one who brought them the Torah, or the 'Law' as this Hebrew word is usually translated (though it is perhaps

[20] See *The Cambridge Companion to the Bible*, gen. ed. Bruce Chilton (2nd edn., Cambridge, 2008), 517–18.

[21] The Hebrew word *'almah* in Isaiah means simply 'young woman', but in the Greek translation (the Septuagint) followed by Matthew, the word is *parthenos*, meaning 'virgin'.

better understood as 'teaching' or 'instruction'). Jesus, in Matthew's Gospel, is the new Moses. He does not replace, but rather 'fulfils' the old Moses, and is the true interpreter of the 'old' Law. The followers of Jesus, according to Matthew, are not to cast aside the Law, but are to understand it in a different way, one taught to them by Jesus. 'Think not that I am come to destroy the Law,' he says, 'I am not come to destroy, but to fulfil' (5:17).

It is even possible that Matthew has structured his Gospel in a way meant to recall the five books of Moses, because it is dominated by five lengthy discourses of Jesus. These are: the Sermon on the Mount (chapters 5–7); the commissioning of the twelve disciples (chapter 10); a collection of parables of the kingdom (chapter 13); instructions for the disciples (chapter 18); and teachings about the end of time (chapters 24–5). The connection with Moses is an important key to understanding the Sermon on the Mount. Just as Moses ascended Mount Sinai to receive the Law—God's guidance to the people of Israel—and to give instruction to God's people (Exodus 19:3), so Jesus ascends a mountain to deliver his Sermon, offering a new way of understanding the old Law.

The Sermon on the Mount is the most famous and influential of all the moral teachings of Jesus (a version of it is included also in Luke 6:20–49). He opens by pronouncing a list of 'blessings', known as the 'Beatitudes', on the 'poor in spirit', those who 'mourn', the 'meek', those who 'hunger and thirst after righteousness', the 'merciful', the 'pure in heart', those who are 'peacemakers', those who endure persecution 'for righteousness' sake'. To give a positive moral dynamic to such qualities is a startlingly new approach to ethics, and indeed is altogether revolutionary. By contrast with Roman civilization, which glorified power and military strength, the 'kingdom of heaven'—God's rule or reign on earth—will be characterized, Jesus says, by a dramatic reversal of the existing social order, one in which the poor, the weak, and the persecuted will be exalted, and in which the rich and powerful will be brought low.

The Beatitudes are followed by a set of ethical demands which are much higher than those of the Mosaic Law, as Jesus emphasizes by setting them out as antitheses. The Law says do not commit murder; Jesus says you should not even be angry without good cause (5:21–2). The Law says do not commit adultery; Jesus says you should not even harbour lustful thoughts (27–8). The Law says you may divorce your wife; Jesus says that if you do so you make her an adulterer (31–2). The Law says you should keep oaths; Jesus says you should not swear oaths at all (33–7). The Law says take an eye for an eye, a tooth for a tooth (meaning seek justice, but not excessive or disproportionate retribution); Jesus says you should not seek any retribution for a wrong done to you, but if you are struck on one cheek, turn the other to be struck as well (38–9). Finally, the Law says love your neighbour; Jesus says that you should also love your enemies (43–4). The requirement to 'turn the other cheek' and practise non-resistance to evil is perhaps the best-known and most radical of all the teachings of Jesus, and he himself lives out his own doctrine when his enemies come to put him to death and he does not resist them.

In his mission as preacher and healer Jesus frequently finds himself opposed by Jewish religious leaders. Judaism at this time was a ferment of many different sects and religious groupings.[22] Two of the most important of these, frequently mentioned in the Gospels, were the Pharisees and the Sadducees. Although often spoken of together, they held differing views and were hostile to each other. The key difference concerned their beliefs about the Torah (or Law). Pharisees believed in a twofold Torah: the written Torah (as set out in the Pentateuch, or five books of Moses: Genesis, Exodus, Leviticus, Numbers, and Deuteronomy) and the oral Torah, or 'Tradition of the Elders', which comprised teachings about ethics, religious ritual, and sexual morality, as well as interpretations of the written Torah. These oral traditions were promulgated by highly esteemed scholars known as 'scribes', who devoted themselves to study and interpretation of the Torah.[23] The Pharisees were notable for the rigour with which they expected the Law, as interpreted by the scribes, to be applied in everyday living. Jesus differed from them in this (see 15:1–20), but he shared their belief in the resurrection of the body and in rewards and punishments in the next life, and their expectation

---

[22] A good deal is known about this diverse religious culture following the chance discovery in 1947 of the Dead Sea Scrolls, texts dating from the first century BCE which set out the beliefs and rules of an ascetic group, not directly mentioned in the Gospels, known as the Essenes. See *The Complete Dead Sea Scrolls in English*, ed. and trans. Geza Vermes (rev. edn., London, 2004).

[23] The oral Torah was eventually written down around the year 200 CE, and later formed part of a lengthy collection of texts known as the Talmud, completed in the fifth century CE. See *The Talmud: A Selection*, trans. and ed. Norman Solomon (London, 2009).

of a new age when God would establish his reign on earth and justice would be done.

The Sadducees were a group of powerful priests from aristocratic families dwelling in and around the Temple at Jerusalem (their name is thought to have derived from Zadok, a priest in the time of David and Solomon). Unlike the Pharisees, they adhered strictly to the written Torah, rejecting the authority of the oral Torah, and were concerned mainly with the proper observance of Temple ritual. They also differed with the Pharisees over bodily resurrection (rejecting this because it was not mentioned in the Torah, but was a later development within Judaism). Information about the Pharisees and Sadducees is provided by the first-century Jewish historian Flavius Josephus (37–100 CE). According to the account in his *Jewish Antiquities* (93–4 CE), the Sadducees persuaded 'none but the rich', while the Pharisees had 'the multitude on their side'.[24]

It is a striking, and apparently paradoxical, feature of Matthew's Gospel that while on the one hand the Jewishness of Jesus and his role in 'fulfilling' the Hebrew scriptures is emphasized, on the other hand he is portrayed as in fierce conflict with the Jewish religious leaders of his time. In the Sermon on the Mount he refers to the scribes and Pharisees as hypocrites (5:20), who ostentatiously give alms, and make a great show of praying in public (6:1–5). Later he has disputes with them about Sabbath observance (12:1–14), and about the laws on divorce (19:3–9). These disputes become ever more ferocious in chapters 21 to 23, following the episode in the Temple where Jesus overturns the tables of traders and money-changers (21:12–16). Their opposition to him becomes intense, and he responds with a series of parables whose point is that God will visit his wrath on them. Finally, in chapter 23, Jesus pronounces seven 'woes' on them, condemning them in quite vitriolic terms for their hypocrisy and their concern with the minutiae of religious observance.

This excoriation of the Pharisees leads into an apocalyptic discourse where Jesus foretells a time of trouble that will precede the return of the 'Son of Man' to earth at the end of time.[25] A similar discourse is included in Mark (chapter 13), in which Jesus prophesies

[24] See Josephus, *Jewish Antiquities*, trans. William Whiston, ed. Brian McGing (London, 2006), 13:293–8, 18:12–17.

[25] On the significance of the term 'Son of Man', see Explanatory Note to Matt. 8:20, below, p. 211.

the destruction of the Temple (which in fact happened in 70 CE, when the Romans crushed a Jewish revolt), and describes a period of intense persecution that will end only with the appearance of the 'Son of Man' in the clouds. In Mark's account Jesus says that no one knows when that day will come, except God (13:32), but according to the account in Matthew this great final day of judgement will take place within a generation or so (24:34), and in that day the wicked will be sent to 'everlasting punishment' but the righteous will be granted 'life eternal' (25:46).

Matthew's Gospel then moves towards its climax, the account of the crucifixion. In Matthew's presentation of this the emphasis falls heavily on the guilt of the Jewish leaders who demand the death of Jesus. Jesus is brought before Caiaphas, the High Priest, who condemns Jesus as a blasphemer for claiming to be the Messiah, the Son of God (26:63–5) and sends him to appear before the Roman prefect, Pontius Pilate. According to Matthew, however, Pilate is reluctant to allow Jesus to be crucified—and, moreover, is warned against doing so by his wife (27:19)—but when he sees that 'he could prevail nothing' he washes his hands and declares that he is 'innocent of the blood of this just person' (27:24). Although Jesus is sentenced and executed by the Romans, who alone had the authority to carry out capital punishment, the blame is shifted to the Jews who repeatedly call for Jesus to be crucified. Matthew specifically holds the religious leaders of the Jews primarily responsible for turning the 'multitude' against Jesus (see 27:20). Nevertheless, the cry 'His blood be on us, and on our children', ascribed to 'all the people' (27:25), is a chilling one, and the idea that 'Christ was killed by the Jews', based on verses such as this one, contributed much to the development and persistence of Christian anti-Semitism over the succeeding centuries.[26]

At the end of Matthew the paradox of this most Jewish of the Gospels which is also the most critical of the Jews is resolved. Having earlier portrayed Jesus as concerned only with his own people—'I am not sent, but unto the lost sheep of the house of Israel' (15:24)—and as sending his disciples only to the Jews—'go rather to the lost sheep of the house of Israel' (10:6)—Matthew now accepts that the Messiah

---

[26] See also John 8:44 and 1 Thess. 2:14–16 for similarly hostile comments about 'the Jews', reflecting, in part, the increasingly bitter conflict between Jewish Christians and the wider Jewish community as Christianity gradually separated itself from Judaism.

has been rejected by his own people, and that followers of Jesus will have to separate themselves from their Jewish origins and look to the wider Gentile world for converts. After the resurrection his followers go to meet Jesus on a mountain in Galilee, where he gives them the 'Great Commission': 'Go ye therefore, and teach all nations, baptizing them in the name of the Father, and of the Son, and of the Holy Ghost' (28:19). It is not so much an ending as a programme for the establishment of a new Church.

The Gospel According to Mark

Unlike Matthew, the author of Mark—almost certainly the earliest of the Gospels to be written—does not include any account of the birth or origins of the person he is going to write about. His Gospel opens with a straightforward declaration: 'The beginning of the gospel of Jesus Christ, the Son of God'. By 'Christ', as we have seen, Mark means 'Messiah', and according to an ancient prophecy in the Jewish scriptures, the Messiah would be preceded by a forerunner who would preach in the wilderness (Isaiah 40:3). This had come to pass in the ministry of John the Baptist, whose baptism of Jesus in the waters of the Jordan had been accompanied by a voice from heaven confirming that Jesus was the 'beloved Son' of God (1:11). However, as Mark and his readers knew very well, Jesus had not turned out to be a Messiah in any of the expected forms. He had not been a warrior-king, or a powerful priestly figure, or a cosmic deliverer from heaven. Instead, he had been arrested, tried by the Roman authorities for treason against the state, and executed. In human terms, his life and ministry could be thought to have been an utter failure. One of the key purposes of Mark's Gospel was to explain why, nevertheless, Jesus was indeed the promised Messiah, one who had come to deliver his people not by military power or warfare, but by suffering and dying as a sacrifice for their sins in accordance with the will of God. Indeed, it might be said that this is a central concern in all four Gospels. As John puts it, his reason for writing is 'that ye might believe that Jesus is the Christ, the Son of God' (John 20:31).

Having established in the minds of his readers that Jesus was the Messiah/Christ, Mark turns without further preamble to an account of his activities in Galilee, following the imprisonment of John the Baptist. It is a dramatic story, full of vivid, telling detail and vigorously presented in a succession of short episodes moving swiftly from one to another (a favourite word is 'straightway'). More frequently than in the other Synoptic Gospels, Mark presents a Jesus who experiences intense human emotions: compassion (1:41); anger and grief (3:5); astonishment (6:6); displeasure (10:14); great sorrow (14:34). We see him calling his disciples, casting out evil spirits, healing people, and going about proclaiming the coming of the kingdom (or rule) of God. He comes across as a figure of great authority, one who commands obedience, who can forgive sins, and to whom people listen with respect. His message is a challenging one, and it brings him into conflict with religious authorities who regard him as violating Jewish laws and tradition by, for example, working on the Sabbath, or not observing rules governing ritual purification.[27] Many people whom Jesus heals and chooses to associate with are on the margins of society, and would have been regarded as ritually 'unclean'. According to Jesus, however, the essence of true 'purity' is not outward observance of ritual laws, but is an inward moral condition (7:1–23). His fame spreads far and wide, and he attracts great crowds, teaching them by means of parables, stories based on everyday events, like a farmer sowing seed (4:3–8) or managing a vineyard (12:1–9).

By contrast with Matthew and Luke, however, where the teaching of Jesus is given great prominence, the emphasis in the early part of Mark is more on Jesus as a miracle-worker, healer and exorcist. It is clear that contemporaries attached great significance to his miracles, and indeed, in one of the earliest recorded Christian sermons, Jesus is described as 'a man approved of God among you by miracles and wonders and signs' (Acts 2:22). It is important to understand, however, that miracle-working and healing abilities would not in themselves at this time have been regarded as evidence of superhuman status. It was generally accepted that miracles could and did take place (many miracles are reported in the Hebrew Bible), and there are other examples of miracle-workers among Jews and non-Jews. A famous example from the Greek world is Apollonius of Tyana, who was reported to have been able to heal and to expel demons.[28]

---

[27] Jewish purity laws focused on food (various animals being listed as not permitted for consumption), and on ritual washing before and after certain activities or following contact with diseases such as leprosy, or with corpses, etc. It is important to note that the terms 'clean' and 'unclean', used in the AV to translate the Hebrew words for 'pure' and 'impure', refer to *ritual* 'cleanliness' and have nothing to do with dirt or hygiene.

[28] See Sanders, *The Historical Figure of Jesus*, 137–8.

We know, too, of Jewish miracle-workers in the periods just before and just after Jesus. In the middle of the first century BCE 'Honi the Circle-drawer' was able to bring rain by praying to God (standing within a circle, hence his name). In the period just after Jesus, a Galilean, Hanina ben Dosa, was known for remarkable healings, including bringing a dying boy back to life, and for miracles such as turning vinegar into oil.[29] The contemporaries of Jesus in rural Galilee would have regarded him as a charismatic holy man, an itinerant prophet figure like John the Baptist, and would not have found it surprising that he could work miracles, exorcize demons, and heal the sick. As we learn from Mark, his reputation attracted throngs of people, something that would eventually arouse alarm among the authorities. (According to Josephus, John the Baptist was executed because it was feared that he might lead an uprising against Roman rule.[30])

Despite his fame as a miracle-worker, a motif of 'secrecy' about the status and destiny of Jesus runs throughout Mark. People who are healed are told not to speak about it (1:44, 5:43, 7:36, 8:26); demons who know who Jesus really is are silenced by him (1:34, 3:12); even the disciples are sworn to secrecy (8:29–30, 9:30). People speculate endlessly about his identity: was he John the Baptist come back from the dead, or was he Elijah, or one of the other prophets returned to earth (6:14–16)? No one seems to recognize that Jesus is the promised Messiah, not even his own disciples. When they witness him calming a storm at sea, they ask themselves, 'What manner of man is this, that even the wind and the sea obey him?' (4:41), and to the exasperation of Jesus, they cannot understand the significance of miracles such as the Feeding of the Five Thousand (8:17–21). At the climax of the Gospel, when he is brought before the High Priest and asked straight out, 'Art thou the Christ [i.e. the Messiah], the Son of the Blessed?' Jesus gives an unequivocal response: 'I am' (14:61–2). Even here, however, his 'secret' is not really revealed, because the High Priest and those present do not believe him.

One of the most striking features of Mark is its frequent criticism of the disciples. At every turn they seem to lack understanding, even though on several occasions Jesus takes them aside to give them special instruction (see 7:17–23, 10:10–12). They try to prevent people

[29] See Geza Vermes, *The Changing Faces of Jesus* (London, 2000), 236–46.
[30] See Josephus, *Jewish Antiquities*, 18:116–19.

bringing their children to be blessed by Jesus, evoking from him one of his most memorable rebukes: 'Suffer the little children to come unto me, and forbid them not: for of such is the kingdom of God' (10:14). Peter, the leader among the disciples, and the one who finally recognizes that Jesus is the Messiah (8:29), when Jesus had been taken for questioning by the High Priest shamefully denies knowing him, and weeps when he remembers how Jesus had predicted he would deny him three times before the cock had crowed twice (14:67–72). All this is to say that Mark presents the disciples as thoroughly human in their weaknesses and proneness to error. What they have to learn, and by extension what Mark wants his readers to learn, is that following Jesus is not easy. They must learn humility (9:35, 10:42–5), and must be willing to suffer, and even to lose their lives (8:34–5).

Everything in Mark leads inexorably to the crucifixion of Jesus and his ultimate vindication in his resurrection. From about the middle of the Gospel Jesus begins to speak explicitly of his approaching death (8:31, 9:31, 10:33). The narrative hastens towards this, and in some ways, in its starkness Mark's is the most harrowing account of the four. After giving his answer to the High Priest Jesus says virtually nothing until, hanging from the cross, in his moment of greatest agony, he cries out, 'with a loud voice', words from Psalm 22: 'My God, my God, why hast thou forsaken me?' (15:34). It is not till after his death that the 'secret' of Jesus is finally revealed, by the Roman centurion who declares: 'Truly this man was the Son of God' (15:39).

There are many puzzles in Mark's Gospel. Some of them are references to otherwise unknown people, such as the mysterious young man who runs away naked at the arrest of Jesus (14:51–2), or the reference to Simon of Cyrene as 'the father of Alexander and Rufus' (15:21); others, apparently, are caused by faults of style, especially his occasional misplacing of clauses.[31] But the greatest puzzle comes right at the end. In the most reliable early manuscripts the text ends at chapter 16, verse 8, with the women fleeing from the empty tomb: 'they trembled, and were amazed, neither said they any thing to any man, for they were afraid.' Scholars are generally agreed that the verses which follow, from 9 to 20, were added later, by scribes who presumably felt that it was not proper for a Gospel to end so abruptly,

---

[31] See Craig A. Evans, 'How Mark Writes', in *The Written Gospel*, ed. Markus Bockmuehl and Donald A. Hagner (Cambridge, 2005), 135–48. See also Explanatory Notes to Mark 11:13–14 and 16:4, below, pp. 241, 243.

and on such an enigmatic note. (In modern translations these verses are omitted, or placed within square brackets or in an appendix.) The question whether Mark really intended his Gospel to finish at verse 8, or whether, as some have conjectured, the final pages of the manuscript may have been lost, has been debated at length. Whatever the truth may be, it seems somehow appropriate that this earliest Gospel, with its stress on human frailty and weakness, should end on a note of awe and astonishment.

The Gospel According to Luke

From its opening words, it is clear that Luke's Gospel is going to be very different in style and approach from the Gospels of Mark and Matthew. By contrast with Mark's abrupt, no-frills statement of his subject, and Matthew's plunge into a detailed genealogy, Luke opens with an elegant, formally structured sentence, written in his own voice to a named individual, Theophilus, explaining that he, Luke, as someone who is aware of earlier attempts to tell the story, and of the testimony of eyewitnesses, is going to provide Theophilus with an orderly account of 'those things, wherein thou hast been instructed'.[32] This measured, unhurried approach will be characteristic of Luke. His manner is less urgent than Mark's, and less stern than Matthew's. He will place more stress than they do on the humanity of Jesus, emphasizing his concern for the poor and socially marginalized, and the importance of women among his followers. The keynote will be the universal nature of the salvation brought to humankind by Jesus. First offered to the Jews, it is now open to all who will receive it.

These characteristics of Luke are prominent in the famous opening chapters which start, in fact, not with the birth of Jesus, but with the birth of John the Baptist to an aged and hitherto childless couple, Zacharias, a priest in the Temple at Jerusalem, and his wife Elizabeth. The angel Gabriel appears to Zacharias while he is carrying out his priestly duties to tell him that Elizabeth will conceive and bear a son whose destiny it will be to 'make ready a people prepared for the Lord' (1:17). Six months later the same angel appears to a

---

[32] Luke's Gospel was the first of two volumes by the same author, the second being the Acts of the Apostles. This provides the earliest historical account of how the Christian Church spread from its beginnings in Jerusalem across the Roman empire. Acts is included as the fifth book in the New Testament.

virgin named Mary, from Nazareth in Galilee, with the news that she will give birth to a son to be called Jesus, who 'shall be great, and shall be called the Son of the Highest' (1:32). Mary's hymn of joy and gratitude, known as the 'Magnificat', is an exultant celebration of the power of God, who brings down the mighty and lifts up the poor (1:46–55). Like Matthew, Luke has Jesus being born in Bethlehem,[33] but in other respects their accounts of the birth of Jesus could hardly be more different. In Matthew, it might be said, we get the story from Joseph's point of view (it is to Joseph, not Mary, that the angel comes), whereas Luke presents the story from Mary's point of view and with her at the centre. There is nothing in Matthew about where exactly Jesus is born, but from Luke we learn that his mother laid him 'in a manger, because there was no room for them in the inn' (2:7). Matthew features wise men and kings, but Luke features women, pious people, and shepherds. In Matthew, Jesus will 'save his people' (1:21); in Luke, the birth of Jesus heralds 'tidings of great joy . . . to all people' (2:10).

As in Matthew, the whole context of the birth and early life of Jesus is Jewish. He is circumcised after eight days, as was the custom for all Jewish boys, and his parents make the customary offerings of doves or pigeons at the Temple. Even here, however, Luke hints that the message of Jesus will not be restricted to his own people but will be offered to Gentiles as well. A man at the Temple named Simeon, to whom it had been promised that he would not die until he had seen the Messiah, takes the child Jesus in his arms and pronounces over him the beautiful benediction known as the 'Nunc Dimittis': 'Lord now lettest thou thy servant depart in peace . . . for mine eyes have seen thy salvation . . . a light to lighten the Gentiles, and the glory of thy people Israel' (2:29–32). John the Baptist, likewise, in his preaching quotes the words of the prophet Isaiah: 'all flesh shall see the salvation of God' (3:6). It is significant that, by contrast with the genealogy in Matthew, which linked Jesus to Abraham, the founder of the Jewish nation, the genealogy included in Luke links him to 'Adam, which was the Son of God' (3:38). For Luke, Jesus, the Son of God, is also the son of Adam, the founder of the whole human race.

---

[33] See Explanatory Note to Luke 2:4, p. 245 below, and see also entry on Quirinius in the Glossary of Persons for a note on the difficulties in reconciling the dates given by Luke and Matthew for the birth of Jesus.

In the first major episode in his ministry recorded by Luke, Jesus reads the scriptures and preaches in the synagogue in his home town of Nazareth (4:14–29). It is a skilfully presented scene, much longer than the equivalent scenes in Mark (6:1–6) and Matthew (13:54–8). As was the custom, Jesus stands up to read from the scroll given to him by the attendant. The passage he reads is from Isaiah 61:1–2: 'The Spirit of the Lord is upon me, because he hath anointed me to preach the gospel to the poor . . . to heal the broken hearted, to preach deliverance to the captives.' Then, as was also customary, he sits down to begin teaching. 'And the eyes of all them that were in the synagogue were fastened on him. And he began to say unto them, "This day is this scripture fulfilled in your ears".' This is received with incredulity ('Is not this Joseph's son?'), but when Jesus begins to elaborate on how 'no prophet is accepted in his own country' and to imply that he is to be compared with Elijah and Elisha, great prophets who found themselves sent to non-Jews, the mood changes to anger. They drive Jesus out of the city, intending to throw him down a hill 'headlong', but, mysteriously, 'he passing through the midst of them went his way'.

This is not the last time that Jesus will be rejected by conventionally religious Jews, and a major theme in Luke is how the kingdom of God will be opened up to the marginalized in society, and to Gentiles as well as Jews. Luke's Jesus does not hesitate to touch 'impure' people such as lepers (5:12–13), he invites even tax collectors—hated as agents of Roman rule as well as for their corrupt practices—to be disciples (5:27–8), and he shows compassion for people suffering from paralysis (5:18–20), withered limbs (6:6–10), blindness (18:35–43), deformity (13:11–13), and dropsy (14:2–4). He is frequently found eating with sinners (5:29–32, 19:7), and when criticized by the scribes and Pharisees for this, defends himself by means of three linked parables emphasizing the mercy shown to sinners by God. The first, the parable of the Lost Sheep (15:3–7), is also found in Matthew (18:12–13), but the other two are only included in Luke. The parables of the Lost Sheep and the Lost Coin (15:8–10) are similar in form. In the first, a shepherd leaves his flock to search for a sheep that is lost; in the second, a woman sweeps her house searching for a coin she has lost. In both, the emphasis is on the yearning of God toward 'lost' sinners, and his joy—'Rejoice with me'—when they are 'found' and brought back to him. The third, the parable of the Prodigal

Son (15:11–32), is a masterpiece of narrative detail, structure, and richly imagined character-drawing. The father's emotion when his 'lost' son returns, expressed in his repeated refrain that his son 'was dead, and is alive again . . . was lost, and is found', is so humanly moving that this is deservedly one of the most famous of the parables of Jesus.

Parables are included in all three of the Synoptic Gospels, and are indeed the characteristic form of teaching used by Jesus, but it is fair to say that they are given a more central place, and are more memorable in Luke than in Matthew or Mark. Whereas in Matthew and Mark the parables are often allegorical, and sometimes quite obscure, the parables in Luke more often take the form of extended narratives full of 'realistic' detail, and which invite the listener (or reader) to identify with the characters being described. Perhaps the most famous of all the parables found only in Luke is that of the Good Samaritan (10:29–37). This is told by Jesus as a way of explaining to a scribe, or 'lawyer', the meaning of the commandment to love your neighbour as yourself (Leviticus 19:18). What is most striking about this parable is not the act of kindness in going to the help of someone who has been attacked and left for dead, as opposed to walking past and offering no assistance. It is that the exemplar of true 'neighbourliness', far from being a highly respected Jewish figure like a priest or a Levite (an attendant to the priest in the Temple), is in fact a Samaritan, one of the most hated 'outsiders' in Jewish society. Samaritans were the descendants of people who lived in Samaria, the ancient capital of the northern kingdom of Israel, who had split off from mainstream Judaism and had built their own sanctuary on Mount Gerizim, in opposition to the Temple in Jerusalem which they regarded as corrupt. Josephus records an incident during a Passover around 6 CE when Samaritans desecrated the Temple by scattering human bones in the sanctuary, which led to great hostility.[34] Jews would avoid travelling through Samaria so as not to have any form of contact with Samaritans. For Jesus to commend the compassion and generosity of a member of a group so despised was a shockingly radical statement.

Another radical feature of Luke's Gospel is its sustained condemnation of those who seek after worldly wealth. In his version of the Sermon on the Mount, the Beatitudes are followed by a list of 'woes' directed at the rich, the well fed, and those held in high esteem in

[34] Josephus, *Jewish Antiquities*, 18:30.

society (6:24–6). For Luke's Jesus, 'a man's life consisteth not in the abundance of the things which he possesseth' (12:15). One of his parables is about a rich fool, who 'layeth up treasure for himself, and is not rich towards God' (12:16–21), and another portrays in stark terms the contrast between a rich man, who 'was clothed in purple and fine linen, and fared sumptuously every day', and a beggar, named Lazarus, who had only 'crumbs which fell from the rich man's table: moreover the dogs came and licked his sores'. But when they die, the rich man is taken down into hell fire, whereas Lazarus is 'carried by the angels into Abraham's bosom' (16:19–31). To a rich young ruler, who thinks he has lived a good life and kept the commandments, Jesus says that the one thing he must also do is give away all his money to the poor. The young man is 'very sorrowful', but Jesus is unbending, remarking that 'it is easier for a camel to go through a needle's eye, than for a rich man to enter into the kingdom of God' (18:18–25). The followers of Jesus are to renounce not only the pursuit of money, but even all concern with food and clothing, placing their trust in God who feeds the ravens and clothes the lilies: 'seek ye the kingdom of God, and all these things shall be added unto you' (12:22–31).

Journeys are important in Luke, especially the journey Jesus makes from Galilee to Jerusalem, which takes up something like 40 per cent of the narrative. His decision to set out on this journey is a deliberate and resolute one—'he steadfastly set his face to go to Jerusalem' (9:51)—and his destination is frequently mentioned as the journey progresses (13:31–5, 17:11, 18:31, 19:11, 28). When Jesus does eventually enter Jerusalem, his main conflict is with the powerful religious leaders in the Temple, who repeatedly question him about his authority to preach and teach (20:1–8), and try to trap him with questions about political allegiance (vv. 21–6). Jesus, however, remains calm and in control, as indeed he will remain in the events leading up to his trial and crucifixion. Luke makes a number of significant changes to the Passion narrative (the term 'Passion' comes from the Greek word for 'suffering'). For example, he describes no fewer than four trials: one before the supreme council of the Jews, the Sanhedrin (22:66–71); one before Pilate (23:1–5); one before Herod (23:6–12); and a final one before Pilate, again (23:13–25). In each trial scene, but particularly the last one, it is evident that Jesus is wholly innocent, but he remains composed throughout. When led to his crucifixion, he tells the women following him not to weep for him, but instead to weep because worse times would come (23:27–31). On the cross, he offers forgiveness to his enemies—exemplifying his teaching in the Sermon on the Mount. He comforts one of the criminals being executed alongside him: 'today shalt thou be with me in paradise' (v. 43). There is no note of despondency here, no cry of agony as in Mark and Matthew. At the moment of death, we are told, he cries out 'Father, into thy hands I commend my spirit' (v. 46), words bespeaking confidence, not dereliction.

Luke's Gospel closes with another journey, when the risen Jesus walks with two of the disciples to Emmaus (24:13–32). Here, and again when he appears to the rest of the disciples in Jerusalem, Luke has Jesus recapitulate his ministry, and the significance of his death and resurrection. The story ends, as it began, with 'great joy' (v. 52), and in Jerusalem, the city from whence the disciples are to begin their missionary work 'among all nations' (v. 47).

The Gospel According to John

As we noted earlier, John's Gospel differs in many respects from the Synoptic Gospels, and this is immediately evident in its extraordinary prologue: 'In the beginning was the Word, and the Word was with God, and the Word was God . . . And the Word was made flesh, and dwelt among us, and we beheld his glory, the glory as of the only begotten of the Father, full of grace and truth' (1:1–14). Nowhere else in the Gospels, or indeed in the New Testament, is there such an exalted, powerfully poetic, philosophical statement of the theme of incarnation—the Christian doctrine that in the person of Jesus (the 'Word') God took on human form (literally 'became flesh'). The Greek word translated here as 'Word' is *logos*, a term which referred not only to the spoken word but to inward thought as well. It was used by Stoic philosophers to signify the active principle of reason or order which governed the whole universe. It was also an important concept in the thought of the Hellenized Jewish philosopher Philo of Alexandria (*c.*20 BCE–*c.*50 CE), for whom the *logos*, the word or wisdom of God, represented both the creative power which orders the world and the means by which human beings know God. It has been suggested that John uses the term here because he was influenced by Greek thought, or because his Gospel was directed to a Greek readership which would have been familiar with the term *logos*.[35] However, the expression 'the word of God' is also found in the Hebrew scriptures, where it refers not simply to communications from God, whether directly or through the prophets, but seems also to be an independent entity possessing creative power and agency in itself (see, for example, Psalm 107:20; Isaiah 55:11). In the first chapter of Genesis everything is brought into being by God's word, and it is significant that, in expressing the idea of the full presence of God in Jesus, John echoes in his own opening words the opening words of Genesis, 'In the beginning . . .', and goes on to identify the 'Word' as the agent of God's creation: 'All things were made by him' (v. 3). This 'Word', the Son of God, is sent into the world, manifesting the 'glory' of God in the human form of Jesus.

The cosmic range and transcendent grandeur of this prologue indicate that the author is an accomplished writer, one very much in control of his material and able to order and rework it creatively. It introduces his main themes, and the perspective from which the reader is to understand them. The remainder of his Gospel is divided into two major sections. From chapters 1:19 to 12:50 the public ministry of Jesus is presented in a selection of narratives, dialogues, and discourses. In chapters 13 to 20 the focus is on the private discourses of Jesus with his disciples, leading into the Last Supper and his subsequent trial, crucifixion, and resurrection. Chapter 21 forms a kind of epilogue, or closing statement.

The account of the ministry of Jesus in the first main section is presented as a series of lengthy scenes in which he reveals his identity as the Christ/Messiah and the Son of God by doing miracles, referred to as 'signs' (though in the AV the Greek word *semeion* is often translated 'miracle'). This is another way in which John differs from the Synoptic Gospels, where we are told that Jesus explicitly disapproved of such 'signs' and refused to comply with demands that he give them.[36] In John, however, miracles always convey a deeper spiritual significance. In the first 'sign', for example, the turning of water into wine at the marriage at Cana (2:1–11), the point is not the miracle itself. What is significant is that the water changed into wine is water used for Jewish

[35] The fact that common Hebrew words such as 'Rabbi', 'Messiah', and 'Cephas' are interpreted by the author (1:38, 41, 42) suggests that John's Gospel was primarily intended for a non-Jewish readership.

[36] See Matt. 12:38–9, 16:1–4; Mark 8:11–12; Luke 11:29.

purification rites, the washing of hands and vessels as required by the Law (see Leviticus 15). The exchange of water, a symbol of the 'old' purity, cleansing the outside, for wine which is imbibed, and becomes therefore internal, symbolizes the inauguration of the new Messianic age when the purification rites of the Law give way to the 'good wine' offered by Jesus. Similarly, the Cleansing of the Temple (placed much earlier in John than in the Synoptic Gospels) is designed to demonstrate how the institutions of Judaism are to be replaced by Jesus, whose own body will become the new 'temple' (2:18–21).

'Signs' in John are often connected to a declaration of Jesus about himself. The Feeding of the Five Thousand is followed by 'I am the bread of life' (6:35); giving sight to a blind man, Jesus says 'I am the light of the world' (9:5); when he raises Lazarus from the dead, he says 'I am the resurrection, and the life' (11:25). There are four other such declarations: 'I am the door' (10:9); 'I am the good shepherd' (10:11); 'I am the way, the truth, and the life' (14:6); 'I am the true vine' (15:1). These 'I am' declarations are among the most characteristic features of John's Gospel, making memorable in richly symbolic form how Jesus is establishing a new way to God and a new community of believers. So, for example, 'bread', the giver of life, evokes the miraculous bread known as 'manna', provided for the people of Israel in the wilderness (Exodus 16:15).

In several other places Jesus simply refers to himself as 'I am', without any predicate.[37] The most striking of these comes in a passage where a group of Jews has challenged him over his claim that his followers will 'never see death' (8:51–9), because, they say, even Abraham himself had died. Jesus responds by declaring: 'Before Abraham was, I am'. This enrages them, because they regard it as Jesus taking to himself the mysterious words spoken by God when Moses had asked him to reveal his name: 'I AM THAT I AM . . . say unto the children of Israel, I AM hath sent me unto you' (Exodus 3:13–15). The Hebrew for 'I am' is *ehyeh*, which would sound like *yahweh*, which was probably the way YHWH, the name of God, would have been pronounced.[38] In fact, however, the name YHWH was regarded as so sacred by Jews that it was never spoken, *adonai*

---

[37] See 8:24, 28, 13:19, 18:5–8. In each of these cases, the Greek words are simply 'I am'; the 'he' is added by translators.

[38] See *The Oxford Bible Commentary*, ed. John Barton and John Muddiman (Oxford, 2001), 71. YHWH is translated as 'the LORD' throughout the AV.

(Lord) being used instead. For Jesus to refer to himself as 'I am' is seen as blasphemy, and his opponents pick up stones to put him to death (the punishment for blasphemy laid down in Leviticus 24:16).

These astounding claims and actions of Jesus culminate in the raising of Lazarus from the dead, designed as proof that he is 'the resurrection, and the life' (11:25). Many Jews, we are told, having 'seen the things which Jesus did, believed on him' (v. 45). Evidently alarmed by his growing popularity, the religious authorities call a meeting of the governing body, the Sanhedrin, to discuss how to be rid of him. Their fear is that popular support for Jesus could spark off a revolt, which could lead to a military crackdown by the Romans, ending, perhaps, in the destruction of the Temple and even of the Jewish people (v. 48). In 66–70 CE, a generation after Jesus's time, a Jewish revolt against Roman rule had indeed led to the destruction of Jerusalem, including the Temple, and the death or captivity of thousands of Jews. Caiaphas, the High Priest, is made to say here that it would be better for one man to be given up to the Romans than that the whole nation be destroyed (v. 50). For John, this cynical piece of political expediency contains a profound theological truth: Jesus *will* die, not only for the Jewish nation but for all the 'children of God that were scattered abroad' (v. 52).

The account of the subsequent trial and crucifixion of Jesus is similar in many respects to that in the Synoptic Gospels. The same people are mentioned, many of the same events occur. But the differences are more significant. In John's narrative Jesus is presented as in full control of the situation, unlike the passive Jesus of Mark. There are no hours of agony in the garden, no sadness or pathos, as in the other Gospels. Here Jesus knows exactly what is going to happen, and voluntarily offers himself to the soldiers who have come to arrest him (18:4). At his trial before Pilate he responds calmly and firmly: 'My kingdom is not of this world . . . for this cause came I into the world, that I should bear witness unto the truth' (vv. 36–7). Even after he has been crowned with thorns and beaten, he defiantly tells Pilate that he could have no power over him 'except it were given thee from above' (19:11)—a remark that evidently troubles Pilate (v. 12). He carries his own cross to the place of execution (v. 17), and even while on the cross continues to direct events, arranging for the care of his mother (vv. 25–7). There is no cry of dereliction at the final moment, no 'My God, my God, why hast thou forsaken me?' as in Mark (15:34) and

Matthew (27:46), not even Luke's 'Father, into thy hands I commend my spirit' (23:46). Here, Jesus simply says, 'It is finished', and with that 'he bowed his head, and gave up the ghost' (19:30). His work on earth has been accomplished.

The most important of all the differences between the account of the Passion in John and that of the other three Gospels concerns its dating and timing of the events described. In the Synoptic Gospels the Last Supper is very clearly a Passover meal, and Jesus is crucified the day after. Passover (Hebrew *Pesach*) was the great festival held in Jerusalem every year, beginning on the fourteenth day of the month of Nisan (March/April), to commemorate the liberation of the Jewish people from slavery in Egypt. On the afternoon of the fourteenth every Jewish family had to take a lamb to be ritually slaughtered at the Temple by the priest, who would sprinkle its blood on the altar in commemoration of the blood of lambs sprinkled on the doorposts which had protected the Jewish people in Egypt (Exodus 12:1–28). The carcass of the lamb was then brought home and roasted to be eaten with unleavened bread and bitter herbs at the Passover meal that evening. There are minor differences between the Synoptic Gospels on the details of what took place at the Last Supper, but they all report that at it Jesus instituted the Eucharist, transforming the Passover into what would become for Christians a commemoration of his own redeeming sacrifice for all humanity.

In John, by contrast, the Last Supper is not a Passover meal; it is held on the evening 'before the Feast of the Passover' (13:1). The reason why John placed the Last Supper before Passover is that for theological reasons he wanted the crucifixion of Jesus to be taking place at the very moment when the Passover lambs were being slaughtered in the Temple. Jesus would thus be the ultimate Passover lamb, encapsulating in a single symbol the Christian theology of universal expiation of sin through his sacrificial death. This interpretation had been carefully prepared for right at the start of the Gospel, when John the Baptist says of Jesus, 'Behold the Lamb of God, which taketh away the sin of the world' (1:29). It also explains an otherwise puzzling detail in John's account of the crucifixion. We are told that the Jews asked the Roman soldiers to break the legs of the three men being crucified, so that they would die more quickly (because unable to push themselves up to breathe), allowing their bodies to be removed for burial before evening (as Jewish Law required). However, when the soldiers came to Jesus he was already dead and so they did not break his legs (19:33). In this, we are told, the scripture was fulfilled: 'A bone of him shall not be broken' (v. 36, quoting from Psalm 34:20). But it was also a further way in which Jesus embodied the Passover lamb, because the Passover lamb had to be 'without blemish . . . neither shall ye break a bone thereof' (Exodus 12:5, 46).

It is not surprising that the Gospel of John has always been one of the most popular and cherished books of the New Testament. It includes many unforgettable stories, like Nicodemus coming to talk to Jesus by night (3:1–21), the encounter with the Samaritan woman at the well (4:5–30), the woman taken in adultery (8:1–11), the raising of Lazarus (11:1–44), Jesus washing the feet of his disciples (13:1–17), Mary Magdalene's meeting with the risen Jesus at the empty sepulchre (20:1–18). It abounds in passages memorable for their beauty of expression as well as thought. 'Let not your heart be troubled: ye believe in God, believe also in me. In my Father's house are many mansions; if it were not so, I would have told you: I go to prepare a place for you. And if I go and prepare a place for you, I will come again, and receive you unto myself; that where I am, there ye may be also' (14:1–3). 'For God so loved the world, that he gave his only begotten Son: that whosoever believeth in him, should not perish, but have everlasting life' (3:16). 'Ye shall know the truth, and the truth shall make you free' (8:32). A central text in the development of Christian doctrine and a major work of world literature, John's Gospel is also, as translated in the Authorized Version, one of the greatest and most influential works of literature in English.

The Gospels in the Authorized Version

Although the AV would become the most famous translation of the Bible into English ever made, it was by no means the first. It was in fact the culmination of nearly a century of intensive translation activity which had begun with William Tyndale (?1494–1536), a young Protestant scholar who, inspired by the success of Martin Luther's translation of the New Testament into German in 1522, conceived of making a similar translation into English. His New Testament—the first to be printed in English, and also the first in English to have been translated directly from the Greek—appeared in 1526, followed by a revised edition in 1534. Tyndale's influence as a Bible translator was enormous, and his clear, vigorous English rendering became the basis of all subsequent translations, including, to a very large extent, the AV.[39]

Complete Bibles incorporating Tyndale's work were published in 1535, 1537, and 1539, but these were large and expensive volumes, designed mainly for public use in churches.[40] In 1560, however, early in the reign of Elizabeth I, a new translation aimed at individual readers was produced by a group of English Protestant scholars working in Geneva. The 'Geneva Bible', as it was known, became very popular partly because it was published in smaller formats, and partly because it provided an elaborate apparatus of aids for readers, including extensive marginal notes giving a strongly Protestant explication of the text. It was printed in clear roman type (as opposed to 'black letter'), and it was the first Bible in English to divide the chapters into numbered verses.[41] Its notes, however, were greatly disapproved of by the Church of England hierarchy, and in 1568 a group of bishops published what became known as the 'Bishops' Bible' in an attempt to supplant the Geneva Bible. In 1571 it was ordered that copies of the Bishops' Bible were to be placed in every cathedral, and it was to be used in church services, but despite this official backing it never rivalled the Geneva Bible in popularity. Over eighty editions of the Geneva Bible appeared between 1568 and 1611, compared with only about nineteen editions of the Bishops' Bible.

When James VI of Scotland ascended to the throne of England in 1603 as James I, he made it clear that he shared the bishops' dislike of the Geneva Bible, regarding its notes as 'very partial, untrue, seditious, and savouring too much of dangerous, and traitorous conceits'.[42] Early in 1604, at a conference of church dignitaries and theologians which met with the new king at Hampton Court to discuss contentious religious issues, it was resolved that 'a translation be made of the whole Bible . . . to be set out and printed, without any marginal notes, and only to be used in all Churches of England in

[39] See David Daniell, *William Tyndale: A Biography* (New Haven and London, 1994).

[40] For accounts, see F. F. Bruce, *History of the Bible in English* (3rd edn., Cambridge, 1979), 53–80; David Daniell, *The Bible in English* (New Haven and London, 2003), 173–220.

[41] See *The Geneva Bible: A Facsimile of the 1560 Edition*, ed. Lloyd E. Berry (Madison, Milwaukee, and London, 1969).

[42] Cited in Daniell, *The Bible in English*, 434.

time of divine service'.[43] The resulting Bible, first published in 1611, is the one that has become known as the 'Authorized Version' or the 'King James Bible'.

A good deal is known about the making of the 1611 Bible. With James's support, Richard Bancroft, bishop of London, assembled a panel of fifty-four of the leading biblical scholars of the time, divided into six 'companies' of nine men each.[44] The translators were to work within a strict set of rules, drawn up by Bancroft, but almost certainly with the involvement of James himself.[45] They were not starting from a blank slate, but were to take the text of the Bishops' Bible as their starting point, only revising this when it seemed necessary. They were to retain the traditional forms of names and important words such as 'church' (which had been translated as 'congregation' by Tyndale), and were not to disturb the division of the text into chapters and verses. Marginal notes were to be confined to the provision of cross-references, or alternative readings of the texts: there was to be no interpretative commentary.

The translators did have freedom to draw on earlier translations, including those of Tyndale and of the Geneva Bible, and to go back to the original Hebrew and Greek in pursuit of the most accurate rendering of the text. As they explained in their preface, their aim was not to make a new translation, 'but to make a good one better, or out of many good ones one principal good one'. They made a crucial decision not to feel constrained to translate the same Hebrew or Greek word with exactly the same English word each time, or, as they put it, not to tie themselves 'to an uniformity of phrasing or to an identity of words'.[46] This gave their translation a richness and freedom of expression that would have been impossible with a more mechanical approach.

We have some insight into how the translators worked from an account given by the jurist and scholar John Selden (1584–1654). According to Selden, at their meetings each translator would read aloud the passage he had been working on while the others followed

---

[43] Cited in Bruce, *History of the Bible in English*, 96.

[44] For an engaging account of these scholars, see Adam Nicolson, *Power and Glory: Jacobean England and the Making of the King James Bible* (London, 2003).

[45] The rules are reproduced in David Norton, *A Textual History of the King James Bible* (Cambridge, 2005), 7–8.

[46] 'The Translators to the Reader', in *The Bible: Authorized King James Version*, ed. Robert Carroll and Stephen Prickett (Oxford, 1997), pp. lxv, lxviii.

the text in the original languages: 'if they found any fault, they spoke, if not, he read on.'[47] It is clear from this that faithfulness to the original text was of paramount importance, but care was also taken that the new translation would sound dignified when read aloud. John Bois, who kept verbatim notes of meetings, records one of the translators arguing for a reordering of the words in a particular passage: 'If the words be arranged in this manner, the statement will be more majestic.'[48] For an example of the care taken to achieve the most 'majestic' and beautiful way of arranging the words, here is a single verse, Matthew 11:28, as rendered successively in Tyndale, the Geneva, the Bishops' Bible, and the AV.

Come unto me all ye that labour and are laden, and I will ease you.

(Tyndale, 1534)

Come unto me, all ye that are weary and laden, and I will ease you.

(Geneva, 1560)

Come unto me all ye that labour sore, and are laden, and I will ease you.

(Bishops' Bible, 1568)

Come unto me all ye that labour, and are heavy laden, and I will give you rest.

(AV, 1611)

The tiny changes made by the AV translators achieve a marvellous rhythmic enactment of the meaning of the words. The Geneva and Bishops' Bible translators sense that something is not quite right with Tyndale's 'labour and are laden', but their attempts to improve it are not very successful. It is the AV's addition of the word 'heavy' to Tyndale's original version, and the substitution of 'I will give you rest' for his 'I will ease you', that give the sentence its beautiful cadence.[49]

One of the consequences of basing their work on earlier translations was that the AV translators often adopted word-forms and phraseology that had already become archaic in 1611. This is most immediately obvious in their use of 'thee', 'thou', 'thy', and 'thine' where a

[47] John Selden, *The Table-Talk*, ed. S. W. Singer (London, 1890), 6.

[48] Ward S. Allen, *Translating for King James: Notes Made by a Translator of King James's Bible* (London, 1970), 87. See also the valuable discussion in Gerald Hammond, *The Making of the English Bible* (Manchester, 1982), 179–92.

[49] A record of the process of revision survives in a copy of the Bishops' Bible, now in the Bodleian Library, with the changes marked up by translators. The annotations for the four Gospels are transcribed in full in Ward S. Allen and Edward C. Jacobs, *The Coming of the King James Gospels: A Collation of the Translators' Work-in-Progress* (Fayetteville, NC, 1995).

modern reader would expect 'you', 'your' and 'yours'. This usage had practically disappeared in southern English by the sixteenth century, when 'you' became the standard form of address except to a child or social inferior. The AV's application of 'thee' and 'thou' to God and humans without discrimination must have seemed old-fashioned even in 1611. The same is true of verb endings, where '-eth' was being replaced by '-s' by the time of the AV. When Tyndale writes in 1534 that the hireling shepherd 'seeth the wolf coming, and leaveth the sheep, and fleeth: and the wolf catcheth them, and scattereth the sheep' (John 10:12), these verb endings were in general use. By 1611, when the AV translators follow Tyndale's wording, they were pretty much obsolete.[50]

It took some time for the AV to become established in the affections of readers. A number of critics pointed out what they regarded as faults in translation, and editions of the Geneva Bible continued to be published up until 1644, indicating a continuing demand for its notes. From the beginning, however, the AV was an undoubted commercial success. Something like 140 separate editions, in a variety of formats, were published between 1611 and 1640—as many as all other complete versions of the Bible published since 1535 put together.[51] After 1660, for reasons that were political and commercial as well as aesthetic, the AV became the only text of the Bible that people bought and read, or that they heard read in churches.[52] In the revision of the Book of Common Prayer published in 1662, which continued to be used in the Church of England until well into the twentieth century, the text of the AV was adopted for the readings from the Gospels (and indeed for all the Bible readings except the Psalms). From about the middle of the eighteenth century the merits of the AV as a translation—and indeed as a work of literature in its own right— began to be praised by literary scholars, and by the nineteenth century its central place in English culture was universally acknowledged.

The influence of the AV on the development of the English language has been incalculable. Phrases from it have been taken into everyday speech so completely that their original source is often unrecognized. Examples from the Gospels alone would include: 'the salt of the

[50] A number of other archaic usages are pointed out in the Explanatory Notes, below. See also A. C. Partridge, *English Biblical Translation* (London, 1973), 115–38.

[51] See Ian Green, *Print and Protestantism in Early Modern England* (Oxford, 2000), 52.

[52] For the process of acceptance, see David Norton, *A History of the Bible as Literature*, 2 vols. (Cambridge, 1993), i. 210–36.

earth' (Matthew 5:13); 'no man can serve two masters' (6:24); 'signs of the times' (16:3); 'made light of it' (22:5); 'the spirit indeed is willing, but the flesh is weak' (26:41); 'in his right mind' (Mark 5:15); 'a den of thieves' (11:17); 'eat, drink, and be merry' (Luke 12:19). Curiously, the extraordinary popularity and ubiquity of the AV in the nineteenth century even meant that words which had dropped out of general use in the seventeenth and eighteenth centuries came back into use. The word 'laden', for example, which is used six times in the AV, seems to have been already archaic in 1611 (Shakespeare prefers 'loaden'), but by the nineteenth century it had come back into general currency, no doubt in large measure because of its use in Matthew 11:28. 'Ponder', in the sense of 'meditate deeply upon', seems to have become common again on the strength of occurrences in the AV, particularly its use in the story of the Annunciation in Luke 2:19: 'Mary kept all these things, and pondered them in her heart.' Other examples include 'stricken' (as in 'stricken ship'), 'bitten', 'ridden' (of horses), 'ate', 'unwittingly', 'heritage', 'eschew', 'change' (as in 'change of garment'), 'avenge' (rather than 'revenge').[53]

If its effect on the development of the English language has been incalculably large, so, too, has been the influence of the AV on English literature. The Bible had of course been a pervasive presence in early and medieval English literature, long before the advent of the AV. In one of the most celebrated of Old English poems, *The Dream of the Rood* (dating from the ninth century or perhaps earlier) the crucifixion of Jesus is recounted with much feeling by the rood (the cross). From the thirteenth to the sixteenth centuries great cycles of biblical plays were regularly performed by members of the craft guilds in places such as York, Chester, and Coventry. Portions of the Bible, including the Nativity and the Passion, would be acted in the streets, enlivened with folklore and 'stock' comic characters.

It was only with the advent of printed translations, however, that the whole Bible became part of everyday life, that its words, stories, and ideas began to sink deep into the consciousness not only of writers, but of ordinary people as well. By the time Shakespeare was writing he and his audience were among the second generation of those with access to the Bible in English, which meant that he could refer to biblical sayings and characters in the knowledge that these would be understood.[54] A whole play, *Measure for Measure*, could be written to explore the complexities of some words of Jesus in the Sermon on the Mount (Matthew 7:1–2). In the seventeenth century the work of poets like John Donne, George Herbert, and John Milton is permeated by allusions to the Bible—indeed many of their poems could hardly be understood without some knowledge of the Bible. John Bunyan, a writer with little formal education, absorbed the Bible to such an extent that his own prose was saturated with it. Bible-reading forms one of the central themes of his famous allegory of the Christian life, *The Pilgrim's Progress* (1678), itself for centuries the most widely read book in English apart from the Bible.[55]

Throughout the eighteenth century—with its flowering of English hymns based on the Bible, by the poets Isaac Watts, Charles Wesley, William Cowper, and others—and even more so throughout the nineteenth century, the Bible remained omnipresent in English culture, though it was beginning to be read and understood in more historically informed and sceptical ways.[56] In the imagination and mythology of a radical Christian poet like William Blake, Jesus becomes a central figure, one who brings love and forgiveness rather than formal moral precepts, and who, in *The Everlasting Gospel* (c.1818), sends out his disciples 'Against Religion & Government'. Many 'lives' of Jesus were written, some notorious, such as David Friedrich Strauss's *Das Leben Jesu* (1835), translated into English in 1846 by the young George Eliot, others vastly popular, such as *The Life of Christ* (1874) by Frederic W. Farrar, later dean of Canterbury Cathedral. Victorian poetry and fiction abounds with allusions to the Gospels, and indeed whole novels taking Jesus as their subject began to be written, among them such popular works as Lew Wallace's *Ben-Hur: A Tale of the Christ* (1880) and Hall Caine's *The Christian* (1897).

In 1870 the Church of England took the momentous decision to establish a panel of scholars to revise the AV. When the Revised Version of the New Testament was eventually published in 1881 it was a sensation, with over 3 million copies being sold in the first

---

[54] See Naseeb Shaheen, *Biblical References in Shakespeare's Plays* (Newark, Del., 1999).

[55] See W. R. Owens, 'John Bunyan and the Bible', in Anne Dunan-Page (ed.), *The Cambridge Companion to Bunyan* (Cambridge, 2010), 39–50.

[56] See David Jasper, 'Biblical Hermeneutics and Literary Theory', in Rebecca Lemon and others (eds.), *The Blackwell Companion to the Bible in English Literature* (Oxford, 2009), 22–37.

year alone. Although the new translation was based on the most up-to-date textual scholarship, and made over 36,000 changes to the AV, it was not a literary success.[57] What it did do, however, was open the way to what would become a flood of new translations in the twentieth century. Among the most influential versions of the New Testament by individual scholars were those published by James Moffat in 1913, J. B. Phillips in 1958, and William Barclay in 1968–9. A revision of the Revised Version was published in 1946 as the *Revised Standard Version*, and this in turn was revised to become the *New Revised Standard Version*, published in 1990, now regarded as the standard text for scholarly purposes. A decisive break with the language and style of the AV came with the publication of the *New English Bible* (New Testament, 1961) and *Good News for Modern Man* (1966), which presented the New Testament in 'today's English'. Translations were made for the use of Protestant evangelicals, such as the *New International Version* (New Testament, 1973), and for Roman Catholics, such as *The Jerusalem Bible* (1966; rev. 1985). Altogether, it has been calculated that eighty new translations of the New Testament into English appeared between 1945 and 1990.[58]

The AV has continued to appear alongside all these modern versions, and indeed it was the best-selling Bible in the United States right up to 1988, when it lost its position to the *New International Version*.[59] Its influence on writers remains strong, and its words continue to echo throughout modern literature. It is a rich and complex intertextual presence throughout Margaret Atwood's satirical dystopian fantasy, *The Handmaid's Tale* (1985), where she imagines a future society in which direct access to the Bible is forbidden. Young women enslaved as 'handmaids' for the sole purpose of producing children have the Gospels read aloud to them by a 'Commander' at mealtimes: 'For lunch it was the Beatitudes. Blessed be this, blessed be that . . . *Blessed be the poor in spirit, for theirs is the kingdom of heaven. Blessed are the merciful. Blessed are the meek. Blessed are the silent.* I knew they made that up, I knew it was wrong, and they left things out too, but there was no way of checking.'[60]

The Gospels may no longer be kept out of the hands of ordinary

[57] See Norton, *History of the Bible as Literature*, ii. 218–39.
[58] Daniell, *The Bible in English*, 764.
[59] John Riches, *The Bible: A Very Short Introduction* (Oxford, 2000), 39.
[60] Margaret Atwood, *The Handmaid's Tale* (London, 1986), 100.

readers as they once were, and as Atwood imagines they might be again, but it is perhaps the case that they have not been read through and responded to as a whole as often as they might. For centuries sections of them have been used in church services as part of the liturgy, and countless sermons have been preached on individual verses, often taken out of context. Scenes from them have been represented in innumerable works of art, music, and film, as well as in literature. But the purpose of the present edition is to encourage reading of the four Gospels as a whole—as if they were a single work. For that is in a sense what they are, despite the many variations between them. In fact it is precisely these variations that give an insight into the historical pressures and constraints affecting the birth of Christianity. Readers who approach the Gospels in this spirit will find themselves engaging with one of the most amazing and inexhaustible stories ever told: the story of the historical Jesus and the Christ of faith.

NOTE ON THE TEXT

THE text on which this Oxford World's Classics edition of *The Gospels* is based is that of the first edition of the Authorized Version of the Bible, published in 1611. This was a large folio volume, with an elaborately engraved title-page, reading as follows:

THE HOLY BIBLE, Conteyning the Old Testament, *AND THE NEW: Newly Translated out of the Originall tongues: & with the former Translations diligently compared and revised: by his Maiesties speciall Commandement. Appointed to be read in Churches. Imprinted at London by Robert Barker, Printer to the Kings most Excellent Maiestie.* ANNO DOM. 1611.

A detailed account of the printing and publishing history of this first edition, and of subsequent editions, is given by David Norton in *A Textual History of the King James Bible* (Cambridge, 2005). As he shows, the first edition, though far from perfect, reproduces more accurately than any other the text as it was prepared by the translators and given to the printers. The second edition was set from the first edition, and although it corrected some typographical and other errors in the first edition, it introduced many further errors. This process continued as successive editions appeared, with changes being introduced by printers and editors. Eventually, in 1769, Benjamin Blayney, later to become Regius Professor of Hebrew at Oxford, was commissioned to carry out a comprehensive review of the text. He not only corrected what he regarded as mistakes, but normalized spelling and presentation according to mid-eighteenth-century practice and added over 30,000 new marginal references. This 1769 edition has been the standard text of the AV ever since: modern copies are essentially 1611 as modified by Blayney. According to Norton (p. 115), only six further significant changes to the text were introduced after 1769.

The present edition follows the copy-text, except that some twenty obvious printer's errors have been corrected, and the spelling of some proper names has been regularized. The only other significant emendations to the text are as follows:

Matthew
   8:25   awoke him, saying] awoke, saying
   13:4   way side] wayes side

26:51 Priest] Priests
27:46 *lama sabachthani*] *Lamasabachthani*

Mark

10:46 highway side] high wayes side
14:47 Priest] Priests
15:34 lama sabachthani] lamasabachthani

Luke

3:21 baptized, it] baptized, and it
8:5 way side] wayes side
15:17 father] fathers
22:50 Priest] Priests

John

8:30 these] those
8:33 Abraham's] Abraham
15:4 and I in] and in

The punctuation of 1611 has also been followed as closely as possible and only altered where, even allowing for the fact that conventions of punctuation were different, it is plainly wrong or liable to be confusing. It will be seen that colons are often used where we would now expect a full stop, and there are many more commas than we would now use. It does not take very long to get used to these conventions, and it will be found that they help enormously in giving a sense of the rhythm and cadence of sentences when the text is read aloud, as it was designed to be.

The 1611 text has, however, been modernized in various ways for this edition. In particular, spelling and use of capitals has been brought into line with modern usage, and direct speech has been placed within inverted commas. Word-forms have usually not been changed. Definitions of words or word-forms which have become obsolete, or which have changed their meaning since 1611, are provided in the Glossary of Words and Terms. A rather odd feature of the 1611 text, which it took over from the Geneva Bible, was that English words added to complete the sense of the original Hebrew or Greek were placed in italics; these italics are not reproduced here.

A significant change in the way the text is presented in this edition is that it is not, as is traditional in Bibles, printed in double columns with each verse starting on a new line. This practice was originally designed to enable what was a very large book to be printed more cheaply, because on fewer pages, and to facilitate reference to the numbered verses, but it makes it difficult for a modern reader to respond to the text as a connected sequence of prose. As a consequence of presenting the text across the whole width of the page, paragraphing has been introduced, with verses being indicated by unobtrusive superscript numerals. The beginnings of new paragraphs were in fact marked in the first edition with a ¶ sign (though not, it must be said, in a very systematic or logical fashion). Finally, the 1611 text included some marginal notes, mainly cross-references to other texts in the Bible, or alternative translations of words or phrases. These have not been included in the present edition, but the more significant cross-references are given in the Explanatory Notes.

SELECT BIBLIOGRAPHY

THE list of works here has been confined, for the most part, to introductory studies, accessible to non-specialist readers. Many of them include details of works recommended for those who wish to undertake further study.

Critical and Historical Studies of Jesus, the Gospels, and the New Testament

Barton, Stephen C. (ed.), *The Cambridge Companion to the Gospels* (Cambridge, 2006).

Bockmuehl, Markus (ed.), *The Cambridge Companion to Jesus* (Cambridge, 2001).

Burridge, Richard A., *Four Gospels, One Jesus?* (2nd edn., London, 2005).

Caird, G. B., *The Gospel of Saint Luke* (Harmondsworth, 1963).

Charlesworth, James H., *The Historical Jesus* (Nashville, Tenn., 2008).

Dunn, James D. G., *A New Perspective on Jesus* (London, 2005).

Ehrman, Bart D., *The New Testament: A Historical Introduction to the Early Christian Writings* (4th edn., New York and Oxford, 2008).

Fenton, J. C., *The Gospel of Saint Matthew* (Harmondsworth, 1963).

Hedrick, Charles W., *Many Things in Parables: Jesus and his Modern Critics* (Louisville and London, 2004).

Marsh, John, *The Gospel of Saint John* (Harmondsworth, 1968).

Miles, Jack, *Christ: A Crisis in the Life of God* (London, 2001).

Nineham, D. E., *The Gospel of Saint Mark* (Harmondsworth, 1963).

Pelikan, Jaroslav, *Jesus Through the Centuries: His Place in the History of Culture* (New Haven and London, 1985).

Sanders, E. P., *The Historical Figure of Jesus* (London, 1993).

Stanton, Graham, *The Gospels and Jesus* (2nd edn., Oxford, 2002).

Vermes, Geza, *Jesus the Jew: A Historian's Reading of the Gospels* (3rd edn., London, 2001).

—— *The Changing Faces of Jesus* (London, 2000).

—— *The Authentic Gospel of Jesus* (London, 2003).

Wilson, A. N., *Jesus* (London, 1992).

Ziolkowski, Theodore, *Fictional Transfigurations of Jesus* (Princeton, 1972).

Critical and Historical Studies of the Bible

Allen, Ward S., *Translating for King James: Notes Made by a Translator of King James's Bible* (London, 1970).

—— and Edward C. Jacobs, *The Coming of the King James Gospels: A Collation of the Translators' Work-in-Progress* (Fayetteville, NC, 1995).

Alter, Robert, and Frank Kermode (eds.), *The Literary Guide to the Bible* (London, 1987).

Armstrong, Karen, *The Bible: The Biography* (London, 2007).

Brettler, Marc Zvi, *How to Read the Jewish Bible* (Oxford and New York, 2007).

Bruce, F. F., *History of the Bible in English* (3rd edn., Cambridge, 1979).

—— *The Books and the Parchments* (rev. edn., London, 1991).

Daniell, David, *The Bible in English: Its History and Influence* (New Haven and London, 2003).

De Hamel, Christopher, *The Book: A History of the Bible* (London and New York, 2001).

Dyas, Dee, and Esther Hughes, *The Bible in Western Culture: The Student's Guide* (London and New York, 2005).

Ferrell, Lori Anne, *The Bible and the People* (New Haven and London, 2008).

Frye, Northrop, *The Great Code: The Bible and Literature* (London, 1982).

Gabel, John B., Charles B. Wheeler, Anthony D. York, and David Citino, *The Bible as Literature: An Introduction* (New York and Oxford, 2006).

Hammond, Gerald, *The Making of the English Bible* (Manchester, 1982).

Hill, Christopher, *The English Bible and the Seventeenth-Century Revolution* (London, 1993).

Jasper, David, *The New Testament and the Literary Imagination* (Basingstoke, 1987).

—— and Stephen Prickett (eds.), *The Bible and Literature: A Reader* (Oxford, 1999).

Lawton, David, *Faith, Text and History: The Bible in English* (Charlottesville, Va., 1990).

Lemon, Rebecca, Emma Mason, Jonathan Roberts, and Christopher Rowland (eds.), *The Blackwell Companion to the Bible in English Literature* (Oxford, 2009).

Lewis, Jack P., *The English Bible from KJV to NIV: A History and Evaluation* (2nd edn., Grand Rapids, Mich., 1991).

Metzger, Bruce M., *The Text of the New Testament: Its Transmission, Corruption, and Restoration* (2nd edn., Oxford, 1968).

Nicolson, Adam, *Power and Glory: Jacobean England and the Making of the King James Bible* (London, 2003).

Norton, David, *A History of the Bible as Literature*, 2 vols. (Cambridge, 1993).

—— *A Textual History of the King James Bible* (Cambridge, 2005).

Pelikan, Jaroslav, *Whose Bible Is It? A History of Scripture Through the Ages* (London, 2005).

Riches, John, *The Bible: A Very Short Introduction* (Oxford, 2000).

Reference Works

Barton, John, and John Muddiman (ed.), *The Oxford Bible Commentary* (Oxford, 2001).

Chilton, Bruce (gen. ed.), *The Cambridge Companion to the Bible* (2nd edn., Cambridge, 2008).

Hass, Andrew W., David Jasper, and Elisabeth Jay (eds.), *The Oxford Handbook of English Literature and Theology* (Oxford, 2007).

Houlden, Leslie (ed.), *Jesus: The Complete Guide* (London and New York, 2003).

Jeffrey, David Lyle (ed.), *A Dictionary of Biblical Tradition in English Literature* (Grand Rapids, Mich., 1992).

Metzger, Bruce M., and Michael D. Coogan (eds.), *The Oxford Companion to the Bible* (New York and Oxford, 1993).

Rogerson, J. W., and Judith M. Lieu (eds.), *The Oxford Handbook of Biblical Studies* (Oxford, 2006).

Further Reading in Oxford World's Classics

The Bible, Authorized King James Version with Apocrypha, ed. Robert Carroll and Stephen Prickett.

A CHRONOLOGY OF JESUS AND EARLY CHRISTIANITY

BCE

63   Conquest of Judea by Roman general Pompey the Great.

37–4   Herod the Great appointed king of the Jews by the Romans.

31 BCE–14 CE   Octavian first emperor, as Caesar Augustus; beginning of the Roman empire.

20   Rebuilding of Temple at Jerusalem begun by Herod the Great.

*c.*6/5 BCE   **Birth of Jesus.**

4–3   Varus, Roman governor of Syria, crushes Jewish uprisings in Galilee and Jerusalem following the death of Herod the Great; 2,000 rebels crucified.

4 BCE–6 CE   Herod Archelaus ethnarch of Judea, Idumea, and Samaria.

4 BCE–33/4 CE   Herod Philip tetrarch of Iturea and regions north-east and east of Galilee.

4 BCE–39 CE   Herod Antipas tetrarch of Galilee and Perea.

CE

6   Quirinius appointed Roman governor of Syria, with authority over Judea.

6–7   Census organized by Quirinius in Judea leads to revolt led by Judas the Galilean.

6–18   Annas/Ananus Jewish High Priest.

6–41   Judea governed by Roman prefects.

14–37   Tiberius emperor.

18–36   Caiaphas Jewish High Priest.

26–36   Pontius Pilate prefect of Judea.

29?   Execution of John the Baptist.

29?   **Public ministry of Jesus begins in Galilee and Judea.**

30?   **Trial and crucifixion of Jesus by the Romans.**

30   Start of Jesus movement within Judaism.

32?   Conversion of Paul.

34–64   Paul's missionary activities among Gentiles.

36   Pontius Pilate dismissed from office as prefect of Judea; Caiaphas removed from office as Jewish High Priest.

37	Birth of Flavius Josephus, Jewish historian.
37–41	Caligula emperor.
39	Herod Antipas deposed and exiled.
41–4	Herod Agrippa I, ruler over most of Palestine; Council of Apostles held at Jerusalem; Apostle James, son of Zebedee, beheaded in Jerusalem.
41–54	Claudius emperor.
44–66	Roman procurators rule Judea, Samaria, and part of Galilee.
49–62?	1 Thessalonians, earliest letter of Paul, and earliest surviving Christian writing, followed by his letters to Philippians, Galatians, 1 and 2 Corinthians, and Romans.
51–2	Paul in Corinth.
53	Herod Agrippa II, ruler over most of Palestine.
54–68	Nero emperor.
58	Paul arrested for preaching in Jerusalem and kept in Caesarea.
60–2	Paul brought before Festus (procurator) and Agrippa II; is sent to Rome to be tried.
60–95?	Letter to the Hebrews.
62	Execution of James, the brother of Jesus.
64	Fire of Rome; fierce persecution of Christians; martyrdom of Paul and Peter.
66–70	Jewish revolt against Rome leads to fall of Jerusalem and the destruction of the Temple.
68	Nero commits suicide.
68–9	Galba, Otho, and Vitellius emperors.
69–79	Vespasian emperor.
*c.*70?	**Gospel of Mark.**
73/74	Fall of Masada to Romans after lengthy siege and suicide of 960 Jewish defenders.
77–8	Josephus, *Jewish War*.
79–81	Titus emperor.
80–90?	**Gospel of Matthew; Gospel of Luke.**
80–110?	Letters of James, Peter, and John.
81–96	Domitian emperor.
85–95?	Acts of the Apostles.
93–4	Josephus, *Jewish Antiquities*.

95–110?   **Gospel of John.**

96–8   Nerva emperor.

98–117   Trajan emperor.

100   *The Didache* [teaching] *of the Twelve Apostles* (earliest description of religious practices of early Christians).

100–10?   Revelation.

106/107   Symeon (son of Clopas the uncle of Jesus), who had succeeded James the brother of Jesus as bishop of Jerusalem, crucified.

117–38   Hadrian emperor.

120–50   Gospels of Thomas, Peter, Philip, Mary, Judas, and other such non-canonical writings.

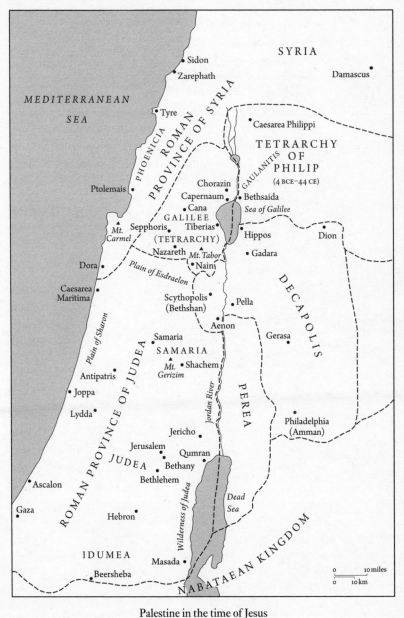

Palestine in the time of Jesus

THE GOSPELS

THE GOSPEL ACCORDING TO
SAINT MATTHEW

Chapter 1

1 *The genealogy of Christ from Abraham to Joseph.* 18 *He was conceived by the Holy Ghost, and born of the virgin Mary when she was espoused to Joseph.* 19 *The angel satisfieth the misdeeming thoughts of Joseph, and interpreteth the names of Christ.*

THE book of the generation of Jesus Christ, the son of David, the son of Abraham.

2 Abraham begat Isaac, and Isaac begat Jacob, and Jacob begat Judas and his brethren. 3 And Judas begat Phares and Zara of Thamar, and Phares begat Esrom, and Esrom begat Aram. 4 And Aram begat Aminadab, and Aminadab begat Naasson, and Naasson begat Salmon. 5 And Salmon begat Booz of Rachab, and Booz begat Obed of Ruth, and Obed begat Jesse. 6 And Jesse begat David the king, and David the king begat Solomon of her that had been the wife of Urias. 7 And Solomon begat Roboam, and Roboam begat Abia, and Abia begat Asa. 8 And Asa begat Josaphat, and Josaphat begat Joram, and Joram begat Ozias. 9 And Ozias begat Joatham, and Joatham begat Achaz, and Achaz begat Ezekias. 10 And Ezekias begat Manasses, and Manasses begat Amon, and Amon begat Josias. 11 And Josias begat Jechonias and his brethren, about the time they were carried away to Babylon. 12 And after they were brought to Babylon, Jechonias begat Salathiel, and Salathiel begat Zorobabel. 13 And Zorobabel begat Abiud, and Abiud begat Eliakim, and Eliakim begat Azor. 14 And Azor begat Sadoc, and Sadoc begat Achim, and Achim begat Eliud. 15 And Eliud begat Eleazar, and Eleazar begat Matthan, and Matthan begat Jacob. 16 And Jacob begat Joseph the husband of Mary, of whom was born Jesus, who is called Christ.

17 So all the generations from Abraham to David, are fourteen generations: and from David until the carrying away into Babylon, are fourteen generations: and from the carrying away into Babylon unto Christ, are fourteen generations.

18 Now the birth of Jesus Christ was on this wise: when as his

mother Mary was espoused to Joseph (before they came together) she was found with child of the Holy Ghost. [19] Then Joseph her husband, being a just man, and not willing to make her a public example, was minded to put her away privily. [20] But while he thought on these things, behold, the angel of the Lord appeared unto him in a dream, saying, 'Joseph thou son of David, fear not to take unto thee Mary thy wife; for that which is conceived in her, is of the Holy Ghost. [21] And she shall bring forth a son, and thou shalt call his name Jesus: for he shall save his people from their sins.' [22] (Now all this was done, that it might be fulfilled which was spoken of the Lord by the prophet, saying, [23] 'Behold, a virgin shall be with child, and shall bring forth a son, and they shall call his name Emmanuel', which being interpreted, is, God with us.) [24] Then Joseph, being raised from sleep, did as the angel of the Lord had bidden him, and took unto him his wife: [25] and knew her not, till she had brought forth her first born son, and he called his name Jesus.

Chapter 2

1 The wise men out of the east, are directed to Christ by a star. 11 They worship him, and offer their presents. 14 Joseph fleeth into Egypt, with Jesus and his mother. 16 Herod slayeth the children: 20 himself dieth. 23 Christ is brought back again into Galilee to Nazareth.

Now when Jesus was born in Bethlehem of Judea, in the days of Herod the king, behold, there came wise men from the east to Jerusalem, [2] saying, 'Where is he that is born King of the Jews? for we have seen his star in the east, and are come to worship him'. [3] When Herod the king had heard these things, he was troubled, and all Jerusalem with him. [4] And when he had gathered all the chief priests and scribes of the people together, he demanded of them where Christ should be born. [5] And they said unto him, 'In Bethlehem of Judea: for thus it is written by the prophet, [6] "And thou Bethlehem in the land of Juda, art not the least among the princes of Juda: for out of thee shall come a governor, that shall rule my people Israel"'.

[7] Then Herod, when he had privily called the wise men, enquired of them diligently what time the star appeared. [8] And he sent them to Bethlehem, and said, 'Go, and search diligently for the young

child, and when ye have found him, bring me word again, that I may come and worship him also'. [9] When they had heard the king, they departed, and lo, the star which they saw in the east, went before them, till it came and stood over where the young child was. [10] When they saw the star, they rejoiced with exceeding great joy.

[11] And when they were come into the house, they saw the young child with Mary his mother, and fell down, and worshipped him: and when they had opened their treasures, they presented unto him gifts, gold, and frankincense, and myrrh. [12] And being warned of God in a dream, that they should not return to Herod, they departed into their own country another way.

[13] And when they were departed, behold, the angel of the Lord appeareth to Joseph in a dream, saying, 'Arise and take the young child, and his mother, and flee into Egypt, and be thou there until I bring thee word: for Herod will seek the young child, to destroy him'. [14] When he arose, he took the young child and his mother by night, and departed into Egypt: [15] and was there until the death of Herod, that it might be fulfilled which was spoken of the Lord by the prophet, saying, 'Out of Egypt have I called my son'.

[16] Then Herod, when he saw that he was mocked of the wise men, was exceeding wroth, and sent forth, and slew all the children that were in Bethlehem, and in all the coasts thereof, from two years old and under, according to the time which he had diligently enquired of the wise men. [17] Then was fulfilled that which was spoken by Jeremy the prophet, saying, [18] 'In Rama was there a voice heard, lamentation, and weeping, and great mourning, Rachel weeping for her children, and would not be comforted, because they are not'.

[19] But when Herod was dead, behold, an angel of the Lord appeareth in a dream to Joseph in Egypt, [20] saying, 'Arise, and take the young child and his mother, and go into the land of Israel: for they are dead which sought the young child's life'. [21] And he arose, and took the young child and his mother, and came into the land of Israel. [22] But when he heard that Archelaus did reign in Judea in the room of his father Herod, he was afraid to go thither: notwithstanding, being warned of God in a dream, he turned aside into the parts of Galilee: [23] and he came and dwelt in a city called Nazareth, that it might be fulfilled which was spoken by the prophets, 'He shall be called a Nazarene'.

Chapter 3

1 John preacheth: his office: life, and baptism. 7 He reprehendeth the Pharisees, 13 and baptizeth Christ in Jordan.

IN those days came John the Baptist, preaching in the wilderness of Judea, ² and saying, 'Repent ye: for the kingdom of heaven is at hand'. ³ For this is he that was spoken of by the prophet Esaias, saying, 'The voice of one crying in the wilderness, "Prepare ye the way of the Lord, make his paths straight" '. ⁴ And the same John had his raiment of camel's hair, and a leathern girdle about his loins, and his meat was locusts and wild honey. ⁵ Then went out to him Jerusalem, and all Judea, and all the region round about Jordan, ⁶ and were baptized of him in Jordan, confessing their sins.

⁷ But when he saw many of the Pharisees and Sadducees come to his baptism, he said unto them, 'O generation of vipers, who hath warned you to flee from the wrath to come? ⁸ Bring forth therefore fruits meet for repentance. ⁹ And think not to say within yourselves, "We have Abraham to our father": for I say unto you, that God is able of these stones to raise up children unto Abraham. ¹⁰ And now also the axe is laid unto the root of the trees: therefore every tree which bringeth not forth good fruit, is hewn down, and cast into the fire. ¹¹ I indeed baptize you with water unto repentance: but he that cometh after me, is mightier than I, whose shoes I am not worthy to bear, he shall baptize you with the Holy Ghost, and with fire. ¹² Whose fan is in his hand, and he will thoroughly purge his floor, and gather his wheat into the garner: but will burn up the chaff with unquenchable fire.'

¹³ Then cometh Jesus from Galilee to Jordan, unto John, to be baptized of him: ¹⁴ but John forbade him, saying, 'I have need to be baptized of thee, and comest thou to me?' ¹⁵ And Jesus answering, said unto him, 'Suffer it to be so now: for thus it becometh us to fulfil all righteousness'. Then he suffered him. ¹⁶ And Jesus, when he was baptized, went up straightway out of the water: and lo, the heavens were opened unto him, and he saw the Spirit of God descending like a dove, and lighting upon him. ¹⁷ And lo, a voice from heaven, saying, 'This is my beloved Son, in whom I am well pleased'.

Chapter 4

1 *Christ fasteth, and is tempted.* 11 *The angels minister unto him.* 13 *He dwelleth in Capernaum,* 17 *beginneth to preach,* 18 *calleth Peter, and Andrew,* 21 *James, and John:* 23 *and healeth all the diseased.*

THEN was Jesus led up of the Spirit into the wilderness, to be tempted of the devil. ² And when he had fasted forty days and forty nights, he was afterward an hungered. ³ And when the tempter came to him, he said, 'If thou be the Son of God, command that these stones be made bread'. ⁴ But he answered, and said, 'It is written, "Man shall not live by bread alone, but by every word that proceedeth out of the mouth of God"'.

⁵ Then the devil taketh him up into the holy city, and setteth him on a pinnacle of the Temple, ⁶ and saith unto him, 'If thou be the Son of God, cast thyself down: for it is written, "He shall give his angels charge concerning thee, and in their hands they shall bear thee up, lest at any time thou dash thy foot against a stone"'. ⁷ Jesus said unto him, 'It is written again, "Thou shalt not tempt the Lord thy God"'.

⁸ Again the devil taketh him up into an exceeding high mountain, and showeth him all the kingdoms of the world, and the glory of them: ⁹ and saith unto him, 'All these things will I give thee, if thou wilt fall down and worship me'. ¹⁰ Then saith Jesus unto him, 'Get thee hence, Satan: for it is written, "Thou shalt worship the Lord thy God, and him only shalt thou serve"'. ¹¹ Then the devil leaveth him, and behold, angels came and ministered unto him.

¹² Now when Jesus had heard that John was cast into prison, he departed into Galilee. ¹³ And leaving Nazareth, he came and dwelt in Capernaum, which is upon the sea coast, in the borders of Zabulon and Nephthali: ¹⁴ that it might be fulfilled which was spoken by Esaias the prophet, saying, ¹⁵ 'The land of Zabulon, and the land of Nephthali, by the way of the sea beyond Jordan, Galilee of the Gentiles: ¹⁶ the people which sat in darkness, saw great light: and to them which sat in the region and shadow of death, light is sprung up'. ¹⁷ From that time Jesus began to preach, and to say, 'Repent: for the kingdom of heaven is at hand'.

¹⁸ And Jesus walking by the Sea of Galilee, saw two brethren, Simon, called Peter, and Andrew his brother, casting a net into the

sea (for they were fishers): ¹⁹ and he saith unto them, 'Follow me: and I will make you fishers of men'. ²⁰ And they straightway left their nets, and followed him. ²¹ And going on from thence, he saw other two brethren, James the son of Zebedee, and John his brother, in a ship with Zebedee their father, mending their nets: and he called them. ²² And they immediately left the ship and their father, and followed him.

²³ And Jesus went about all Galilee, teaching in their synagogues, and preaching the gospel of the kingdom, and healing all manner of sickness, and all manner of disease among the people. ²⁴ And his fame went throughout all Syria: and they brought unto him all sick people that were taken with divers diseases and torments, and those which were possessed with devils, and those which were lunatic, and those that had the palsy, and he healed them. ²⁵ And there followed him great multitudes of people, from Galilee, and from Decapolis, and from Jerusalem, and from Judea, and from beyond Jordan.

Chapter 5

Christ beginneth his Sermon in the Mount: 3 declaring who are blessed, 13 who are the salt of the earth, 14 the light of the world, the city on an hill, 15 the candle: 17 that he came to fulfil the Law: 21 what it is to kill, 27 to commit adultery, 33 to swear: 38 exhorteth to suffer wrong, 44 to love even our enemies, 48 and to labour after perfectness.

AND seeing the multitudes, he went up into a mountain: and when he was set, his disciples came unto him. ² And he opened his mouth, and taught them, saying,

³ 'Blessed are the poor in spirit: for theirs is the kingdom of heaven.

⁴ 'Blessed are they that mourn: for they shall be comforted.

⁵ 'Blessed are the meek: for they shall inherit the earth.

⁶ 'Blessed are they which do hunger and thirst after righteousness: for they shall be filled.

⁷ 'Blessed are the merciful: for they shall obtain mercy.

⁸ 'Blessed are the pure in heart: for they shall see God.

⁹ 'Blessed are the peacemakers: for they shall be called the children of God.

¹⁰ 'Blessed are they which are persecuted for righteousness' sake: for theirs is the kingdom of heaven.

[11] 'Blessed are ye, when men shall revile you, and persecute you, and shall say all manner of evil against you falsely, for my sake. [12] Rejoice, and be exceeding glad: for great is your reward in heaven: for so persecuted they the prophets which were before you.

[13] 'Ye are the salt of the earth: but if the salt have lost his savour, wherewith shall it be salted? It is thenceforth good for nothing, but to be cast out, and to be trodden under foot of men.

[14] 'Ye are the light of the world. A city that is set on an hill, cannot be hid. [15] Neither do men light a candle, and put it under a bushel: but on a candlestick, and it giveth light unto all that are in the house. [16] Let your light so shine before men, that they may see your good works, and glorify your Father which is in heaven.

[17] 'Think not that I am come to destroy the Law or the Prophets. I am not come to destroy, but to fulfil. [18] For verily I say unto you, till heaven and earth pass, one jot or one tittle shall in no wise pass from the Law, till all be fulfilled. [19] Whosoever therefore shall break one of these least commandments, and shall teach men so, he shall be called the least in the kingdom of heaven: but whosoever shall do, and teach them, the same shall be called great in the kingdom of heaven. [20] For I say unto you, that except your righteousness shall exceed the righteousness of the scribes and Pharisees, ye shall in no case enter into the kingdom of heaven.

[21] 'Ye have heard that it was said by them of old time, "Thou shalt not kill": and, "Whosoever shall kill shall be in danger of the judgement". [22] But I say unto you, that whosoever is angry with his brother without a cause, shall be in danger of the judgement: and whosoever shall say to his brother, "Raca", shall be in danger of the council: but whosoever shall say, "Thou fool", shall be in danger of hell fire. [23] Therefore if thou bring thy gift to the altar, and there rememberest that thy brother hath ought against thee: [24] leave there thy gift before the altar, and go thy way; first be reconciled to thy brother, and then come and offer thy gift. [25] Agree with thine adversary quickly, whiles thou art in the way with him: lest at any time the adversary deliver thee to the judge, and the judge deliver thee to the officer, and thou be cast into prison. [26] Verily I say unto thee, thou shalt by no means come out thence, till thou hast paid the uttermost farthing.

[27] 'Ye have heard that it was said by them of old time, "Thou shalt not commit adultery". [28] But I say unto you, that whosoever looketh

on a woman to lust after her, hath committed adultery with her already in his heart. [29] And if thy right eye offend thee, pluck it out, and cast it from thee. For it is profitable for thee that one of thy members should perish, and not that thy whole body should be cast into hell. [30] And if thy right hand offend thee, cut it off, and cast it from thee. For it is profitable for thee that one of thy members should perish, and not that thy whole body should be cast into hell.

[31] 'It hath been said, "Whosoever shall put away his wife, let him give her a writing of divorcement". [32] But I say unto you, that whosoever shall put away his wife, saving for the cause of fornication, causeth her to commit adultery: and whosoever shall marry her that is divorced, committeth adultery.

[33] 'Again, ye have heard that it hath been said by them of old time, "Thou shalt not forswear thyself, but shalt perform unto the Lord thine oaths". [34] But I say unto you, swear not at all, neither by heaven, for it is God's throne: [35] nor by the earth, for it is his footstool: neither by Jerusalem, for it is the city of the great King. [36] Neither shalt thou swear by thy head, because thou canst not make one hair white or black. [37] But let your communication be "Yea, yea": "Nay, nay": for whatsoever is more than these, cometh of evil.

[38] 'Ye have heard that it hath been said, "An eye for an eye, and a tooth for a tooth". [39] But I say unto you, that ye resist not evil: but whosoever shall smite thee on thy right cheek, turn to him the other also. [40] And if any man will sue thee at the law, and take away thy coat, let him have thy cloak also. [41] And whosoever shall compel thee to go a mile, go with him twain. [42] Give to him that asketh thee: and from him that would borrow of thee, turn not thou away.

[43] 'Ye have heard that it hath been said, "Thou shalt love thy neighbour, and hate thine enemy". [44] But I say unto you, love your enemies, bless them that curse you, do good to them that hate you, and pray for them which despitefully use you, and persecute you: [45] that ye may be the children of your Father which is in heaven: for he maketh his sun to rise on the evil, and on the good, and sendeth rain on the just, and on the unjust. [46] For if ye love them which love you, what reward have ye? Do not even the publicans the same? [47] And if ye salute your brethren only, what do you more than others? Do not even the publicans so? [48] Be ye therefore perfect, even as your Father, which is in heaven, is perfect.'

Chapter 6

1 *Christ continueth his Sermon in the Mount, speaking of alms,* 5 *prayer,*
14 *forgiving our brethren,* 16 *fasting,* 19 *where our treasure is to be laid*
up, 24 *of serving God, and mammon,* 25 *exhorteth not to be carefull for*
worldly things: 33 *but to seek God's kingdom.*

'TAKE heed that ye do not your alms before men, to be seen
    of them: otherwise ye have no reward of your Father which is
in heaven. ² Therefore, when thou doest thine alms, do not sound
a trumpet before thee, as the hypocrites do, in the synagogues, and
in the streets, that they may have glory of men. Verily I say unto
you, they have their reward. ³ But when thou doest alms, let not thy
left hand know what thy right doeth: ⁴ that thine alms may be in
secret: and thy Father which seeth in secret, himself shall reward thee
openly.

⁵ 'And when thou prayest, thou shalt not be as the hypocrites are:
for they love to pray standing in the synagogues, and in the corners
of the streets, that they may be seen of men. Verily I say unto you,
they have their reward. ⁶But thou when thou prayest, enter into thy
closet, and when thou hast shut thy door, pray to thy Father which
is in secret, and thy Father which seeth in secret, shall reward thee
openly. ⁷ But when ye pray, use not vain repetitions, as the heathen do.
For they think that they shall be heard for their much speaking. ⁸ Be
not ye therefore like unto them: for your Father knoweth what things
ye have need of, before ye ask him.

⁹ 'After this manner therefore pray ye: "Our Father which art in
heaven, hallowed be thy name. ¹⁰ Thy kingdom come. Thy will be
done, in earth, as it is in heaven. ¹¹ Give us this day our daily bread.
¹² And forgive us our debts, as we forgive our debtors. ¹³ And lead
us not into temptation, but deliver us from evil: for thine is the
kingdom, and the power, and the glory, for ever, Amen." ¹⁴ For, if ye
forgive men their trespasses, your heavenly Father will also forgive
you. ¹⁵ But, if ye forgive not men their trespasses, neither will your
Father forgive your trespasses.

¹⁶ 'Moreover, when ye fast, be not as the hypocrites, of a sad countenance: for they disfigure their faces, that they may appear unto men
to fast: verily I say unto you, they have their reward. ¹⁷ But thou, when
thou fastest, anoint thine head, and wash thy face: ¹⁸ that thou appear

not unto men to fast, but unto thy Father which is in secret: and thy Father which seeth in secret, shall reward thee openly.

¹⁹ 'Lay not up for yourselves treasures upon earth, where moth and rust doth corrupt, and where thieves break through, and steal. ²⁰ But lay up for yourselves treasures in heaven, where neither moth nor rust doth corrupt, and where thieves do not break through, nor steal. ²¹ For where your treasure is, there will your heart be also.

²² 'The light of the body is the eye: if therefore thine eye be single, thy whole body shall be full of light. ²³ But if thine eye be evil, thy whole body shall be full of darkness. If therefore the light that is in thee be darkness, how great is that darkness?

²⁴ 'No man can serve two masters: for either he will hate the one and love the other, or else he will hold to the one, and despise the other. Ye cannot serve God and mammon. ²⁵ Therefore I say unto you, take no thought for your life, what ye shall eat, or what ye shall drink, nor yet for your body, what ye shall put on: is not the life more than meat? and the body than raiment? ²⁶ Behold the fowls of the air: for they sow not, neither do they reap, nor gather into barns, yet your heavenly Father feedeth them. Are ye not much better than they? ²⁷ Which of you by taking thought, can add one cubit unto his stature? ²⁸ And why take ye thought for raiment? Consider the lilies of the field, how they grow: they toil not, neither do they spin. ²⁹ And yet I say unto you, that even Solomon in all his glory, was not arrayed like one of these. ³⁰ Wherefore, if God so clothe the grass of the field, which today is, and tomorrow is cast into the oven: shall he not much more clothe you, O ye of little faith? ³¹ Therefore take no thought, saying, "What shall we eat?" or, "What shall we drink?" or "Wherewithal shall we be clothed?" ³² (for after all these things do the Gentiles seek): for your heavenly Father knoweth that ye have need of all these things. ³³ But seek ye first the kingdom of God, and his righteousness, and all these things shall be added unto you. ³⁴ Take therefore no thought for the morrow: for the morrow shall take thought for the things of itself: sufficient unto the day is the evil thereof.'

Chapter 7

1 *Christ ending his Sermon in the Mount, reproveth rash judgement,*
6 *forbiddeth to cast holy things to dogs,* 7 *exhorteth to prayer,* 13 *to enter*
in at the strait gate, 15 *to beware of false prophets,* 21 *not to be hearers,*
but doers of the word: 24 *like houses builded on a rock,* 26 *and not on*
the sand.

'JUDGE not, that ye be not judged. ² For with what judgement ye
judge, ye shall be judged: and with what measure ye mete, it shall
be measured to you again. ³ And why beholdest thou the mote that is
in thy brother's eye, but considerest not the beam that is in thine own
eye? ⁴ Or how wilt thou say to thy brother, "Let me pull out the mote
out of thine eye", and behold, a beam is in thine own eye? ⁵ Thou
hypocrite, first cast out the beam out of thine own eye: and then shalt
thou see clearly to cast out the mote out of thy brother's eye.

⁶ 'Give not that which is holy unto the dogs, neither cast ye your
pearls before swine: lest they trample them under their feet, and turn
again and rend you.

⁷ 'Ask, and it shall be given you: seek, and ye shall find: knock, and
it shall be opened unto you. ⁸ For every one that asketh, receiveth: and
he that seeketh, findeth: and to him that knocketh, it shall be opened.
⁹ Or what man is there of you, whom if his son ask bread, will he give
him a stone? ¹⁰ Or if he ask a fish, will he give him a serpent? ¹¹ If ye
then being evil, know how to give good gifts unto your children, how
much more shall your Father which is in heaven, give good things to
them that ask him? ¹² Therefore all things whatsoever ye would that
men should do to you, do ye even so to them: for this is the Law and
the Prophets.

¹³ 'Enter ye in at the strait gate, for wide is the gate, and broad is
the way that leadeth to destruction, and many there be which go in
thereat: ¹⁴ because strait is the gate, and narrow is the way which leadeth unto life, and few there be that find it.

¹⁵ 'Beware of false prophets which come to you in sheep's clothing,
but inwardly they are ravening wolves. ¹⁶ Ye shall know them by their
fruits: do men gather grapes of thorns, or figs of thistles? ¹⁷ Even so,
every good tree bringeth forth good fruit: but a corrupt tree bringeth
forth evil fruit. ¹⁸ A good tree cannot bring forth evil fruit, neither can
a corrupt tree bring forth good fruit. ¹⁹ Every tree that bringeth not

forth good fruit, is hewn down, and cast into the fire. [20] Wherefore by their fruits ye shall know them.

[21] 'Not every one that saith unto me, "Lord, Lord", shall enter into the kingdom of heaven: but he that doth the will of my Father which is in heaven. [22] Many will say to me in that day, "Lord, Lord, have we not prophesied in thy name? and in thy name have cast out devils? and in thy name done many wonderful works?" [23] And then will I profess unto them, "I never knew you: depart from me, ye that work iniquity".

[24] 'Therefore, whosoever heareth these sayings of mine, and doeth them, I will liken him unto a wise man, which built his house upon a rock: [25] and the rain descended, and the floods came, and the winds blew, and beat upon that house: and it fell not, for it was founded upon a rock. [26] And every one that heareth these sayings of mine, and doeth them not, shall be likened unto a foolish man, which built his house upon the sand: [27] and the rain descended, and the floods came, and the winds blew, and beat upon that house, and it fell, and great was the fall of it.'

[28] And it came to pass, when Jesus had ended these sayings, the people were astonished at his doctrine. [29] For he taught them as one having authority, and not as the scribes.

Chapter 8

2 Christ cleanseth the leper, 5 healeth the centurion's servant, 14 Peter's mother-in-law, 16 and many other diseased: 18 showeth how he is to be followed; 23 stilleth the tempest on the sea, 28 driveth the devils out of two men possessed, 31 and suffereth them to go into the swine.

WHEN he was come down from the mountain, great multitudes followed him. [2] And behold, there came a leper, and worshipped him, saying, 'Lord, if thou wilt, thou canst make me clean'. [3] And Jesus put forth his hand, and touched him, saying, 'I will, be thou clean'. And immediately his leprosy was cleansed. [4] And Jesus saith unto him, 'See thou tell no man, but go thy way, show thyself to the priest, and offer the gift that Moses commanded, for a testimony unto them'.

[5] And when Jesus was entered into Capernaum, there came unto him a centurion, beseeching him, [6] and saying, 'Lord, my servant lieth at home sick of the palsy, grievously tormented'. [7] And Jesus

saith unto him, 'I will come, and heal him'. [8] The centurion answered, and said, 'Lord, I am not worthy that thou shouldst come under my roof: but speak the word only, and my servant shall be healed. [9] For I am a man under authority, having soldiers under me: and I say to this man, "Go", and he goeth: and to another, "Come", and he cometh: and to my servant, "Do this", and he doeth it.' [10] When Jesus heard it, he marvelled, and said to them that followed, 'Verily, I say unto you, I have not found so great faith, no not in Israel. [11] And I say unto you, that many shall come from the east and west, and shall sit down with Abraham, and Isaac, and Jacob, in the kingdom of heaven: [12] but the children of the kingdom shall be cast out into outer darkness: there shall be weeping and gnashing of teeth.' [13] And Jesus said unto the centurion, 'Go thy way, and as thou hast believed, so be it done unto thee'. And his servant was healed in the self same hour.

[14] And when Jesus was come into Peter's house, he saw his wife's mother laid, and sick of a fever: [15] and he touched her hand, and the fever left her: and she arose, and ministered unto them. [16] When the even was come, they brought unto him many that were possessed with devils: and he cast out the spirits with his word, and healed all that were sick, [17] that it might be fulfilled which was spoken by Esaias the prophet, saying, 'Himself took our infirmities, and bare our sicknesses'.

[18] Now when Jesus saw great multitudes about him, he gave commandment to depart unto the other side. [19] And a certain scribe came, and said unto him, 'Master, I will follow thee whithersoever thou goest'. [20] And Jesus saith unto him, 'The foxes have holes, and the birds of the air have nests: but the Son of Man hath not where to lay his head'. [21] And another of his disciples said unto him, 'Lord, suffer me first to go and bury my father'. [22] But Jesus said unto him, 'Follow me, and let the dead bury their dead'.

[23] And when he was entered into a ship, his disciples followed him. [24] And behold, there arose a great tempest in the sea, insomuch that the ship was covered with the waves: but he was asleep. [25] And his disciples came to him, and awoke him, saying, 'Lord, save us: we perish'. [26] And he saith unto them, 'Why are ye fearful, O ye of little faith?' Then he arose, and rebuked the winds and the sea, and there was a great calm. [27] But the men marvelled, saying, 'What manner of man is this, that even the winds and the sea obey him?'

[28] And when he was come to the other side, into the country of the Gergesenes, there met him two possessed with devils, coming

out of the tombs, exceeding fierce, so that no man might pass by that way. [29] And behold, they cried out, saying, 'What have we to do with thee, Jesus thou Son of God? Art thou come hither to torment us before the time?' [30] And there was a good way off from them, an herd of many swine, feeding. [31] So the devils besought him, saying, 'If thou cast us out, suffer us to go away into the herd of swine'. [32] And he said unto them, 'Go'. And when they were come out, they went into the herd of swine: and behold, the whole herd of swine ran violently down a steep place into the sea, and perished in the waters. [33] And they that kept them, fled, and went their ways into the city, and told everything, and what was befallen to the possessed of the devils. [34] And behold, the whole city came out to meet Jesus: and when they saw him, they besought him that he would depart out of their coasts.

Chapter 9

2 Christ curing one sick of the palsy, 9 calleth Matthew from the receipt of custom, 10 eateth with publicans, and sinners, 14 defendeth his disciples for not fasting, 20 cureth the bloody issue, 23 raiseth from death Jairus's daughter, 27 giveth sight to two blind men, 32 healeth a dumb man possessed of a devil, 36 and hath compassion of the multitude.

AND he entered into a ship, and passed over, and came into his own city. [2] And behold, they brought to him a man sick of the palsy, lying on a bed: and Jesus seeing their faith, said unto the sick of the palsy, 'Son, be of good cheer, thy sins be forgiven thee'. [3] And behold, certain of the scribes said within themselves, 'This man blasphemeth'. [4] And Jesus knowing their thoughts, said, 'Wherefore think ye evil in your hearts? [5] For whether is easier to say, "Thy sins be forgiven thee": or to say, "Arise, and walk"? [6] But that ye may know that the Son of Man hath power on earth to forgive sins' (then saith he to the sick of the palsy), 'Arise, take up thy bed, and go unto thine house.' [7] And he arose, and departed to his house. [8] But when the multitudes saw it, they marvelled, and glorified God, which had given such power unto men.

[9] And as Jesus passed forth from thence, he saw a man named Matthew, sitting at the receipt of custom: and he saith unto him, 'Follow me'. And he arose and followed him.

[10] And it came to pass, as Jesus sat at meat in the house, behold, many publicans and sinners came and sat down with him and his disciples. [11] And when the Pharisees saw it, they said unto his disciples, 'Why eateth your master with publicans and sinners?' [12] But when Jesus heard that, he said unto them, 'They that be whole need not a physician, but they that are sick. [13] But go ye and learn what that meaneth, "I will have mercy, and not sacrifice": for I am not come to call the righteous, but sinners to repentance.'

[14] Then came to him the disciples of John, saying, 'Why do we and the Pharisees fast oft, but thy disciples fast not?' [15] And Jesus said unto them, 'Can the children of the bride-chamber mourn, as long as the bridegroom is with them? But the days will come when the bridegroom shall be taken from them, and then shall they fast. [16] No man putteth a piece of new cloth unto an old garment: for that which is put in to fill it up, taketh from the garment, and the rent is made worse. [17] Neither do men put new wine into old bottles: else the bottles break, and the wine runneth out, and the bottles perish: but they put new wine into new bottles, and both are preserved.'

[18] While he spake these things unto them, behold, there came a certain ruler and worshipped him, saying, 'My daughter is even now dead: but come, and lay thy hand upon her, and she shall live'. [19] And Jesus arose, and followed him, and so did his disciples.

[20] And behold, a woman which was diseased with an issue of blood twelve years, came behind him, and touched the hem of his garment. [21] For she said within herself, 'If I may but touch his garment, I shall be whole'. [22] But Jesus turned him about, and when he saw her, he said, 'Daughter, be of good comfort, thy faith hath made thee whole'. And the woman was made whole from that hour.

[23] And when Jesus came into the ruler's house, and saw the minstrels and the people making a noise, [24] he said unto them, 'Give place, for the maid is not dead, but sleepeth'. And they laughed him to scorn. [25] But when the people were put forth, he went in, and took her by the hand: and the maid arose. [26] And the fame hereof went abroad into all that land.

[27] And when Jesus departed thence, two blind men followed him, crying, and saying, 'Thou Son of David, have mercy on us'. [28] And when he was come into the house, the blind men came to him: and Jesus saith unto them, 'Believe ye that I am able to do this?' They said unto him, 'Yea, Lord'. [29] Then touched he their eyes, saying,

'According to your faith, be it unto you'. ³⁰ And their eyes were opened: and Jesus straitly charged them, saying, 'See that no man know it'. ³¹ But they, when they were departed, spread abroad his fame in all that country.

³² As they went out, behold, they brought to him a dumb man possessed with a devil. ³³ And when the devil was cast out, the dumb spake, and the multitudes marvelled, saying, 'It was never so seen in Israel'. ³⁴ But the Pharisees said, 'He casteth out the devils through the prince of the devils'.

³⁵ And Jesus went about all the cities and villages, teaching in their synagogues, and preaching the gospel of the kingdom, and healing every sickness, and every disease among the people. ³⁶ But when he saw the multitudes, he was moved with compassion on them, because they fainted, and were scattered abroad, as sheep having no shepherd. ³⁷ Then saith he unto his disciples, 'The harvest truly is plenteous, but the labourers are few. ³⁸ Pray ye therefore the Lord of the harvest, that he will send forth labourers into his harvest.'

Chapter 10

1 Christ sendeth out his twelve apostles, enabling them with power to do miracles, 5 giveth them their charge, teacheth them, 16 comforteth them against persecutions: 40 and promiseth a blessing to those that receive them.

AND when he had called unto him his twelve disciples, he gave them power against unclean spirits, to cast them out, and to heal all manner of sickness, and all manner of disease. ² Now the names of the twelve apostles are these: the first, Simon, who is called Peter, and Andrew his brother; James the son of Zebedee, and John his brother; ³ Philip, and Bartholomew; Thomas, and Matthew the publican; James the son of Alphaeus, and Lebbaeus, whose surname was Thaddaeus; ⁴ Simon the Canaanite, and Judas Iscariot, who also betrayed him.

⁵ These twelve Jesus sent forth, and commanded them, saying, 'Go not into the way of the Gentiles, and into any city of the Samaritans enter ye not: ⁶ but go rather to the lost sheep of the house of Israel. ⁷ And as ye go, preach, saying, "The kingdom of heaven is at hand": ⁸ heal the sick, cleanse the lepers, raise the dead, cast out devils: freely

ye have received, freely give. ⁹ Provide neither gold, nor silver, nor brass in your purses: ¹⁰ nor scrip for your journey, neither two coats, neither shoes, nor yet staves: for the workman is worthy of his meat. ¹¹ And into whatsoever city or town ye shall enter, enquire who in it is worthy, and there abide till ye go thence. ¹² And when ye come into an house, salute it. ¹³ And if the house be worthy, let your peace come upon it: but if it be not worthy, let your peace return to you. ¹⁴ And whosoever shall not receive you, nor hear your words: when ye depart out of that house, or city, shake off the dust of your feet. ¹⁵ Verily I say unto you, it shall be more tolerable for the land of Sodom and Gomorrha in the day of judgement, than for that city.

¹⁶ 'Behold, I send you forth as sheep in the midst of wolves: be ye therefore wise as serpents, and harmless as doves. ¹⁷ But beware of men: for they will deliver you up to the councils, and they will scourge you in their synagogues, ¹⁸ and ye shall be brought before governors and kings for my sake, for a testimony against them, and the Gentiles. ¹⁹ But when they deliver you up, take no thought, how or what ye shall speak, for it shall be given you in that same hour what ye shall speak. ²⁰ For it is not ye that speak, but the Spirit of your Father, which speaketh in you. ²¹ And the brother shall deliver up the brother to death, and the father the child: and the children shall rise up against their parents, and cause them to be put to death. ²² And ye shall be hated of all men for my name's sake: but he that endureth to the end, shall be saved. ²³ But when they persecute you in this city, flee ye into another: for verily I say unto you, ye shall not have gone over the cities of Israel, till the Son of Man be come.

²⁴ 'The disciple is not above his master, nor the servant above his lord. ²⁵ It is enough for the disciple that he be as his master, and the servant as his lord: if they have called the master of the house Beelzebub, how much more shall they call them of his household?

²⁶ 'Fear them not therefore: for there is nothing covered, that shall not be revealed; and hid, that shall not be known. ²⁷ What I tell you in darkness, that speak ye in light: and what ye hear in the ear, that preach ye upon the house tops. ²⁸ And fear not them which kill the body, but are not able to kill the soul: but rather fear him which is able to destroy both soul and body in hell. ²⁹ Are not two sparrows sold for a farthing? And one of them shall not fall on the ground without your Father. ³⁰ But the very hairs of your head are all numbered. ³¹ Fear ye not therefore, ye are of more value than many sparrows.

³² 'Whosoever therefore shall confess me before men, him will I confess also before my Father which is in heaven. ³³ But whosoever shall deny me before men, him will I also deny before my Father which is in heaven.

³⁴ 'Think not that I am come to send peace on earth: I came not to send peace, but a sword. ³⁵ For I am come to set a man at variance against his father, and the daughter against her mother, and the daughter-in-law against her mother-in-law. ³⁶ And a man's foes shall be they of his own household. ³⁷ He that loveth father or mother more than me, is not worthy of me: and he that loveth son or daughter more than me, is not worthy of me. ³⁸ And he that taketh not his cross, and followeth after me, is not worthy of me. ³⁹ He that findeth his life, shall lose it: and he that loseth his life for my sake, shall find it.

⁴⁰ 'He that receiveth you, receiveth me: and he that receiveth me, receiveth him that sent me. ⁴¹ He that receiveth a prophet in the name of a prophet, shall receive a prophet's reward: and he that receiveth a righteous man, in the name of a righteous man, shall receive a righteous man's reward. ⁴² And whosoever shall give to drink unto one of these little ones, a cup of cold water only, in the name of a disciple, verily I say unto you, he shall in no wise lose his reward.'

Chapter 11

2 *John sendeth his disciples to Christ.* 7 *Christ's testimony concerning John.* 18 *The opinion of the people, both concerning John, and Christ.* 20 *Christ upbraideth the unthankfulness, and unrepentance of Chorazin, Bethsaida, and Capernaum:* 25 *and praising his Father's wisdom in revealing the gospel to the simple,* 28 *he calleth to him all such as feel the burden of their sins.*

AND it came to pass, when Jesus had made an end of commanding his twelve disciples, he departed thence to teach and to preach in their cities. ² Now when John had heard in the prison the works of Christ, he sent two of his disciples, ³ and said unto him, 'Art thou he that should come? Or do we look for another?' ⁴ Jesus answered and said unto them, 'Go and show John again those things which ye do hear and see: ⁵ the blind receive their sight, and the lame walk, the lepers are cleansed, and the deaf hear, the dead are raised up, and the poor have the gospel preached to them. [6] And blessed is he, whosoever shall not be offended in me.'

[7] And as they departed, Jesus began to say unto the multitudes concerning John, 'What went ye out into the wilderness to see? A reed shaken with the wind? [8] But what went ye out for to see? A man clothed in soft raiment? Behold, they that wear soft clothing, are in kings' houses. [9] But what went ye out for to see? A prophet? Yea, I say unto you, and more than a prophet. [10] For this is he of whom it is written, "Behold, I send my messenger before thy face, which shall prepare thy way before thee". [11] Verily I say unto you, among them that are born of women, there hath not risen a greater than John the Baptist: notwithstanding, he that is least in the kingdom of heaven, is greater than he. [12] And from the days of John the Baptist, until now, the kingdom of heaven suffereth violence, and the violent take it by force. [13] For all the Prophets, and the Law prophesied until John. [14] And if ye will receive it, this is Elias which was for to come. [15] He that hath ears to hear, let him hear.

[16] 'But whereunto shall I liken this generation? It is like unto children, sitting in the markets, and calling unto their fellows, [17] and saying, "We have piped unto you, and ye have not danced: we have mourned unto you, and ye have not lamented". [18] For John came neither eating nor drinking, and they say, "He hath a devil". [19] The Son of Man came eating and drinking, and they say, "Behold a man gluttonous, and a wine bibber, a friend of publicans and sinners". But wisdom is justified of her children.'

[20] Then began he to upbraid the cities wherein most of his mighty works were done, because they repented not. [21] 'Woe unto thee Chorazin, woe unto thee, Bethsaida: for if the mighty works which were done in you, had been done in Tyre and Sidon, they would have repented long ago in sackcloth and ashes. [22] But I say unto you, it shall be more tolerable for Tyre and Sidon at the day of judgement, than for you. [23] And thou Capernaum, which art exalted unto heaven, shalt be brought down to hell: for if the mighty works which have been done in thee, had been done in Sodom, it would have remained until this day. [24] But I say unto you, that it shall be more tolerable for the land of Sodom, in the day of judgement, than for thee.'

[25] At that time Jesus answered, and said, 'I thank thee, O Father, Lord of heaven and earth, because thou hast hid these things from the wise and prudent, and hast revealed them unto babes. [26] Even so,

Father, for so it seemed good in thy sight. ²⁷ All things are delivered
unto me of my Father: and no man knoweth the Son but the Father:
neither knoweth any man the Father, save the Son, and he to whomsoever the Son will reveal him.

²⁸ 'Come unto me all ye that labour, and are heavy laden, and I will
give you rest. ²⁹ Take my yoke upon you, and learn of me, for I am
meek and lowly in heart: and ye shall find rest unto your souls. ³⁰ For
my yoke is easy, and my burden is light.'

Chapter 12

1 *Christ reproveth the blindness of the Pharisees concerning the breach*
of the Sabbath, 3 by scriptures, 9 by reason, 13 and by a miracle. 22 He
healeth the man possessed that was blind, and dumb. 31 Blasphemy
against the Holy Ghost shall never be forgiven. 36 Account shall be made
of idle words. 38 He rebuketh the unfaithfull, who seek after a sign:
49 and showeth who is his brother, sister, and mother.

A^T that time, Jesus went on the Sabbath day through the corn,
and his disciples were an hungered, and began to pluck the ears
of corn, and to eat. ² But when the Pharisees saw it, they said unto
him, 'Behold, thy disciples do that which is not lawful to do upon the
Sabbath day'. ³ But he said unto them, 'Have ye not read what David
did when he was an hungered, and they that were with him, ⁴ how he
entered into the house of God, and did eat the shewbread, which was
not lawful for him to eat, neither for them which were with him, but
only for the priests? ⁵ Or have ye not read in the Law, how that on the
Sabbath days the priests in the Temple profane the Sabbath, and are
blameless? ⁶ But I say unto you, that in this place is one greater than
the Temple. ⁷ But if ye had known what this meaneth, "I will have
mercy, and not sacrifice", ye would not have condemned the guiltless.
⁸ For the Son of Man is Lord even of the Sabbath day.'

⁹ And when he was departed thence, he went into their synagogue.
¹⁰ And behold, there was a man which had his hand withered, and
they asked him, saying, 'Is it lawful to heal on the Sabbath days?' that
they might accuse him. ¹¹ And he said unto them, 'What man shall
there be among you, that shall have one sheep: and if it fall into a pit
on the Sabbath day, will he not lay hold on it, and lift it out? ¹² How
much then is a man better than a sheep? Wherefore it is lawful to do

well on the Sabbath days.' ¹³ Then saith he to the man, 'Stretch forth thine hand': and he stretched it forth, and it was restored whole, like as the other.

¹⁴ Then the Pharisees went out, and held a council against him, how they might destroy him. ¹⁵ But when Jesus knew it, he withdrew himself from thence: and great multitudes followed him, and he healed them all, ¹⁶ and charged them that they should not make him known: ¹⁷ that it might be fulfilled which was spoken by Esaias the prophet, saying, ¹⁸ 'Behold, my servant whom I have chosen, my beloved in whom my soul is well pleased: I will put my spirit upon him, and he shall show judgement to the Gentiles. ¹⁹ He shall not strive, nor cry, neither shall any man hear his voice in the streets. ²⁰ A bruised reed shall he not break, and smoking flax shall he not quench, till he send forth judgement unto victory. ²¹ And in his name shall the Gentiles trust.'

²² Then was brought unto him one possessed with a devil, blind, and dumb: and he healed him, insomuch that the blind and dumb both spake and saw. ²³ And all the people were amazed, and said, 'Is this the Son of David?' ²⁴ But when the Pharisees heard it, they said, 'This fellow doth not cast out devils, but by Beelzebub the prince of the devils'. ²⁵ And Jesus knew their thoughts, and said unto them, 'Every kingdom divided against itself, is brought to desolation: and every city or house divided against itself, shall not stand. ²⁶ And if Satan cast out Satan, he is divided against himself; how shall then his kingdom stand? ²⁷ And if I by Beelzebub cast out devils, by whom do your children cast them out? Therefore they shall be your judges. ²⁸ But if I cast out devils by the Spirit of God, then the kingdom of God is come unto you. ²⁹ Or else, how can one enter into a strong man's house, and spoil his goods, except he first bind the strong man, and then he will spoil his house. ³⁰ He that is not with me, is against me: and he that gathereth not with me, scattereth abroad.

³¹ 'Wherefore I say unto you, all manner of sin and blasphemy shall be forgiven unto men: but the blasphemy against the Holy Ghost, shall not be forgiven unto men. ³² And whosoever speaketh a word against the Son of Man, it shall be forgiven him: but whosoever speaketh against the Holy Ghost, it shall not be forgiven him, neither in this world, neither in the world to come. ³³ Either make the tree good, and his fruit good: or else make the tree corrupt, and his fruit corrupt: for the tree is known by his fruit. ³⁴ O generation of vipers, how can ye, being evil, speak good things? For out of the abundance of the

heart the mouth speaketh. ³⁵ A good man out of the good treasure of the heart, bringeth forth good things: and an evil man out of the evil treasure, bringeth forth evil things. ³⁶ But I say unto you, that every idle word that men shall speak, they shall give accompt thereof in the day of judgement. ³⁷ For by thy words thou shalt be justified, and by thy words thou shalt be condemned.'

³⁸ Then certain of the scribes, and of the Pharisees, answered, saying, 'Master, we would see a sign from thee'. ³⁹ But he answered, and said unto them, 'An evil and adulterous generation seeketh after a sign, and there shall no sign be given to it, but the sign of the prophet Jonas. ⁴⁰ For as Jonas was three days and three nights in the whale's belly: so shall the Son of Man be three days and three nights in the heart of the earth. ⁴¹ The men of Nineveh shall rise in judgement with this generation, and shall condemn it, because they repented at the preaching of Jonas, and behold, a greater than Jonas is here. ⁴² The queen of the south shall rise up in the judgement with this generation, and shall condemn it: for she came from the uttermost parts of the earth to hear the wisdom of Solomon, and behold, a greater than Solomon is here.

⁴³ 'When the unclean spirit is gone out of a man, he walketh through dry places, seeking rest, and findeth none. ⁴⁴ Then he saith, "I will return into my house from whence I came out"; and when he is come, he findeth it empty, swept, and garnished. ⁴⁵ Then goeth he, and taketh with himself seven other spirits more wicked than himself, and they enter in and dwell there: and the last state of that man is worse than the first. Even so shall it be also unto this wicked generation.'

⁴⁶ While he yet talked to the people, behold, his mother and his brethren stood without, desiring to speak with him. ⁴⁷ Then one said unto him, 'Behold, thy mother and thy brethren stand without, desiring to speak with thee'. ⁴⁸ But he answered, and said unto him that told him, 'Who is my mother? And who are my brethren?' ⁴⁹ And he stretched forth his hand toward his disciples, and said, 'Behold, my mother and my brethren. ⁵⁰ For whosoever shall do the will of my Father which is in heaven, the same is my brother, and sister, and mother.'

Chapter 13

3 The parable of the sower and the seed: 18 the exposition of it. 24 The parable of the tares, 31 of the mustard seed, 33 of the leaven, 44 of the hidden treasure, 45 of the pearl, 47 of the drawnet cast into the sea, 53 and how Christ is contemned of his own countrymen.

THE same day went Jesus out of the house, and sat by the sea side. ² And great multitudes were gathered together unto him, so that he went into a ship, and sat, and the whole multitude stood on the shore. ³ And he spake many things unto them in parables, saying, 'Behold, a sower went forth to sow. ⁴ And when he sowed, some seeds fell by the way side, and the fowls came, and devoured them up. ⁵ Some fell upon stony places, where they had not much earth: and forthwith they sprung up, because they had no deepness of earth. ⁶ And when the sun was up, they were scorched: and because they had not root, they withered away. ⁷ And some fell among thorns: and the thorns sprung up, and choked them. ⁸ But other fell into good ground, and brought forth fruit, some an hundred fold, some sixty fold, some thirty fold. ⁹ Who hath ears to hear, let him hear.'

¹⁰ And the disciples came, and said unto him, 'Why speakest thou unto them in parables?' ¹¹ He answered, and said unto them, 'Because it is given unto you to know the mysteries of the kingdom of heaven, but to them it is not given. ¹² For whosoever hath, to him shall be given, and he shall have more abundance: but whosoever hath not, from him shall be taken away, even that he hath. ¹³ Therefore speak I to them in parables: because they seeing, see not: and hearing, they hear not, neither do they understand. ¹⁴ And in them is fulfilled the prophecy of Esaias, which saith, "By hearing ye shall hear, and shall not understand: and seeing ye shall see, and shall not perceive. ¹⁵ For this people's heart is waxed gross, and their ears are dull of hearing, and their eyes they have closed, lest at any time they should see with their eyes, and hear with their ears, and should under-stand with their heart, and should be converted, and I should heal them." ¹⁶ But blessed are your eyes, for they see: and your ears, for they hear. ¹⁷ For verily I say unto you, that many prophets, and right-eous men have desired to see those things which ye see, and have not seen them: and to hear those things which ye hear, and have not heard them.

[18] 'Hear ye therefore the parable of the sower. [19] When any one heareth the word of the kingdom, and understandeth it not, then cometh the wicked one, and catcheth away that which was sown in his heart: this is he which received seed by the way side. [20] But he that received the seed into stony places, the same is he that heareth the word, and anon with joy receiveth it: [21] yet hath he not root in himself, but dureth for a while: for when tribulation or persecution ariseth because of the word, by and by he is offended. [22] He also that received seed among the thorns, is he that heareth the word, and the care of this world, and the deceitfulness of riches choke the word, and he becometh unfruitful. [23] But he that received seed into the good ground, is he that heareth the word, and understandeth it; which also beareth fruit, and bringeth forth, some an hundred fold, some sixty, some thirty.'

[24] Another parable put he forth unto them, saying, 'The kingdom of heaven is likened unto a man which sowed good seed in his field: [25] but while men slept, his enemy came and sowed tares among the wheat, and went his way. [26] But when the blade was sprung up, and brought forth fruit, then appeared the tares also. [27] So the servants of the householder came, and said unto him, "Sir, didst not thou sow good seed in thy field? from whence then hath it tares?" [28] He said unto them, "An enemy hath done this". The servants said unto him, "Wilt thou then that we go and gather them up?" [29] But he said, "Nay: lest while ye gather up the tares, ye root up also the wheat with them. [30] Let both grow together until the harvest: and in the time of harvest, I will say to the reapers, 'Gather ye together first the tares, and bind them in bundles to burn them: but gather the wheat into my barn'."'

[31] Another parable put he forth unto them, saying, 'The kingdom of heaven is like to a grain of mustard seed, which a man took, and sowed in his field. [32] Which indeed is the least of all seeds: but when it is grown, it is the greatest among herbs, and becometh a tree: so that the birds of the air come and lodge in the branches thereof.'

[33] Another parable spake he unto them, 'The kingdom of heaven is like unto leaven, which a woman took, and hid in three measures of meal, till the whole was leavened'.

[34] All these things spake Jesus unto the multitude in parables, and without a parable spake he not unto them: [35] that it might be fulfilled which was spoken by the prophet, saying, 'I will open my mouth

in parables, I will utter things which have been kept secret from the foundation of the world'.

[36] Then Jesus sent the multitude away, and went into the house: and his disciples came unto him, saying, 'Declare unto us the parable of the tares of the field'. [37] He answered, and said unto them, 'He that soweth the good seed, is the Son of Man. [38] The field is the world. The good seed, are the children of the kingdom: but the tares are the children of the wicked one. [39] The enemy that sowed them, is the devil. The harvest, is the end of the world. And the reapers are the angels. [40] As therefore the tares are gathered and burned in the fire: so shall it be in the end of this world. [41] The Son of Man shall send forth his angels, and they shall gather out of his kingdom all things that offend, and them which do iniquity: [42] and shall cast them into a furnace of fire: there shall be wailing and gnashing of teeth. [43] Then shall the righteous shine forth as the sun, in the kingdom of their Father. Who hath ears to hear, let him hear.

[44] 'Again, the kingdom of heaven is like unto treasure hid in a field: the which when a man hath found, he hideth, and for joy thereof goeth and selleth all that he hath, and buyeth that field.

[45] 'Again, the kingdom of heaven is like unto a merchant man, seeking goodly pearls: [46] who when he had found one pearl of great price, he went and sold all that he had, and bought it.

[47] 'Again, the kingdom of heaven is like unto a net that was cast into the sea, and gathered of every kind, [48] which, when it was full, they drew to shore, and sat down, and gathered the good into vessels, but cast the bad away. [49] So shall it be at the end of the world: the angels shall come forth, and sever the wicked from among the just, [50] and shall cast them into the furnace of fire: there shall be wailing, and gnashing of teeth.'

[51] Jesus saith unto them, 'Have ye understood all these things?' They say unto him, 'Yea, Lord'. [52] Then said he unto them, 'Therefore every scribe which is instructed unto the kingdom of heaven, is like unto a man that is an householder, which bringeth forth out of his treasure things new and old'.

[53] And it came to pass, that when Jesus had finished these parables, he departed thence. [54] And when he was come into his own country, he taught them in their synagogue, insomuch that they were astonished, and said, 'Whence hath this man this wisdom, and these mighty works? [55] Is not this the carpenter's son? Is not his mother called

Mary? and his brethren, James, and Joses, and Simon, and Judas? [56] And his sisters, are they not all with us? Whence then hath this man all these things?' [57] And they were offended in him. But Jesus said unto them, 'A prophet is not without honour, save in his own country, and in his own house'. [58] And he did not many mighty works there, because of their unbelief.

Chapter 14

1 Herod's opinion of Christ. 3 Wherefore John Baptist was beheaded. 13 Jesus departeth into a desert place: 15 where he feedeth five thousand men with five loaves, and two fishes: 22 he walketh on the sea to his disciples: 34 and landing at Gennesaret, healeth the sick by the touch of the hem of his garment.

A T that time Herod the Tetrarch heard of the fame of Jesus, [2] and said unto his servants, 'This is John the Baptist, he is risen from the dead, and therefore mighty works do show forth themselves in him'. [3] For Herod had laid hold on John, and bound him, and put him in prison for Herodias's sake, his brother Philip's wife. [4] For John said unto him, 'It is not lawful for thee to have her'. [5] And when he would have put him to death, he feared the multitude, because they counted him as a prophet. [6] But when Herod's birthday was kept, the daughter of Herodias danced before them, and pleased Herod. [7] Whereupon he promised with an oath, to give her whatsoever she would ask. [8] And she, being before instructed of her mother, said, 'Give me here John Baptist's head in a charger'. [9] And the king was sorry: nevertheless for the oath's sake, and them which sat with him at meat, he commanded it to be given her: [10] and he sent, and beheaded John in the prison. [11] And his head was brought in a charger, and given to the damsel: and she brought it to her mother. [12] And his disciples came, and took up the body, and buried it, and went and told Jesus.

[13] When Jesus heard of it, he departed thence by ship, into a desert place apart: and when the people had heard thereof, they followed him on foot, out of the cities. [14] And Jesus went forth, and saw a great multitude, and was moved with compassion toward them, and he healed their sick.

[15] And when it was evening, his disciples came to him, saying, 'This is a desert place, and the time is now past; send the multitude

away, that they may go into the villages, and buy themselves victuals'. [16] But Jesus said unto them, 'They need not depart; give ye them to eat'. [17] And they say unto him, 'We have here but five loaves, and two fishes'. [18] He said, 'Bring them hither to me'. [19] And he commanded the multitude to sit down on the grass, and took the five loaves, and the two fishes, and looking up to heaven, he blessed, and brake, and gave the loaves to his disciples, and the disciples to the multitude. [20] And they did all eat, and were filled: and they took up of the fragments that remained twelve baskets full. [21] And they that had eaten were about five thousand men, beside women and children.

[22] And straightway Jesus constrained his disciples to get into a ship, and to go before him unto the other side, while he sent the multitudes away. [23] And when he had sent the multitudes away, he went up into a mountain apart to pray: and when the evening was come, he was there alone. [24] But the ship was now in the midst of the sea, tossed with waves: for the wind was contrary. [25] And in the fourth watch of the night, Jesus went unto them, walking on the sea. [26] And when the disciples saw him walking on the sea, they were troubled, saying, 'It is a spirit': and they cried out for fear. [27] But straightway Jesus spake unto them, saying, 'Be of good cheer: it is I, be not afraid'. [28] And Peter answered him, and said, 'Lord, if it be thou, bid me come unto thee on the water'. [29] And he said, 'Come'. And when Peter was come down out of the ship, he walked on the water, to go to Jesus. [30] But when he saw the wind boisterous, he was afraid: and beginning to sink, he cried, saying, 'Lord, save me'. [31] And immediately Jesus stretched forth his hand, and caught him, and said unto him, 'O thou of little faith, wherefore didst thou doubt?' [32] And when they were come into the ship, the wind ceased. [33] Then they that were in the ship, came and worshipped him, saying, 'Of a truth thou art the Son of God'.

[34] And when they were gone over, they came into the land of Gennesaret. [35] And when the men of that place had knowledge of him, they sent out into all that country round about, and brought unto him all that were diseased, [36] and besought him, that they might only touch the hem of his garment; and as many as touched, were made perfectly whole.

Chapter 15

*3 Christ reproveth the scribes, and Pharisees, for transgressing God's
commandments through their own traditions: 11 teacheth how that which
goeth into the mouth, doth not defile a man. 21 He healeth the daughter
of the woman of Canaan, 30 and other great multitudes: 32 and with
seven loaves and a few little fishes feedeth four thousand men, beside
women and children.*

THEN came to Jesus scribes and Pharisees, which were of
Jerusalem, saying, ² 'Why do thy disciples transgress the tradition
of the elders? for they wash not their hands when they eat bread'.
³ But he answered, and said unto them, 'Why do you also transgress
the commandment of God by your tradition? ⁴ For God commanded,
saying, "Honour thy father and mother", and, "He that curseth father
or mother, let him die the death". ⁵ But ye say, "Whosoever shall say
to his father or his mother, 'It is a gift, by whatsoever thou mightest
be profited by me', ⁶ and honour not his father or his mother, he shall
be free". Thus have ye made the commandment of God of none effect
by your tradition. ⁷ Ye hypocrites, well did Esaias prophesy of you,
saying, ⁸ "This people draweth nigh unto me with their mouth, and
honoureth me with their lips: but their heart is far from me. ⁹ But in
vain they do worship me, teaching for doctrines, the commandments
of men." '

¹⁰ And he called the multitude, and said unto them, 'Hear, and
understand. ¹¹ Not that which goeth into the mouth defileth a man:
but that which cometh out of the mouth, this defileth a man.' ¹² Then
came his disciples, and said unto him, 'Knowest thou that the
Pharisees were offended after they heard this saying?' ¹³ But he
answered, and said, 'Every plant which my heavenly Father hath not
planted, shall be rooted up. ¹⁴ Let them alone: they be blind leaders
of the blind. And if the blind lead the blind, both shall fall into the
ditch.'

¹⁵ Then answered Peter, and said unto him, 'Declare unto us this
parable'. ¹⁶ And Jesus said, 'Are ye also yet without understanding?
¹⁷ Do not ye yet understand, that whatsoever entereth in at the mouth,
goeth into the belly, and is cast out into the draught? ¹⁸ But those
things which proceed out of the mouth, come forth from the heart,
and they defile the man. ¹⁹ For out of the heart proceed evil thoughts,

murders, adulteries, fornications, thefts, false witness, blasphemies.
[20] These are the things which defile a man: but to eat with unwashen
hands, defileth not a man.'

[21] Then Jesus went thence, and departed into the coasts of Tyre
and Sidon. [22] And behold, a woman of Canaan came out of the same
coasts, and cried unto him, saying, 'Have mercy on me, O Lord, thou
Son of David, my daughter is grievously vexed with a devil'. [23] But
he answered her not a word. And his disciples came, and besought
him, saying, 'Send her away, for she crieth after us'. [24] But he answered,
and said, 'I am not sent, but unto the lost sheep of the house of
Israel'. [25] Then came she, and worshipped him, saying, 'Lord, help
me'. [26] But he answered, and said, 'It is not meet to take the children's bread, and to cast it to dogs'. [27] And she said, 'Truth, Lord:
yet the dogs eat of the crumbs which fall from their master's table'.
[28] Then Jesus answered, and said unto her, 'O woman, great is thy
faith: be it unto thee even as thou wilt'. And her daughter was made
whole from that very hour.

[29] And Jesus departed from thence, and came nigh unto the Sea
of Galilee, and went up into a mountain, and sat down there. [30] And
great multitudes came unto him, having with them those that were
lame, blind, dumb, maimed, and many others, and cast them down at
Jesus's feet, and he healed them: [31] insomuch that the multitude wondered, when they saw the dumb to speak, the maimed to be whole,
the lame to walk, and the blind to see: and they glorified the God of
Israel.

[32] Then Jesus called his disciples unto him, and said, 'I have compassion on the multitude, because they continue with me now three
days, and have nothing to eat: and I will not send them away fasting,
lest they faint in the way'. [33] And his disciples say unto him, 'Whence
should we have so much bread in the wilderness, as to fill so great a
multitude?' [34] And Jesus saith unto them, 'How many loaves have ye?'
And they said, 'Seven, and a few little fishes'. [35] And he commanded
the multitude to sit down on the ground. [36] And he took the seven
loaves and the fishes, and gave thanks, and brake them, and gave to
his disciples, and the disciples to the multitude. [37] And they did all
eat, and were filled: and they took up of the broken meat that was left,
seven baskets full. [38] And they that did eat, were four thousand men,
beside women and children. [39] And he sent away the multitude, and
took ship, and came into the coasts of Magdala.

Chapter 16

1 The Pharisees require a sign. 6 Jesus warneth his disciples of the leaven of the Pharisees and Sadducees. 13 The people's opinion of Christ, 16 and Peter's confession of him. 21 Jesus foreshoweth his death, 23 reproving Peter for dissuading him from it: 24 and admonisheth those that will follow him, to bear the cross.

THE Pharisees also, with the Sadducees, came, and tempting, desired him that he would show them a sign from heaven. ² He answered, and said unto them, 'When it is evening, ye say, "It will be fair weather: for the sky is red". ³ And in the morning, "It will be foul weather today: for the sky is red and lowering". O ye hypocrites, ye can discern the face of the sky, but can ye not discern the signs of the times? ⁴ A wicked and adulterous generation seeketh after a sign; and there shall no sign be given unto it, but the sign of the prophet Jonas.' And he left them, and departed.

⁵ And when his disciples were come to the other side, they had forgotten to take bread. ⁶ Then Jesus said unto them, 'Take heed and beware of the leaven of the Pharisees and of the Sadducees'. ⁷ And they reasoned among themselves, saying, 'It is because we have taken no bread'. ⁸ Which when Jesus perceived, he said unto them, 'O ye of little faith, why reason ye among yourselves, because ye have brought no bread? ⁹ Do ye not yet understand, neither remember the five loaves of the five thousand, and how many baskets ye took up? ¹⁰ Neither the seven loaves of the four thousand, and how many baskets ye took up? ¹¹ How is it that ye do not understand, that I spake it not to you concerning bread, that ye should beware of the leaven of the Pharisees, and of the Sadducees?' ¹² Then understood they how that he bade them not beware of the leaven of bread, but of the doctrine of the Pharisees, and of the Sadducees.

¹³ When Jesus came into the coasts of Caesarea Philippi, he asked his disciples, saying, 'Whom do men say, that I, the Son of Man, am?' ¹⁴ And they said, 'Some say that thou art John the Baptist, some, Elias, and others, Jeremias, or one of the prophets'. ¹⁵ He saith unto them, 'But whom say ye that I am?' ¹⁶ And Simon Peter answered, and said, 'Thou art Christ, the Son of the living God'. ¹⁷ And Jesus answered, and said unto him, 'Blessed art thou, Simon bar Jona: for flesh and blood hath not revealed it unto thee, but my Father which

is in heaven. [18] And I say also unto thee, that thou art Peter, and upon this rock I will build my church: and the gates of hell shall not prevail against it. [19] And I will give unto thee the keys of the kingdom of heaven: and whatsoever thou shalt bind on earth, shall be bound in heaven: whatsoever thou shalt loose on earth, shall be loosed in heaven.' [20] Then charged he his disciples that they should tell no man that he was Jesus the Christ.

[21] From that time forth began Jesus to show unto his disciples, how that he must go unto Jerusalem, and suffer many things of the elders and chief priests and scribes, and be killed, and be raised again the third day. [22] Then Peter took him, and began to rebuke him, saying, 'Be it far from thee, Lord: this shall not be unto thee'. [23] But he turned, and said unto Peter, 'Get thee behind me, Satan: thou art an offence unto me: for thou savourest not the things that be of God, but those that be of men'.

[24] Then said Jesus unto his disciples, 'If any man will come after me, let him deny himself, and take up his cross, and follow me. [25] For whosoever will save his life shall lose it: and whosoever will lose his life for my sake, shall find it. [26] For what is a man profited, if he shall gain the whole world, and lose his own soul? Or what shall a man give in exchange for his soul? [27] For the Son of Man shall come in the glory of his Father, with his angels: and then he shall reward every man according to his works. [28] Verily I say unto you, there be some standing here, which shall not taste of death, till they see the Son of Man coming in his kingdom.'

Chapter 17

1 The transfiguration of Christ. 14 He healeth the lunatic, 22 foretelleth his own passion, 24 and payeth tribute.

AND after six days Jesus taketh Peter, James, and John his brother, and bringeth them up into an high mountain apart, [2] and was transfigured before them, and his face did shine as the sun, and his raiment was white as the light. [3] And behold, there appeared unto them Moses and Elias talking with him. [4] Then answered Peter, and said unto Jesus, 'Lord, it is good for us to be here: if thou wilt, let us make here three tabernacles: one for thee, and one for Moses, and one for Elias'. [5] While he yet spake, behold, a bright cloud overshadowed them: and behold, a voice out of the cloud, which said, 'This is my beloved Son, in whom I am well pleased; hear ye him'. [6] And when the disciples heard it, they fell on their face, and were sore afraid. [7] And Jesus came and touched them, and said, 'Arise, and be not afraid'. [8] And when they had lifted up their eyes, they saw no man, save Jesus only.

[9] And as they came down from the mountain, Jesus charged them, saying, 'Tell the vision to no man, until the Son of Man be risen again from the dead'. [10] And his disciples asked him, saying, 'Why then say the scribes that Elias must first come?' [11] And Jesus answered, and said unto them, 'Elias truly shall first come, and restore all things. [12] But I say unto you, that Elias is come already, and they knew him not, but have done unto him whatsoever they listed: likewise shall also the Son of Man suffer of them.' [13] Then the disciples understood that he spake unto them of John the Baptist.

[14] And when they were come to the multitude, there came to him a certain man, kneeling down to him, and saying, [15] 'Lord, have mercy on my son: for he is lunatic, and sore vexed: for oft times he falleth into the fire, and oft into the water. [16] And I brought him to thy disciples, and they could not cure him.' [17] Then Jesus answered, and said, 'O faithless and perverse generation, how long shall I be with you? how long shall I suffer you? bring him hither to me'. [18] And Jesus rebuked the devil, and he departed out of him: and the child was cured from that very hour. [19] Then came the disciples to Jesus apart, and said, 'Why could not we cast him out?' [20] And Jesus said unto them, 'Because of your unbelief: for verily I say unto you, if ye have faith as a grain of mustard seed, ye shall say unto this mountain, "Remove hence to yonder place": and it shall remove, and nothing shall be impossible unto you. [21] Howbeit, this kind goeth not out, but by prayer and fasting.'

[22] And while they abode in Galilee, Jesus said unto them, 'The Son of Man shall be betrayed into the hands of men: [23] and they shall kill him, and the third day he shall be raised again': and they were exceeding sorry.

[24] And when they were come to Capernaum, they that received tribute money, came to Peter, and said, 'Doth not your master pay tribute?' [25] He saith, 'Yes'. And when he was come into the house, Jesus prevented him, saying, 'What thinkest thou, Simon? of whom do the kings of the earth take custom or tribute? of their own children, or of

strangers?' ²⁶ Peter saith unto him, 'Of strangers'. Jesus saith unto him, 'Then are the children free. ²⁷ Notwithstanding, lest we should offend them, go thou to the sea, and cast an hook, and take up the fish that first cometh up: and when thou hast opened his mouth, thou shalt find a piece of money: that take, and give unto them for me, and thee.'

Chapter 18

1 Christ warneth his disciples to be humble and harmless: 7 to avoid offences, and not to despise the little ones: 15 teacheth how we are to deal with our brethren, when they offend us: 21 and how oft to forgive them: 23 which he setteth forth by a parable of the king, that took account of his servants, 32 and punished him who showed no mercy to his fellow.

AT the same time came the disciples unto Jesus, saying, 'Who is the greatest in the kingdom of heaven?' ² And Jesus called a little child unto him, and set him in the midst of them, ³ and said, 'Verily I say unto you, except ye be converted, and become as little children, ye shall not enter into the kingdom of heaven. ⁴ Whosoever therefore shall humble himself as this little child, the same is greatest in the kingdom of heaven. ⁵ And who so shall receive one such little child in my name, receiveth me. ⁶ But who so shall offend one of these little ones which believe in me, it were better for him that a millstone were hanged about his neck, and that he were drowned in the depth of the sea.

⁷ 'Woe unto the world because of offences: for it must needs be that offences come: but woe to that man by whom the offence cometh. ⁸ Wherefore if thy hand or thy foot offend thee, cut them off, and cast them from thee: it is better for thee to enter into life halt or maimed, rather than having two hands or two feet, to be cast into everlasting fire. ⁹ And if thine eye offend thee, pluck it out, and cast it from thee: it is better for thee to enter into life with one eye, rather than having two eyes, to be cast into hell fire.

¹⁰ 'Take heed that ye despise not one of these little ones: for I say unto you, that in heaven their angels do always behold the face of my Father which is in heaven. ¹¹ For the Son of Man is come to save that which was lost. ¹² How think ye? if a man have an hundred sheep, and one of them be gone astray, doth he not leave the ninety and

nine, and goeth into the mountains, and seeketh that which is gone astray? ¹³ And if so be that he find it, verily I say unto you, he rejoiceth more of that sheep, than of the ninety and nine which went not astray. ¹⁴ Even so, it is not the will of your Father which is in heaven, that one of these little ones should perish.

¹⁵ 'Moreover, if thy brother shall trespass against thee, go and tell him his fault between thee and him alone: if he shall hear thee, thou hast gained thy brother. ¹⁶ But if he will not hear thee, then take with thee one or two more, that in the mouth of two or three witnesses, every word may be established. ¹⁷ And if he shall neglect to hear them, tell it unto the church: but if he neglect to hear the church, let him be unto thee as an heathen man and a publican. ¹⁸ Verily I say unto you, whatsoever ye shall bind on earth, shall be bound in heaven: and whatsoever ye shall loose on earth, shall be loosed in heaven. ¹⁹ Again I say unto you, that if two of you shall agree on earth as touching any thing that they shall ask, it shall be done for them of my Father which is in heaven. ²⁰ For where two or three are gathered together in my name, there am I in the midst of them.'

²¹ Then came Peter to him, and said, 'Lord, how oft shall my brother sin against me, and I forgive him? till seven times?' ²² Jesus saith unto him, 'I say not unto thee, until seven times: but, until seventy times seven.

²³ 'Therefore is the kingdom of heaven likened unto a certain king, which would take accompt of his servants. ²⁴ And when he had begun to reckon, one was brought unto him, which ought him ten thousand talents. ²⁵ But forasmuch as he had not to pay, his lord commanded him to be sold, and his wife, and children, and all that he had, and payment to be made. ²⁶ The servant therefore fell down, and worshipped him, saying, "Lord, have patience with me, and I will pay thee all". ²⁷ Then the lord of that servant was moved with compassion, and loosed him, and forgave him the debt. ²⁸ But the same servant went out, and found one of his fellow-servants, which ought him an hundred pence: and he laid hands on him, and took him by the throat, saying, "Pay me that thou owest". ²⁹ And his fellow-servant fell down at his feet, and besought him, saying, "Have patience with me, and I will pay thee all". ³⁰ And he would not: but went and cast him into prison, till he should pay the debt. ³¹ So when his fellow-servants saw what was done, they were very sorry, and came, and told unto their lord all that was done. ³² Then his lord, after that he had called him, said unto him, "O thou wicked servant, I forgave thee all that debt

because thou desiredst me: ³³ shouldst not thou also have had compassion on thy fellow-servant, even as I had pity on thee?" ³⁴ And his lord was wroth, and delivered him to the tormentors, till he should pay all that was due unto him. ³⁵ So likewise shall my heavenly Father do also unto you, if ye from your hearts forgive not every one his brother their trespasses.'

Chapter 19

2 Christ healeth the sick: 3 answereth the Pharisees concerning divorcement: 10 showeth when marriage is necessary: 13 receiveth little children: 16 instructeth the young man how to attain eternal life, 20 and how to be perfect: 23 telleth his disciples how hard it is for a rich man to enter into the kingdom of God, 27 and promiseth reward to those that forsake any thing, to follow him.

AND it came to pass, that when Jesus had finished these sayings, he departed from Galilee, and came into the coasts of Judea, beyond Jordan: ² and great multitudes followed him; and he healed them there.

³ The Pharisees also came unto him, tempting him, and saying unto him, 'Is it lawful for a man to put away his wife for every cause?' ⁴ And he answered, and said unto them, 'Have ye not read, that he which made them at the beginning, made them male and female, ⁵ and said, "For this cause shall a man leave father and mother, and shall cleave to his wife: and they twain shall be one flesh"? ⁶ Wherefore they are no more twain, but one flesh. What therefore God hath joined together, let not man put asunder.' ⁷ They say unto him, 'Why did Moses then command to give a writing of divorcement, and to put her away?' ⁸ He saith unto them, 'Moses, because of the hardness of your hearts, suffered you to put away your wives: but from the beginning it was not so. ⁹ And I say unto you, whosoever shall put away his wife, except it be for fornication, and shall marry another, committeth adultery: and whoso marrieth her which is put away doth commit adultery.'

¹⁰ His disciples say unto him, 'If the case of the man be so with his wife, it is not good to marry'. ¹¹ But he said unto them, 'All men cannot receive this saying, save they to whom it is given. ¹² For there are some eunuchs, which were so born from their mother's womb:

and there are some eunuchs, which were made eunuchs of men: and there be eunuchs, which have made themselves eunuchs for the kingdom of heaven's sake. He that is able to receive it, let him receive it.'

[13] Then were there brought unto him little children, that he should put his hands on them, and pray: and the disciples rebuked them. [14] But Jesus said, 'Suffer little children, and forbid them not to come unto me: for of such is the kingdom of heaven'. [15] And he laid his hands on them, and departed thence.

[16] And behold, one came and said unto him, 'Good Master, what good thing shall I do, that I may have eternal life?' [17] And he said unto him, 'Why callest thou me good? there is none good but one, that is, God: but if thou wilt enter into life, keep the commandments'. [18] He saith unto him, 'Which?' Jesus said, 'Thou shalt do no murder, thou shalt not commit adultery, thou shalt not steal, thou shalt not bear false witness, [19] honour thy father and thy mother: and, thou shalt love thy neighbour as thyself'. [20] The young man saith unto him, 'All these things have I kept from my youth up: what lack I yet?' [21] Jesus said unto him, 'If thou wilt be perfect, go and sell that thou hast, and give to the poor, and thou shalt have treasure in heaven: and come and follow me'. [22] But when the young man heard that saying, he went away sorrowful: for he had great possessions.

[23] Then said Jesus unto his disciples, 'Verily I say unto you, that a rich man shall hardly enter into the kingdom of heaven. [24] And again I say unto you, it is easier for a camel to go through the eye of a needle, than for a rich man to enter into the kingdom of God.' [25] When his disciples heard it, they were exceedingly amazed, saying, 'Who then can be saved?' [26] But Jesus beheld them, and said unto them, 'With men this is unpossible; but with God all things are possible'.

[27] Then answered Peter, and said unto him, 'Behold, we have forsaken all, and followed thee, what shall we have therefore?' [28] And Jesus said unto them, 'Verily I say unto you, that ye which have followed me, in the regeneration when the Son of Man shall sit in the throne of his glory, ye also shall sit upon twelve thrones, judging the twelve tribes of Israel. [29] And every one that hath forsaken houses, or brethren, or sisters, or father, or mother, or wife, or children, or lands, for my name's sake, shall receive an hundred fold, and shall inherit everlasting life. [30] But many that are first, shall be last, and the last shall be first.'

Chapter 20

1 *Christ by the similitude of the labourers in the vineyard, showeth that God is debtor unto no man:* 17 *foretelleth his passion:* 20 *by answering the mother of Zebedee's children, teacheth his disciples to be lowly:* 30 *and giveth two blind men their sight.*

'FOR the kingdom of heaven is like unto a man that is an householder, which went out early in the morning to hire labourers into his vineyard. ² And when he had agreed with the labourers for a penny a day, he sent them into his vineyard. ³ And he went out about the third hour, and saw others standing idle in the market place, ⁴ and said unto them, "Go ye also into the vineyard, and whatsoever is right, I will give you". And they went their way. ⁵ Again he went out about the sixth and ninth hour, and did likewise. ⁶ And about the eleventh hour he went out, and found others standing idle, and saith unto them, "Why stand ye here all the day idle?" ⁷ They say unto him, "Because no man hath hired us". He saith unto them, "Go ye also into the vineyard: and whatsoever is right, that shall ye receive". ⁸ So when even was come, the lord of the vineyard saith unto his steward, "Call the labourers, and give them their hire, beginning from the last unto the first". ⁹ And when they came that were hired about the eleventh hour, they received every man a penny. ¹⁰ But when the first came, they supposed that they should have received more, and they likewise received every man a penny. ¹¹ And when they had received it, they murmured against the goodman of the house, ¹² saying, "These last have wrought but one hour, and thou hast made them equal unto us, which have borne the burden, and heat of the day". ¹³ But he answered one of them and said, "Friend, I do thee no wrong: didst not thou agree with me for a penny? ¹⁴ Take that thine is, and go thy way: I will give unto this last, even as unto thee. ¹⁵ Is it not lawful for me to do what I will with mine own? Is thine eye evil, because I am good?" ¹⁶ So the last shall be first, and the first last: for many be called, but few chosen.'

¹⁷ And Jesus going up to Jerusalem, took the twelve disciples apart in the way, and said unto them, ¹⁸ 'Behold, we go up to Jerusalem, and the Son of Man shall be betrayed unto the chief priests, and unto the scribes, and they shall condemn him to death, ¹⁹ and shall deliver him to the Gentiles to mock, and to scourge, and to crucify him: and the third day he shall rise again'.

[20] Then came to him the mother of Zebedee's children, with her sons, worshipping him, and desiring a certain thing of him. [21] And he said unto her, 'What wilt thou?' She saith unto him, 'Grant, that these my two sons may sit, the one on thy right hand, and the other on the left in thy kingdom'. [22] But Jesus answered, and said, 'Ye know not what ye ask. Are ye able to drink of the cup that I shall drink of, and to be baptized with the baptism that I am baptized with?' They say unto him, 'We are able'. [23] And he saith unto them, 'Ye shall drink indeed of my cup, and be baptized with the baptism that I am baptized with: but to sit on my right hand, and on my left, is not mine to give, but it shall be given to them for whom it is prepared of my Father'.

[24] And when the ten heard it, they were moved with indignation against the two brethren. [25] But Jesus called them unto him, and said, 'Ye know that the princes of the Gentiles exercise dominion over them, and they that are great, exercise authority upon them. [26] But it shall not be so among you: but whosoever will be great among you, let him be your minister: [27] and whosoever will be chief among you, let him be your servant: [28] even as the Son of Man came not to be ministered unto, but to minister, and to give his life a ransom for many.'

[29] And as they departed from Jericho, a great multitude followed him. [30] And behold, two blind men sitting by the way side, when they heard that Jesus passed by, cried out, saying, 'Have mercy on us, O Lord, thou Son of David'. [31] And the multitude rebuked them, because they should hold their peace: but they cried the more, saying, 'Have mercy on us, O Lord, thou Son of David'. [32] And Jesus stood still, and called them, and said, 'What will ye that I shall do unto you?' [33] They say unto him, 'Lord, that our eyes may be opened'. [34] So Jesus had compassion on them, and touched their eyes: and immediately their eyes received sight, and they followed him.

Chapter 21

1 Christ rideth into Jerusalem upon an ass, 12 driveth the buyers and sellers out of the Temple, 17 curseth the fig tree, 23 putteth to silence the priests and elders, 28 and rebuketh them by the similitude of the two sons, 35 and the husbandmen, who slew such as were sent unto them.

AND when they drew nigh unto Jerusalem, and were come to Bethphage, unto the Mount of Olives, then sent Jesus two disciples, [2] saying unto them, 'Go into the village over against you, and straightway ye shall find an ass tied, and a colt with her: loose them, and bring them unto me. [3] And if any man say ought unto you, ye shall say, "The Lord hath need of them", and straightway he will send them.' [4] All this was done, that it might be fulfilled which was spoken by the prophet, saying, [5] 'Tell ye the daughter of Sion, "Behold, thy King cometh unto thee, meek, and sitting upon an ass, and a colt, the foal of an ass" '.

[6] And the disciples went, and did as Jesus commanded them, [7] and brought the ass, and the colt, and put on them their clothes, and they set him thereon. [8] And a very great multitude spread their garments in the way, others cut down branches from the trees, and strawed them in the way. [9] And the multitudes that went before, and that followed, cried, saying, 'Hosanna to the Son of David: blessed is he that cometh in the name of the Lord, Hosanna in the highest'. [10] And when he was come into Jerusalem, all the city was moved, saying, 'Who is this?' [11] And the multitude said, 'This is Jesus the prophet of Nazareth of Galilee'.

[12] And Jesus went into the Temple of God, and cast out all them that sold and bought in the Temple, and overthrew the tables of the money changers, and the seats of them that sold doves, [13] and said unto them, 'It is written, "My house shall be called the house of prayer", but ye have made it a den of thieves'.

[14] And the blind and the lame came to him in the Temple, and he healed them. [15] And when the chief priests and scribes saw the wonderful things that he did, and the children crying in the Temple, and saying, 'Hosanna to the Son of David', they were sore displeased, [16] and said unto him, 'Hearest thou what these say?' And Jesus saith unto them, 'Yea, have ye never read, "Out of the mouth of babes and sucklings thou hast perfected praise"?' [17] And he left them, and went out of the city into Bethany, and he lodged there.

[18] Now in the morning, as he returned into the city, he hungered. [19] And when he saw a fig tree in the way, he came to it, and found nothing thereon, but leaves only, and said unto it, 'Let no fruit grow on thee hence forward for ever'. And presently the fig tree withered away. [20] And when the disciples saw it, they marvelled, saying, 'How soon is the fig tree withered away?' [21] Jesus answered, and said unto them, 'Verily I say unto you, if ye have faith, and doubt not, ye shall not only do this which is done to the fig tree, but also, if ye shall say unto this

mountain, "Be thou removed, and be thou cast into the sea", it shall be done. [22] And all things whatsoever ye shall ask in prayer, believing, ye shall receive.'

[23] And when he was come into the Temple, the chief priests and the elders of the people came unto him as he was teaching, and said, 'By what authority doest thou these things? and who gave thee this authority?' [24] And Jesus answered and said unto them, 'I also will ask you one thing, which if ye tell me, I in like wise will tell you by what authority I do these things. [25] The baptism of John, whence was it? from heaven, or of men?' And they reasoned with themselves saying, 'If we shall say, "From heaven", he will say unto us, "Why did ye not then believe him?" [26] But if we shall say, "Of men", we fear the people, for all hold John as a prophet.' [27] And they answered Jesus, and said, 'We cannot tell'. And he said unto them, 'Neither tell I you by what authority I do these things.

[28] 'But what think you? A certain man had two sons, and he came to the first, and said, "Son, go work today in my vineyard". [29] He answered, and said, "I will not": but afterward he repented, and went. [30] And he came to the second, and said likewise: and he answered, and said, "I go, sir", and went not. [31] Whether of them twain did the will of his father?' They say unto him, 'The first'. Jesus saith unto them, 'Verily I say unto you, that the publicans and the harlots go into the kingdom of God before you. [32] For John came unto you in the way of righteousness, and ye believed him not: but the publicans and the harlots believed him. And ye when ye had seen it, repented not afterward, that ye might believe him.

[33] 'Hear another parable. There was a certain house-holder, which planted a vineyard, and hedged it round about, and digged a wine-press in it, and built a tower, and let it out to husbandmen, and went into a far country. [34] And when the time of the fruit drew near, he sent his servants to the husbandmen, that they might receive the fruits of it. [35] And the husbandmen took his servants, and beat one, and killed another, and stoned another. [36] Again he sent other servants, moe than the first, and they did unto them likewise. [37] But last of all he sent unto them his son, saying, "They will reverence my son". [38] But when the husbandmen saw the son, they said among themselves, "This is the heir, come, let us kill him, and let us seize on his inheritance". [39] And they caught him, and cast him out of the vineyard, and slew him. [40] When the lord therefore of the vineyard cometh, what

will he do unto those husbandmen?' [41] They say unto him, 'He will miserably destroy those wicked men, and will let out his vineyard unto other husbandmen, which shall render him the fruits in their seasons'.

[42] Jesus saith unto them, 'Did ye never read in the scriptures, "The stone which the builders rejected, the same is become the head of the corner: this is the Lord's doing, and it is marvellous in our eyes"? [43] Therefore say I unto you, the kingdom of God shall be taken from you, and given to a nation bringing forth the fruits thereof. [44] And whosoever shall fall on this stone, shall be broken: but on whom soever it shall fall, it will grind him to powder.' [45] And when the chief priests and Pharisees had heard his parables, they perceived that he spake of them. [46] But when they sought to lay hands on him, they feared the multitude, because they took him for a prophet.

Chapter 22

1 *The parable of the marriage of the king's son.* 9 *The vocation of the Gentiles.* 12 *The punishment of him that wanted the wedding garment.* 15 *Tribute ought to be paid to Caesar.* 23 *Christ confuteth the Sadducees for the resurrection:* 34 *answereth the lawyer, which is the first and great commandment:* 41 *and poseth the Pharisees about the Messiah.*

AND Jesus answered, and spake unto them again by parables, and said, [2] 'The kingdom of heaven is like unto a certain king, which made a marriage for his son, [3] and sent forth his servants to call them that were bidden to the wedding, and they would not come. [4] Again, he sent forth other servants, saying, "Tell them which are bidden, 'Behold, I have prepared my dinner; my oxen and my fatlings are killed, and all things are ready: come unto the marriage' ". [5] But they made light of it, and went their ways, one to his farm, another to his merchandise: [6] and the remnant took his servants, and intreated them spitefully, and slew them. [7] But when the king heard thereof, he was wroth, and he sent forth his armies, and destroyed those murderers, and burnt up their city. [8] Then saith he to his servants, "The wedding is ready, but they which were bidden, were not worthy. [9] Go ye therefore into the high ways, and as many as ye shall find, bid to the marriage." [10] So those servants went out into the high ways, and gathered together all as many as they found, both bad and good, and the wedding was furnished with guests.

[11] 'And when the king came in to see the guests, he saw there a man, which had not on a wedding garment, [12] and he saith unto him, "Friend, how camest thou in hither, not having a wedding garment?" And he was speechless. [13] Then said the king to the servants, "Bind him hand and foot, and take him away, and cast him into outer darkness, there shall be weeping and gnashing of teeth". [14] For many are called, but few are chosen.'

[15] Then went the Pharisees, and took counsel, how they might entangle him in his talk. [16] And they sent out unto him their disciples, with the Herodians, saying, 'Master, we know that thou art true, and teachest the way of God in truth, neither carest thou for any man; for thou regardest not the person of men. [17] Tell us therefore, what thinkest thou? is it lawful to give tribute unto Caesar, or not?' [18] But Jesus perceived their wickedness, and said, 'Why tempt ye me, ye hypocrites? [19] Show me the tribute money.' And they brought unto him a penny. [20] And he saith unto them, 'Whose is this image and superscription?' [21] They say unto him, 'Caesar's'. Then saith he unto them, 'Render therefore unto Caesar, the things which are Caesar's: and unto God, the things that are God's'. [22] When they had heard these words, they marvelled, and left him, and went their way.

[23] The same day came to him the Sadducees, which say that there is no resurrection, and asked him, [24] saying, 'Master, Moses said, "If a man die, having no children, his brother shall marry his wife, and raise up seed unto his brother". [25] Now there were with us seven brethren: and the first, when he had married a wife, deceased, and, having no issue, left his wife unto his brother. [26] Likewise the second also, and the third, unto the seventh. [27] And last of all the woman died also. [28] Therefore in the resurrection whose wife shall she be of the seven? for they all had her.' [29] Jesus answered, and said unto them, 'Ye do err, not knowing the scriptures, nor the power of God. [30] For in the resurrection they neither marry, nor are given in marriage, but are as the angels of God in heaven. [31] But as touching the resurrection of the dead, have ye not read that which was spoken unto you by God, saying, [32] "I am the God of Abraham, and the God of Isaac, and the God of Jacob"? God is not the God of the dead, but of the living.' [33] And when the multitude heard this, they were astonished at his doctrine.

[34] But when the Pharisees had heard that he had put the Sadducees to silence, they were gathered together. [35] Then one of them, which was a lawyer, asked him a question, tempting him, and saying, [36] 'Master, which is the great commandment in the Law?' [37] Jesus said unto him, 'Thou shalt love the Lord thy God with all thy heart, and with all thy soul, and with all thy mind. [38] This is the first and great commandment. [39] And the second is like unto it, thou shalt love thy neighbour as thyself. [40] On these two commandments hang all the Law and the Prophets.'

[41] While the Pharisees were gathered together, Jesus asked them, [42] saying, 'What think ye of Christ? whose son is he?' They say unto him, 'The Son of David'. [43] He saith unto them, 'How then doth David in Spirit call him Lord, saying, [44] "The Lord said unto my Lord, 'Sit thou on my right hand, till I make thine enemies thy footstool' "? [45] If David then call him Lord, how is he his son?' [46] And no man was able to answer him a word, neither durst any man (from that day forth) ask him any moe questions.

Chapter 23

1 *Christ admonisheth the people to follow the good doctrine, not the evil examples of the scribes and Pharisees. 5 His disciples must beware of their ambition. 13 He denounceth eight woes against their hypocrisy and blindness: 34 and prophesieth of the destruction of Jerusalem.*

THEN spake Jesus to the multitude, and to his disciples, [2] saying, 'The scribes and the Pharisees sit in Moses' seat: [3] all therefore whatsoever they bid you observe, that observe and do, but do not ye after their works: for they say, and do not. [4] For they bind heavy burdens, and grievous to be borne, and lay them on men's shoulders, but they themselves will not move them with one of their fingers. [5] But all their works they do, for to be seen of men: they make broad their phylacteries, and enlarge the borders of their garments, [6] and love the uppermost rooms at feasts, and the chief seats in the synagogues, [7] and greetings in the markets, and to be called of men, "Rabbi, Rabbi". [8] But be not ye called Rabbi: for one is your Master, even Christ, and all ye are brethren. [9] And call no man your father upon the earth: for one is your Father which is in heaven. [10] Neither be ye called masters: for one is your Master, even Christ. [11] But he that is greatest among you shall be your servant. ¹² And whosoever shall exalt himself shall be abased: and he that shall humble himself, shall be exalted.

¹³ 'But woe unto you, scribes and Pharisees, hypocrites; for ye shut up the kingdom of heaven against men: for ye neither go in yourselves, neither suffer ye them that are entering, to go in. ¹⁴ Woe unto you scribes and Pharisees, hypocrites; for ye devour widows' houses, and for a pretence make long prayer; therefore ye shall receive the greater damnation. ¹⁵ Woe unto you scribes and Pharisees, hypocrites; for ye compass sea and land to make one proselyte, and when he is made, ye make him two fold more the child of hell than yourselves.

¹⁶ 'Woe unto you, ye blind guides, which say, "Whosoever shall swear by the Temple, it is nothing: but whosoever shall swear by the gold of the Temple, he is a debtor". ¹⁷ Ye fools and blind: for whether is greater, the gold, or the Temple that sanctifieth the gold? ¹⁸ And, "Whosoever shall swear by the altar, it is nothing: but whosoever sweareth by the gift that is upon it, he is guilty". ¹⁹ Ye fools and blind: for whether is greater, the gift, or the altar that sanctifieth the gift? ²⁰ Who so therefore shall swear by the altar, sweareth by it, and by all things thereon. ²¹ And who so shall swear by the Temple, sweareth by it, and by him that dwelleth therein. ²² And he that shall swear by heaven, sweareth by the throne of God, and by him that sitteth thereon.

²³ 'Woe unto you scribes and Pharisees, hypocrites; for ye pay tithe of mint, and anise, and cummin, and have omitted the weightier matters of the Law, judgement, mercy, and faith: these ought ye to have done, and not to leave the other undone. ²⁴ Ye blind guides, which strain at a gnat, and swallow a camel.

²⁵ 'Woe unto you scribes and Pharisees, hypocrites; for ye make clean the outside of the cup, and of the platter, but within they are full of extortion and excess. ²⁶ Thou blind Pharisee, cleanse first that which is within the cup and platter, that the outside of them may be clean also.

²⁷ 'Woe unto you scribes and Pharisees, hypocrites; for ye are like unto whited sepulchres, which indeed appear beautiful outward, but are within full of dead men's bones, and of all uncleanness. ²⁸ Even so ye also outwardly appear righteous unto men, but within ye are full of hypocrisy and iniquity.

²⁹ 'Woe unto you scribes and Pharisees, hypocrites; because ye build the tombs of the prophets, and garnish the sepulchres of the righteous, ³⁰ and say, "If we had been in the days of our fathers, we would

not have been partakers with them in the blood of the prophets". [31] Wherefore ye be witnesses unto yourselves, that ye are the children of them which killed the prophets. [32] Fill ye up then the measure of your fathers. [33] Ye serpents, ye generation of vipers, how can ye escape the damnation of hell? [34] Wherefore behold, I send unto you prophets, and wisemen, and scribes, and some of them ye shall kill and crucify, and some of them shall ye scourge in your synagogues, and persecute them from city to city: [35] that upon you may come all the righteous blood shed upon the earth, from the blood of righteous Abel unto the blood of Zacharias, son of Barachias, whom ye slew between the Temple and the altar. [36] Verily I say unto you, all these things shall come upon this generation.

[37] 'O Jerusalem, Jerusalem, thou that killest the prophets, and stonest them which are sent unto thee, how often would I have gathered thy children together, even as a hen gathereth her chickens under her wings, and ye would not? [38] Behold, your house is left unto you desolate. [39] For I say unto you, ye shall not see me henceforth, till ye shall say, "Blessed is he that cometh in the name of the Lord".'

Chapter 24

1 Christ foretelleth the destruction of the Temple: 3 what, and how great calamities shall be before it: 29 the signs of his coming to judgement. 36 And because that day and hour is unknown, 42 we ought to watch like good servants expecting every moment our master's coming.

AND Jesus went out, and departed from the Temple, and his disciples came to him, for to show him the buildings of the Temple. [2] And Jesus said unto them, 'See ye not all these things? Verily I say unto you, there shall not be left here one stone upon another, that shall not be thrown down.'

[3] And as he sat upon the Mount of Olives, the disciples came unto him privately, saying, 'Tell us, when shall these things be? and what shall be the sign of thy coming, and of the end of the world?' [4] And Jesus answered, and said unto them, 'Take heed that no man deceive you. [5] For many shall come in my name, saying, "I am Christ": and shall deceive many. [6] And ye shall hear of wars, and rumours of wars: see that ye be not troubled: for all these things must come to pass, but the end is not yet. [7] For nation shall rise against nation, and kingdom

against kingdom, and there shall be famines, and pestilences, and earthquakes in divers places. [8] All these are the beginning of sorrows.

[9] 'Then shall they deliver you up to be afflicted, and shall kill you: and ye shall be hated of all nations for my name's sake. [10] And then shall many be offended, and shall betray one another, and shall hate one another. [11] And many false prophets shall rise, and shall deceive many. [12] And because iniquity shall abound, the love of many shall wax cold. [13] But he that shall endure unto the end, the same shall be saved. [14] And this gospel of the kingdom shall be preached in all the world, for a witness unto all nations, and then shall the end come.

[15] 'When ye therefore shall see the abomination of desolation, spoken of by Daniel the prophet, stand in the holy place (who so readeth, let him understand), [16] then let them which be in Judea flee into the mountains. [17] Let him which is on the house top not come down, to take any thing out of his house: [18] neither let him which is in the field, return back to take his clothes. [19] And woe unto them that are with child, and to them that give suck in those days. [20] But pray ye that your flight be not in the winter, neither on the Sabbath day: [21] for then shall be great tribulation, such as was not since the beginning of the world to this time, no, nor ever shall be. [22] And except those days should be shortened, there should no flesh be saved: but for the elect's sake those days shall be shortened. [23] Then if any man shall say unto you, "Lo, here is Christ", or "there": believe it not. [24] For there shall arise false Christs, and false prophets, and shall show great signs and wonders: insomuch that (if it were possible), they shall deceive the very elect. [25] Behold, I have told you before. [26] Wherefore, if they shall say unto you, "Behold, he is in the desert", go not forth: "Behold, he is in the secret chambers", believe it not. [27] For as the lightning cometh out of the east, and shineth even unto the west: so shall also the coming of the Son of Man be. [28] For wheresoever the carcass is, there will the eagles be gathered together.

[29] 'Immediately after the tribulation of those days, shall the sun be darkened, and the moon shall not give her light, and the stars shall fall from heaven, and the powers of the heavens shall be shaken. [30] And then shall appear the sign of the Son of Man in heaven: and then shall all the tribes of the earth mourn, and they shall see the Son of Man coming in the clouds of heaven, with power and great glory. [31] And he shall send his angels with a great sound of a trumpet, and they shall gather together his elect from the four winds, from one end of heaven to the other.

³² 'Now learn a parable of the fig tree: when his branch is yet tender, and putteth forth leaves, ye know that summer is nigh: ³³ so likewise ye, when ye shall see all these things, know that it is near, even at the doors. ³⁴ Verily I say unto you, this generation shall not pass, till all these things be fulfilled. ³⁵ Heaven and earth shall pass away, but my words shall not pass away.

³⁶ 'But of that day and hour knoweth no man, no, not the angels of heaven, but my Father only. ³⁷ But as the days of Noe were, so shall also the coming of the Son of Man be. ³⁸ For as in the days that were before the flood, they were eating, and drinking, marrying, and giving in marriage, until the day that Noe entered into the ark, ³⁹ and knew not until the flood came, and took them all away: so shall also the coming of the Son of Man be. ⁴⁰ Then shall two be in the field: the one shall be taken, and the other left. ⁴¹ Two women shall be grinding at the mill: the one shall be taken, and the other left. ⁴² Watch therefore, for ye know not what hour your Lord doth come. ⁴³ But know this, that if the goodman of the house had known in what watch the thief would come, he would have watched, and would not have suffered his house to be broken up. ⁴⁴ Therefore be ye also ready: for in such an hour as ye think not, the Son of Man cometh.

⁴⁵ 'Who then is a faithful and wise servant, whom his lord hath made ruler over his household, to give them meat in due season? ⁴⁶ Blessed is that servant, whom his lord when he cometh, shall find so doing. ⁴⁷ Verily I say unto you, that he shall make him ruler over all his goods. ⁴⁸ But and if that evil servant shall say in his heart, "My lord delayeth his coming", ⁴⁹ and shall begin to smite his fellow servants, and to eat and drink with the drunken: ⁵⁰ the lord of that servant shall come in a day when he looketh not for him, and in an hour that he is not ware of: ⁵¹ and shall cut him asunder, and appoint him his portion with the hypocrites: there shall be weeping and gnashing of teeth.'

Chapter 25

'THEN shall the kingdom of heaven be likened unto ten virgins, which took their lamps, and went forth to meet the bridegroom.

[2] And five of them were wise, and five were foolish. [3] They that were foolish took their lamps, and took no oil with them: [4] but the wise took oil in their vessels with their lamps. [5] While the bridegroom tarried, they all slumbered and slept. [6] And at midnight there was a cry made, "Behold, the bridegroom cometh, go ye out to meet him". [7] Then all those virgins arose, and trimmed their lamps. [8] And the foolish said unto the wise, "Give us of your oil, for our lamps are gone out". [9] But the wise answered, saying, "Not so, lest there be not enough for us and you: but go ye rather to them that sell, and buy for yourselves". [10] And while they went to buy, the bridegroom came, and they that were ready, went in with him to the marriage, and the door was shut. [11] Afterward came also the other virgins, saying, "Lord, lord, open to us". [12] But he answered and said, "Verily I say unto you, I know you not". [13] Watch therefore, for ye know neither the day, nor the hour, wherein the Son of Man cometh.

[14] 'For the kingdom of heaven is as a man travelling into a far country, who called his own servants, and delivered unto them his goods: [15] and unto one he gave five talents, to another two, and to another one, to every man according to his several ability, and straightway took his journey. [16] Then he that had received the five talents, went and traded with the same, and made them other five talents. [17] And likewise he that had received two, he also gained other two. [18] But he that had received one, went and digged in the earth, and hid his lord's money. [19] After a long time, the lord of those servants cometh, and reckoneth with them. [20] And so he that had received five talents, came and brought other five talents, saying, "Lord, thou deliveredst unto me five talents: behold, I have gained beside them five talents moe". [21] His lord said unto him, "Well done, thou good and faithful servant, thou hast been faithful over a few things, I will make thee ruler over many things: enter thou into the joy of thy lord". [22] He also that had received two talents, came and said, "Lord, thou deliveredst unto me two talents: behold, I have gained two other talents besides them". [23] His lord said unto him, "Well done, good and faithful servant, thou hast been faithful over a few things, I will make thee ruler over many things: enter thou into the joy of thy lord". [24] Then he which had received the one talent, came and said, "Lord, I knew thee that thou art an hard man, reaping where thou hast not sown, and gathering where thou hast not strawed: [25] and I was afraid, and went and hid thy talent in the earth: lo, there thou hast that is thine". [26] His lord

answered, and said unto him, "Thou wicked and slothful servant, thou knewest that I reap where I sowed not, and gather where I have not strawed: [27] thou oughtest therefore to have put my money to the exchangers, and then at my coming I should have received mine own with usury. [28] Take therefore the talent from him, and give it unto him which hath ten talents. [29] For unto every one that hath shall be given, and he shall have abundance: but from him that hath not, shall be taken away, even that which he hath. [30] And cast ye the unprofitable servant into outer darkness, there shall be weeping and gnashing of teeth."

[31] 'When the Son of Man shall come in his glory, and all the holy angels with him, then shall he sit upon the throne of his glory: [32] and before him shall be gathered all nations, and he shall separate them one from another, as a shepherd divideth his sheep from the goats. [33] And he shall set the sheep on his right hand, but the goats on the left. [34] Then shall the King say unto them on his right hand, "Come, ye blessed of my Father, inherit the kingdom prepared for you from the foundation of the world. [35] For I was an hungered, and ye gave me meat: I was thirsty, and ye gave me drink: I was a stranger, and ye took me in: [36] naked, and ye clothed me: I was sick, and ye visited me: I was in prison, and ye came unto me". [37] Then shall the righteous answer him, saying, "Lord, when saw we thee an hungered, and fed thee? or thirsty, and gave thee drink? [38] When saw we thee a stranger, and took thee in? or naked, and clothed thee? [39] Or when saw we thee sick, or in prison, and came unto thee?" [40] And the King shall answer, and say unto them, "Verily I say unto you, in as much as ye have done it unto one of the least of these my brethren, ye have done it unto me". [41] Then shall he say also unto them on the left hand, "Depart from me, ye cursed, into everlasting fire, prepared for the devil and his angels. [42] For I was an hungered, and ye gave me no meat: I was thirsty, and ye gave me no drink: [43] I was a stranger, and ye took me not in: naked, and ye clothed me not: sick, and in prison, and ye visited me not". [44] Then shall they also answer him, saying, "Lord, when saw we thee an hungred, or athirst, or a stranger, or naked, or sick, or in prison, and did not minister unto thee?" [45] Then shall he answer them, saying, "Verily I say unto you, in as much as ye did it not to one of the least of these, ye did it not to me". [46] And these shall go away into everlasting punishment: but the righteous into life eternal.'

Chapter 26

1 *The rulers conspire against Christ.* 6 *The woman anointeth his feet.*
14 *Judas selleth him.* 17 *Christ eateth the Passover:* 26 *instituteth his holy supper:* 36 *prayeth in the garden:* 47 *and being betrayed with a kiss,* 57 *is carried to Caiaphas,* 69 *and denied of Peter.*

AND it came to pass, when Jesus had finished all these sayings, he said unto his disciples, ² 'Ye know that after two days is the Feast of the Passover, and the Son of Man is betrayed to be crucified'. ³ Then assembled together the chief priests, and the scribes, and the elders of the people, unto the palace of the High Priest, who was called Caiaphas, ⁴ and consulted that they might take Jesus by subtlety, and kill him. ⁵ But they said, 'Not on the feast day, lest there be an uproar among the people'.

⁶ Now when Jesus was in Bethany, in the house of Simon the leper, ⁷ there came unto him a woman, having an alabaster box of very precious ointment, and poured it on his head, as he sat at meat. ⁸ But when his disciples saw it, they had indignation, saying, 'To what purpose is this waste? ⁹ For this ointment might have been sold for much, and given to the poor.' ¹⁰ When Jesus understood it, he said unto them, 'Why trouble ye the woman? for she hath wrought a good work upon me. ¹¹ For ye have the poor always with you, but me ye have not always. ¹² For in that she hath poured this ointment on my body, she did it for my burial. ¹³ Verily I say unto you, wheresoever this gospel shall be preached in the whole world, there shall also this, that this woman hath done, be told for a memorial of her.'

¹⁴ Then one of the twelve, called Judas Iscariot, went unto the chief priests, ¹⁵ and said unto them, 'What will ye give me, and I will deliver him unto you?' And they covenanted with him for thirty pieces of silver. ¹⁶ And from that time he sought opportunity to betray him.

¹⁷ Now the first day of the Feast of Unleavened Bread, the disciples came to Jesus, saying unto him, 'Where wilt thou that we prepare for thee to eat the Passover?' ¹⁸ And he said, 'Go into the city to such a man, and say unto him, "The master saith, 'My time is at hand, I will keep the Passover at thy house with my disciples' "'. ¹⁹ And the disciples did as Jesus had appointed them, and they made ready the Passover.

²⁰ Now when the even was come, he sat down with the twelve. ²¹ And as they did eat, he said, 'Verily I say unto you, that one of you

shall betray me'. ²² And they were exceeding sorrowful, and began every one of them to say unto him, 'Lord, is it I?' ²³ And he answered and said, 'He that dippeth his hand with me in the dish, the same shall betray me. ²⁴ The Son of Man goeth as it is written of him: but woe unto that man by whom the Son of Man is betrayed: it had been good for that man if he had not been born.' ²⁵ Then Judas, which betrayed him, answered, and said, 'Master, is it I?' He said unto him, 'Thou hast said'.

²⁶ And as they were eating, Jesus took bread, and blessed it, and brake it, and gave it to the disciples, and said, 'Take, eat, this is my body'. ²⁷ And he took the cup, and gave thanks, and gave it to them, saying, 'Drink ye all of it: ²⁸ for this is my blood of the new testament, which is shed for many for the remission of sins. ²⁹ But I say unto you, I will not drink henceforth of this fruit of the vine, until that day when I drink it new with you in my Father's kingdom.'

³⁰ And when they had sung an hymn, they went out into the Mount of Olives. ³¹ Then saith Jesus unto them, 'All ye shall be offended because of me this night, for it is written, "I will smite the shepherd, and the sheep of the flock shall be scattered abroad". ³² But after I am risen again, I will go before you into Galilee.' ³³ Peter answered, and said unto him, 'Though all men shall be offended because of thee, yet will I never be offended'. ³⁴ Jesus said unto him, 'Verily I say unto thee, that this night before the cock crow, thou shalt deny me thrice'. ³⁵ Peter said unto him, 'Though I should die with thee, yet will I not deny thee'. Likewise also said all the disciples.

³⁶ Then cometh Jesus with them unto a place called Gethsemane, and saith unto the disciples, 'Sit ye here, while I go and pray yonder'. ³⁷ And he took with him Peter, and the two sons of Zebedee, and began to be sorrowful, and very heavy. ³⁸ Then saith he unto them, 'My soul is exceeding sorrowful, even unto death: tarry ye here, and watch with me'. ³⁹ And he went a little further, and fell on his face, and prayed, saying, 'O my Father, if it be possible, let this cup pass from me: nevertheless, not as I will, but as thou wilt'.

⁴⁰ And he cometh unto the disciples, and findeth them asleep, and saith unto Peter, 'What, could ye not watch with me one hour? ⁴¹ Watch and pray, that ye enter not into temptation: the spirit indeed is willing, but the flesh is weak.' ⁴² He went away again the second time, and prayed, saying, 'O my Father, if this cup may not pass away from me, except I drink it, thy will be done'. ⁴³ And he came and found them

asleep again: for their eyes were heavy. [44] And he left them, and went away again, and prayed the third time, saying the same words. [45] Then cometh he to his disciples, and saith unto them, 'Sleep on now, and take your rest: behold, the hour is at hand, and the Son of Man is betrayed into the hands of sinners. [46] Rise, let us be going: behold, he is at hand that doth betray me.'

[47] And while he yet spake, lo, Judas one of the twelve came, and with him a great multitude with swords and staves, from the chief priests and elders of the people. [48] Now he that betrayed him, gave them a sign, saying, 'Whomsoever I shall kiss, that same is he, hold him fast'. [49] And forthwith he came to Jesus, and said, 'Hail, master', and kissed him. [50] And Jesus said unto him, 'Friend, wherefore art thou come?' Then came they, and laid hands on Jesus, and took him.

[51] And behold, one of them which were with Jesus, stretched out his hand, and drew his sword, and struck a servant of the High Priest, and smote off his ear. [52] Then said Jesus unto him, 'Put up again thy sword into his place: for all they that take the sword, shall perish with the sword. [53] Thinkest thou that I cannot now pray to my Father, and he shall presently give me more than twelve legions of angels? [54] But how then shall the scriptures be fulfilled, that thus it must be?' [55] In that same hour said Jesus to the multitudes, 'Are ye come out as against a thief with swords and staves for to take me? I sat daily with you teaching in the Temple, and ye laid no hold on me. [56] But all this was done, that the scriptures of the prophets might be fulfilled.' Then all the disciples forsook him, and fled.

[57] And they that had laid hold on Jesus, led him away to Caiaphas the High Priest, where the scribes and the elders were assembled. [58] But Peter followed him afar off, unto the High Priest's palace, and went in, and sat with the servants to see the end. [59] Now the chief priests and elders, and all the council, sought false witness against Jesus, to put him to death, [60] but found none: yea, though many false witnesses came, yet found they none. At the last came two false witnesses, [61] and said, 'This fellow said, "I am able to destroy the Temple of God, and to build it in three days"'. [62] And the High Priest arose, and said unto him, 'Answerest thou nothing? what is it which these witness against thee?' [63] But Jesus held his peace. And the High Priest answered, and said unto him, 'I adjure thee by the living God, that thou tell us, whether thou be the Christ the Son of God'. [64] Jesus saith unto him, 'Thou hast said: nevertheless I say unto you, hereafter shall ye see

the Son of Man sitting on the right hand of power, and coming in the clouds of heaven'. ⁶⁵ Then the High Priest rent his clothes, saying, 'He hath spoken blasphemy: what further need have we of witnesses? Behold, now ye have heard his blasphemy. ⁶⁶ What think ye?' They answered and said, 'He is guilty of death'.⁶⁷ Then did they spit in his face, and buffeted him, and others smote him with the palms of their hands, ⁶⁸ saying, 'Prophesy unto us, thou Christ, who is he that smote thee?'

⁶⁹ Now Peter sat without in the palace: and a damsel came unto him, saying, 'Thou also wast with Jesus of Galilee'. ⁷⁰ But he denied before them all, saying, 'I know not what thou sayest'. ⁷¹ And when he was gone out into the porch, another maid saw him, and said unto them that were there, 'This fellow was also with Jesus of Nazareth'. ⁷² And again he denied with an oath, 'I do not know the man'. ⁷³ And after a while came unto him they that stood by, and said to Peter, 'Surely thou also art one of them, for thy speech bewrayeth thee'. ⁷⁴ Then began he to curse and to swear, saying, 'I know not the man'. And immediately the cock crew. ⁷⁵ And Peter remembered the words of Jesus, which said unto him, 'Before the cock crow, thou shalt deny me thrice'. And he went out, and wept bitterly.

Chapter 27

1 Christ is delivered bound to Pilate. 3 Judas hangeth himself. 19 Pilate admonished of his wife, 24 washeth his hands: 26 and looseth Barabbas. 29 Christ is crowned with thorns, 34 crucified, 40 reviled, 50 dieth, and is buried: 66 his sepulchre is sealed, and watched.

WHEN the morning was come, all the chief priests and elders of the people took counsel against Jesus to put him to death. ² And when they had bound him, they led him away, and delivered him to Pontius Pilate the governor.

³ Then Judas, which had betrayed him, when he saw that he was condemned, repented himself, and brought again the thirty pieces of silver to the chief priests and elders, ⁴ saying, 'I have sinned, in that I have betrayed the innocent blood'. And they said, 'What is that to us? see thou to that'. ⁵ And he cast down the pieces of silver in the Temple, and departed, and went and hanged himself. ⁶ And the chief priests took the silver pieces, and said, 'It is not lawful for to put them into

the treasury, because it is the price of blood'. [7] And they took counsel, and bought with them the potter's field, to bury strangers in. [8] Wherefore that field was called the Field of Blood unto this day. [9] (Then was fulfilled that which was spoken by Jeremy the prophet, saying, 'And they took the thirty pieces of silver, the price of him that was valued, whom they of the children of Israel did value: [10] and gave them for the potter's field, as the Lord appointed me'.)

[11] And Jesus stood before the governor, and the governor asked him, saying, 'Art thou the King of the Jews?' And Jesus said unto him, 'Thou sayest'. [12] And when he was accused of the chief priests and elders, he answered nothing. [13] Then saith Pilate unto him, 'Hearest thou not how many things they witness against thee?' [14] And he answered him to never a word: insomuch that the governor marvelled greatly.

[15] Now at that feast the governor was wont to release unto the people a prisoner, whom they would. [16] And they had then a notable prisoner, called Barabbas. [17] Therefore when they were gathered together, Pilate said unto them, 'Whom will ye that I release unto you? Barabbas, or Jesus, which is called Christ?' [18] For he knew that for envy they had delivered him. [19] When he was set down on the judgement seat, his wife sent unto him, saying, 'Have thou nothing to do with that just man: for I have suffered many things this day in a dream, because of him'. [20] But the chief priests and elders persuaded the multitude that they should ask Barabbas, and destroy Jesus. [21] The governor answered, and said unto them, 'Whether of the twain will ye that I release unto you?' They said, 'Barabbas'. [22] Pilate said unto them, 'What shall I do then with Jesus, which is called Christ?' They all said unto him, 'Let him be crucified'. [23] And the governor said, 'Why, what evil hath he done?' But they cried out the more, saying, 'Let him be crucified'.

[24] When Pilate saw that he could prevail nothing, but that rather a tumult was made, he took water, and washed his hands before the multitude, saying, 'I am innocent of the blood of this just person: see ye to it'. [25] Then answered all the people, and said, 'His blood be on us, and on our children'. [26] Then released he Barabbas unto them, and when he had scourged Jesus, he delivered him to be crucified.

[27] Then the soldiers of the governor took Jesus into the common hall, and gathered unto him the whole band of soldiers. [28] And they stripped him, and put on him a scarlet robe. [29] And when they had plaited a crown of thorns, they put it upon his head, and a reed in his right hand:

and they bowed the knee before him, and mocked him, saying, 'Hail, King of the Jews'. [30] And they spit upon him, and took the reed, and smote him on the head. [31] And after that they had mocked him, they took the robe off from him, and put his own raiment on him, and led him away to crucify him. [32] And as they came out, they found a man of Cyrene, Simon by name: him they compelled to bear his cross.

[33] And when they were come unto a place called Golgotha, that is to say, a Place of a Skull, [34] they gave him vinegar to drink, mingled with gall: and when he had tasted thereof, he would not drink. [35] And they crucified him, and parted his garments, casting lots: that it might be fulfilled which was spoken by the prophet, 'They parted my garments among them, and upon my vesture did they cast lots'. [36] And sitting down, they watched him there: [37] and set up over his head his accusation written, '*THIS IS JESUS THE KING OF THE JEWS*'.

[38] Then were there two thieves crucified with him: one on the right hand, and another on the left. [39] And they that passed by, reviled him, wagging their heads, [40] and saying, 'Thou that destroyest the Temple, and buildest it in three days, save thyself: if thou be the Son of God, come down from the cross'. [41] Likewise also the chief priests mocking him, with the scribes and elders, said, [42] 'He saved others, himself he cannot save: if he be the King of Israel, let him now come down from the cross, and we will believe him. [43] He trusted in God, let him deliver him now if he will have him: for he said, "I am the Son of God".' [44] The thieves also which were crucified with him, cast the same in his teeth.

[45] Now from the sixth hour there was darkness over all the land unto the ninth hour. [46] And about the ninth hour, Jesus cried with a loud voice, saying, '*Eli, Eli, lama sabachthani?*', that is to say, 'My God, my God, why hast thou forsaken me?' [47] Some of them that stood there, when they heard that, said, 'This man calleth for Elias'. [48] And straightway one of them ran, and took a sponge, and filled it with vinegar, and put it on a reed, and gave him to drink. [49] The rest said, 'Let be, let us see whether Elias will come to save him'.

[50] Jesus, when he had cried again with a loud voice, yielded up the ghost. [51] And behold, the veil of the Temple was rent in twain, from the top to the bottom, and the earth did quake, and the rocks rent. [52] And the graves were opened, and many bodies of saints which slept, arose, [53] and came out of the graves after his resurrection, and went into the holy city, and appeared unto many. [54] Now when the centurion,

and they that were with him, watching Jesus, saw the earthquake, and those things that were done, they feared greatly, saying, 'Truly this was the Son of God'.

⁵⁵ And many women were there (beholding afar off) which followed Jesus from Galilee, ministering unto him. ⁵⁶ Among which was Mary Magdalene, and Mary the mother of James and Joses, and the mother of Zebedee's children.

⁵⁷ When the even was come, there came a rich man of Arimathea, named Joseph, who also himself was Jesus's disciple: ⁵⁸ he went to Pilate, and begged the body of Jesus: then Pilate commanded the body to be delivered. ⁵⁹ And when Joseph had taken the body, he wrapped it in a clean linen cloth, ⁶⁰ and laid it in his own new tomb, which he had hewn out in the rock: and he rolled a great stone to the door of the sepulchre, and departed. ⁶¹ And there was Mary Magdalene, and the other Mary, sitting over against the sepulchre.

⁶² Now the next day that followed the day of the Preparation, the chief priests and Pharisees came together unto Pilate, ⁶³ saying, 'Sir, we remember that that deceiver said, while he was yet alive, "After three days I will rise again". ⁶⁴ Command therefore that the sepulchre be made sure, until the third day, lest his disciples come by night, and steal him away, and say unto the people, "He is risen from the dead": so the last error shall be worse than the first.' ⁶⁵ Pilate said unto them, 'Ye have a watch, go your way, make it as sure as ye can'. ⁶⁶ So they went, and made the sepulchre sure, sealing the stone, and setting a watch.

Chapter 28

¹ *Christ's resurrection is declared by an angel, to the women.* 9 *He himself appeareth unto them.* 11 *The high priests give the soldiers money to say that he was stolen out of his sepulchre.* 16 *Christ appeareth to his disciples,* 12 *and sendeth them to baptize and teach all nations.*

I<small>N</small> the end of the Sabbath, as it began to dawn towards the first day of the week, came Mary Magdalene, and the other Mary, to see the sepulchre. ² And behold, there was a great earthquake, for the angel of the Lord descended from heaven, and came and rolled back the stone from the door, and sat upon it. ³ His countenance was like lightning, and his raiment white as snow. ⁴ And for fear of him, the keepers did shake, and became as dead men. [5] And the angel answered, and said unto the women, 'Fear not ye: for I know that ye seek Jesus, which was crucified. [6] He is not here: for he is risen, as he said: come, see the place where the Lord lay. [7] And go quickly, and tell his disciples that he is risen from the dead. And behold, he goeth before you into Galilee, there shall ye see him: lo, I have told you.' [8] And they departed quickly from the sepulchre, with fear and great joy, and did run to bring his disciples word. [9] And as they went to tell his disciples, behold, Jesus met them, saying, 'All hail'. And they came, and held him by the feet, and worshipped him. [10] Then said Jesus unto them, 'Be not afraid: go tell my brethren that they go into Galilee, and there shall they see me'.

[11] Now when they were going, behold, some of the watch came into the city, and showed unto the chief priests all the things that were done. [12] And when they were assembled with the elders, and had taken counsel, they gave large money unto the soldiers, [13] saying, 'Say ye, "His disciples came by night, and stole him away while we slept". [14] And if this come to the governor's ears, we will persuade him, and secure you.' [15] So they took the money, and did as they were taught. And this saying is commonly reported among the Jews until this day.

[16] Then the eleven disciples went away into Galilee, into a mountain where Jesus had appointed them. [17] And when they saw him, they worshipped him: but some doubted. [18] And Jesus came, and spake unto them, saying, 'All power is given unto me in heaven and in earth. [19] Go ye therefore, and teach all nations, baptizing them in the name of the Father, and of the Son, and of the Holy Ghost: [20] teaching them to observe all things, whatsoever I have commanded you: and lo, I am with you alway, even unto the end of the world.' Amen.

THE GOSPEL ACCORDING TO
SAINT MARK

Chapter 1

THE beginning of the gospel of Jesus Christ, the Son of God, ²as it is written in the Prophets, 'Behold, I send my messenger before thy face, which shall prepare thy way before thee'. ³'The voice of one crying in the wilderness, "Prepare ye the way of the Lord, make his paths straight".'

⁴John did baptize in the wilderness, and preach the baptism of repentance, for the remission of sins. ⁵And there went out unto him all the land of Judea, and they of Jerusalem, and were all baptized of him in the river of Jordan, confessing their sins. ⁶And John was clothed with camel's hair, and with a girdle of a skin about his loins: and he did eat locusts and wild honey, ⁷and preached, saying, 'There cometh one mightier than I after me, the latchet of whose shoes I am not worthy to stoop down and unloose. ⁸I indeed have baptized you with water: but he shall baptize you with the Holy Ghost.'

⁹And it came to pass in those days, that Jesus came from Nazareth of Galilee, and was baptized of John in Jordan. ¹⁰And straightway coming up out of the water, he saw the heavens opened, and the Spirit like a dove descending upon him. ¹¹And there came a voice from heaven, saying, 'Thou art my beloved Son, in whom I am well pleased'.

¹²And immediately the Spirit driveth him into the wilderness. ¹³And he was there in the wilderness forty days tempted of Satan, and was with the wild beasts, and the angels ministered unto him.

¹⁴Now after that John was put in prison, Jesus came into Galilee, preaching the gospel of the kingdom of God, ¹⁵and saying, 'The time is fulfilled, and the kingdom of God is at hand: repent ye, and believe the gospel'. ¹⁶Now as he walked by the Sea of Galilee, he saw Simon,

and Andrew his brother, casting a net into the sea (for they were fishers). ¹⁷ And Jesus said unto them, 'Come ye after me; and I will make you to become fishers of men'. ¹⁸ And straightway they forsook their nets, and followed him. ¹⁹ And when he had gone a little further thence, he saw James the son of Zebedee, and John his brother, who also were in the ship mending their nets. ²⁰ And straightway he called them: and they left their father Zebedee in the ship with the hired servants, and went after him.

²¹ And they went into Capernaum, and straightway on the Sabbath day he entered into the synagogue, and taught. ²² And they were astonished at his doctrine: for he taught them as one that had authority, and not as the scribes. ²³ And there was in their synagogue a man with an unclean spirit, and he cried out, ²⁴ saying, 'Let us alone, what have we to do with thee, thou Jesus of Nazareth? Art thou come to destroy us? I know thee who thou art, the Holy One of God.' ²⁵ And Jesus rebuked him, saying, 'Hold thy peace, and come out of him'. ²⁶ And when the unclean spirit had torn him, and cried with a loud voice, he came out of him. ²⁷ And they were all amazed, insomuch that they questioned among themselves, saying, 'What thing is this? What new doctrine is this? For with authority commandeth he even the unclean spirits, and they do obey him.' ²⁸ And immediately his fame spread abroad throughout all the region round about Galilee.

²⁹ And forthwith, when they were come out of the synagogue, they entered into the house of Simon and Andrew, with James and John. ³⁰ But Simon's wife's mother lay sick of a fever, and anon they tell him of her. ³¹ And he came and took her by the hand, and lift her up, and immediately the fever left her, and she ministered unto them.

³² And at even, when the sun did set, they brought unto him all that were diseased, and them that were possessed with devils: ³³ and all the city was gathered together at the door. ³⁴ And he healed many that were sick of divers diseases, and cast out many devils, and suffered not the devils to speak, because they knew him.

³⁵ And in the morning, rising up a great while before day, he went out, and departed into a solitary place, and there prayed. ³⁶ And Simon, and they that were with him, followed after him: ³⁷ and when they had found him, they said unto him, 'All men seek for thee'. ³⁸ And he said unto them, 'Let us go into the next towns, that I may preach there also: for therefore came I forth'. ³⁹ And he preached in their synagogues throughout all Galilee, and cast out devils.

⁴⁰ And there came a leper to him, beseeching him, and kneeling down to him, and saying unto him, 'If thou wilt, thou canst make me clean'. ⁴¹ And Jesus moved with compassion, put forth his hand, and touched him, and saith unto him, 'I will, be thou clean'. ⁴² And as soon as he had spoken, immediately the leprosy departed from him, and he was cleansed. ⁴³ And he straitly charged him, and forthwith sent him away, ⁴⁴ and saith unto him, 'See thou say nothing to any man: but go thy way, show thyself to the priest, and offer for thy cleansing those things which Moses commanded, for a testimony unto them'. ⁴⁵ But he went out, and began to publish it much, and to blaze abroad the matter: insomuch that Jesus could no more openly enter into the city, but was without in desert places: and they came to him from every quarter.

Chapter 2

1 Christ healeth one sick of the palsy, 14 calleth Matthew from the receipt of custom, 15 eateth with publicans, and sinners, 18 excuseth his disciples for not fasting, 23 and for plucking the ears of corn on the Sabbath day.

AND again he entered into Capernaum after some days, and it was noised that he was in the house. ² And straightway many were gathered together, insomuch that there was no room to receive them, no not so much as about the door: and he preached the word unto them. ³ And they come unto him, bringing one sick of the palsy, which was borne of four. ⁴ And when they could not come nigh unto him for press, they uncovered the roof where he was: and when they had broken it up, they let down the bed wherein the sick of the palsy lay. ⁵ When Jesus saw their faith, he said unto the sick of the palsy, 'Son, thy sins be forgiven thee'. ⁶ But there were certain of the scribes sitting there, and reasoning in their hearts, ⁷ 'Why doth this man thus speak blasphemies? Who can forgive sins but God only?' ⁸ And immediately, when Jesus perceived in his spirit that they so reasoned within themselves, he said unto them, 'Why reason ye these things in your hearts? ⁹ Whether is it easier to say to the sick of the palsy, "Thy sins be forgiven thee": or to say, "Arise, and take up thy bed and walk"? ¹⁰ But that ye may know that the Son of Man hath power on earth to forgive sins' (he saith to the sick of the palsy), ¹¹ 'I say unto thee, "Arise, and take up thy bed, and go thy way into thine house".'

[12] And immediately he arose, took up the bed, and went forth before them all, insomuch that they were all amazed, and glorified God, saying, 'We never saw it on this fashion'.

[13] And he went forth again by the sea side, and all the multitude resorted unto him, and he taught them. [14] And as he passed by, he saw Levi the son of Alphaeus sitting at the receipt of custom, and said unto him, 'Follow me'. And he arose, and followed him.

[15] And it came to pass, that as Jesus sat at meat in his house, many publicans and sinners sat also together with Jesus and his disciples: for there were many, and they followed him. [16] And when the scribes and Pharisees saw him eat with publicans and sinners, they said unto his disciples, 'How is it that he eateth and drinketh with publicans and sinners?' [17] When Jesus heard it, he saith unto them, 'They that are whole, have no need of the physician, but they that are sick: I came not to call the righteous, but sinners to repentance'.

[18] And the disciples of John, and of the Pharisees used to fast; and they come, and say unto him, 'Why do the disciples of John, and of the Pharisees fast, but thy disciples fast not?' [19] And Jesus said unto them, 'Can the children of the bride-chamber fast, while the bridegroom is with them? As long as they have the bridegroom with them, they cannot fast. [20] But the days will come, when the bridegroom shall be taken away from them, and then shall they fast in those days.

[21] 'No man also seweth a piece of new cloth on an old garment: else the new piece that filled it up, taketh away from the old, and the rent is made worse. [22] And no man putteth new wine into old bottles, else the new wine doth burst the bottles, and the wine is spilled, and the bottles will be marred: but new wine must be put into new bottles.'

[23] And it came to pass, that he went through the corn fields on the Sabbath day, and his disciples began, as they went, to pluck the ears of corn. [24] And the Pharisees said unto him, 'Behold, why do they on the Sabbath day that which is not lawful?' [25] And he said unto them, 'Have ye never read what David did, when he had need, and was an hungered, he, and they that were with him? [26] How he went into the house of God in the days of Abiathar the High Priest, and did eat the shewbread, which is not lawful to eat, but for the priests, and gave also to them which were with him?' [27] And he said unto them, 'The Sabbath was made for man, and not man for the Sabbath: [28] therefore the Son of Man is Lord also of the Sabbath'.

Chapter 3

*1 Christ healeth the withered hand, 10 and many other infirmities:
11 rebuketh the unclean spirits: 13 chooseth his twelve apostles: 22 convinceth the blasphemy of casting out devils by Beelzebub: 31 and showeth
who are his brother, sister, and mother.*

AND he entered again into the synagogue, and there was a man there
which had a withered hand: ² and they watched him, whether he
would heal him on the Sabbath day, that they might accuse him. ³ And
he saith unto the man which had the withered hand, 'Stand forth'.
⁴ And he saith unto them, 'Is it lawful to do good on the Sabbath days,
or to do evil? to save life, or to kill?' But they held their peace. ⁵ And
when he had looked round about on them with anger, being grieved for
the hardness of their hearts, he saith unto the man, 'Stretch forth thine
hand'. And he stretched it out: and his hand was restored whole as
the other. ⁶ And the Pharisees went forth, and straightway took counsel
with the Herodians against him, how they might destroy him.

⁷ But Jesus withdrew himself with his disciples to the sea: and a
great multitude from Galilee followed him, and from Judea, ⁸ and
from Jerusalem, and from Idumea, and from beyond Jordan, and they
about Tyre and Sidon, a great multitude, when they had heard what
great things he did, came unto him. ⁹ And he spake to his disciples
that a small ship should wait on him, because of the multitude, lest
they should throng him. ¹⁰ For he had healed many, insomuch that
they pressed upon him, for to touch him, as many as had plagues.
¹¹ And unclean spirits, when they saw him, fell down before him, and
cried, saying, 'Thou art the Son of God'. ¹² And he straitly charged
them, that they should not make him known.

¹³ And he goeth up into a mountain, and calleth unto him whom he
would: and they came unto him. ¹⁴ And he ordained twelve, that they
should be with him, and that he might send them forth to preach:
¹⁵ and to have power to heal sicknesses, and to cast out devils. ¹⁶ And
Simon he surnamed Peter. ¹⁷ And James the son of Zebedee, and John
the brother of James (and he surnamed them Boanerges, which is,
the sons of thunder). ¹⁸ And Andrew, and Philip, and Bartholomew,
and Matthew, and Thomas, and James the son of Alphaeus, and
Thaddaeus, and Simon the Canaanite, ¹⁹ and Judas Iscariot, which
also betrayed him: and they went into an house.

²⁰ And the multitude cometh together again, so that they could not so much as eat bread. ²¹ And when his friends heard of it, they went out to lay hold on him, for they said, 'He is beside himself'. ²² And the scribes which came down from Jerusalem, said, 'He hath Beelzebub, and by the prince of the devils, casteth he out devils'. ²³ And he called them unto him, and said unto them in parables, 'How can Satan cast out Satan? ²⁴ And if a kingdom be divided against itself, that kingdom cannot stand. ²⁵ And if a house be divided against itself, that house cannot stand. ²⁶ And if Satan rise up against himself, and be divided, he cannot stand, but hath an end. ²⁷ No man can enter into a strong man's house, and spoil his goods, except he will first bind the strong man, and then he will spoil his house. ²⁸ Verily I say unto you, all sins shall be forgiven unto the sons of men, and blasphemies, wherewith soever they shall blaspheme: ²⁹ but he that shall blaspheme against the Holy Ghost, hath never forgiveness, but is in danger of eternal damnation.' ³⁰ Because they said, 'He hath an unclean spirit'.

³¹ There came then his brethren, and his mother, and standing without, sent unto him, calling him. ³² And the multitude sat about him, and they said unto him, 'Behold, thy mother and thy brethren without seek for thee'. ³³ And he answered them, saying, 'Who is my mother, or my brethren?' ³⁴ And he looked round about on them which sat about him, and said, 'Behold my mother and my brethren. ³⁵ For whosoever shall do the will of God, the same is my brother, and my sister, and mother.'

Chapter 4

1 The parable of the sower, 14 and the meaning thereof. 21 We must communicate the light of our knowledge to others. 26 The parable of the seed growing secretly, 30 and of the mustard seed. 35 Christ stilleth the tempest on the sea.

AND he began again to teach by the sea side: and there was gathered unto him a great multitude, so that he entered into a ship, and sat in the sea; and the whole multitude was by the sea on the land. ² And he taught them many things by parables, and said unto them in his doctrine, ³ 'Hearken, behold, there went out a sower to sow: ⁴ and it came to pass as he sowed, some fell by the way side, and the fowls of the air came, and devoured it up. ⁵ And some fell on stony ground, where it had not much earth: and immediately it sprang up, because it had no

depth of earth:[6] but when the sun was up, it was scorched, and because it had no root, it withered away.[7] And some fell among thorns, and the thorns grew up, and choked it, and it yielded no fruit.[8] And other fell on good ground, and did yield fruit that sprang up, and increased, and brought forth some thirty, and some sixty, and some an hundred.'
[9] And he said unto them, 'He that hath ears to hear, let him hear'.

[10] And when he was alone, they that were about him, with the twelve, asked of him the parable. [11] And he said unto them, 'Unto you it is given to know the mystery of the kingdom of God: but unto them that are without, all these things are done in parables: [12] that seeing they may see, and not perceive, and hearing they may hear, and not understand, lest at any time they should be converted, and their sins should be forgiven them'. [13] And he said unto them, 'Know ye not this parable? And how then will you know all parables? [14] The sower soweth the word. [15] And these are they by the way side, where the word is sown, but when they have heard, Satan cometh immediately, and taketh away the word that was sown in their hearts. [16] And these are they likewise which are sown on stony ground, who when they have heard the word, immediately receive it with gladness: [17] and have no root in themselves, and so endure but for a time: afterward, when affliction or persecution ariseth for the word's sake, immediately they are offended. [18] And these are they which are sown among thorns: such as hear the word, [19] and the cares of this world, and the deceitfulness of riches, and the lusts of other things entering in, choke the word, and it becometh unfruitful. [20] And these are they which are sown on good ground, such as hear the word, and receive it, and bring forth fruit, some thirty fold, some sixty, and some an hundred.'

[21] And he said unto them, 'Is a candle brought to be put under a bushel, or under a bed? and not to be set on a candlestick? [22] For there is nothing hid, which shall not be manifested: neither was any thing kept secret, but that it should come abroad. [23] If any man have ears to hear, let him hear.' [24] And he said unto them, 'Take heed what ye hear: with what measure ye mete, it shall be measured to you: and unto you that hear, shall more be given. [25] For he that hath, to him shall be given: and he that hath not, from him shall be taken, even that which he hath.'

[26] And he said, 'So is the kingdom of God, as if a man should cast seed into the ground, [27] and should sleep, and rise night and day, and the seed should spring, and grow up, he knoweth not how. [28] For the earth bringeth forth fruit of herself, first the blade, then the ear, after

that the full corn in the ear. ²⁹ But when the fruit is brought forth, immediately he putteth in the sickle, because the harvest is come.'

³⁰ And he said, 'Whereunto shall we liken the kingdom of God? Or with what comparison shall we compare it? ³¹ It is like a grain of mustard seed: which when it is sown in the earth, is less than all the seeds that be in the earth. ³² But when it is sown, it groweth up, and becometh greater than all herbs, and shooteth out great branches, so that the fowls of the air may lodge under the shadow of it.' ³³ And with many such parables spake he the word unto them, as they were able to hear it. ³⁴ But without a parable spake he not unto them, and when they were alone, he expounded all things to his disciples.

³⁵ And the same day, when the even was come, he saith unto them, 'Let us pass over unto the other side'. ³⁶ And when they had sent away the multitude, they took him, even as he was in the ship, and there were also with him other little ships. ³⁷ And there arose a great storm of wind, and the waves beat into the ship, so that it was now full. ³⁸ And he was in the hinder part of the ship asleep on a pillow: and they awake him, and say unto him, 'Master, carest thou not that we perish?' ³⁹ And he arose, and rebuked the wind, and said unto the sea, 'Peace, be still': and the wind ceased, and there was a great calm. ⁴⁰ And he said unto them, 'Why are ye so fearful? How is it that you have no faith?' ⁴¹ And they feared exceedingly, and said one to another, 'What manner of man is this, that even the wind and the sea obey him?'

Chapter 5

1 *Christ delivering the possessed of the legion of devils,* 13 *they enter into the swine,* 25 *he healeth the woman of the bloody issue,* 35 *and raiseth from death Jairus's daughter.*

AND they came over unto the other side of the sea, into the country of the Gadarenes. ² And when he was come out of the ship, immediately there met him out of the tombs, a man with an unclean spirit, ³ who had his dwelling among the tombs, and no man could bind him, no not with chains: ⁴ because that he had been often bound with fetters and chains, and the chains had been plucked asunder by him, and the fetters broken in pieces: neither could any man tame him. ⁵ And always night and day, he was in the mountains, and in the tombs, crying, and cutting himself with stones. ⁶ But when he saw Jesus afar off, he came and worshipped him, [7] and cried with a loud voice, and said, 'What have I to do with thee, Jesus, thou Son of the most high God? I adjure thee by God, that thou torment me not.' [8] (For he said unto him, 'Come out of the man, thou unclean spirit'.) [9] And he asked him, 'What is thy name?' And he answered, saying, 'My name is Legion: for we are many'. [10] And he besought him much, that he would not send them away out of the country. [11] Now there was there nigh unto the mountains a great herd of swine, feeding. [12] And all the devils besought him, saying, 'Send us into the swine, that we may enter into them'. [13] And forthwith Jesus gave them leave. And the unclean spirits went out, and entered into the swine, and the herd ran violently down a steep place into the sea (they were about two thousand) and were choked in the sea.

[14] And they that fed the swine fled, and told it in the city, and in the country. And they went out to see what it was that was done. [15] And they come to Jesus, and see him that was possessed with the devil, and had the legion, sitting, and clothed, and in his right mind: and they were afraid. [16] And they that saw it, told them how it befell to him that was possessed with the devil, and also concerning the swine. [17] And they began to pray him to depart out of their coasts. [18] And when he was come into the ship, he that had been possessed with the devil prayed him that he might be with him. [19] Howbeit Jesus suffered him not, but saith unto him, 'Go home to thy friends, and tell them how great things the Lord hath done for thee, and hath had compassion on thee'. [20] And he departed, and began to publish in Decapolis, how great things Jesus had done for him: and all men did marvel.

[21] And when Jesus was passed over again by ship unto the other side, much people gathered unto him, and he was nigh unto the sea. [22] And behold, there cometh one of the rulers of the synagogue, Jairus by name, and when he saw him, he fell at his feet, [23] and besought him greatly, saying, 'My little daughter lieth at the point of death, I pray thee come and lay thy hands on her, that she may be healed, and she shall live'. [24] And Jesus went with him, and much people followed him, and thronged him.

[25] And a certain woman which had an issue of blood twelve years, [26] and had suffered many things of many physicians, and had spent all that she had, and was nothing bettered, but rather grew worse, [27] when she had heard of Jesus, came in the press behind, and touched his garment. [28] For she said, 'If I may touch but his clothes, I shall be whole'.

²⁹ And straightway the fountain of her blood was dried up: and she felt in her body that she was healed of that plague. ³⁰ And Jesus immediately knowing in himself that virtue had gone out of him, turned him about in the press, and said, 'Who touched my clothes?' ³¹ And his disciples said unto him, 'Thou seest the multitude thronging thee, and sayest thou, "Who touched me?"' ³² And he looked round about to see her that had done this thing. ³³ But the woman fearing and trembling, knowing what was done in her, came and fell down before him, and told him all the truth. ³⁴ And he said unto her, 'Daughter, thy faith hath made thee whole, go in peace, and be whole of thy plague'.

³⁵ While he yet spake, there came from the ruler of the synagogue's house, certain which said, 'Thy daughter is dead, why troublest thou the Master any further?' ³⁶ As soon as Jesus heard the word that was spoken, he saith unto the ruler of the synagogue, 'Be not afraid, only believe'. ³⁷ And he suffered no man to follow him, save Peter, and James, and John the brother of James. ³⁸ And he cometh to the house of the ruler of the synagogue, and seeth the tumult, and them that wept and wailed greatly. ³⁹ And when he was come in, he saith unto them, 'Why make ye this ado, and weep? the damsel is not dead, but sleepeth'. ⁴⁰ And they laughed him to scorn: but when he had put them all out, he taketh the father and the mother of the damsel, and them that were with him, and entereth in where the damsel was lying. ⁴¹ And he took the damsel by the hand, and said unto her, '*Talitha cumi*', which is, being interpreted, 'Damsel (I say unto thee) arise'. ⁴² And straightway the damsel arose, and walked, for she was of the age of twelve years: and they were astonished with a great astonishment. ⁴³ And he charged them straitly, that no man should know it: and commanded that something should be given her to eat.

Chapter 6

1 *Christ is contemned of his countrymen.* 7 *He giveth the twelve power over unclean spirits.* 14 *Divers opinions of Christ.* 18 *John Baptist is beheaded,* 29 *and buried.* 30 *The apostles return from preaching.* 34 *The miracle of five loaves and two fishes.* 45 *Christ walketh on the sea:* 53 *and healeth all that touch him.*

AND he went out from thence, and came into his own country, and his disciples follow him. ² And when the Sabbath day was come, he began to teach in the synagogue: and many hearing him, were astonished, saying, 'From whence hath this man these things? And what wisdom is this which is given unto him, that even such mighty works are wrought by his hands? ³ Is not this the carpenter, the son of Mary, the brother of James and Joses, and of Juda, and Simon? And are not his sisters here with us?' And they were offended at him. ⁴ But Jesus said unto them, 'A prophet is not without honour, but in his own country, and among his own kin, and in his own house'. ⁵ And he could there do no mighty work, save that he laid his hands upon a few sick folk, and healed them. ⁶ And he marvelled because of their unbelief. And he went round about the villages, teaching.

⁷ And he calleth unto him the twelve, and began to send them forth, by two and two, and gave them power over unclean spirits, ⁸ and commanded them that they should take nothing for their journey, save a staff only: no scrip, no bread, no money in their purse: ⁹ but be shod with sandals: and not put on two coats. ¹⁰ And he said unto them, 'In what place soever ye enter into an house, there abide till ye depart from that place. ¹¹ And whosoever shall not receive you, nor hear you, when ye depart thence, shake off the dust under your feet, for a testimony against them: verily I say unto you, it shall be more tolerable for Sodom and Gomorrha in the Day of Judgement, than for that city.' ¹² And they went out, and preached that men should repent. ¹³ And they cast out many devils, and anointed with oil many that were sick, and healed them.

¹⁴ And King Herod heard of him (for his name was spread abroad): and he said that John the Baptist was risen from the dead, and therefore mighty works do show forth themselves in him. ¹⁵ Others said, that it is Elias. And others said, that it is a prophet, or as one of the prophets. ¹⁶ But when Herod heard thereof, he said, 'It is John, whom I beheaded, he is risen from the dead'.

¹⁷ For Herod himself had sent forth and laid hold upon John, and bound him in prison for Herodias's sake, his brother Philip's wife, for he had married her. ¹⁸ For John had said unto Herod, 'It is not lawful for thee to have thy brother's wife'. ¹⁹ Therefore Herodias had a quarrel against him, and would have killed him, but she could not. ²⁰ For Herod feared John, knowing that he was a just man, and an holy, and observed him: and when he heard him, he did many things, and heard him gladly. ²¹ And when a convenient day was come, that Herod on his birth day made a supper to his lords, high captains, and

chief estates of Galilee: [22] and when the daughter of the said Herodias came in, and danced, and pleased Herod, and them that sat with him, the king said unto the damsel, 'Ask of me whatsoever thou wilt, and I will give it thee'. [23] And he sware unto her, 'Whatsoever thou shalt ask of me, I will give it thee, unto the half of my kingdom'. [24] And she went forth, and said unto her mother, 'What shall I ask?' And she said, 'The head of John the Baptist'. [25] And she came in straightway with haste, unto the king, and asked, saying, 'I will that thou give me by and by in a charger, the head of John the Baptist'. [26] And the king was exceeding sorry, yet for his oath's sake, and for their sakes which sat with him, he would not reject her. [27] And immediately the king sent an executioner, and commanded his head to be brought, and he went, and beheaded him in the prison, [28] and brought his head in a charger, and gave it to the damsel, and the damsel gave it to her mother. [29] And when his disciples heard of it, they came and took up his corpse, and laid it in a tomb.

[30] And the apostles gathered themselves together unto Jesus, and told him all things, both what they had done, and what they had taught. [31] And he said unto them, 'Come ye yourselves apart into a desert place, and rest a while'. For there were many coming and going, and they had no leisure so much as to eat. [32] And they departed into a desert place by ship privately. [33] And the people saw them departing, and many knew him, and ran afoot thither out of all cities, and outwent them, and came together unto him. [34] And Jesus when he came out, saw much people, and was moved with compassion toward them, because they were as sheep not having a shepherd: and he began to teach them many things. [35] And when the day was now far spent, his disciples came unto him, and said, 'This is a desert place, and now the time is far passed. [36] Send them away, that they may go into the country round about, and into the villages, and buy themselves bread: for they have nothing to eat.' [37] He answered and said unto them, 'Give ye them to eat'. And they say unto him, 'Shall we go and buy two hundred pennyworth of bread, and give them to eat?' [38] He saith unto them, 'How many loaves have ye? go, and see'. And when they knew, they say, 'Five, and two fishes'. [39] And he commanded them to make all sit down by companies upon the green grass. [40] And they sat down in ranks by hundreds, and by fifties. [41] And when he had taken the five loaves, and the two fishes, he looked up to heaven, and blessed, and brake the loaves, and gave them to his disciples to set before them;

and the two fishes divided he among them all. ⁴² And they did all eat, and were filled. ⁴³ And they took up twelve baskets full of the fragments, and of the fishes. ⁴⁴ And they that did eat of the loaves, were about five thousand men.

⁴⁵ And straightway he constrained his disciples to get into the ship, and to go to the other side before unto Bethsaida, while he sent away the people. ⁴⁶ And when he had sent them away, he departed into a mountain to pray. ⁴⁷ And when even was come, the ship was in the midst of the sea, and he alone on the land. ⁴⁸ And he saw them toiling in rowing (for the wind was contrary unto them): and about the fourth watch of the night, he cometh unto them, walking upon the sea, and would have passed by them. ⁴⁹ But when they saw him walking upon the sea, they supposed it had been a spirit, and cried out ⁵⁰ (for they all saw him, and were troubled). And immediately he talked with them, and saith unto them, 'Be of good cheer, it is I, be not afraid'. ⁵¹ And he went up unto them into the ship, and the wind ceased: and they were sore amazed in themselves beyond measure, and wondered. ⁵² For they considered not the miracle of the loaves, for their heart was hardened.

⁵³ And when they had passed over, they came into the land of Gennesaret, and drew to the shore. ⁵⁴ And when they were come out of the ship, straightway they knew him, ⁵⁵ and ran through that whole region round about, and began to carry about in beds, those that were sick, where they heard he was. ⁵⁶ And whithersoever he entered, into villages, or cities, or country, they laid the sick in the streets, and besought him that they might touch if it were but the border of his garment: and as many as touched him, were made whole.

Chapter 7

1 *The Pharisees find fault at the disciples for eating with unwashen hands.* 8 *They break the commandment of God, by the traditions of men.* 4 *Meat defileth not the man.* 24 *He healeth the Syrophoenician woman's daughter of an unclean spirit,* 31 *and one that was deaf, and stammered in his speech.*

THEN came together unto him the Pharisees, and certain of the scribes, which came from Jerusalem. ² And when they saw some of his disciples eat bread with defiled (that is to say, with unwashen) hands, they found fault. ³ For the Pharisees and all the Jews, except

they wash their hands oft, eat not, holding the tradition of the elders.
[4] And when they come from the market, except they wash, they eat not.
And many other things there be, which they have received to hold, as
the washing of cups and pots, brazen vessels, and of tables. [5] Then the
Pharisees and scribes asked him, 'Why walk not thy disciples according to the tradition of the elders, but eat bread with unwashen hands?'
[6] He answered and said unto them, 'Well hath Esaias prophesied of
you hypocrites, as it is written, "This people honoureth me with their
lips, but their heart is far from me. [7] Howbeit in vain do they worship
me, teaching for doctrines, the commandments of men." [8] For laying
aside the commandment of God, ye hold the tradition of men, as the
washing of pots, and cups: and many other such like things ye do.'

[9] And he said unto them, 'Full well ye reject the commandment of
God, that ye may keep your own tradition. [10] For Moses said, "Honour
thy father and thy mother: and, whoso curseth father or mother, let
him die the death". [11] But ye say, "If a man shall say to his father or
mother, 'It is Corban', that is to say, a gift, by whatsoever thou mightest be profited by me: he shall be free". [12] And ye suffer him no more
to do ought for his father, or his mother: [13] making the word of God
of none effect through your tradition, which ye have delivered: and
many such like things do ye.'

[14] And when he had called all the people unto him, he said unto
them, 'Hearken unto me every one of you, and understand. [15] There
is nothing from without a man that entering into him, can defile him:
but the things which come out of him, those are they that defile the
man. [16] If any man have ears to hear, let him hear.'

[17] And when he was entered into the house from the people, his disciples asked him concerning the parable. [18] And he saith unto them,
'Are ye so without understanding also? Do ye not perceive that whatsoever thing from without entereth into the man, it cannot defile him,
[19] because it entereth not into his heart, but into the belly, and goeth
out into the draught, purging all meats?' [20] And he said, 'That which
cometh out of the man, that defileth the man. [21] For from within, out
of the heart of men, proceed evil thoughts, adulteries, fornications,
murders, [22] thefts, covetousness, wickedness, deceit, lasciviousness,
an evil eye, blasphemy, pride, foolishness: [23] all these evil things come
from within, and defile the man.'

[24] And from thence he arose, and went into the borders of Tyre and
Sidon, and entered into an house, and would have no man know it,

but he could not be hid. ²⁵ For a certain woman, whose young daughter had an unclean spirit, heard of him, and came and fell at his feet. ²⁶ The woman was a Greek, a Syrophoenician by nation: and she besought him that he would cast forth the devil out of her daughter. ²⁷ But Jesus said unto her, 'Let the children first be filled: for it is not meet to take the children's bread, and to cast it unto the dogs'. ²⁸ And she answered and said unto him, 'Yes Lord, yet the dogs under the table eat of the children's crumbs'. ²⁹ And he said unto her, 'For this saying, go thy way, the devil is gone out of thy daughter'. ³⁰ And when she was come to her house, she found the devil gone out, and her daughter laid upon the bed.

³¹ And again departing from the coasts of Tyre and Sidon, he came unto the Sea of Galilee, through the midst of the coasts of Decapolis. ³² And they bring unto him one that was deaf, and had an impediment in his speech: and they beseech him to put his hand upon him. ³³ And he took him aside from the multitude, and put his fingers into his ears, and he spit, and touched his tongue, ³⁴ and looking up to heaven, he sighed, and saith unto him, 'Ephphatha', that is, 'Be opened'. ³⁵ And straightway his ears were opened, and the string of his tongue was loosed, and he spake plain. ³⁶ And he charged them that they should tell no man: but the more he charged them, so much the more a great deal they published it, ³⁷ and were beyond measure astonished, saying, 'He hath done all things well: he maketh both the deaf to hear, and the dumb to speak'.

Chapter 8

1 Christ feedeth the people miraculously: 10 refuseth to give a sign to the Pharisees: 14 admonisheth his disciples to beware of the leaven of the Pharisees, and of the leaven of Herod: 22 giveth a blind man his sight: 27 acknowledgeth that he is the Christ, who should suffer and rise again: 34 and exhorteth to patience in persecution for the profession of the gospel.

IN those days the multitude being very great, and having nothing to eat, Jesus called his disciples unto him, and saith unto them, ² 'I have compassion on the multitude, because they have now been with me three days, and have nothing to eat: ³ and if I send them away fasting to their own houses, they will faint by the way: for divers of them came from far'. [4] And his disciples answered him, 'From whence can a man satisfy these men with bread here in the wilderness?' [5] And he asked them, 'How many loaves have ye?' And they said, 'Seven'. [6] And he commanded the people to sit down on the ground: and he took the seven loaves, and gave thanks, and brake, and gave to his disciples to set before them: and they did set them before the people. [7] And they had a few small fishes: and he blessed, and commanded to set them also before them. [8] So they did eat, and were filled: and they took up, of the broken meat that was left, seven baskets. [9] And they that had eaten were about four thousand, and he sent them away.

[10] And straightway he entered into a ship with his disciples, and came into the parts of Dalmanutha. [11] And the Pharisees came forth, and began to question with him, seeking of him a sign from heaven, tempting him. [12] And he sighed deeply in his spirit, and saith, 'Why doth this generation seek after a sign? Verily I say unto you, there shall no sign be given unto this generation.' [13] And he left them, and entering into the ship again, departed to the other side.

[14] Now the disciples had forgotten to take bread, neither had they in the ship with them more than one loaf. [15] And he charged them, saying, 'Take heed, beware of the leaven of the Pharisees, and of the leaven of Herod'. [16] And they reasoned among themselves, saying, 'It is because we have no bread'. [17] And when Jesus knew it, he saith unto them, 'Why reason ye, because ye have no bread? Perceive ye not yet, neither understand? Have ye your heart yet hardened? [18] Having eyes, see ye not? and having ears hear ye not? And do ye not remember? [19] When I brake the five loaves among five thousand, how many baskets full of fragments took ye up?' They say unto him, 'Twelve'. [20] 'And when the seven among four thousand: how many baskets full of fragments took ye up?' And they said, 'Seven'. [21] And he said unto them, 'How is it that ye do not understand?'

[22] And he cometh to Bethsaida, and they bring a blind man unto him, and besought him to touch him: [23] and he took the blind man by the hand, and led him out of the town, and when he had spit on his eyes, and put his hands upon him, he asked him if he saw ought. [24] And he looked up, and said, 'I see men as trees, walking'. [25] After that he put his hands again upon his eyes, and made him look up: and he was restored, and saw every man clearly. [26] And he sent him away to his house, saying, 'Neither go into the town, nor tell it to any in the town'.

[27] And Jesus went out, and his disciples, into the towns of Caesarea Philippi: and by the way he asked his disciples, saying unto them, 'Whom do men say that I am?' [28] And they answered, 'John the Baptist: but some say, Elias: and others, one of the prophets'. [29] And he saith unto them, 'But whom say ye that I am?' And Peter answereth and saith unto him, 'Thou art the Christ'. [30] And he charged them that they should tell no man of him. [31] And he began to teach them, that the Son of Man must suffer many things, and be rejected of the elders, and of the chief priests, and scribes, and be killed, and after three days rise again. [32] And he spake that saying openly. And Peter took him, and began to rebuke him. [33] But when he had turned about, and looked on his disciples, he rebuked Peter, saying, 'Get thee behind me, Satan: for thou savourest not the things that be of God, but the things that be of men'.

[34] And when he had called the people unto him, with his disciples also, he said unto them, 'Whosoever will come after me, let him deny himself, and take up his cross and follow me. [35] For whosoever will save his life shall lose it, but whosoever shall lose his life for my sake and the gospel's, the same shall save it. [36] For what shall it profit a man, if he shall gain the whole world, and lose his own soul? [37] Or what shall a man give in exchange for his soul? [38] Whosoever therefore shall be ashamed of me, and of my words, in this adulterous and sinful generation, of him also shall the Son of Man be ashamed, when he cometh in the glory of his Father, with the holy angels.'

Chapter 9

2 Jesus is transfigured. 11 He instructeth his disciples, concerning the coming of Elias: 14 casteth forth a dumb, and deaf spirit: 30 foretelleth his death and resurrection: 33 exhorteth his disciples to humility: 38 bidding them, not to prohibit such as be not against them, nor to give offence to any of the faithfull.

AND he said unto them, 'Verily I say unto you, that there be some of them that stand here, which shall not taste of death, till they have seen the kingdom of God come with power'.

[2] And after six days, Jesus taketh with him Peter, and James, and John, and leadeth them up into an high mountain apart by themselves: and he was transfigured before them. [3] And his raiment became

shining, exceeding white as snow: so as no fuller on earth can white them. [4] And there appeared unto them Elias with Moses: and they were talking with Jesus. [5] And Peter answered, and said to Jesus, 'Master, it is good for us to be here, and let us make three tabernacles; one for thee, and one for Moses, and one for Elias'. [6] For he wist not what to say, for they were sore afraid. [7] And there was a cloud that overshadowed them: and a voice came out of the cloud, saying, 'This is my beloved Son: hear him'. [8] And suddenly when they had looked round about, they saw no man any more, save Jesus only with themselves.

[9] And as they came down from the mountain, he charged them that they should tell no man, what things they had seen, till the Son of Man were risen from the dead. [10] And they kept that saying with themselves, questioning one with another, what the rising from the dead should mean. [11] And they asked him, saying, 'Why say the scribes that Elias must first come?' [12] And he answered, and told them, 'Elias verily cometh first, and restoreth all things, and how it is written of the Son of Man, that he must suffer many things, and be set at nought. [13] But I say unto you, that Elias is indeed come, and they have done unto him whatsoever they listed, as it is written of him.'

[14] And when he came to his disciples, he saw a great multitude about them, and the scribes questioning with them. [15] And straightway all the people, when they beheld him, were greatly amazed, and running to him, saluted him. [16] And he asked the scribes, 'What question ye with them?' [17] And one of the multitude answered, and said, 'Master, I have brought unto thee my son, which hath a dumb spirit: [18] and wheresoever he taketh him, he teareth him, and he foameth, and gnasheth with his teeth, and pineth away: and I spake to thy disciples, that they should cast him out, and they could not'. [19] He answereth him, and saith, 'O faithless generation, how long shall I be with you, how long shall I suffer you? Bring him unto me.' [20] And they brought him unto him: and when he saw him, straightway the spirit tare him, and he fell on the ground, and wallowed, foaming. [21] And he asked his father, 'How long is it ago since this came unto him?' And he said, 'Of a child. [22] And oft times it hath cast him into the fire, and into the waters to destroy him: but if thou canst do any thing, have compassion on us, and help us.' [23] Jesus said unto him, 'If thou canst believe, all things are possible to him that believeth'. [24] And straightway the father of the child cried out and said with tears, 'Lord, I believe, help

thou mine unbelief'. [25] When Jesus saw that the people came running together, he rebuked the foul spirit, saying unto him, 'Thou dumb and deaf spirit, I charge thee come out of him, and enter no more into him'. [26] And the spirit cried, and rent him sore, and came out of him, and he was as one dead, insomuch that many said, 'He is dead'. [27] But Jesus took him by the hand, and lifted him up, and he arose. [28] And when he was come into the house, his disciples asked him privately, 'Why could not we cast him out?' [29] And he said unto them, 'This kind can come forth by nothing, but by prayer, and fasting'.

[30] And they departed thence, and passed through Galilee, and he would not that any man should know it. [31] For he taught his disciples, and said unto them, 'The Son of Man is delivered into the hands of men, and they shall kill him, and after that he is killed, he shall rise the third day'. [32] But they understood not that saying, and were afraid to ask him.

[33] And he came to Capernaum; and being in the house, he asked them, 'What was it that ye disputed among yourselves by the way?' [34] But they held their peace: for by the way they had disputed among themselves, who should be the greatest. [35] And he sat down, and called the twelve, and saith unto them, 'If any man desire to be first, the same shall be last of all, and servant of all'. [36] And he took a child, and set him in the midst of them: and when he had taken him in his arms, he said unto them, [37] 'Whosoever shall receive one of such children in my name, receiveth me: and whosoever shall receive me, receiveth not me, but him that sent me'.

[38] And John answered him, saying, 'Master, we saw one casting out devils in thy name, and he followeth not us, and we forbad him, because he followeth not us'. [39] But Jesus said, 'Forbid him not, for there is no man, which shall do a miracle in my name, that can lightly speak evil of me. [40] For he that is not against us, is on our part. [41] For whosoever shall give you a cup of water to drink in my name, because ye belong to Christ, verily I say unto you, he shall not lose his reward.

[42] 'And whosoever shall offend one of these little ones that believe in me, it is better for him, that a millstone were hanged about his neck, and he were cast into the sea. [43] And if thy hand offend thee, cut it off: it is better for thee to enter into life maimed, than having two hands to go into hell, into the fire that never shall be quenched: [44] where their worm dieth not, and the fire is not quenched. [45] And if thy foot offend thee, cut it off: it is better for thee to enter halt into life, than

having two feet, to be cast into hell, into the fire that never shall be quenched: [46] where their worm dieth not, and the fire is not quenched. [47] And if thine eye offend thee, pluck it out: it is better for thee to enter into the kingdom of God with one eye, than having two eyes, to be cast into hell fire: [48] where their worm dieth not, and the fire is not quenched.

[49] 'For every one shall be salted with fire, and every sacrifice shall be salted with salt. [50] Salt is good: but if the salt have lost his saltness, wherewith will ye season it? Have salt in yourselves, and have peace one with another.'

Chapter 10

2 Christ disputeth with the Pharisees, touching divorcement: 13 blesseth the children that are brought unto him: 17 resolveth a rich man how he may inherit life everlasting: 23 telleth his disciples of the danger of riches: 28 promiseth rewards to them that forsake any thing for the gospel: 32 foretelleth his death, and resurrection: 35 biddeth the two ambitious suitors to think rather of suffering with him: 46 and restoreth to Bartimaeus his sight.

AND he arose from thence, and cometh into the coasts of Judea by the farther side of Jordan: and the people resort unto him again, and as he was wont, he taught them again.

[2] And the Pharisees came to him, and asked him, 'Is it lawful for a man to put away his wife?' tempting him. [3] And he answered, and said unto them, 'What did Moses command you?' [4] And they said, 'Moses suffered to write a bill of divorcement, and to put her away'. [5] And Jesus answered, and said unto them, 'For the hardness of your heart, he wrote you this precept. [6] But from the beginning of the creation, God made them male, and female. [7] For this cause shall a man leave his father and mother, and cleave to his wife, [8] and they twain shall be one flesh: so then they are no more twain, but one flesh. [9] What therefore God hath joined together, let not man put asunder.'

[10] And in the house his disciples asked him again of the same matter. [11] And he saith unto them, 'Whosoever shall put away his wife, and marry another, committeth adultery against her. [12] And if a woman shall put away her husband, and be married to another, she committeth adultery.'

¹³ And they brought young children to him, that he should touch them, and his disciples rebuked those that brought them. ¹⁴ But when Jesus saw it, he was much displeased, and said unto them, 'Suffer the little children to come unto me, and forbid them not: for of such is the kingdom of God. ¹⁵ Verily I say unto you, whosoever shall not receive the kingdom of God as a little child, he shall not enter therein.' ¹⁶ And he took them up in his arms, put his hands upon them, and blessed them.

¹⁷ And when he was gone forth into the way, there came one running, and kneeled to him, and asked him, 'Good Master, what shall I do that I may inherit eternal life?' ¹⁸ And Jesus said unto him, 'Why callest thou me good? there is no man good, but one, that is God. ¹⁹ Thou knowest the commandments, do not commit adultery, do not kill, do not steal, do not bear false witness, defraud not, honour thy father and mother.' ²⁰ And he answered, and said unto him, 'Master, all these have I observed from my youth'. ²¹ Then Jesus beholding him, loved him, and said unto him, 'One thing thou lackest; go thy way, sell whatsoever thou hast, and give to the poor, and thou shalt have treasure in heaven, and come, take up the cross and follow me'. ²² And he was sad at that saying, and went away grieved: for he had great possessions.

²³ And Jesus looked round about, and saith unto his disciples, 'How hardly shall they that have riches enter into the kingdom of God?' ²⁴ And the disciples were astonished at his words. But Jesus answereth again, and saith unto them, 'Children, how hard is it for them that trust in riches, to enter into the kingdom of God? ²⁵ It is easier for a camel to go through the eye of a needle, than for a rich man to enter into the kingdom of God.' ²⁶ And they were astonished out of measure, saying among themselves, 'Who then can be saved?' ²⁷ And Jesus looking upon them, saith, 'With men it is impossible, but not with God: for with God all things are possible'.

²⁸ Then Peter began to say unto him, 'Lo, we have left all, and have followed thee'. ²⁹ And Jesus answered, and said, 'Verily I say unto you, there is no man that hath left house, or brethren, or sisters, or father, or mother, or wife, or children, or lands, for my sake, and the gospel's, ³⁰ but he shall receive an hundred fold now in this time, houses, and brethren, and sisters, and mothers, and children, and lands, with persecutions; and in the world to come eternal life. ³¹ But many that are first, shall be last: and the last, first.'

³² And they were in the way going up to Jerusalem: and Jesus went before them, and they were amazed, and as they followed, they were afraid: and he took again the twelve, and began to tell them what things should happen unto him, ³³ saying, 'Behold, we go up to Jerusalem, and the Son of Man shall be delivered unto the chief priests, and unto the scribes: and they shall condemn him to death, and shall deliver him to the Gentiles. ³⁴ And they shall mock him, and shall scourge him, and shall spit upon him, and shall kill him, and the third day he shall rise again.'

³⁵ And James and John, the sons of Zebedee come unto him, saying, 'Master, we would that thou shouldst do for us whatsoever we shall desire'. ³⁶ And he said unto them, 'What would ye that I should do for you?' ³⁷ They said unto him, 'Grant unto us that we may sit, one on thy right hand, and the other on thy left hand, in thy glory'. ³⁸ But Jesus said unto them, 'Ye know not what ye ask: can ye drink of the cup that I drink of? and be baptized with the baptism that I am baptized with?' ³⁹ And they said unto him, 'We can'. And Jesus said unto them, 'Ye shall indeed drink of the cup that I drink of: and with the baptism that I am baptized withal, shall ye be baptized: ⁴⁰ but to sit on my right hand and on my left hand, is not mine to give, but it shall be given to them for whom it is prepared'.

⁴¹ And when the ten heard it, they began to be much displeased with James and John. ⁴² But Jesus called them to him, and saith unto them, 'Ye know that they which are accompted to rule over the Gentiles, exercise lordship over them: and their great ones exercise authority upon them. ⁴³ But so shall it not be among you: but whosoever will be great among you, shall be your minister: ⁴⁴ and whosoever of you will be the chiefest, shall be servant of all. ⁴⁵ For even the Son of Man came not to be ministered unto, but to minister, and to give his life a ransom for many.'

⁴⁶ And they came to Jericho: and as he went out of Jericho with his disciples, and a great number of people, blind Bartimaeus, the son of Timaeus, sat by the highway side, begging. ⁴⁷ And when he heard that it was Jesus of Nazareth, he began to cry out, and say, 'Jesus thou Son of David, have mercy on me'. ⁴⁸ And many charged him, that he should hold his peace: but he cried the more a great deal, 'Thou Son of David, have mercy on me'. ⁴⁹ And Jesus stood still, and commanded him to be called: and they call the blind man, saying unto him, 'Be of good comfort, rise, he calleth thee'. ⁵⁰ And he casting

away his garment, rose, and came to Jesus. [51] And Jesus answered, and said unto him, 'What wilt thou that I should do unto thee?' The blind man said unto him, 'Lord, that I might receive my sight'. [52] And Jesus said unto him, 'Go thy way, thy faith hath made thee whole': and immediately he received his sight, and followed Jesus in the way.

Chapter 11

1 Christ rideth with triumph into Jerusalem: 12 curseth the fruitless leafy tree: 15 purgeth the Temple: 20 exhorteth his disciples to steadfastness of faith, and to forgive their enemies: 27 and defendeth the lawfulness of his actions, by the witness of John, who was a man sent of God.

AND when they came nigh to Jerusalem, unto Bethphage, and Bethany, at the Mount of Olives, he sendeth forth two of his disciples, [2] and saith unto them, 'Go your way into the village over against you, and as soon as ye be entered into it, ye shall find a colt tied, whereon never man sat, loose him, and bring him. [3] And if any man say unto you, "Why do ye this?" say ye, that the Lord hath need of him: and straightway he will send him hither.' [4] And they went their way, and found the colt tied by the door without, in a place where two ways met: and they loose him. [5] And certain of them that stood there, said unto them, 'What do ye loosing the colt?' [6] And they said unto them even as Jesus had commanded: and they let them go. [7] And they brought the colt to Jesus, and cast their garments on him, and he sat upon him. [8] And many spread their garments in the way: and others cut down branches of the trees, and strawed them in the way. [9] And they that went before, and they that followed, cried, saying, '*Hosanna*, blessed is he that cometh in the name of the Lord. [10] Blessed be the kingdom of our father David, that cometh in the name of the Lord, *Hosanna* in the highest.' [11] And Jesus entered into Jerusalem, and into the Temple, and when he had looked round about upon all things, and now the eventide was come, he went out unto Bethany with the twelve.

[12] And on the morrow when they were come from Bethany, he was hungry. [13] And seeing a fig tree a far off, having leaves, he came, if haply he might find any thing thereon, and when he came to it, he found nothing but leaves: for the time of figs was not yet. [14] And Jesus

answered, and said unto it, 'No man eat fruit of thee hereafter for ever'. And his disciples heard it.

¹⁵ And they come to Jerusalem, and Jesus went into the Temple, and began to cast out them that sold and bought in the Temple, and overthrew the tables of the money changers, and the seats of them that sold doves, ¹⁶ and would not suffer that any man should carry any vessel through the Temple. ¹⁷ And he taught, saying unto them, 'Is it not written, "My house shall be called of all nations the house of prayer"? but ye have made it a den of thieves'. ¹⁸ And the scribes and chief priests heard it, and sought how they might destroy him: for they feared him, because all the people was astonished at his doctrine. ¹⁹ And when even was come, he went out of the city.

²⁰ And in the morning, as they passed by, they saw the fig tree dried up from the roots. ²¹ And Peter calling to remembrance saith unto him, 'Master, behold, the fig tree which thou cursedst, is withered away'. ²² And Jesus answering, saith unto them, 'Have faith in God. ²³ For verily I say unto you, that whosoever shall say unto this mountain, "Be thou removed, and be thou cast into the sea", and shall not doubt in his heart, but shall believe that those things which he saith, shall come to pass: he shall have whatsoever he saith. ²⁴ Therefore I say unto you, what things soever ye desire when ye pray, believe that ye receive them, and ye shall have them. ²⁵ And when ye stand praying, forgive, if ye have ought against any: that your Father also which is in heaven, may forgive you your trespasses. ²⁶ But if you do not forgive, neither will your Father which is in heaven, forgive your trespasses.'

²⁷ And they come again to Jerusalem, and as he was walking in the Temple, there come to him the chief priests, and the scribes, and the elders, ²⁸ and say unto him, 'By what authority doest thou these things? and who gave thee this authority to do these things?' ²⁹ And Jesus answered, and said unto them, 'I will also ask of you one question, and answer me, and I will tell you by what authority I do these things. ³⁰ The baptism of John, was it from heaven, or of men? Answer me.' ³¹ And they reasoned with themselves, saying, if we shall say, 'From heaven', he will say, 'Why then did ye not believe him?' ³² But if we shall say, 'Of men', they feared the people: for all men counted John, that he was a prophet indeed. ³³ And they answered and said unto Jesus, 'We cannot tell'. And Jesus answering, saith unto them, 'Neither do I tell you by what authority I do these things'.

Chapter 12

*1 In a parable of the vineyard let out to unthankful husbandmen, Christ
foretelleth the reprobation of the Jews, and the calling of the Gentiles:
13 he avoideth the snare of the Pharisees and Herodians about paying
tribute to Caesar: 18 convinceth the error of the Sadducees, who denied
the resurrection: 28 resolveth the scribe who questioned of the first
commandment: 35 refuteth the opinion that the scribes held of Christ:
38 bidding the people to beware of their ambition, and hypocrisy: 41 and
commendeth the poor widow for her two mites, above all.*

AND he began to speak unto them by parables. 'A certain man
planted a vineyard, and set an hedge about it, and digged a place
for the wine fat, and built a tower, and let it out to husbandmen, and
went into a far country. ² And at the season, he sent to the husbandmen a servant, that he might receive from the husbandmen of the
fruit of the vineyard. ³ And they caught him, and beat him, and sent
him away empty. ⁴ And again, he sent unto them another servant; and
at him they cast stones, and wounded him in the head, and sent him
away shamefully handled. ⁵ And again, he sent another, and him they
killed: and many others, beating some, and killing some. ⁶ Having yet
therefore one son, his wellbeloved, he sent him also last unto them,
saying, "They will reverence my son". ⁷ But those husbandmen said
amongst themselves, "This is the heir, come, let us kill him, and the
inheritance shall be ours". ⁸ And they took him, and killed him, and
cast him out of the vineyard. ⁹ What shall therefore the lord of the
vineyard do? He will come and destroy the husbandmen, and will give
the vineyard unto others. ¹⁰ And have ye not read this scripture? "The
stone which the builders rejected, is become the head of the corner:
¹¹ this was the Lord's doing, and it is marvellous in our eyes".' ¹² And
they sought to lay hold on him, but feared the people, for they knew
that he had spoken the parable against them: and they left him, and
went their way.

¹³ And they send unto him certain of the Pharisees, and of the
Herodians, to catch him in his words. ¹⁴ And when they were come,
they say unto him, 'Master, we know that thou art true, and carest
for no man: for thou regardest not the person of men, but teachest
the way of God in truth. Is it lawful to give tribute to Caesar, or not?
¹⁵ Shall we give, or shall we not give?' But he knowing their hypocrisy,

said unto them, 'Why tempt ye me? Bring me a penny that I may see it.' ¹⁶ And they brought it: and he saith unto them, 'Whose is this image and superscription?' And they said unto him, 'Caesar's'. ¹⁷ And Jesus answering, said unto them, 'Render to Caesar the things that are Caesar's: and to God the things that are God's'. And they marvelled at him.

¹⁸ Then come unto him the Sadducees, which say there is no resurrection, and they asked him, saying, ¹⁹ 'Master, Moses wrote unto us, if a man's brother die, and leave his wife behind him, and leave no children, that his brother should take his wife, and raise up seed unto his brother. ²⁰ Now there were seven brethren: and the first took a wife, and dying left no seed. ²¹ And the second took her, and died, neither left he any seed, and the third likewise. ²² And the seven had her, and left no seed: last of all the woman died also. ²³ In the resurrection therefore, when they shall rise, whose wife shall she be of them? For the seven had her to wife.'

²⁴ And Jesus answering, said unto them, 'Do ye not therefore err, because ye know not the scriptures, neither the power of God? ²⁵ For when they shall rise from the dead, they neither marry, nor are given in marriage: but are as the angels which are in heaven. ²⁶ And as touching the dead, that they rise: have ye not read in the book of Moses, how in the bush God spake unto him, saying, "I am the God of Abraham, and the God of Isaac, and the God of Jacob?" ²⁷ He is not the God of the dead, but the God of the living: ye therefore do greatly err.'

²⁸ And one of the scribes came, and having heard them reasoning together, and perceiving that he had answered them well, asked him which is the first commandment of all. ²⁹ And Jesus answered him, 'The first of all the commandments is, "Hear, O Israel, the Lord our God is one Lord: ³⁰ and thou shalt love the Lord thy God with all thy heart, and with all thy soul, and with all thy mind, and with all thy strength": this is the first commandment. ³¹ And the second is like, namely this, "Thou shalt love thy neighbour as thyself": there is none other commandment greater than these.' ³² And the scribe said unto him, 'Well, Master, thou hast said the truth: for there is one God, and there is none other but he. ³³ And to love him with all the heart, and with all the understanding, and with all the soul, and with all the strength, and to love his neighbour as himself, is more than all whole burnt offerings and sacrifices.' ³⁴ And when Jesus saw that he answered

discreetly, he said unto him, 'Thou art not far from the kingdom of God'. And no man after that durst ask him any question.

³⁵ And Jesus answered, and said, while he taught in the Temple, 'How say the scribes that Christ is the Son of David? ³⁶ For David himself said by the Holy Ghost, "The Lord said to my Lord, 'Sit thou on my right hand, till I make thine enemies thy footstool'". ³⁷ David therefore himself calleth him Lord, and whence is he then his Son?' And the common people heard him gladly.

³⁸ And he said unto them in his doctrine, 'Beware of the scribes, which love to go in long clothing, and love salutations in the market places, ³⁹ and the chief seats in the synagogues, and the uppermost rooms at feasts: ⁴⁰ which devour widows' houses, and for a pretence make long prayers: these shall receive greater damnation'.

⁴¹ And Jesus sat over against the treasury, and beheld how the people cast money into the treasury: and many that were rich, cast in much. ⁴² And there came a certain poor widow, and she threw in two mites, which make a farthing. ⁴³ And he called unto him his disciples, and saith unto them, 'Verily I say unto you, that this poor widow hath cast more in, than all they which have cast into the treasury. ⁴⁴ For all they did cast in of their abundance: but she of her want, did cast in all that she had, even all her living.'

Chapter 13

1 Christ foretelleth the destruction of the Temple: 9 the persecutions for the gospel: 10 that the gospel must be preached to all nations: 14 that great calamities shall happen to the Jews: 24 and the manner of his coming to Judgement: 32 the hour whereof, being known to none, every man is to watch and pray, that we be not found unprovided, when he cometh to each one particularly by death.

AND as he went out of the Temple, one of his disciples saith unto him, 'Master, see what manner of stones and what buildings are here'. ² And Jesus answering, said unto him, 'Seest thou these great buildings? there shall not be left one stone upon another, that shall not be thrown down'.

³ And as he sat upon the Mount of Olives, over against the Temple, Peter, and James, and John, and Andrew asked him privately, ⁴ 'Tell us, when shall these things be? And what shall be the sign when all

these things shall be fulfilled?' [5] And Jesus answering them, began to say, 'Take heed lest any man deceive you. [6] For many shall come in my name, saying, "I am Christ": and shall deceive many. [7] And when ye shall hear of wars, and rumours of wars, be ye not troubled: for such things must needs be, but the end shall not be yet. [8] For nation shall rise against nation, and kingdom against kingdom: and there shall be earthquakes in divers places, and there shall be famines, and troubles: these are the beginnings of sorrows.

[9] 'But take heed to yourselves: for they shall deliver you up to councils, and in the synagogues ye shall be beaten, and ye shall be brought before rulers and kings for my sake, for a testimony against them. [10] And the gospel must first be published among all nations. [11] But when they shall lead you, and deliver you up, take no thought before hand what ye shall speak, neither do ye premeditate: but whatsoever shall be given you in that hour, that speak ye: for it is not ye that speak, but the Holy Ghost. [12] Now the brother shall betray the brother to death, and the father the son: and children shall rise up against their parents, and shall cause them to be put to death. [13] And ye shall be hated of all men for my name's sake: but he that shall endure unto the end, the same shall be saved.

[14] 'But when ye shall see the abomination of desolation spoken of by Daniel the prophet, standing where it ought not (let him that readeth understand) then let them that be in Judea, flee to the mountains: [15] and let him that is on the house top, not go down into the house, neither enter therein, to take any thing out of his house. [16] And let him that is in the field, not turn back again for to take up his garment. [17] But woe to them that are with child, and to them that give suck in those days. [18] And pray ye that your flight be not in the winter. [19] For in those days shall be affliction, such as was not from the beginning of the creation which God created, unto this time, neither shall be. [20] And except that the Lord had shortened those days, no flesh should be saved: but for the elect's sake whom he hath chosen, he hath shortened the days. [21] And then, if any man shall say to you, "Lo, here is Christ"; or, "Lo, he is there": believe him not. [22] For false Christs and false prophets shall rise, and shall show signs and wonders, to seduce, if it were possible, even the elect. [23] But take ye heed: behold, I have foretold you all things.

[24] 'But in those days, after that tribulation, the sun shall be darkened, and the moon shall not give her light. [25] And the stars of heaven

shall fall, and the powers that are in heaven shall be shaken. [26] And then shall they see the Son of Man coming in the clouds, with great power and glory. [27] And then shall he send his angels, and shall gather together his elect from the four winds, from the uttermost part of the earth, to the uttermost part of heaven.

[28] 'Now learn a parable of the fig tree. When her branch is yet tender, and putteth forth leaves, ye know that summer is near: [29] so ye in like manner, when ye shall see these things come to pass, know that it is nigh, even at the doors. [30] Verily I say unto you, that this generation shall not pass, till all these things be done. [31] Heaven and earth shall pass away: but my words shall not pass away.

[32] 'But of that day and that hour knoweth no man, no not the angels which are in heaven, neither the Son, but the Father. [33] Take ye heed, watch and pray: for ye know not when the time is. [34] For the Son of Man is as a man taking a far journey, who left his house, and gave authority to his servants, and to every man his work, and commanded the porter to watch: [35] watch ye therefore (for ye know not when the master of the house cometh, at even, or at midnight, or at the cock crowing, or in the morning). [36] Lest coming suddenly, he find you sleeping. [37] And what I say unto you, I say unto all, "Watch".'

Chapter 14

[1] *A conspiracy against Christ.* [3] *Precious ointment is poured on his head by a woman.* [10] *Judas selleth his master for money.* [12] *Christ himself foretelleth how he shall be betrayed of one of his disciples:* [22] *after the Passover prepared, and eaten, instituteth his Supper:* [26] *declareth aforehand the flight of all his disciples, and Peter's denial.* [43] *Judas betrayeth him with a kiss.* [46] *He is apprehended in the garden,* [53] *falsely accused, and impiously condemned of the Jews' council:* [65] *shamefully abused by them:* [66] *and thrice denied of Peter.*

AFTER two days was the Feast of the Passover, and of Unleavened Bread: and the chief priests and the scribes sought how they might take him by craft, and put him to death. [2] But they said, 'Not on the feast day, lest there be an uproar of the people'.

[3] And being in Bethany, in the house of Simon the leper, as he sat at meat, there came a woman, having an alabaster box of ointment of spikenard very precious, and she brake the box, and poured it on his

head. [4] And there were some that had indignation within themselves, and said, 'Why was this waste of the ointment made? [5] For it might have been sold for more than three hundred pence, and have been given to the poor': and they murmured against her. [6] And Jesus said, 'Let her alone, why trouble you her? She hath wrought a good work on me. [7] For ye have the poor with you always, and whensoever ye will ye may do them good: but me ye have not always. [8] She hath done what she could: she is come aforehand to anoint my body to the burying. [9] Verily I say unto you, wheresoever this gospel shall be preached throughout the whole world, this also that she hath done, shall be spoken of for a memorial of her.'

[10] And Judas Iscariot, one of the twelve, went unto the chief priests, to betray him unto them. [11] And when they heard it, they were glad, and promised to give him money. And he sought how he might conveniently betray him.

[12] And the first day of Unleavened Bread, when they killed the Passover, his disciples said unto him, 'Where wilt thou that we go, and prepare, that thou mayest eat the Passover?' [13] And he sendeth forth two of his disciples, and saith unto them, 'Go ye into the city, and there shall meet you a man bearing a pitcher of water: follow him. [14] And wheresoever he shall go in, say ye to the good man of the house, "The Master saith, 'Where is the guest chamber, where I shall eat the Passover with my disciples?' " [15] And he will show you a large upper room furnished, and prepared: there make ready for us.' [16] And his disciples went forth, and came into the city, and found as he had said unto them: and they made ready the Passover.

[17] And in the evening he cometh with the twelve. [18] And as they sat, and did eat, Jesus said, 'Verily I say unto you, one of you which eateth with me, shall betray me'. [19] And they began to be sorrowful, and to say unto him, one by one, 'Is it I?' And another said, 'Is it I?' [20] And he answered, and said unto them, 'It is one of the twelve, that dippeth with me in the dish. [21] The Son of Man indeed goeth, as it is written of him: but woe to that man by whom the Son of Man is betrayed: good were it for that man, if he had never been born.'

[22] And as they did eat, Jesus took bread, and blessed, and brake it, and gave to them, and said, 'Take, eat: this is my body'. [23] And he took the cup, and when he had given thanks, he gave it to them: and they all drank of it. [24] And he said unto them, 'This is my blood of the new testament, which is shed for many. [25] Verily I say unto you, I will drink

no more of the fruit of the vine, until that day that I drink it new in the kingdom of God.'

²⁶ And when they had sung an hymn, they went out into the Mount of Olives. ²⁷ And Jesus saith unto them, 'All ye shall be offended because of me this night: for it is written, "I will smite the shepherd, and the sheep shall be scattered". ²⁸ But after that I am risen, I will go before you into Galilee.' ²⁹ But Peter said unto him, 'Although all shall be offended, yet will not I'. ³⁰ And Jesus saith unto him, 'Verily I say unto thee, that this day, even in this night before the cock crow twice, thou shalt deny me thrice'. ³¹ But he spake the more vehemently, 'If I should die with thee, I will not deny thee in any wise'. Likewise also said they all.

³² And they came to a place which was named Gethsemane, and he saith to his disciples, 'Sit ye here, while I shall pray'. ³³ And he taketh with him Peter, and James, and John, and began to be sore amazed, and to be very heavy, ³⁴ and saith unto them, 'My soul is exceeding sorrowful unto death: tarry ye here, and watch'. ³⁵ And he went forward a little, and fell on the ground, and prayed, that if it were possible, the hour might pass from him. ³⁶ And he said, 'Abba, Father, all things are possible unto thee, take away this cup from me: nevertheless, not that I will, but what thou wilt'. ³⁷ And he cometh, and findeth them sleeping, and saith unto Peter, 'Simon, sleepest thou? Couldst not thou watch one hour? ³⁸ Watch ye and pray, lest ye enter into temptation: the spirit truly is ready, but the flesh is weak.' ³⁹ And again he went away, and prayed, and spake the same words. ⁴⁰ And when he returned, he found them asleep again (for their eyes were heavy), neither wist they what to answer him. ⁴¹ And he cometh the third time, and saith unto them, 'Sleep on now, and take your rest: it is enough, the hour is come, behold, the Son of Man is betrayed into the hands of sinners. ⁴² Rise up, let us go; lo, he that betrayeth me, is at hand.'

⁴³ And immediately, while he yet spake, cometh Judas, one of the twelve, and with him a great multitude with swords and staves, from the chief priests, and the scribes, and the elders. ⁴⁴ And he that betrayed him, had given them a token, saying, 'Whomsoever I shall kiss, that same is he; take him, and lead him away safely'. ⁴⁵ And as soon as he was come, he goeth straightway to him, and saith, 'Master, master', and kissed him. ⁴⁶ And they laid their hands on him, and took him. ⁴⁷ And one of them that stood by, drew a sword, and smote a

servant of the High Priest, and cut off his ear. [48] And Jesus answered, and said unto them, 'Are ye come out as against a thief, with swords, and with staves to take me? [49] I was daily with you in the Temple, teaching, and ye took me not; but the scriptures must be fulfilled.' [50] And they all forsook him, and fled.

[51] And there followed him a certain young man, having a linen cloth cast about his naked body, and the young men laid hold on him: [52] and he left the linen cloth, and fled from them naked.

[53] And they led Jesus away to the High Priest, and with him were assembled all the chief priests, and the elders, and the scribes. [54] And Peter followed him a far off, even into the palace of the High Priest: and he sat with the servants, and warmed himself at the fire. [55] And the chief priests, and all the council sought for witness against Jesus, to put him to death, and found none. [56] For many bare false witness against him, but their witness agreed not together. [57] And there arose certain, and bare false witness against him, saying, [58] 'We heard him say, "I will destroy this Temple that is made with hands, and within three days I will build another made without hands"'. [59] But neither so did their witness agree together. [60] And the High Priest stood up in the mids, and asked Jesus, saying, 'Answerest thou nothing? What is it which these witness against thee?' [61] But he held his peace, and answered nothing. Again, the High Priest asked him, and said unto him, 'Art thou the Christ, the Son of the Blessed?' [62] And Jesus said, 'I am: and ye shall see the Son of Man sitting on the right hand of power, and coming in the clouds of heaven'. [63] Then the High Priest rent his clothes, and saith, 'What need we any further witnesses? [64] Ye have heard the blasphemy: what think ye?' And they all condemned him to be guilty of death. [65] And some began to spit on him, and to cover his face, and to buffet him, and to say unto him, 'Prophesy': and the servants did strike him with the palms of their hands.

[66] And as Peter was beneath in the palace, there cometh one of the maids of the High Priest. [67] And when she saw Peter warming himself, she looked upon him, and said, 'And thou also wast with Jesus of Nazareth'. [68] But he denied, saying, 'I know not, neither understand I what thou sayest'. And he went out into the porch, and the cock crew. [69] And a maid saw him again, and began to say to them that stood by, 'This is one of them'. [70] And he denied it again. And a little after, they that stood by said again to Peter, 'Surely thou art one of them: for thou art a Galilean, and thy speech agreeth thereto'. [71] But he began

to curse and to swear, saying, 'I know not this man of whom ye speak'. [72] And the second time the cock crew: and Peter called to mind the word that Jesus said unto him, 'Before the cock crow twice, thou shalt deny me thrice'. And when he thought thereon, he wept.

Chapter 15

1 Jesus brought bound, and accused before Pilate. 15 Upon the clamour of the common people, the murderer Barabbas is loosed, and Jesus delivered up to be crucified: 17 he is crowned with thorns, 19 spit on, and mocked: 21 fainteth in bearing his cross: 27 hangeth between two thieves, 29 suffereth the triumphing reproaches of the Jews: 39 but confessed by the centurion, to be the Son of God: 43 and is honourably buried by Joseph.

AND straightway in the morning the chief priests held a consultation with the elders and scribes, and the whole council, and bound Jesus, and carried him away, and delivered him to Pilate. [2] And Pilate asked him, 'Art thou the King of the Jews?' And he answering, said unto him, 'Thou sayest it'. [3] And the chief priests accused him of many things: but he answered nothing. [4] And Pilate asked him again, saying, 'Answerest thou nothing? behold how many things they witness against thee'. [5] But Jesus yet answered nothing, so that Pilate marvelled.

[6] Now at that feast he released unto them one prisoner, whomsoever they desired. [7] And there was one named Barabbas, which lay bound with them that had made insurrection with him, who had committed murder in the insurrection. [8] And the multitude crying aloud, began to desire him to do as he had ever done unto them. [9] But Pilate answered them, saying, 'Will ye that I release unto you the King of the Jews?' [10] (For he knew that the chief priests had delivered him for envy.) [11] But the chief priests moved the people, that he should rather release Barabbas unto them. [12] And Pilate answered, and said again unto them, 'What will ye then that I shall do unto him whom ye call the King of the Jews?' [13] And they cried out again, 'Crucify him'. [14] Then Pilate said unto them, 'Why, what evil hath he done?' And they cried out the more exceedingly, 'Crucify him'. [15] And so Pilate, willing to content the people, released Barabbas unto them, and delivered Jesus, when he had scourged him, to be crucified.

¹⁶ And the soldiers led him away into the hall, called Praetorium, and they call together the whole band. ¹⁷ And they clothed him with purple, and platted a crown of thorns, and put it about his head, ¹⁸ and began to salute him, 'Hail, King of the Jews'. ¹⁹ And they smote him on the head with a reed, and did spit upon him, and bowing their knees, worshipped him. ²⁰ And when they had mocked him, they took off the purple from him, and put his own clothes on him, and led him out to crucify him. ²¹ And they compel one Simon a Cyrenian, who passed by, coming out of the country, the father of Alexander and Rufus, to bear his cross.

²² And they bring him unto the place Golgotha, which is, being interpreted, The Place of a Skull. ²³ And they gave him to drink, wine mingled with myrrh: but he received it not. ²⁴ And when they had crucified him, they parted his garments, casting lots upon them, what every man should take. ²⁵ And it was the third hour, and they cruci-fied him. ²⁶ And the superscription of his accusation was written over, 'THE KING OF THE JEWS'. ²⁷ And with him they crucify two thieves, the one on his right hand, and the other on his left. ²⁸ And the scripture was fulfilled, which saith, 'And he was numbered with the transgressors'.

²⁹ And they that passed by, railed on him, wagging their heads, and saying, 'Ah thou that destroyest the Temple, and buildest it in three days, ³⁰ save thyself, and come down from the cross'. ³¹ Likewise also the chief priests mocking, said among themselves with the scribes, 'He saved others, himself he cannot save. ³² Let Christ the King of Israel descend now from the cross, that we may see and believe': and they that were crucified with him, reviled him.

³³ And when the sixth hour was come, there was darkness over the whole land, until the ninth hour. ³⁴ And at the ninth hour, Jesus cried with a loud voice, saying, 'Eloi, Eloi, lama sabachthani?' which is, being interpreted, 'My God, my God, why hast thou forsaken me?' ³⁵ And some of them that stood by, when they heard it, said, 'Behold, he calleth Elias'. ³⁶ And one ran, and filled a sponge full of vinegar, and put it on a reed, and gave him to drink, saying, 'Let alone, let us see whether Elias will come to take him down'. ³⁷ And Jesus cried with a loud voice, and gave up the ghost. ³⁸ And the veil of the Temple was rent in twain, from the top to the bottom. ³⁹ And when the centurion which stood over against him, saw that he so cried out, and gave up the ghost, he said, 'Truly this man was the Son of God'.

⁴⁰ There were also women looking on afar off, among whom was Mary Magdalene, and Mary the mother of James the less and of Joses, and Salome: ⁴¹ who also when he was in Galilee, followed him, and ministered unto him, and many other women which came up with him unto Jerusalem.

⁴² And now when the even was come (because it was the Preparation, that is, the day before the Sabbath), ⁴³ Joseph of Arimathea, an honourable counsellor, which also waited for the kingdom of God, came, and went in boldly unto Pilate, and craved the body of Jesus. ⁴⁴ And Pilate marvelled if he were already dead, and calling unto him the centurion, he asked him whether he had been any while dead. ⁴⁵ And when he knew it of the centurion, he gave the body to Joseph. ⁴⁶ And he bought fine linen, and took him down, and wrapped him in the linen, and laid him in a sepulchre, which was hewn out of a rock, and rolled a stone unto the door of the sepulchre. ⁴⁷ And Mary Magdalene, and Mary the mother of Joses beheld where he was laid.

Chapter 16

1 *An angel declareth the resurrection of Christ to three women.* 9 *Christ himself appeareth to Mary Magdalene:* 12 *to two going into the country:* 14 *then, to the apostles,* 15 *whom he sendeth forth to preach the gospel:* 19 *and ascendeth into heaven.*

AND when the Sabbath was past, Mary Magdalene, and Mary the mother of James, and Salome, had bought sweet spices, that they might come and anoint him. ² And very early in the morning, the first day of the week they came unto the sepulchre, at the rising of the sun: ³ and they said among themselves, 'Who shall roll us away the stone from the door of the sepulchre?' ⁴ And when they looked, they saw that the stone was rolled away: for it was very great. ⁵ And entering into the sepulchre, they saw a young man sitting on the right side, clothed in a long white garment, and they were affrighted. ⁶ And he saith unto them, 'Be not affrighted; ye seek Jesus of Nazareth, which was crucified: he is risen, he is not here: behold the place where they laid him. ⁷ But go your way, tell his disciples, and Peter, that he goeth before you into Galilee, there shall ye see him, as he said unto you.' ⁸ And they went out quickly, and fled from the sepulchre, for they trembled, and were amazed, neither said they any thing to any man, for they were afraid.

⁹ Now when Jesus was risen early, the first day of the week, he appeared first to Mary Magdalene, out of whom he had cast seven devils. ¹⁰ And she went and told them that had been with him, as they mourned and wept. ¹¹ And they, when they had heard that he was alive, and had been seen of her, believed not.

¹² After that, he appeared in another form unto two of them, as they walked, and went into the country. ¹³ And they went and told it unto the residue, neither believed they them.

¹⁴ Afterward he appeared unto the eleven, as they sat at meat, and upbraided them with their unbelief, and hardness of heart, because they believed not them, which had seen him after he was risen. ¹⁵ And he said unto them, 'Go ye into all the world, and preach the gospel to every creature. ¹⁶ He that believeth and is baptized, shall be saved, but he that believeth not, shall be damned. ¹⁷ And these signs shall follow them that believe, in my name shall they cast out devils, they shall speak with new tongues, ¹⁸ they shall take up serpents, and if they drink any deadly thing, it shall not hurt them, they shall lay hands on the sick, and they shall recover.'

¹⁹ So then after the Lord had spoken unto them, he was received up into heaven, and sat on the right hand of God. ²⁰ And they went forth, and preached everywhere, the Lord working with them, and confirming the word with signs following. Amen.

THE GOSPEL ACCORDING TO
SAINT LUKE

Chapter 1

1 *The preface of Luke to his whole Gospel.* 5 *The conception of John the Baptist,* 26 *and of Christ.* 39 *The prophesy of Elizabeth, and of Mary, concerning Christ.* 57 *The nativity and circumcision of John.* 67 *The prophesy of Zachary both of Christ,* 76 *and of John.*

FORASMUCH as many have taken in hand to set forth in order a declaration of those things which are most surely believed among us, ² even as they delivered them unto us, which from the beginning were eye-witnesses, and ministers of the word: ³ it seemed good to me also, having had perfect understanding of things from the very first, to write unto thee in order, most excellent Theophilus, ⁴ that thou mightest know the certainty of those things, wherein thou hast been instructed.

⁵ THERE was in the days of Herod the king of Judea, a certain priest, named Zacharias, of the course of Abia, and his wife was of the daughters of Aaron, and her name was Elizabeth. ⁶ And they were both righteous before God, walking in all the commandments and ordinances of the Lord, blameless. ⁷ And they had no child, because that Elizabeth was barren, and they both were now well stricken in years.

⁸ And it came to pass, that while he executed the priest's office before God in the order of his course, ⁹ according to the custom of the priest's office, his lot was to burn incense when he went into the Temple of the Lord. ¹⁰ And the whole multitude of the people were praying without, at the time of incense. ¹¹ And there appeared unto him an angel of the Lord, standing on the right side of the altar of incense. ¹² And when Zacharias saw him, he was troubled, and fear fell upon him. ¹³ But the angel said unto him, 'Fear not, Zacharias, for thy prayer is heard; and thy wife Elizabeth shall bear thee a son, and thou shalt call his name John. ¹⁴ And thou shalt have joy and gladness, and many shall rejoice at his birth: ¹⁵ for he shall be great in the sight of the Lord, and shall drink neither wine, nor strong drink, and he

shall be filled with the Holy Ghost, even from his mother's womb.
[16] And many of the children of Israel shall he turn to the Lord their
God. [17] And he shall go before him in the spirit and power of Elias,
to turn the hearts of the fathers to the children, and the disobedient
to the wisdom of the just, to make ready a people prepared for the
Lord.' [18] And Zacharias said unto the angel, 'Whereby shall I know
this? For I am an old man, and my wife well stricken in years'. [19] And
the angel answering, said unto him, 'I am Gabriel that stand in the
presence of God, and am sent to speak unto thee, and to show thee
these glad tidings. [20] And behold, thou shalt be dumb, and not able
to speak, until the day that these things shall be performed, because
thou believest not my words, which shall be fulfilled in their season.'

[21] And the people waited for Zacharias, and marvelled that he tarried so long in the Temple. [22] And when he came out, he could not
speak unto them: and they perceived that he had seen a vision in
the Temple: for he beckoned unto them, and remained speechless.
[23] And it came to pass, that as soon as the days of his ministration were
accomplished, he departed to his own house.

[24] And after those days his wife Elizabeth conceived, and hid herself
five months, saying, [25] 'Thus hath the Lord dealt with me in the days
wherein he looked on me, to take away my reproach among men'.

[26] And in the sixth month, the angel Gabriel was sent from God,
unto a city of Galilee, named Nazareth, [27] to a virgin espoused to a man
whose name was Joseph, of the house of David; and the virgin's name
was Mary. [28] And the angel came in unto her, and said, 'Hail thou that
art highly favoured, the Lord is with thee: blessed art thou among
women'. [29] And when she saw him, she was troubled at his saying, and
cast in her mind what manner of salutation this should be. [30] And the
angel said unto her, 'Fear not, Mary, for thou hast found favour with
God. [31] And behold, thou shalt conceive in thy womb, and bring forth
a son, and shalt call his name Jesus. [32] He shall be great, and shall be
called the Son of the Highest, and the Lord God shall give unto him
the throne of his father David. [33] And he shall reign over the house of
Jacob for ever, and of his kingdom there shall be no end.' [34] Then said
Mary unto the angel, 'How shall this be, seeing I know not a man?'
[35] And the angel answered and said unto her, 'The Holy Ghost shall
come upon thee, and the power of the Highest shall overshadow thee.
Therefore also that holy thing which shall be born of thee, shall be
called the Son of God. [36] And behold, thy cousin Elizabeth, she hath

also conceived a son in her old age, and this is the sixth month with her, who was called barren. [37] For with God no thing shall be unpossible.' [38] And Mary said, 'Behold the handmaid of the Lord, be it unto me according to thy word': and the angel departed from her.

[39] And Mary arose in those days, and went into the hill country with haste, into a city of Juda, [40] and entered into the house of Zacharias, and saluted Elizabeth. [41] And it came to pass that when Elizabeth heard the salutation of Mary, the babe leaped in her womb, and Elizabeth was filled with the Holy Ghost. [42] And she spake out with a loud voice, and said, 'Blessed art thou among women, and blessed is the fruit of thy womb. [43] And whence is this to me, that the mother of my Lord should come to me? [44] For lo, as soon as the voice of thy salutation sounded in mine ears, the babe leaped in my womb for joy. [45] And blessed is she that believed, for there shall be a performance of those things, which were told her from the Lord.'

[46] And Mary said, 'My soul doth magnify the Lord, [47] and my spirit hath rejoiced in God my Saviour. [48] For he hath regarded the low estate of his handmaiden: for behold, from henceforth all generations shall call me blessed. [49] For he that is mighty hath done to me great things, and holy is his name. [50] And his mercy is on them that fear him, from generation to generation. [51] He hath showed strength with his arm, he hath scattered the proud, in the imagination of their hearts. [52] He hath put down the mighty from their seats, and exalted them of low degree. [53] He hath filled the hungry with good things, and the rich he hath sent empty away. [54] He hath holpen his servant Israel, in remembrance of his mercy, [55] as he spake to our fathers, to Abraham, and to his seed for ever.' [56] And Mary abode with her about three months, and returned to her own house.

[57] Now Elizabeth's full time came, that she should be delivered, and she brought forth a son. [58] And her neighbours and her cousins heard how the Lord had showed great mercy upon her, and they rejoiced with her. [59] And it came to pass, that on the eighth day they came to circumcise the child, and they called him Zacharias, after the name of his father. [60] And his mother answered, and said, 'Not so, but he shall be called John'. [61] And they said unto her, 'There is none of thy kindred that is called by this name'. [62] And they made signs to his father, how he would have him called. [63] And he asked for a writing table, and wrote, saying, 'His name is John': and they marvelled all. [64] And his mouth was opened immediately, and his tongue loosed, and

he spake, and praised God. [65] And fear came on all that dwelt round about them, and all these sayings were noised abroad throughout all the hill country of Judea. [66] And all they that had heard them, laid them up in their hearts, saying, 'What manner of child shall this be?' And the hand of the Lord was with him.

[67] And his father Zacharias was filled with the Holy Ghost, and prophesied, saying, [68] 'Blessed be the Lord God of Israel, for he hath visited and redeemed his people, [69] and hath raised up an horn of salvation for us, in the house of his servant David, [70] as he spake by the mouth of his holy prophets, which have been since the world began: [71] that we should be saved from our enemies, and from the hand of all that hate us, [72] to perform the mercy promised to our fathers, and to remember his holy covenant, [73] the oath which he sware to our father Abraham, [74] that he would grant unto us, that we being delivered out of the hands of our enemies, might serve him without fear, [75] in holiness and righteousness before him, all the days of our life. [76] And thou child shalt be called the Prophet of the Highest: for thou shalt go before the face of the Lord to prepare his ways, [77] to give knowledge of salvation unto his people, by the remission of their sins, [78] through the tender mercy of our God, whereby the day-spring from on high hath visited us, [79] to give light to them that sit in darkness, and in the shadow of death, to guide our feet into the way of peace.' [80] And the child grew, and waxed strong in spirit, and was in the deserts, till the day of his showing unto Israel.

Chapter 2

1 Augustus taxeth all the Roman empire: 6 the nativity of Christ: 3 one angel relateth it to the shepherds: 13 many sing praises to God for it. 21 Christ is circumcised. 22 Mary purified: 28 Simeon and Anna prophesy of Christ: 40 who increaseth in wisdom, 46 questioneth in the Temple with the doctors, 51 and is obedient to his parents.

AND it came to pass in those days, that there went out a decree from Caesar Augustus, that all the world should be taxed. [2] (And this taxing was first made when Cyrenius was governor of Syria.) [3] And all went to be taxed, every one into his own city. [4] And Joseph also went up from Galilee, out of the city of Nazareth, into Judea, unto the city of David, which is called Bethlehem (because he was of the house and lineage of David), [5] to be taxed with Mary his espoused wife, being great with child. ⁶ And so it was, that while they were there, the days were accomplished that she should be delivered. ⁷ And she brought forth her first born son, and wrapped him in swaddling clothes, and laid him in a manger, because there was no room for them in the inn.

⁸ And there were in the same country shepherds abiding in the field, keeping watch over their flock by night. ⁹ And lo, the angel of the Lord came upon them, and the glory of the Lord shone round about them, and they were sore afraid. ¹⁰ And the angel said unto them, 'Fear not: for behold, I bring you good tidings of great joy, which shall be to all people. ¹¹ For unto you is born this day, in the city of David, a saviour, which is Christ the Lord. ¹² And this shall be a sign unto you; ye shall find the babe wrapped in swaddling clothes lying in a manger.' ¹³ And suddenly there was with the angel a multitude of the heavenly host praising God, and saying, ¹⁴ 'Glory to God in the highest, and on earth peace, good will towards men'.

¹⁵ And it came to pass, as the angels were gone away from them into heaven, the shepherds said one to another, 'Let us now go even unto Bethlehem, and see this thing which is come to pass, which the Lord hath made known unto us'. ¹⁶ And they came with haste, and found Mary and Joseph, and the babe lying in a manger. ¹⁷ And when they had seen it, they made known abroad the saying which was told them, concerning this child. ¹⁸ And all they that heard it, wondered at those things, which were told them by the shepherds. ¹⁹ But Mary kept all these things, and pondered them in her heart. ²⁰ And the shepherds returned, glorifying and praising God for all the things that they had heard and seen, as it was told unto them.

²¹ And when eight days were accomplished for the circumcising of the child, his name was called Jesus, which was so named of the angel before he was conceived in the womb.

²² And when the days of her purification according to the Law of Moses were accomplished, they brought him to Jerusalem, to present him to the Lord ²³ (as it is written in the Law of the Lord, 'Every male that openeth the womb, shall be called holy to the Lord'), ²⁴ and to offer a sacrifice according to that which is said in the Law of the Lord, 'A pair of turtle doves, or two young pigeons'. ²⁵ And behold, there was a man in Jerusalem, whose name was Simeon, and the same man was just and devout, waiting for the consolation of Israel: and the Holy Ghost was upon him. ²⁶ And it was revealed unto him by the Holy Ghost, that he should not see death, before he had seen the

Lord's Christ. [27] And he came by the Spirit into the Temple: and when the parents brought in the child Jesus, to do for him after the custom of the Law, [28] then took he him up in his arms, and blessed God, and said, [29] 'Lord now lettest thou thy servant depart in peace, according to thy word. [30] For mine eyes have seen thy salvation, [31] which thou hast prepared before the face of all people; [32] a light to lighten the Gentiles, and the glory of thy people Israel.' [33] And Joseph and his mother marvelled at those things which were spoken of him. [34] And Simeon blessed them, and said unto Mary his mother, 'Behold, this child is set for the fall and rising again of many in Israel: and for a sign which shall be spoken against [35] (yea a sword shall pierce through thy own soul also), that the thoughts of many hearts may be revealed'.

[36] And there was one Anna a prophetess, the daughter of Phanuel, of the tribe of Aser; she was of a great age, and had lived with an husband seven years from her virginity. [37] And she was a widow of about fourscore and four years, which departed not from the Temple, but served God with fastings and prayers night and day. [38] And she coming in that instant, gave thanks likewise unto the Lord, and spake of him to all them that looked for redemption in Jerusalem.

[39] And when they had performed all things according to the Law of the Lord, they returned into Galilee, to their own city Nazareth. [40] And the child grew, and waxed strong in spirit filled with wisdom, and the grace of God was upon him.

[41] Now his parents went to Jerusalem every year, at the Feast of the Passover. [42] And when he was twelve years old, they went up to Jerusalem after the custom of the feast. [43] And when they had fulfilled the days, as they returned, the child Jesus tarried behind in Jerusalem, and Joseph and his mother knew not of it. [44] But they supposing him to have been in the company, went a day's journey, and they sought him among their kinsfolk and acquaintance. [45] And when they found him not, they turned back again to Jerusalem, seeking him. [46] And it came to pass, that after three days they found him in the Temple, sitting in the midst of the doctors, both hearing them, and asking them questions. [47] And all that heard him were astonished at his understanding, and answers. [48] And when they saw him, they were amazed: and his mother said unto him, 'Son, why hast thou thus dealt with us? Behold, thy father and I have sought thee sorrowing.' [49] And he said unto them, 'How is it that ye sought me? Wist ye not that I must be about my Father's business?' [50] And they understood not the saying

which he spake unto them. ⁵¹ And he went down with them, and came to Nazareth, and was subject unto them: but his mother kept all these sayings in her heart. ⁵² And Jesus increased in wisdom and stature, and in favour with God and man.

Chapter 3

1 *The preaching and baptism of John:* 15 *his testimony of Christ.* 20 *Herod imprisoneth John.* 21 *Christ baptized, receiveth testimony from heaven.* 23 *The age, and genealogy of Christ, from Joseph upwards.*

Now in the fifteenth year of the reign of Tiberius Caesar, Pontius Pilate being governor of Judea, and Herod being Tetrarch of Galilee, and his brother Philip Tetrarch of Iturea, and of the region of Trachonitis, and Lysanias the Tetrarch of Abilene, ² Annas and Caiaphas being the High Priests, the word of God came unto John the son of Zacharias, in the wilderness. ³ And he came into all the country about Jordan, preaching the baptism of repentance for the remission of sins, ⁴ as it is written in the book of the words of Esaias the prophet, saying, 'The voice of one crying in the wilderness, "Prepare ye the way of the Lord, make his paths straight. ⁵ Every valley shall be filled, and every mountain and hill shall be brought low, and the crooked shall be made straight, and the rough ways shall be made smooth. ⁶ And all flesh shall see the salvation of God." '

⁷ Then said he to the multitude that came forth to be baptized of him, 'O generation of vipers, who hath warned you to flee from the wrath to come? ⁸ Bring forth therefore fruits worthy of repentance, and begin not to say within yourselves, "We have Abraham to our father": for I say unto you, that God is able of these stones to raise up children unto Abraham. ⁹ And now also the axe is laid unto the root of the trees: every tree therefore which bringeth not forth good fruit, is hewn down, and cast into the fire.'

¹⁰ And the people asked him, saying, 'What shall we do then?' ¹¹ He answereth, and saith unto them, 'He that hath two coats, let him impart to him that hath none, and he that hath meat, let him do likewise'. ¹² Then came also publicans to be baptized, and said unto him, 'Master, what shall we do?' ¹³ And he said unto them, 'Exact no more than that which is appointed you'. ¹⁴ And the soldiers likewise demanded of him, saying, 'And what shall we do?' And he said unto

them, 'Do violence to no man, neither accuse any falsely, and be content with your wages'.

¹⁵ And as the people were in expectation, and all men mused in their hearts of John, whether he were the Christ or not: ¹⁶ John answered, saying unto them all, 'I indeed baptize you with water, but one mightier than I cometh, the latchet of whose shoes I am not worthy to unloose, he shall baptize you with the Holy Ghost, and with fire: ¹⁷ whose fan is in his hand, and he will thoroughly purge his floor, and will gather the wheat into his garner, but the chaff he will burn with fire unquenchable.'

¹⁸ And many other things in his exhortation preached he unto the people. ¹⁹ But Herod the Tetrarch being reproved by him for Herodias his brother Philip's wife, and for all the evils which Herod had done, ²⁰ added yet this above all, that he shut up John in prison.

²¹ Now when all the people were baptized, it came to pass that Jesus also being baptized, and praying, the heaven was opened: ²² and the Holy Ghost descended in a bodily shape like a dove upon him, and a voice came from heaven, which said, 'Thou art my beloved Son, in thee I am well pleased'.

²³ And Jesus himself began to be about thirty years of age, being (as was supposed) the son of Joseph, which was the son of Heli, ²⁴ which was the son of Matthat, which was the son of Levi, which was the son of Melchi, which was the son of Janna, which was the son of Joseph, ²⁵ which was the son of Mattathias, which was the son of Amos, which was the son of Naum, which was the son of Esli, which was the son of Nagge, ²⁶ which was the son of Maath, which was the son of Mattathias, which was the son of Semei, which was the son of Joseph, which was the son of Juda, ²⁷ which was the son of Joanna, which was the son of Rhesa, which was the son of Zorobabel, which was the son of Salathiel, which was the son of Neri, ²⁸ which was the son of Melchi, which was the son of Addi, which was the son of Cosam, which was the son of Elmodam, which was the son of Er, ²⁹ which was the son of Jose, which was the son of Eliezer, which was the son of Jorim, which was the son of Matthat, which was the son of Levi, ³⁰ which was the son of Simeon, which was the son of Juda, which was the son of Joseph, which was the son of Jonan, which was the son of Eliakim, ³¹ which was the son of Melea, which was the son of Menan, which was the son of Mattatha, which was the son of Nathan, which was the son of David, ³² which was the son of Jesse, which was the son of Obed, which was the son of Booz, which was

the son of Salmon, which was the son of Naasson, [33] which was the son
of Aminadab, which was the son of Aram, which was the son of Esrom,
which was the son of Phares, which was the son of Juda, [34] which was the
son of Jacob, which was the son of Isaac, which was the son of Abraham,
which was the son of Thara, which was the son of Nachor, [35] which was
the son of Saruch, which was the son of Ragau, which was the son of
Phalec, which was the son of Heber, which was the son of Sala, [36] which
was the son of Cainan, which was the son of Arphaxad, which was the
son of Sem, which was the son of Noe, which was the son of Lamech,
[37] which was the son of Mathusala, which was the son of Enoch, which
was the son of Jared, which was the son of Maleleel, which was the son
of Cainan, [38] which was the son of Enos, which was the son of Seth,
which was the son of Adam, which was the son of God.

Chapter 4

*1 The temptation and fasting of Christ: 13 he overcometh the devil:
14 beginneth to preach: 16 the people of Nazareth admire his gracious
words: 33 he cureth one possessed of a devil, 38 Peter's mother-in-law,
40 and divers other sick persons. 41 The devils acknowledge Christ, and
are reproved for it: 43 he preacheth through the cities.*

AND Jesus being full of the Holy Ghost, returned from Jordan,
and was led by the Spirit into the wilderness, [2] being forty days
tempted of the devil, and in those days he did eat nothing: and when
they were ended, he afterward hungered. [3] And the devil said unto
him, 'If thou be the Son of God, command this stone that it be made
bread'. [4] And Jesus answered him, saying, 'It is written, that man shall
not live by bread alone, but by every word of God'.

[5] And the devil taking him up into an high mountain, showed unto
him all the kingdoms of the world in a moment of time. [6] And the
devil said unto him, 'All this power will I give thee, and the glory of
them; for that is delivered unto me, and to whomsoever I will, I give
it. [7] If thou therefore wilt worship me, all shall be thine.' [8] And Jesus
answered and said unto him, 'Get thee behind me, Satan: for it is
written, "Thou shalt worship the Lord thy God, and him only shalt
thou serve"'.

[9] And he brought him to Jerusalem, and set him on a pinnacle
of the Temple, and said unto him, 'If thou be the Son of God, cast

thyself down from hence. [10] For it is written, "He shall give his angels charge over thee, to keep thee: [11] and in their hands they shall bear thee up, lest at any time thou dash thy foot against a stone".' [12] And Jesus answering, said unto him, 'It is said, "Thou shalt not tempt the Lord thy God"'. [13] And when the devil had ended all the temptation, he departed from him for a season.

[14] And Jesus returned in the power of the Spirit into Galilee, and there went out a fame of him through all the region round about. [15] And he taught in their synagogues, being glorified of all.

[16] And he came to Nazareth, where he had been brought up, and as his custom was, he went into the synagogue on the Sabbath day, and stood up for to read. [17] And there was delivered unto him the book of the prophet Esaias, and when he had opened the book, he found the place where it was written, [18] 'The Spirit of the Lord is upon me, because he hath anointed me to preach the gospel to the poor, he hath sent me to heal the broken hearted, to preach deliverance to the captives, and recovering of sight to the blind, to set at liberty them that are bruised, [19] to preach the acceptable year of the Lord'. [20] And he closed the book, and he gave it again to the minister, and sat down: and the eyes of all them that were in the synagogue were fastened on him. [21] And he began to say unto them, 'This day is this scripture fulfilled in your ears'. [22] And all bare him witness, and wondered at the gracious words, which proceeded out of his mouth. And they said, 'Is not this Joseph's son?' [23] And he said unto them, 'Ye will surely say unto me this proverb, "Physician, heal thyself": whatsoever we have heard done in Capernaum, do also here in thy country'. [24] And he said, 'Verily I say unto you, no prophet is accepted in his own country. [25] But I tell you of a truth, many widows were in Israel in the days of Elias, when the heaven was shut up three years and six months: when great famine was throughout all the land: [26] but unto none of them was Elias sent, save unto Sarepta a city of Sidon, unto a woman that was a widow. [27] And many lepers were in Israel in the time of Eliseus the prophet: and none of them was cleansed, saving Naaman the Syrian.'

[28] And all they in the synagogue, when they heard these things, were filled with wrath, [29] and rose up, and thrust him out of the city, and led him unto the brow of the hill (whereon their city was built) that they might cast him down headlong. [30] But he passing through the mids of them, went his way: [31] and came down to Capernaum, a city of Galilee,

and taught them on the Sabbath days. ³² And they were astonished at his doctrine: for his word was with power.

³³ And in the synagogue there was a man which had a spirit of an unclean devil, and cried out with a loud voice, ³⁴ saying, 'Let us alone, what have we to do with thee, thou Jesus of Nazareth? Art thou come to destroy us? I know thee who thou art, the Holy One of God.' ³⁵ And Jesus rebuked him, saying, 'Hold thy peace, and come out of him'. And when the devil had thrown him in the mids, he came out of him, and hurt him not. ³⁶ And they were all amazed, and spake among themselves, saying, 'What a word is this? for with authority and power he commandeth the unclean spirits, and they come out'. ³⁷ And the fame of him went out into every place of the country round about.

³⁸ And he arose out of the synagogue, and entered into Simon's house: and Simon's wife's mother was taken with a great fever, and they besought him for her. ³⁹ And he stood over her, and rebuked the fever, and it left her. And immediately she arose, and ministered unto them.

⁴⁰ Now when the sun was setting, all they that had any sick with divers diseases, brought them unto him: and he laid his hands on every one of them, and healed them. ⁴¹ And devils also came out of many, crying out, and saying, 'Thou art Christ the Son of God'. And he rebuking them, suffered them not to speak: for they knew that he was Christ.

⁴² And when it was day, he departed, and went into a desert place: and the people sought him, and came unto him, and stayed him, that he should not depart from them. ⁴³ And he said unto them, 'I must preach the kingdom of God to other cities also: for therefore am I sent'. ⁴⁴ And he preached in the synagogues of Galilee.

Chapter 5

1 Christ teacheth the people out of Peter's ship. 4 In a miraculous taking of fishes, showeth how he will make him and his partners fishers of men: 12 cleanseth the leper: 16 prayeth in the wilderness: 18 healeth one sick of the palsy: 27 calleth Matthew the Publican: 29 eateth with sinners, as being the physician of souls: 34 foretelleth the fastings and afflictions of the apostles after his ascension: 35 and likeneth faint hearted and weak disciples, to old bottles and worn garments.

AND it came to pass, that as the people pressed upon him to hear the word of God, he stood by the lake of Gennesaret, ² and saw two ships standing by the lake: but the fishermen were gone out of them, and were washing their nets. ³ And he entered into one of the ships, which was Simon's, and prayed him that he would thrust out a little from the land: and he sat down, and taught the people out of the ship. ⁴ Now when he had left speaking, he said unto Simon, 'Launch out into the deep, and let down your nets for a draught'. ⁵ And Simon answering, said unto him, 'Master, we have toiled all the night, and have taken nothing: nevertheless at thy word I will let down the net'. ⁶ And when they had this done, they inclosed a great multitude of fishes, and their net brake: ⁷ and they beckoned unto their partners, which were in the other ship, that they should come and help them. And they came, and filled both the ships, so that they began to sink. ⁸ When Simon Peter saw it, he fell down at Jesus's knees, saying, 'Depart from me, for I am a sinful man, O Lord'. ⁹ For he was astonished, and all that were with him, at the draught of the fishes which they had taken: ¹⁰ and so was also James and John, the sons of Zebedee, which were partners with Simon. And Jesus said unto Simon, 'Fear not, from henceforth thou shalt catch men'. ¹¹ And when they had brought their ships to land, they forsook all, and followed him.

¹² And it came to pass, when he was in a certain city, behold a man full of leprosy: who seeing Jesus, fell on his face, and besought him, saying, 'Lord, if thou wilt, thou canst make me clean'. ¹³ And he put forth his hand, and touched him, saying, 'I will: be thou clean'. And immediately the leprosy departed from him. ¹⁴ And he charged him to tell no man: but, 'Go, and show thyself to the priest, and offer for thy cleansing, according as Moses commanded, for a testimony unto them'. ¹⁵ But so much the more went there a fame abroad of him, and great multitudes came together to hear, and to be healed by him of their infirmities. ¹⁶ And he withdrew himself into the wilderness, and prayed.

¹⁷ And it came to pass on a certain day, as he was teaching, that there were Pharisees and doctors of the Law sitting by, which were come out of every town of Galilee, and Judea, and Jerusalem: and the power of the Lord was present to heal them. ¹⁸ And behold, men brought in a bed a man which was taken with a palsy: and they sought means to bring him in, and to lay him before him. ¹⁹ And when they could not find by what way they might bring him in, because of the multitude, they went upon the house top, and let him down through

the tiling with his couch, into the midst before Jesus. [20] And when he saw their faith, he said unto him, 'Man, thy sins are forgiven thee'. [21] And the scribes and the Pharisees began to reason, saying, 'Who is this which speaketh blasphemies? Who can forgive sins, but God alone?' [22] But when Jesus perceived their thoughts, he answering, said unto them, 'What reason ye in your hearts? [23] Whether is easier to say, "Thy sins be forgiven thee": or to say, "Rise up and walk"? [24] But that ye may know that the Son of Man hath power upon earth to forgive sins' (he said unto the sick of the palsy), 'I say unto thee, arise, and take up thy couch, and go into thine house.' [25] And immediately he rose up before them, and took up that whereon he lay, and departed to his own house, glorifying God. [26] And they were all amazed, and they glorified God, and were filled with fear, saying, 'We have seen strange things today'.

[27] And after these things he went forth, and saw a publican, named Levi, sitting at the receipt of custom: and he said unto him, 'Follow me'. [28] And he left all, rose up, and followed him. [29] And Levi made him a great feast in his own house: and there was a great company of publicans, and of others that sat down with them. [30] But their scribes and Pharisees murmured against his disciples, saying, 'Why do ye eat and drink with publicans and sinners?' [31] And Jesus answering, said unto them, 'They that are whole need not a physician: but they that are sick. [32] I came not to call the righteous, but sinners to repentance.'

[33] And they said unto him, 'Why do the disciples of John fast often, and make prayers, and likewise the disciples of the Pharisees: but thine eat and drink?' [34] And he said unto them, 'Can ye make the children of the bride-chamber fast, while the bridegroom is with them? [35] But the days will come, when the bridegroom shall be taken away from them, and then shall they fast in those days.'

[36] And he spake also a parable unto them, 'No man putteth a piece of a new garment upon an old: if otherwise, then both the new maketh a rent, and the piece that was taken out of the new, agreeth not with the old. [37] And no man putteth new wine into old bottles: else the new wine will burst the bottles, and be spilled, and the bottles shall perish. [38] But new wine must be put into new bottles, and both are preserved. [39] No man also having drunk old wine, straightway desireth new: for he saith, "The old is better".'

Chapter 6

1 Christ reproveth the Pharisees' blindness about the observation of the Sabbath, by scripture, reason, and miracle: 13 chooseth twelve apostles: 17 healeth the diseased: 20 preacheth to his disciples before the people of blessings, and curses: 27 how we must love our enemies: 46 and join the obedience of good works, to the hearing of the word: lest in the evil day of temptation, we fall like an house built upon the face of the earth, without any foundation.

AND it came to pass on the second Sabbath after the first, that he went through the corn fields: and his disciples plucked the ears of corn, and did eat, rubbing them in their hands. ² And certain of the Pharisees said unto them, 'Why do ye that which is not lawful to do on the Sabbath days?' ³ And Jesus answering them, said, 'Have ye not read so much as this what David did, when himself was an hungered, and they which were with him: ⁴ how he went into the house of God, and did take and eat the shewbread, and gave also to them that were with him, which it is not lawful to eat but for the priests alone?' ⁵ And he said unto them, 'That the Son of Man is Lord also of the Sabbath'.

⁶ And it came to pass also on another Sabbath, that he entered into the synagogue, and taught: and there was a man whose right hand was withered. ⁷ And the scribes and Pharisees watched him, whether he would heal on the Sabbath day: that they might find an accusation against him. ⁸ But he knew their thoughts, and said to the man which had the withered hand, 'Rise up, and stand forth in the mids'. And he arose, and stood forth. ⁹ Then said Jesus unto them, 'I will ask you one thing, is it lawful on the Sabbath days to do good, or to do evil? to save life, or to destroy it?' ¹⁰ And looking round about upon them all, he said unto the man, 'Stretch forth thy hand'. And he did so: and his hand was restored whole as the other. ¹¹ And they were filled with madness, and communed one with another what they might do to Jesus.

¹² And it came to pass in those days, that he went out into a mountain to pray, and continued all night in prayer to God. ¹³ And when it was day, he called unto him his disciples: and of them he chose twelve, whom also he named apostles: ¹⁴ Simon (whom he also named Peter), and Andrew his brother, James and John, Philip and Bartholomew,

¹⁵ Matthew and Thomas, James the son of Alphaeus, and Simon, called Zelotes, ¹⁶ and Judas the brother of James, and Judas Iscariot, which also was the traitor.

¹⁷ And he came down with them, and stood in the plain, and the company of his disciples, and a great multitude of people, out of all Judea and Jerusalem, and from the sea coast of Tyre and Sidon, which came to hear him, and to be healed of their diseases, ¹⁸ and they that were vexed with unclean spirits: and they were healed. ¹⁹ And the whole multitude sought to touch him: for there went virtue out of him, and healed them all.

²⁰ And he lifted up his eyes on his disciples, and said,

'Blessed be ye poor: for yours is the kingdom of God.

²¹ 'Blessed are ye that hunger now: for ye shall be filled.

'Blessed are ye that weep now: for ye shall laugh.

²² 'Blessed are ye when men shall hate you, and when they shall separate you from their company, and shall reproach you, and cast out your name as evil, for the Son of Man's sake. ²³ Rejoice ye in that day, and leap for joy: for behold, your reward is great in heaven, for in the like manner did their fathers unto the prophets.

²⁴ 'But woe unto you that are rich: for ye have received your consolation.

²⁵ 'Woe unto you that are full: for ye shall hunger.

'Woe unto you that laugh now: for ye shall mourn and weep.

²⁶ 'Woe unto you, when all men shall speak well of you: for so did their fathers to the false prophets.

²⁷ 'But I say unto you which hear, love your enemies, do good to them which hate you, ²⁸ bless them that curse you, and pray for them which despitefully use you. ²⁹ And unto him that smiteth thee on the one cheek, offer also the other: and him that taketh away thy cloak, forbid not to take thy coat also. ³⁰ Give to every man that asketh of thee, and of him that taketh away thy goods, ask them not again. ³¹ And as ye would that men should do to you, do ye also to them likewise.

³² 'For if ye love them which love you, what thank have ye? for sinners also love those that love them. ³³ And if ye do good to them which do good to you, what thank have ye? for sinners also do even the same. ³⁴ And if ye lend to them of whom ye hope to receive, what thank have ye? for sinners also lend to sinners, to receive as much again. ³⁵ But love ye your enemies, and do good, and lend, hoping for nothing again: and your reward shall be great, and ye shall be the children

of the Highest: for he is kind unto the unthankful, and to the evil. [36] Be ye therefore merciful, as your Father also is merciful. [37] Judge not, and ye shall not be judged: condemn not, and ye shall not be condemned: forgive, and ye shall be forgiven: [38] give, and it shall be given unto you, good measure, pressed down, and shaken together, and running over, shall men give into your bosom: for with the same measure that ye mete withal, it shall be measured to you again.'

[39] And he spake a parable unto them, 'Can the blind lead the blind? Shall they not both fall into the ditch? [40] The disciple is not above his master: but every one that is perfect shall be as his master. [41] And why beholdest thou the mote that is in thy brother's eye, but perceivest not the beam that is in thine own eye? [42] Either how canst thou say to thy brother, "Brother, let me pull out the mote that is in thine eye": when thou thyself beholdest not the beam that is in thine own eye? Thou hypocrite, cast out first the beam out of thine own eye, and then shalt thou see clearly to pull out the mote that is in thy brother's eye.

[43] 'For a good tree bringeth not forth corrupt fruit: neither doth a corrupt tree bring forth good fruit. [44] For every tree is known by his own fruit: for of thorns men do not gather figs, nor of a bramble bush gather they grapes. [45] A good man out of the good treasure of his heart, bringeth forth that which is good: and an evil man out of the evil treasure of his heart, bringeth forth that which is evil: for of the abundance of the heart, his mouth speaketh.

[46] 'And why call ye me "Lord, Lord", and do not the things which I say? [47] Whosoever cometh to me, and heareth my sayings, and doeth them, I will show you to whom he is like. [48] He is like a man which built an house, and digged deep, and laid the foundation on a rock. And when the flood arose, the stream beat vehemently upon that house, and could not shake it: for it was founded upon a rock. [49] But he that heareth, and doeth not, is like a man that without a foundation built an house upon the earth: against which the stream did beat vehemently, and immediately it fell, and the ruin of that house was great.'

Chapter 7

1 *Christ findeth a greater faith in the centurion a Gentile, than in any of the Jews:* 10 *healeth his servant being absent:* 11 *raiseth from death the widow's son at Nain:* 10 *answereth John's messengers with the declaration of his miracles:* 24 *testifieth to the people what opinion he held of John:* 30 *inveigheth against the Jews, who with neither the manners of John, nor of Jesus could be won:* 36 *and showeth by occasion of Mary Magdalene, how he is a friend to sinners, not to maintain them in sins, but to forgive them their sins, upon their faith and repentance.*

Now when he had ended all his sayings in the audience of the people, he entered into Capernaum. ² And a certain centurion's servant, who was dear unto him, was sick and ready to die. ³ And when he heard of Jesus, he sent unto him the elders of the Jews, beseeching him that he would come and heal his servant. ⁴ And when they came to Jesus, they besought him instantly, saying, that he was worthy for whom he should do this. ⁵ 'For he loveth our nation, and he hath built us a synagogue.' ⁶ Then Jesus went with them. And when he was now not far from the house, the centurion sent friends to him, saying unto him, 'Lord, trouble not thyself: for I am not worthy that thou shouldst enter under my roof. ⁷ Wherefore neither thought I myself worthy to come unto thee: but say in a word, and my servant shall be healed. ⁸ For I also am a man set under authority, having under me soldiers: and I say unto one, "Go", and he goeth: and to another, "Come", and he cometh: and to my servant, "Do this", and he doeth it.' ⁹ When Jesus heard these things, he marvelled at him, and turned him about, and said unto the people that followed him, 'I say unto you, I have not found so great faith, no, not in Israel'. ¹⁰ And they that were sent, returning to the house, found the servant whole that had been sick.

¹¹ And it came to pass the day after, that he went into a city called Nain: and many of his disciples went with him, and much people. ¹² Now when he came nigh to the gate of the city, behold, there was a dead man carried out, the only son of his mother, and she was a widow: and much people of the city was with her. ¹³ And when the Lord saw her, he had compassion on her, and said unto her, 'Weep not'. ¹⁴ And he came and touched the bier (and they that bare him, stood still). And he said, 'Young man, I say unto thee, arise'. ¹⁵ And

he that was dead, sat up, and began to speak: and he delivered him to his mother. ¹⁶ And there came a fear on all, and they glorified God, saying, that a great prophet is risen up among us, and that God hath visited his people. ¹⁷ And this rumour of him went forth throughout all Judea, and throughout all the region round about.

¹⁸ And the disciples of John showed him of all these things. ¹⁹ And John calling unto him two of his disciples, sent them to Jesus, saying, 'Art thou he that should come, or look we for another?' ²⁰ When the men were come unto him, they said, 'John Baptist hath sent us unto thee, saying, "Art thou he that should come, or look we for another?" ' ²¹ And in that same hour he cured many of their infirmities and plagues, and of evil spirits, and unto many that were blind, he gave sight. ²² Then Jesus answering, said unto them, 'Go your way, and tell John what things ye have seen and heard, how that the blind see, the lame walk, the lepers are cleansed, the deaf hear, the dead are raised, to the poor the gospel is preached. ²³ And blessed is he whosoever shall not be offended in me.'

²⁴ And when the messengers of John were departed, he began to speak unto the people concerning John: 'What went ye out into the wilderness for to see? A reed shaken with the wind? ²⁵ But what went ye out for to see? A man clothed in soft raiment? Behold, they which are gorgeously apparelled, and live delicately, are in kings' courts. ²⁶ But what went ye out for to see? A prophet? Yea, I say unto you, and much more than a prophet. ²⁷ This is he of whom it is written, "Behold, I send my messenger before thy face, which shall prepare thy way before thee". ²⁸ For I say unto you, among those that are born of women, there is not a greater prophet than John the Baptist: but he that is least in the kingdom of God, is greater than he.' ²⁹ And all the people that heard him, and the publicans, justified God, being baptized with the baptism of John. ³⁰ But the Pharisees and lawyers rejected the counsel of God against themselves, being not baptized of him.

³¹ And the Lord said, 'Whereunto then shall I liken the men of this generation? and to what are they like? ³² They are like unto children sitting in the market place, and calling one to another, and saying, "We have piped unto you, and ye have not danced: we have mourned to you, and ye have not wept". ³³ For John the Baptist came, neither eating bread, nor drinking wine, and ye say, "He hath a devil". ³⁴ The Son of Man is come, eating, and drinking, and ye say, "Behold

a gluttonous man, and a wine bibber, a friend of publicans and sinners". ³⁵ But wisdom is justified of all her children.'

³⁶ And one of the Pharisees desired him that he would eat with him. And he went into the Pharisee's house, and sat down to meat. ³⁷ And behold, a woman in the city which was a sinner, when she knew that Jesus sat at meat in the Pharisee's house, brought an alabaster box of ointment, ³⁸ and stood at his feet behind him, weeping, and began to wash his feet with tears, and did wipe them with the hairs of her head, and kissed his feet, and anointed them with the ointment. ³⁹ Now when the Pharisee which had bidden him, saw it, he spake within himself, saying, 'This man, if he were a prophet, would have known who, and what manner of woman this is that toucheth him: for she is a sinner'. ⁴⁰ And Jesus answering, said unto him, 'Simon, I have somewhat to say unto thee'. And he saith, 'Master, say on'. ⁴¹ 'There was a certain creditor, which had two debtors: the one ought five hundred pence, and the other fifty. ⁴² And when they had nothing to pay, he frankly forgave them both. Tell me therefore, which of them will love him most?' ⁴³ Simon answered, and said, 'I suppose that he to whom he forgave most'. And he said unto him, 'Thou hast rightly judged'. ⁴⁴ And he turned to the woman, and said unto Simon, 'Seest thou this woman? I entered into thine house, thou gavest me no water for my feet: but she hath washed my feet with tears, and wiped them with the hairs of her head. ⁴⁵ Thou gavest me no kiss: but this woman since the time I came in, hath not ceased to kiss my feet. ⁴⁶ Mine head with oil thou didst not anoint: but this woman hath anointed my feet with ointment. ⁴⁷ Wherefore, I say unto thee, her sins, which are many, are forgiven, for she loved much: but to whom little is forgiven, the same loveth little.' ⁴⁸ And he said unto her, 'Thy sins are forgiven'. ⁴⁹ And they that sat at meat with him, began to say within themselves, 'Who is this that forgiveth sins also?' ⁵⁰ And he said to the woman, 'Thy faith hath saved thee, go in peace'.

Chapter 8

AND it came to pass afterward, that he went throughout every city and village preaching, and showing the glad tidings of the kingdom of God: and the twelve were with him, [2] and certain women which had been healed of evil spirits and infirmities, Mary called Magdalene, out of whom went seven devils, [3] and Joanna the wife of Chuza, Herod's steward, and Susanna, and many others which ministered unto him of their substance.

[4] And when much people were gathered together, and were come to him out of every city, he spake by a parable: [5] 'A sower went out to sow his seed: and as he sowed, some fell by the way side, and it was trodden down, and the fowls of the air devoured it. [6] And some fell upon a rock, and as soon as it was sprung up, it withered away, because it lacked moisture. [7] And some fell among thorns, and the thorns sprang up with it, and choked it. [8] And other fell on good ground, and sprang up, and bare fruit an hundred fold.' And when he said these things, he cried, 'He that hath ears to hear, let him hear'.

[9] And his disciples asked him, saying, 'What might this parable be?' [10] And he said, 'Unto you it is given to know the mysteries of the kingdom of God: but to others in parables, that seeing, they might not see, and hearing, they might not understand. [11] Now the parable is this: the seed is the word of God. [12] Those by the way side, are they that hear: then cometh the devil, and taketh away the word out of their hearts, lest they should believe, and be saved. [13] They on the rock, are they which when they hear, receive the word with joy; and these have no root, which for a while believe, and in time of temptation fall away. [14] And that which fell among thorns, are they, which when they have heard, go forth, and are choked with cares and riches, and pleasures of this life, and bring no fruit to perfection. [15] But that on the good ground, are they, which in an honest and

good heart, having heard the word, keep it, and bring forth fruit with patience.

[16] 'No man, when he hath lighted a candle, covereth it with a vessel, or putteth it under a bed: but setteth it on a candlestick, that they which enter in, may see the light. [17] For nothing is secret, that shall not be made manifest: neither any thing hid, that shall not be known, and come abroad. [18] Take heed therefore how ye hear: for whosoever hath, to him shall be given; and whosoever hath not, from him shall be taken, even that which he seemeth to have.'

[19] Then came to him his mother and his brethren, and could not come at him for the press. [20] And it was told him by certain which said, 'Thy mother and thy brethren stand without, desiring to see thee'. [21] And he answered and said unto them, 'My mother and my brethren are these which hear the word of God, and do it'.

[22] Now it came to pass on a certain day, that he went into a ship, with his disciples: and he said unto them, 'Let us go over unto the other side of the lake', and they launched forth. [23] But as they sailed, he fell asleep, and there came down a storm of wind on the lake, and they were filled with water, and were in jeopardy. [24] And they came to him, and awoke him, saying, 'Master, master, we perish'. Then he rose, and rebuked the wind, and the raging of the water: and they ceased, and there was a calm. [25] And he said unto them, 'Where is your faith?' And they being afraid wondered, saying one to another, 'What manner of man is this? For he commandeth even the winds and water, and they obey him'.

[26] And they arrived at the country of the Gadarenes, which is over against Galilee. [27] And when he went forth to land, there met him out of the city a certain man which had devils long time, and ware no clothes, neither abode in any house, but in the tombs. [28] When he saw Jesus, he cried out, and fell down before him, and with a loud voice said, 'What have I to do with thee, Jesus, thou Son of God most high? I beseech thee torment me not.' [29] (For he had commanded the unclean spirit to come out of the man: for oftentimes it had caught him, and he was kept bound with chains, and in fetters: and he brake the bands, and was driven of the devil into the wilderness.) [30] And Jesus asked him, saying, 'What is thy name?' And he said, 'Legion': because many devils were entered into him. [31] And they besought him, that he would not command them to go out into the deep. [32] And there was there an herd of many swine feeding on the mountain: and

they besought him that he would suffer them to enter into them: and he suffered them. ³³ Then went the devils out of the man, and entered into the swine: and the herd ran violently down a steep place into the lake, and were choked. ³⁴ When they that fed them saw what was done, they fled, and went, and told it in the city, and in the country. ³⁵ Then they went out to see what was done; and came to Jesus, and found the man, out of whom the devils were departed, sitting at the feet of Jesus, clothed, and in his right mind: and they were afraid. ³⁶ They also which saw it, told them by what means he that was possessed of the devils, was healed.

³⁷ Then the whole multitude of the country of the Gadarenes round about, besought him to depart from them, for they were taken with great fear: and he went up into the ship, and returned back again. ³⁸ Now the man, out of whom the devils were departed, besought him that he might be with him: but Jesus sent him away, saying, ³⁹ 'Return to thine own house, and show how great things God hath done unto thee'. And he went his way, and published throughout the whole city how great things Jesus had done unto him.

⁴⁰ And it came to pass, that when Jesus was returned, the people gladly received him: for they were all waiting for him. ⁴¹ And behold, there came a man named Jairus, and he was a ruler of the synagogue, and he fell down at Jesus's feet, and besought him that he would come into his house: ⁴² for he had one only daughter, about twelve years of age, and she lay a dying.

But as he went the people thronged him. ⁴³ And a woman having an issue of blood twelve years, which had spent all her living upon physicians, neither could be healed of any, ⁴⁴ came behind him, and touched the border of his garment: and immediately her issue of blood stanched. ⁴⁵ And Jesus said, 'Who touched me?' When all denied, Peter and they that were with him said, 'Master, the multitude throng thee, and press thee, and sayest thou, "Who touched me?"' ⁴⁶ And Jesus said, 'Some body hath touched me: for I perceive that virtue is gone out of me'. ⁴⁷ And when the woman saw that she was not hid, she came trembling, and falling down before him, she declared unto him before all the people, for what cause she had touched him, and how she was healed immediately. ⁴⁸ And he said unto her, 'Daughter, be of good comfort, thy faith hath made thee whole, go in peace'.

⁴⁹ While he yet spake, there cometh one from the ruler of the

synagogue's house, saying to him, 'Thy daughter is dead, trouble not the Master'. ⁵⁰ But when Jesus heard it, he answered him, saying, 'Fear not, believe only, and she shall be made whole'. ⁵¹ And when he came into the house, he suffered no man to go in, save Peter, and James, and John, and the father and the mother of the maiden. ⁵² And all wept, and bewailed her: but he said, 'Weep not, she is not dead, but sleepeth'. ⁵³ And they laughed him to scorn, knowing that she was dead. ⁵⁴ And he put them all out, and took her by the hand, and called, saying, 'Maid, arise'. ⁵⁵ And her spirit came again, and she arose straightway: and he commanded to give her meat. ⁵⁶ And her parents were astonished: but he charged them that they should tell no man what was done.

Chapter 9

1 Christ sendeth his apostles to work miracles, and to preach. 7 Herod desired to see Christ. Christ feedeth five thousand: 18 inquireth what opinion the world had of him: foretelleth his Passion: 23 proposeth to all, the pattern of his patience. 28 The transfiguration. 37 He healeth the lunatic: 43 again forwarneth his disciples of his Passion: 46 commendeth humility: 51 biddeth them to show mildness towards all, without desire of revenge. 57 Divers would follow him, but upon conditions.

THEN he called his twelve disciples together, and gave them power and authority over all devils, and to cure diseases. ² And he sent them to preach the kingdom of God, and to heal the sick. ³ And he said unto them, 'Take nothing for your journey, neither staves, nor scrip, neither bread, neither money, neither have two coats apiece. ⁴ And whatsoever house ye enter into, there abide, and thence depart. ⁵ And whosoever will not receive you, when ye go out of that city, shake off the very dust from your feet, for a testimony against them.' ⁶ And they departed, and went through the towns, preaching the gospel, and healing everywhere.

⁷ Now Herod the Tetrarch heard of all that was done by him: and he was perplexed, because that it was said of some, that John was risen from the dead: ⁸ and of some, that Elias had appeared: and of others, that one of the old prophets was risen again. ⁹ And Herod said, 'John have I beheaded: but who is this of whom I hear such things?' And he desired to see him.

[10] And the apostles when they were returned, told him all that they had done. And he took them, and went aside privately into a desert place, belonging to the city called Bethsaida. [11] And the people when they knew it, followed him, and he received them, and spake unto them of the kingdom of God, and healed them that had need of healing. [12] And when the day began to wear away, then came the twelve, and said unto him, 'Send the multitude away, that they may go into the towns and country round about, and lodge, and get victuals: for we are here in a desert place'. [13] But he said unto them, 'Give ye them to eat'. And they said, 'We have no more but five loaves and two fishes, except we should go and buy meat for all this people'. [14] For they were about five thousand men. And he said to his disciples, 'Make them sit down by fifties in a company'. [15] And they did so, and made them all sit down. [16] Then he took the five loaves and the two fishes, and looking up to heaven, he blessed them, and brake, and gave to the disciples to set before the multitude. [17] And they did eat, and were all filled. And there was taken up of fragments that remained to them, twelve baskets.

[18] And it came to pass, as he was alone praying, his disciples were with him: and he asked them, saying, 'Whom say the people that I am?' [19] They answering, said, 'John the Baptist; but some say, Elias: and others say, that one of the old prophets is risen again'. [20] He said unto them, 'But whom say ye that I am?' Peter answering, said, 'The Christ of God'. [21] And he straitly charged them, and commanded them to tell no man that thing, [22] saying, 'The Son of Man must suffer many things, and be rejected of the elders, and chief priests, and scribes, and be slain, and be raised the third day'.

[23] And he said to them all, 'If any man will come after me, let him deny himself, and take up his cross daily, and follow me. [24] For whosoever will save his life, shall lose it: but whosoever will lose his life for my sake, the same shall save it. [25] For what is a man advantaged, if he gain the whole world, and lose himself, or be cast away? [26] For whosoever shall be ashamed of me, and of my words, of him shall the Son of Man be ashamed, when he shall come in his own glory, and in his Father's, and of the holy angels. [27] But I tell you of a truth, there be some standing here, which shall not taste of death, till they see the kingdom of God.'

[28] And it came to pass, about an eight days after these sayings, he took Peter, and John, and James, and went up into a mountain to pray:

[29] and as he prayed, the fashion of his countenance was altered, and his raiment was white and glistering. [30] And behold, there talked with him two men, which were Moses and Elias, [31] who appeared in glory, and spake of his decease, which he should accomplish at Jerusalem. [32] But Peter, and they that were with him, were heavy with sleep: and when they were awake, they saw his glory, and the two men that stood with him. [33] And it came to pass, as they departed from him, Peter said unto Jesus, 'Master, it is good for us to be here, and let us make three tabernacles, one for thee, and one for Moses, and one for Elias': not knowing what he said. [34] While he thus spake, there came a cloud, and overshadowed them: and they feared, as they entered into the cloud. [35] And there came a voice out of the cloud, saying, 'This is my beloved Son, hear him'. [36] And when the voice was past, Jesus was found alone, and they kept it close, and told no man in those days any of those things which they had seen.

[37] And it came to pass, that on the next day, when they were come down from the hill, much people met him. [38] And behold, a man of the company cried out, saying, 'Master, I beseech thee, look upon my son, for he is mine only child. [39] And lo, a spirit taketh him, and he suddenly crieth out, and it teareth him that he foameth again, and bruising him, hardly departeth from him. [40] And I besought thy disciples to cast him out, and they could not.' [41] And Jesus answering, said, 'O faithless, and perverse generation, how long shall I be with you, and suffer you? Bring thy son hither.' [42] And as he was yet a coming, the devil threw him down, and tare him. And Jesus rebuked the unclean spirit, and healed the child, and delivered him again to his father.

[43] And they were all amazed at the mighty power of God: but while they wondered every one at all things which Jesus did, he said unto his disciples, [44] 'Let these sayings sink down into your ears: for the Son of Man shall be delivered into the hands of men'. [45] But they understood not this saying, and it was hid from them, that they perceived it not: and they feared to ask him of that saying.

[46] Then there arose a reasoning among them, which of them should be greatest. [47] And Jesus perceiving the thought of their heart, took a child, and set him by him, [48] and said unto them, 'Whosoever shall receive this child in my name, receiveth me: and whosoever shall receive me, receiveth him that sent me: for he that is least among you all, the same shall be great'.

⁴⁹ And John answered, and said, 'Master, we saw one casting out devils in thy name, and we forbad him, because he followeth not with us'. ⁵⁰ And Jesus said unto him, 'Forbid him not: for he that is not against us, is for us'.

⁵¹ And it came to pass, when the time was come that he should be received up, he steadfastly set his face to go to Jerusalem, ⁵² and sent messengers before his face, and they went and entered into a village of the Samaritans to make ready for him. ⁵³ And they did not receive him, because his face was as though he would go to Jerusalem. ⁵⁴ And when his disciples, James and John saw this, they said, 'Lord, wilt thou that we command fire to come down from heaven, and consume them, even as Elias did?' ⁵⁵ But he turned, and rebuked them, and said, 'Ye know not what manner of spirit ye are of. ⁵⁶ For the Son of Man is not come to destroy men's lives, but to save them.' And they went to another village.

⁵⁷ And it came to pass that as they went in the way, a certain man said unto him, 'Lord, I will follow thee whithersoever thou goest'. ⁵⁸ And Jesus said unto him, 'Foxes have holes, and birds of the air have nests, but the Son of Man hath not where to lay his head'. ⁵⁹ And he said unto another, 'Follow me': but he said, 'Lord, suffer me first to go and bury my father'. ⁶⁰ Jesus said unto him, 'Let the dead bury their dead: but go thou and preach the kingdom of God'. ⁶¹ And another also said, 'Lord, I will follow thee: but let me first go bid them farewell, which are at home at my house'. ⁶² And Jesus said unto him, 'No man having put his hand to the plough, and looking back, is fit for the kingdom of God'.

Chapter 10

1 Christ sendeth out at once, seventy disciples to work miracles, and to preach: 17 admonisheth them to be humble, and wherein to rejoice: 21 thanketh his Father for his grace: 23 magnifieth the happy estate of his church: 25 teacheth the lawyer, how to attain eternal life, and to take every one for his neighbour, that needeth his mercy: 41 reprehendeth Martha, and commendeth Mary her sister.

AFTER these things, the Lord appointed other seventy also, and sent them two and two before his face, into every city and place, whither he himself would come. ² Therefore said he unto them, 'The harvest truly is great, but the labourers are few; pray ye therefore the

Lord of the harvest, that he would send forth labourers into his harvest. [3] Go your ways: behold, I send you forth as lambs among wolves. [4] Carry neither purse nor scrip, nor shoes, and salute no man by the way. [5] And into whatsoever house ye enter, first say, "Peace be to this house". [6] And if the Son of Peace be there, your peace shall rest upon it: if not, it shall turn to you again. [7] And in the same house remain, eating and drinking such things as they give: for the labourer is worthy of his hire. Go not from house to house. [8] And into whatsoever city ye enter, and they receive you, eat such things as are set before you: [9] and heal the sick that are therein, and say unto them, "The kingdom of God is come nigh unto you". [10] But into whatsoever city ye enter, and they receive you not, go your ways out into the streets of the same, and say, [11] "Even the very dust of your city which cleaveth on us, we do wipe off against you: notwithstanding, be ye sure of this, that the kingdom of God is come nigh unto you". [12] But I say unto you, that it shall be more tolerable in that day for Sodom, than for that city.

[13] 'Woe unto thee Chorazin, woe unto thee Bethsaida: for if the mighty works had been done in Tyre and Sidon, which have been done in you, they had a great while ago repented, sitting in sackcloth and ashes. [14] But it shall be more tolerable for Tyre and Sidon at the Judgement, than for you. [15] And thou Capernaum, which art exalted to heaven, shalt be thrust down to hell. [16] He that heareth you, heareth me: and he that despiseth you, despiseth me: and he that despiseth me, despiseth him that sent me.'

[17] And the seventy returned again with joy, saying, 'Lord, even the devils are subject unto us through thy name'. [18] And he said unto them, 'I beheld Satan as lightning fall from heaven. [19] Behold, I give unto you power to tread on serpents and scorpions, and over all the power of the enemy: and nothing shall by any means hurt you. [20] Notwithstanding in this rejoice not, that the spirits are subject unto you: but rather rejoice, because your names are written in heaven.'

[21] In that hour Jesus rejoiced in spirit, and said, 'I thank thee, O Father, Lord of heaven and earth, that thou hast hid these things from the wise and prudent, and hast revealed them unto babes: even so Father, for so it seemed good in thy sight. [22] All things are delivered to me of my Father: and no man knoweth who the Son is, but the Father: and who the Father is, but the Son, and he to whom the Son will reveal him.'

²³ And he turned him unto his disciples, and said privately, 'Blessed are the eyes which see the things that ye see. ²⁴ For I tell you, that many prophets, and kings have desired to see those things which ye see, and have not seen them: and to hear those things which ye hear, and have not heard them.'

²⁵ And behold, a certain lawyer stood up, and tempted him, saying, 'Master, what shall I do to inherit eternal life?' ²⁶ He said unto him, 'What is written in the Law? how readest thou?' ²⁷ And he answering said, 'Thou shalt love the Lord thy God with all thy heart, and with all thy soul, and with all thy strength, and with all thy mind, and thy neighbour as thyself'. ²⁸ And he said unto him, 'Thou hast answered right: this do, and thou shalt live'.

²⁹ But he, willing to justify himself, said unto Jesus, 'And who is my neighbour?' ³⁰ And Jesus answering, said, 'A certain man went down from Jerusalem to Jericho, and fell among thieves, which stripped him of his raiment, and wounded him, and departed, leaving him half dead. ³¹ And by chance there came down a certain priest that way, and when he saw him, he passed by on the other side. ³² And likewise a Levite, when he was at the place, came and looked on him, and passed by on the other side. ³³ But a certain Samaritan as he journeyed, came where he was; and when he saw him, he had compassion on him, ³⁴ and went to him, and bound up his wounds, pouring in oil and wine, and set him on his own beast, and brought him to an inn, and took care of him. ³⁵ And on the morrow when he departed, he took out two pence, and gave them to the host, and said unto him, "Take care of him, and whatsoever thou spendest more, when I come again I will repay thee". ³⁶ Which now of these three, thinkest thou, was neighbour unto him that fell among the thieves?' ³⁷ And he said, 'He that showed mercy on him'. Then said Jesus unto him, 'Go, and do thou likewise'.

³⁸ Now it came to pass, as they went, that he entered into a certain village: and a certain woman named Martha, received him into her house. ³⁹ And she had a sister called Mary, which also sat at Jesus's feet, and heard his word: ⁴⁰ but Martha was cumbered about much serving, and came to him, and said, 'Lord, dost thou not care that my sister hath left me to serve alone? Bid her therefore that she help me.' ⁴¹ And Jesus answered, and said unto her, 'Martha, Martha, thou art careful, and troubled about many things: ⁴² but one thing is needful, and Mary hath chosen that good part, which shall not be taken away from her'.

Chapter 11

1 Christ teacheth to pray, and that instantly: 11 assuring that God so will give us good things. 14 He casting out a dumb devil, rebuketh the blasphemous Pharisees: 28 and showeth who are blessed: 29 preacheth to the people, 37 and reprehendeth the outward show of holiness in the Pharisees, scribes and lawyers.

AND it came to pass, that as he was praying in a certain place, when he ceased, one of his disciples said unto him, 'Lord, teach us to pray, as John also taught his disciples'. ² And he said unto them, 'When ye pray, say, "Our Father which art in heaven, hallowed be thy name, thy kingdom come, thy will be done as in heaven, so in earth. ³ Give us day by day our daily bread. ⁴ And forgive us our sins: for we also forgive every one that is indebted to us. And lead us not into temptation, but deliver us from evil." '

⁵ And he said unto them, 'Which of you shall have a friend, and shall go unto him at midnight, and say unto him, "Friend, lend me three loaves: ⁶ for a friend of mine in his journey is come to me, and I have nothing to set before him", ⁷ and he from within shall answer and say, "Trouble me not: the door is now shut, and my children are with me in bed: I cannot rise and give thee". ⁸ I say unto you, though he will not rise and give him, because he is his friend: yet because of his importunity, he will rise and give him as many as he needeth.

⁹ 'And I say unto you, ask, and it shall be given you: seek, and ye shall find: knock, and it shall be opened unto you. ¹⁰ For every one that asketh, receiveth: and he that seeketh, findeth: and to him that knocketh, it shall be opened. ¹¹ If a son shall ask bread of any of you that is a father, will he give him a stone? Or if he ask a fish, will he for a fish give him a serpent? ¹² Or if he shall ask an egg, will he offer him a scorpion? ¹³ If ye then, being evil, know how to give good gifts unto your children: how much more shall your heavenly Father give the Holy Spirit to them that ask him?'

¹⁴ And he was casting out a devil, and it was dumb. And it came to pass, when the devil was gone out, the dumb spake: and the people wondered. ¹⁵ But some of them said, 'He casteth out devils through Beelzebub the chief of the devils'. ¹⁶ And others tempting him, sought of him a sign from heaven. ¹⁷ But he knowing their thoughts, said unto them, 'Every kingdom divided against itself, is brought to desolation:

and a house divided against a house, falleth. ¹⁸ If Satan also be divided against himself, how shall his kingdom stand? Because ye say that I cast out devils through Beelzebub. ¹⁹ And if I by Beelzebub cast out devils, by whom do your sons cast them out? Therefore shall they be your judges. ²⁰ But if I with the finger of God cast out devils, no doubt the kingdom of God is come upon you. ²¹ When a strong man armed keepeth his palace, his goods are in peace: ²² but when a stronger than he shall come upon him, and overcome him, he taketh from him all his armour wherein he trusted, and divideth his spoils. ²³ He that is not with me, is against me: and he that gathereth not with me, scattereth. ²⁴ When the unclean spirit is gone out of a man, he walketh through dry places, seeking rest: and finding none, he saith, "I will return unto my house whence I came out". ²⁵ And when he cometh, he findeth it swept and garnished. ²⁶ Then goeth he, and taketh to him seven other spirits more wicked than himself, and they enter in, and dwell there, and the last state of that man is worse than the first.'

²⁷ And it came to pass as he spake these things, a certain woman of the company lift up her voice, and said unto him, 'Blessed is the womb that bare thee, and the paps which thou hast sucked'. ²⁸ But he said, 'Yea, rather blessed are they that hear the word of God, and keep it'.

²⁹ And when the people were gathered thick together, he began to say, 'This is an evil generation, they seek a sign, and there shall no sign be given it, but the sign of Jonas the prophet: ³⁰ for as Jonas was a sign unto the Ninevites, so shall also the Son of Man be to this generation. ³¹ The queen of the south shall rise up in the Judgement with the men of this generation, and condemn them: for she came from the utmost parts of the earth, to hear the wisdom of Solomon: and behold, a greater than Solomon is here. ³² The men of Nineveh shall rise up in the Judgement with this generation, and shall condemn it: for they repented at the preaching of Jonas, and behold, a greater than Jonas is here.

³³ 'No man when he hath lighted a candle, putteth it in a secret place, neither under a bushel, but on a candlestick, that they which come in may see the light. ³⁴ The light of the body is the eye: therefore when thine eye is single, thy whole body also is full of light: but when thine eye is evil, thy body also is full of darkness. ³⁵ Take heed therefore, that the light which is in thee, be not darkness. ³⁶ If thy whole body therefore be full of light, having no part dark, the whole shall

be full of light, as when the bright shining of a candle doth give thee light.'

³⁷ And as he spake, a certain Pharisee besought him to dine with him: and he went in, and sat down to meat. ³⁸ And when the Pharisee saw it, he marvelled that he had not first washed before dinner. ³⁹ And the Lord said unto him, 'Now do ye Pharisees make clean the outside of the cup and the platter: but your inward part is full of ravening and wickedness. ⁴⁰ Ye fools, did not he that made that which is without, make that which is within also? ⁴¹ But rather give alms of such things as ye have: and behold, all things are clean unto you. ⁴² But woe unto you Pharisees: for ye tithe mint and rue, and all manner of herbs, and pass over judgement, and the love of God: these ought ye to have done, and not to leave the other undone. ⁴³ Woe unto you Pharisees: for ye love the uppermost seats in the synagogues, and greetings in the markets. ⁴⁴ Woe unto you scribes and Pharisees, hypocrites: for ye are as graves which appear not, and the men that walk over them, are not aware of them.'

⁴⁵ Then answered one of the lawyers, and said unto him, 'Master, thus saying, thou reproachest us also'. ⁴⁶ And he said, 'Woe unto you also ye lawyers: for ye lade men with burdens grievous to be borne, and ye yourselves touch not the burdens with one of your fingers. ⁴⁷ Woe unto you: for ye build the sepulchres of the prophets, and your fathers killed them. ⁴⁸ Truly ye bear witness that ye allow the deeds of your fathers: for they indeed killed them, and ye build their sepulchres. ⁴⁹ Therefore also said the wisdom of God, "I will send them prophets and apostles, and some of them they shall slay and persecute": ⁵⁰ that the blood of all the prophets, which was shed from the foundation of the world, may be required of this generation, ⁵¹ from the blood of Abel unto the blood of Zacharias, which perished between the altar and the Temple: verily I say unto you, it shall be required of this generation. ⁵² Woe unto you lawyers: for ye have taken away the key of knowledge: ye entered not in yourselves, and them that were entering in, ye hindered.'

⁵³ And as he said these things unto them, the scribes and the Pharisees began to urge him vehemently, and to provoke him to speak of many things: ⁵⁴ laying wait for him, and seeking to catch something out of his mouth, that they might accuse him.

Chapter 12

*1 Christ preacheth to his disciples to avoid hypocrisy, and fearfulness in
publishing his doctrine: 13 warneth the people to beware of covetousness,
by the parable of the rich man who set up greater barns. 22 We must
not be over careful of earthly things, 31 but seek the kingdom of God,
33 give alms, 36 be ready at a knock to open to our Lord whensoever he
cometh. 41 Christ's ministers are to see to their charge, 49 and look for
persecution. 54 The people must take this time of grace, 58 because it is
a fearful thing to die without reconciliation.*

I N the meantime, when there were gathered together an innumerable multitude of people, insomuch that they trod one upon another,
he began to say unto his disciples first of all, 'Beware ye of the leaven
of the Pharisees, which is hypocrisy. ² For there is nothing covered,
that shall not be revealed, neither hid, that shall not be known.
³ Therefore, whatsoever ye have spoken in darkness, shall be heard in
the light: and that which ye have spoken in the ear, in closets, shall be
proclaimed upon the house tops.

⁴ 'And I say unto you my friends, be not afraid of them that kill
the body, and after that, have no more that they can do. ⁵ But I will
forewarn you whom ye shall fear: fear him, which after he hath killed,
hath power to cast into hell, yea, I say unto you, fear him.

⁶ 'Are not five sparrows sold for two farthings, and not one of them
is forgotten before God? ⁷ But even the very hairs of your head are all
numbered: fear not therefore, ye are of more value than many sparrows.

⁸ 'Also I say unto you, whosoever shall confess me before men, him
shall the Son of Man also confess before the angels of God. ⁹ But he
that denieth me before men, shall be denied before the angels of God.
¹⁰ And whosoever shall speak a word against the Son of Man, it shall
be forgiven him: but unto him that blasphemeth against the Holy
Ghost, it shall not be forgiven. ¹¹ And when they bring you unto the
synagogues, and unto magistrates, and powers, take ye no thought
how or what thing ye shall answer, or what ye shall say: ¹² for the Holy
Ghost shall teach you in the same hour, what ye ought to say.'

¹³ And one of the company said unto him, 'Master, speak to my
brother, that he divide the inheritance with me'. ¹⁴ And he said unto
him, 'Man, who made me a judge, or a divider over you?' ¹⁵ And he
said unto them, 'Take heed, and beware of covetousness: for a man's

life consisteth not in the abundance of the things which he possesseth'. [16] And he spake a parable unto them, saying, 'The ground of a certain rich man brought forth plentifully. [17] And he thought within himself, saying, "What shall I do, because I have no room where to bestow my fruits?" [18] And he said, "This will I do, I will pull down my barns, and build greater, and there will I bestow all my fruits, and my goods. [19] And I will say to my soul, 'Soul, thou hast much goods laid up for many years, take thine ease, eat, drink, and be merry'." [20] But God said unto him, "Thou fool, this night thy soul shall be required of thee: then whose shall those things be which thou hast provided?" [21] So is he that layeth up treasure for himself, and is not rich towards God.'

[22] And he said unto his disciples, 'Therefore I say unto you, take no thought for your life what ye shall eat, neither for the body what ye shall put on. [23] The life is more than meat, and the body is more than raiment. [24] Consider the ravens, for they neither sow nor reap, which neither have storehouse nor barn, and God feedeth them: how much more are ye better than the fowls? [25] And which of you with taking thought can add to his stature one cubit? [26] If ye then be not able to do that thing which is least, why take ye thought for the rest? [27] Consider the lilies how they grow, they toil not; they spin not: and yet I say unto you, that Solomon in all his glory, was not arrayed like one of these. [28] If then God so clothe the grass, which is today in the field, and tomorrow is cast into the oven: how much more will he clothe you, O ye of little faith? [29] And seek not ye what ye shall eat, or what ye shall drink, neither be ye of doubtful mind. [30] For all these things do the nations of the world seek after: and your Father knoweth that ye have need of these things. [31] But rather seek ye the kingdom of God, and all these things shall be added unto you.

[32] 'Fear not, little flock, for it is your Father's good pleasure to give you the kingdom. [33] Sell that ye have, and give alms: provide yourselves bags which wax not old, a treasure in the heavens that faileth not, where no thief approacheth, neither moth corrupteth. [34] For where your treasure is, there will your heart be also. [35] Let your loins be girded about, and your lights burning, [36] and ye yourselves like unto men that wait for their lord, when he will return from the wedding, that when he cometh and knocketh, they may open unto him immediately. [37] Blessed are those servants, whom the lord when he cometh shall find watching: verily, I say unto you, that he shall gird himself, and make them to sit down to meat, and will come forth and

serve them. ³⁸ And if he shall come in the second watch, or come in the third watch, and find them so, blessed are those servants. ³⁹ And this know, that if the goodman of the house had known what hour the thief would come, he would have watched, and not have suffered his house to be broken through. ⁴⁰ Be ye therefore ready also: for the Son of Man cometh at an hour when ye think not.'

⁴¹ Then Peter said unto him, 'Lord, speakest thou this parable unto us, or even to all?' ⁴² And the Lord said, 'Who then is that faithful and wise steward, whom his lord shall make ruler over his household, to give them their portion of meat in due season? ⁴³ Blessed is that servant, whom his lord when he cometh shall find so doing. ⁴⁴ Of a truth, I say unto you, that he will make him ruler over all that he hath. ⁴⁵ But and if that servant say in his heart, "My lord delayeth his coming"; and shall begin to beat the menservants, and maidens, and to eat and drink, and to be drunken: ⁴⁶ the lord of that servant will come in a day when he looketh not for him, and at an hour when he is not ware, and will cut him in sunder, and will appoint him his portion with the unbelievers. ⁴⁷ And that servant which knew his lord's will, and prepared not himself, neither did according to his will, shall be beaten with many stripes. ⁴⁸ But he that knew not, and did commit things worthy of stripes, shall be beaten with few stripes. For unto whomsoever much is given, of him shall be much required: and to whom men have committed much, of him they will ask the more.

⁴⁹ 'I am come to send fire on the earth, and what will I, if it be already kindled? ⁵⁰ But I have a baptism to be baptized with, and how am I straitened till it be accomplished? ⁵¹ Suppose ye that I am come to give peace on earth? I tell you, nay, but rather division. ⁵² For from henceforth there shall be five in one house divided, three against two, and two against three. ⁵³ The father shall be divided against the son, and the son against the father: the mother against the daughter, and the daughter against the mother: the mother-in-law against her daughter-in-law, and the daughter-in-law against her mother-in-law.'

⁵⁴ And he said also to the people, 'When ye see a cloud rise out of the west, straightway ye say, "There cometh a shower", and so it is. ⁵⁵ And when ye see the south wind blow, ye say, "There will be heat", and it cometh to pass. ⁵⁶ Ye hypocrites, ye can discern the face of the sky, and of the earth: but how is it that ye do not discern this time?

⁵⁷ 'Yea, and why even of yourselves judge ye not what is right? ⁵⁸ When thou goest with thine adversary to the magistrate, as thou art

in the way, give diligence that thou mayest be delivered from him, lest
he hale thee to the judge, and the judge deliver thee to the officer, and
the officer cast thee into prison. [59] I tell thee, thou shalt not depart
thence, till thou hast paid the very last mite.'

Chapter 13

1 *Christ preacheth repentance upon the punishment of the Galileans, and
others.* 6 *The fruitless fig tree may not stand.* 11 *He healeth the crooked
woman:* 18 *showeth the powerful working of the word in the hearts of
his chosen, by the parable of the grain of mustard seed, and of leaven:*
24 *exhorteth to enter in at the strait gate,* 31 *and reproveth Herod, and
Jerusalem.*

THERE were present at that season, some that told him of the
Galileans, whose blood Pilate had mingled with their sacrifices.
[2] And Jesus answering, said unto them, 'Suppose ye that these
Galileans were sinners above all the Galileans, because they suffered
such things? [3] I tell you, nay: but except ye repent, ye shall all likewise
perish. [4] Or those eighteen, upon whom the tower in Siloam fell, and
slew them, think ye that they were sinners above all men that dwelt in
Jerusalem? [5] I tell you, nay; but, except ye repent, ye shall all likewise
perish.'

[6] He spake also this parable, 'A certain man had a fig tree planted in
his vineyard; and he came and sought fruit thereon, and found none.
[7] Then said he unto the dresser of his vineyard, "Behold, these three
years I come seeking fruit on this fig tree, and find none: cut it down,
why cumbereth it the ground?" [8] And he answering, said unto him,
"Lord, let it alone this year also, till I shall dig about it, and dung it:
[9] and if it bear fruit, well: and if not, then after that thou shalt cut it
down".'

[10] And he was teaching in one of the synagogues on the Sabbath.
[11] And behold, there was a woman which had a spirit of infirmity eighteen years, and was bowed together, and could in no wise lift up herself.
[12] And when Jesus saw her, he called her to him, and said unto her,
'Woman, thou art loosed from thine infirmity'. [13] And he laid his hands
on her, and immediately she was made straight, and glorified God.
[14] And the ruler of the synagogue answered with indignation, because
that Jesus had healed on the Sabbath day, and said unto the people,

'There are six days in which men ought to work: in them therefore come and be healed, and not on the Sabbath day'. [15] The Lord then answered him, and said, 'Thou hypocrite, doth not each one of you on the Sabbath loose his ox or his ass from the stall, and lead him away to watering? [16] And ought not this woman, being a daughter of Abraham, whom Satan hath bound, lo these eighteen years, be loosed from this bond on the Sabbath day?' [17] And when he had said these things, all his adversaries were ashamed: and all the people rejoiced for all the glorious things that were done by him.

[18] Then said he, 'Unto what is the kingdom of God like? and whereunto shall I resemble it? [19] It is like a grain of mustard seed, which a man took, and cast into his garden, and it grew, and waxed a great tree: and the fowls of the air lodged in the branches of it.' [20] And again he said, 'Whereunto shall I liken the kingdom of God? [21] It is like leaven, which a woman took and hid in three measures of meal, till the whole was leavened.'

[22] And he went through the cities and villages, teaching and journeying towards Jerusalem. [23] Then said one unto him, 'Lord, are there few that be saved?' And he said unto them, [24] 'Strive to enter in at the strait gate: for many, I say unto you, will seek to enter in, and shall not be able. [25] When once the master of the house is risen up, and hath shut to the door, and ye begin to stand without, and to knock at the door, saying, "Lord, Lord, open unto us", and he shall answer, and say unto you, "I know you not whence ye are": [26] then shall ye begin to say, "We have eaten and drunk in thy presence, and thou hast taught in our streets". [27] But he shall say, "I tell you, I know you not whence ye are; depart from me all ye workers of iniquity". [28] There shall be weeping and gnashing of teeth, when ye shall see Abraham, and Isaac, and Jacob, and all the prophets in the kingdom of God, and you yourselves thrust out. [29] And they shall come from the east, and from the west, and from the north, and from the south, and shall sit down in the kingdom of God. [30] And behold, there are last, which shall be first; and there are first, which shall be last.'

[31] The same day there came certain of the Pharisees, saying unto him, 'Get thee out, and depart hence; for Herod will kill thee'. [32] And he said unto them, 'Go ye and tell that fox, "Behold, I cast out devils, and I do cures today and tomorrow, and the third day I shall be perfected". [33] Nevertheless, I must walk today, and tomorrow, and the day following: for it cannot be that a prophet perish out

of Jerusalem. ³⁴ O Jerusalem, Jerusalem, which killest the prophets, and stonest them that are sent unto thee; how often would I have gathered thy children together, as a hen doth gather her brood under her wings, and ye would not? ³⁵ Behold, your house is left unto you desolate. And verily I say unto you, ye shall not see me, until the time come when ye shall say, "Blessed is he that cometh in the name of the Lord".'

Chapter 14

2 Christ healeth the dropsy on the Sabbath: 7 teacheth humility: 12 to feast the poor: 15 under the parable of the great supper, showeth how worldly minded men, who contemn the word of God, shall be shut out of heaven. 25 Those who will be his disciples, to bear their cross must make their accounts aforehand, lest with shame they revolt from him afterward, 34 and become altogether unprofitable, like salt that has lost his savour.

AND it came to pass, as he went into the house of one of the chief Pharisees to eat bread on the Sabbath day, that they watched him. ² And behold, there was a certain man before him, which had the dropsy. ³ And Jesus answering, spake unto the lawyers and Pharisees, saying, 'Is it lawful to heal on the Sabbath day?' ⁴ And they held their peace. And he took him, and healed him, and let him go, ⁵ and answered them, saying, 'Which of you shall have an ass or an ox fallen into a pit, and will not straightway pull him out on the Sabbath day?' ⁶ And they could not answer him again to these things.

⁷ And he put forth a parable to those which were bidden, when he marked how they chose out the chief rooms, saying unto them, ⁸ 'When thou art bidden of any man to a wedding, sit not down in the highest room: lest a more honourable man than thou be bidden of him, ⁹ and he that bade thee and him, come, and say to thee, "Give this man place": and thou begin with shame to take the lowest room. ¹⁰ But when thou art bidden, go and sit down in the lowest room, that when he that bade thee cometh, he may say unto thee, "Friend, go up higher": then shalt thou have worship in the presence of them that sit at meat with thee. ¹¹ For whosoever exalteth himself, shall be abased: and he that humbleth himself, shall be exalted.'

¹² Then said he also to him that bade him, 'When thou makest a dinner or a supper, call not thy friends, nor thy brethren, neither thy kinsmen, nor thy rich neighbours, lest they also bid thee again, and a recompence be made thee. ¹³ But when thou makest a feast, call the poor, the maimed, the lame, the blind, ¹⁴ and thou shalt be blessed, for they cannot recompense thee: for thou shalt be recompensed at the resurrection of the just.'

¹⁵ And when one of them that sat at meat with him, heard these things, he said unto him, 'Blessed is he that shall eat bread in the kingdom of God'. ¹⁶ Then said he unto him, 'A certain man made a great supper, and bade many: ¹⁷ and sent his servant at supper time, to say to them that were bidden, "Come, for all things are now ready". ¹⁸ And they all with one consent began to make excuse: the first said unto him, "I have bought a piece of ground, and I must needs go and see it: I pray thee have me excused". ¹⁹ And another said, "I have bought five yoke of oxen, and I go to prove them: I pray thee have me excused". ²⁰ And another said, "I have married a wife: and therefore I cannot come". ²¹ So that servant came, and showed his lord these things. Then the master of the house being angry said to his servant, "Go out quickly into the streets and lanes of the city, and bring in hither the poor, and the maimed, and the halt, and the blind". ²² And the servant said, "Lord, it is done as thou hast commanded, and yet there is room". ²³ And the lord said unto the servant, "Go out into the high ways and hedges, and compel them to come in, that my house may be filled. ²⁴ For I say unto you, that none of those men which were bidden, shall taste of my supper."'

²⁵ And there went great multitudes with him: and he turned, and said unto them, ²⁶ 'If any man come to me, and hate not his father, and mother, and wife, and children, and brethren, and sisters, yea, and his own life also, he cannot be my disciple. ²⁷ And whosoever doth not bear his cross, and come after me, cannot be my disciple. ²⁸ For which of you intending to build a tower, sitteth not down first, and counteth the cost, whether he have sufficient to finish it? ²⁹ Lest haply after he hath laid the foundation, and is not able to finish it, all that behold it, begin to mock him, ³⁰ saying, "This man began to build, and was not able to finish". ³¹ Or what king going to make war against another king, sitteth not down first, and consulteth whether he be able with ten thousand, to meet him that cometh against him with twenty thousand? ³² Or else, while the other is yet a great way off, he sendeth an ambassage,

and desireth conditions of peace. ³³ So likewise, whos\
you, that forsaketh not all that he hath, he cannot be my\

³⁴ 'Salt is good: but if the salt have lost his savour, whe\
it be seasoned? ³⁵ It is neither fit for the land, nor yet for the\
but men cast it out. He that hath ears to hear, let him hear.'

Chapter 15

1 *The parable of the lost sheep:* 8 *of the piece of silver:* 11 *of the prodigal son.*

THEN drew near unto him all the publicans and sinners, for to hear him. ² And the Pharisees and scribes murmured, saying, 'This man receiveth sinners, and eateth with them'.

³ And he spake this parable unto them, saying, ⁴ 'What man of you having an hundred sheep, if he lose one of them, doth not leave the ninety and nine in the wilderness, and go after that which is lost, until he find it? ⁵ And when he hath found it, he layeth it on his shoulders, rejoicing. ⁶ And when he cometh home, he calleth together his friends, and neighbours, saying unto them, "Rejoice with me, for I have found my sheep which was lost". ⁷ I say unto you, that likewise joy shall be in heaven over one sinner that repenteth, more than over ninety and nine just persons, which need no repentance.

⁸ 'Either what woman having ten pieces of silver, if she lose one piece, doth not light a candle, and sweep the house, and seek diligently till she find it? ⁹ And when she hath found it, she calleth her friends and her neighbours together, saying, "Rejoice with me, for I have found the piece which I had lost". ¹⁰ Likewise I say unto you, there is joy in the presence of the angels of God, over one sinner that repenteth.'

¹¹ And he said, 'A certain man had two sons: ¹² and the younger of them said to his father, "Father, give me the portion of goods that falleth to me". And he divided unto them his living. ¹³ And not many days after, the younger son gathered all together, and took his journey into a far country, and there wasted his substance with riotous living. ¹⁴ And when he had spent all, there arose a mighty famine in that land, and he began to be in want. ¹⁵ And he went and joined himself to a citizen of that country, and he sent him into his fields to feed swine. ¹⁶ And he would fain have filled his belly with the husks that the swine

..d eat: and no man gave unto him. [17] And when he came to himself, he said, "How many hired servants of my father have bread enough and to spare, and I perish with hunger? [18] I will arise and go to my father, and will say unto him, 'Father, I have sinned against heaven and before thee, [19] and am no more worthy to be called thy son: make me as one of thy hired servants'." [20] And he arose and came to his father. But when he was yet a great way off, his father saw him, and had compassion, and ran, and fell on his neck, and kissed him. [21] And the son said unto him, "Father, I have sinned against heaven, and in thy sight, and am no more worthy to be called thy son". [22] But the father said to his servants, "Bring forth the best robe, and put it on him, and put a ring on his hand, and shoes on his feet. [23] And bring hither the fatted calf, and kill it, and let us eat and be merry. [24] For this my son was dead, and is alive again; he was lost, and is found." And they began to be merry.

[25] 'Now his elder son was in the field, and as he came and drew nigh to the house, he heard music and dancing, [26] and he called one of the servants, and asked what these things meant. [27] And he said unto him, "Thy brother is come, and thy father hath killed the fatted calf, because he hath received him safe and sound". [28] And he was angry, and would not go in: therefore came his father out, and intreated him. [29] And he answering said to his father, "Lo, these many years do I serve thee, neither transgressed I at any time thy commandment: and yet thou never gavest me a kid, that I might make merry with my friends: [30] but as soon as this thy son was come, which hath devoured thy living with harlots, thou hast killed for him the fatted calf". [31] And he said unto him, "Son, thou art ever with me, and all that I have is thine. [32] It was meet that we should make merry, and be glad: for this thy brother was dead, and is alive again: and was lost, and is found." '

Chapter 16

1 The parable of the unjust steward. 14 Christ reproveth the hypocrisy of the covetous Pharisees. 19 The rich glutton, and Lazarus the beggar.

AND he said also unto his disciples, 'There was a certain rich man which had a steward, and the same was accused unto him that he had wasted his goods. [2] And he called him, and said unto him,

"How is it that I hear this of thee? Give an accompt of thy steward-ship: for thou mayest be no longer steward." [3] Then the steward said within himself, "What shall I do, for my lord taketh away from me the stewardship? I cannot dig, to beg I am ashamed. [4] I am resolved what to do, that when I am put out of the stewardship, they may receive me into their houses." [5] So he called every one of his lord's debtors unto him, and said unto the first, "How much owest thou unto my lord?" [6] And he said, "An hundred measures of oil". And he said unto him, "Take thy bill, and sit down quickly, and write fifty". [7] Then said he to another, "And how much owest thou?" And he said, "An hundred measures of wheat". And he said unto him, "Take thy bill and write fourscore". [8] And the lord commended the unjust steward, because he had done wisely: for the children of this world are in their genera-tion wiser than the children of light. [9] And I say unto you, make to yourselves friends of the mammon of unrighteousness, that when ye fail, they may receive you into everlasting habitations. [10] He that is faithful in that which is least, is faithful also in much: and he that is unjust in the least, is unjust also in much. [11] If therefore ye have not been faithful in the unrighteous mammon, who will commit to your trust the true riches? [12] And if ye have not been faithful in that which is another man's, who shall give you that which is your own? [13] No servant can serve two masters, for either he will hate the one, and love the other: or else he will hold to the one, and despise the other: ye cannot serve God and mammon.'

[14] And the Pharisees also who were covetous, heard all these things: and they derided him. [15] And he said unto them, 'Ye are they which justify yourselves before men, but God knoweth your hearts: for that which is highly esteemed among men, is abomination in the sight of God. [16] The Law and the Prophets were until John: since that time the kingdom of God is preached, and every man presseth into it. [17] And it is easier for heaven and earth to pass, than one tittle of the Law to fail. [18] Whosoever putteth away his wife, and marrieth another, com-mitteth adultery: and whosoever marrieth her that is put away from her husband, committeth adultery.

[19] 'There was a certain rich man, which was clothed in purple and fine linen, and fared sumptuously every day. [20] And there was a certain beggar named Lazarus, which was laid at his gate, full of sores, [21] and desiring to be fed with the crumbs which fell from the rich man's table: moreover the dogs came and licked his sores. [22] And it came

to pass that the beggar died, and was carried by the angels into Abraham's bosom: the rich man also died, and was buried. 23 And in hell he lift up his eyes being in torments, and seeth Abraham afar off, and Lazarus in his bosom. 24 And he cried, and said, "Father Abraham, have mercy on me, and send Lazarus, that he may dip the tip of his finger in water, and cool my tongue, for I am tormented in this flame". 25 But Abraham said, "Son, remember that thou in thy lifetime receivedst thy good things, and likewise Lazarus evil things, but now he is comforted, and thou art tormented. 26 And beside all this, between us and you there is a great gulf fixed, so that they which would pass from hence to you, cannot, neither can they pass to us, that would come from thence." 27 Then he said, "I pray thee therefore father, that thou wouldst send him to my father's house: 28 for I have five brethren, that he may testify unto them, lest they also come into this place of torment". 29 Abraham saith unto him, "They have Moses and the Prophets, let them hear them". 30 And he said, "Nay, father Abraham: but if one went unto them from the dead, they will repent". 31 And he said unto him, "If they hear not Moses and the Prophets, neither will they be persuaded, though one rose from the dead".'

Chapter 17

1 *Christ teacheth to avoid occasions of offence.* 3 *One to forgive another.*
6 *The power of faith.* 7 *How we are bound to God, and not he to us.*
11 *He healeth ten lepers.* 22 *Of the kingdom of God, and the coming of the Son of Man.*

THEN said he unto the disciples, 'It is impossible but that offences will come, but woe unto him through whom they come. 2 It were better for him that a millstone were hanged about his neck, and he cast into the sea, than that he should offend one of these little ones. 3 Take heed to yourselves: if thy brother trespass against thee, rebuke him, and if he repent, forgive him. 4 And if he trespass against thee seven times in a day, and seven times in a day turn again to thee, saying, "I repent", thou shalt forgive him.'

5 And the apostles said unto the Lord, 'Increase our faith'. 6 And the Lord said, 'If ye had faith as a grain of mustard seed, ye might

say unto this sycamine tree, "Be thou plucked up by the root, and be thou planted in the sea", and it should obey you. [7] But which of you, having a servant plowing, or feeding cattle, will say unto him by and by when he is come from the field, "Go and sit down to meat?" [8] And will not rather say unto him, "Make ready wherewith I may sup, and gird thyself, and serve me, till I have eaten and drunken: and afterward thou shalt eat and drink." [9] Doth he thank that servant, because he did the things that were commanded him? I trow not. [10] So likewise ye, when ye shall have done all those things which are commanded you, say, "We are unprofitable servants: we have done that which was our duty to do".'

[11] And it came to pass, as he went to Jerusalem, that he passed through the mids of Samaria and Galilee. [12] And as he entered into a certain village, there met him ten men that were lepers, which stood afar off. [13] And they lifted up their voices, and said, 'Jesus, Master, have mercy on us'. [14] And when he saw them, he said unto them, 'Go show yourselves unto the priests'. And it came to pass, that as they went, they were cleansed. [15] And one of them when he saw that he was healed, turned back, and with a loud voice glorified God, [16] and fell down on his face at his feet, giving him thanks: and he was a Samaritan. [17] And Jesus answering, said, 'Were there not ten cleansed, but where are the nine? [18] There are not found that returned to give glory to God, save this stranger.' [19] And he said unto him, 'Arise, go thy way, thy faith hath made thee whole'.

[20] And when he was demanded of the Pharisees, when the kingdom of God should come, he answered them, and said, 'The kingdom of God cometh not with observation. [21] Neither shall they say, "Lo here", or "Lo there": for behold, the kingdom of God is within you.'

[22] And he said unto the disciples, 'The days will come, when ye shall desire to see one of the days of the Son of Man, and ye shall not see it. [23] And they shall say to you, "See here", or "See there": go not after them, nor follow them. [24] For as the lightning that lighteneth out of the one part under heaven, shineth unto the other part under heaven: so shall also the Son of Man be in his day. [25] But first must he suffer many things, and be rejected of this generation.

[26] 'And as it was in the days of Noe: so shall it be also in the days of the Son of Man. [27] They did eat, they drank, they married wives, they were given in marriage, until the day that Noe entered into the ark: and the flood came, and destroyed them all. [28] Likewise also

as it was in the days of Lot, they did eat, they drank, they bought, they sold, they planted, they builded: [29] but the same day that Lot went out of Sodom, it rained fire and brimstone from heaven, and destroyed them all: [30] even thus shall it be in the day when the Son of Man is revealed. [31] In that day he which shall be upon the house top, and his stuff in the house, let him not come down to take it away: and he that is in the field, let him likewise not return back. [32] Remember Lot's wife. [33] Whosoever shall seek to save his life, shall lose it, and whosoever shall lose his life, shall preserve it. [34] I tell you, in that night there shall be two men in one bed; the one shall be taken, the other shall be left. [35] Two women shall be grinding together; the one shall be taken, and the other left. [36] Two men shall be in the field; the one shall be taken, and the other left.' [37] And they answered, and said unto him, 'Where, Lord?' And he said unto them, 'Wheresoever the body is, thither will the eagles be gathered together'.

Chapter 18

AND he spake a parable unto them, to this end, that men ought always to pray, and not to faint, [2] saying, 'There was in a city a judge, which feared not God, neither regarded man. [3] And there was a widow in that city, and she came unto him, saying, "Avenge me of mine adversary": [4] and he would not for a while. But afterward he said within himself, "Though I fear not God, nor regard man, [5] yet because this widow troubleth me, I will avenge her, lest by her continual coming, she weary me".' [6] And the Lord said, 'Hear what the unjust judge saith. [7] And shall not God avenge his own elect, which cry day and night unto him, though he bear long with them? [8] I tell you that he will avenge them speedily. Nevertheless, when the Son of Man cometh, shall he find faith on the earth?'

[9] And he spake this parable unto certain which trusted in themselves that they were righteous, and despised other: [10] 'Two men went up into the Temple to pray, the one a Pharisee, and the other a publican. [11] The Pharisee stood and prayed thus with himself, "God, I

thank thee, that I am not as other men are, extortioners, unjust, adulterers, or even as this publican. [12] I fast twice in the week, I give tithes of all that I possess." [13] And the publican, standing afar off, would not lift up so much as his eyes unto heaven: but smote upon his breast, saying, "God be merciful to me a sinner". [14] I tell you, this man went down to his house justified rather than the other: for every one that exalteth himself, shall be abased: and he that humbleth himself, shall be exalted.'

[15] And they brought unto him also infants, that he would touch them: but when his disciples saw it, they rebuked them. [16] But Jesus called them unto him, and said, 'Suffer little children to come unto me, and forbid them not: for of such is the kingdom of God. [17] Verily I say unto you, whosoever shall not receive the kingdom of God as a little child, shall in no wise enter therein.'

[18] And a certain ruler asked him, saying, 'Good Master, what shall I do to inherit eternal life?' [19] And Jesus said unto him, 'Why callest thou me good? None is good save one, that is God. [20] Thou knowest the commandments, do not commit adultery, do not kill, do not steal, do not bear false witness, honour thy father and thy mother.' [21] And he said, 'All these have I kept from my youth up'. [22] Now when Jesus heard these things, he said unto him, 'Yet lackest thou one thing: sell all that thou hast, and distribute unto the poor, and thou shalt have treasure in heaven, and come, follow me'. [23] And when he heard this, he was very sorrowful, for he was very rich. [24] And when Jesus saw that he was very sorrowful, he said, 'How hardly shall they that have riches, enter into the kingdom of God? [25] For it is easier for a camel to go through a needle's eye, than for a rich man to enter into the kingdom of God.' [26] And they that heard it, said, 'Who then can be saved?' [27] And he said, 'The things which are unpossible with men, are possible with God'. [28] Then Peter said, 'Lo, we have left all, and followed thee'. [29] And he said unto them, 'Verily, I say unto you, there is no man that hath left house, or parents, or brethren, or wife, or children, for the kingdom of God's sake, [30] who shall not receive manifold more in this present time, and in the world to come life everlasting'.

[31] Then he took unto him the twelve, and said unto them, 'Behold, we go up to Jerusalem, and all things that are written by the prophets concerning the Son of Man, shall be accomplished. [32] For he shall be delivered unto the Gentiles, and shall be mocked, and spitefully

intreated, and spitted on: ³³ and they shall scourge him, and put him to death, and the third day he shall rise again.' ³⁴ And they understood none of these things: and this saying was hid from them, neither knew they the things which were spoken.

³⁵ And it came to pass, that as he was come nigh unto Jericho, a certain blind man sat by the way side, begging, ³⁶ and hearing the multitude pass by, he asked what it meant. ³⁷ And they told him that Jesus of Nazareth passeth by. ³⁸ And he cried, saying, 'Jesus, thou Son of David, have mercy on me'. ³⁹ And they which went before, rebuked him, that he should hold his peace: but he cried so much the more, 'Thou Son of David, have mercy on me'. ⁴⁰ And Jesus stood and commanded him to be brought unto him: and when he was come near, he asked him, ⁴¹ saying, 'What wilt thou that I shall do unto thee?' And he said, 'Lord, that I may receive my sight'. ⁴² And Jesus said unto him, 'Receive thy sight, thy faith hath saved thee'. ⁴³ And immediately he received his sight, and followed him, glorifying God: and all the people when they saw it, gave praise unto God.

Chapter 19

1 *Of Zachaeus a publican.* 11 *The ten pieces of money.* 28 *Christ rideth into Jerusalem with triumph:* 41 *weepeth over it:* 45 *driveth the buyers and sellers out of the Temple:* 47 *teaching daily in it. The rulers would have destroyed him, but for fear of the people.*

AND Jesus entered, and passed through Jericho. ² And behold, there was a man named Zacchaeus, which was the chief among the publicans, and he was rich. ³ And he sought to see Jesus who he was, and could not for the press, because he was little of stature. ⁴ And he ran before, and climbed up into a sycamore tree to see him, for he was to pass that way. ⁵ And when Jesus came to the place, he looked up and saw him, and said unto him, 'Zacchaeus, make haste, and come down, for today I must abide at thy house'. ⁶ And he made haste, and came down, and received him joyfully. ⁷ And when they saw it, they all murmured, saying, that he was gone to be guest with a man that is a sinner. ⁸ And Zacchaeus stood, and said unto the Lord, 'Behold, Lord, the half of my goods I give to the poor, and if I have taken any thing from any man by false accusation, I restore him four fold'. ⁹ And Jesus said unto him, 'This day is salvation come to this house, forsomuch as he also is the son of Abraham. [10] For the Son of Man is come to seek and to save that which was lost.'

[11] And as they heard these things, he added, and spake a parable, because he was nigh to Jerusalem, and because they thought that the kingdom of God should immediately appear. [12] He said therefore, 'A certain nobleman went into a far country, to receive for himself a kingdom, and to return. [13] And he called his ten servants, and delivered them ten pounds, and said unto them, "Occupy till I come". [14] But his citizens hated him, and sent a message after him, saying, "We will not have this man to reign over us". [15] And it came to pass, that when he was returned, having received the kingdom, then he commanded these servants to be called unto him, to whom he had given the money, that he might know how much every man had gained by trading. [16] Then came the first, saying, "Lord, thy pound hath gained ten pounds". [17] And he said unto him, "Well, thou good servant: because thou hast been faithful in a very little, have thou authority over ten cities". [18] And the second came, saying, "Lord, thy pound hath gained five pounds". [19] And he said likewise to him, "Be thou also over five cities". [20] And another came, saying, "Lord, behold, here is thy pound which I have kept laid up in a napkin: [21] for I feared thee, because thou art an austere man: thou takest up that thou layedst not down, and reapest that thou didst not sow". [22] And he saith unto him, "Out of thine own mouth will I judge thee, thou wicked servant: thou knewest that I was an austere man, taking up that I laid not down, and reaping that I did not sow. [23] Wherefore then gavest not thou my money into the bank, that at my coming I might have required mine own with usury?" [24] And he said unto them that stood by, "Take from him the pound, and give it to him that hath ten pounds". [25] And they said unto him, "Lord, he hath ten pounds". [26] "For I say unto you, that unto every one which hath, shall be given, and from him that hath not, even that he hath shall be taken away from him. [27] But those mine enemies which would not that I should reign over them, bring hither, and slay them before me." '

[28] And when he had thus spoken, he went before, ascending up to Jerusalem. [29] And it came to pass when he was come nigh to Bethphage and Bethany, at the mount called the Mount of Olives, he sent two of his disciples, [30] saying, 'Go ye into the village over against you, in the which at your entering ye shall find a colt tied, whereon yet never man sat: loose him, and bring him hither. [31] And if any man ask you,

"Why do ye loose him?" thus shall ye say unto him, "Because the Lord hath need of him".' [32] And they that were sent, went their way, and found even as he had said unto them. [33] And as they were loosing the colt, the owners thereof said unto them, 'Why loose ye the colt?' [34] And they said, 'The Lord hath need of him'. [35] And they brought him to Jesus: and they cast their garments upon the colt, and they set Jesus thereon. [36] And as he went, they spread their clothes in the way. [37] And when he was come nigh, even now at the descent of the Mount of Olives, the whole multitude of the disciples began to rejoice and praise God with a loud voice, for all the mighty works that they had seen, [38] saying, 'Blessed be the King that cometh in the name of the Lord, peace in heaven, and glory in the highest'. [39] And some of the Pharisees from among the multitude said unto him, 'Master, rebuke thy disciples'. [40] And he answered, and said unto them, 'I tell you, that if these should hold their peace, the stones would immediately cry out'.

[41] And when he was come near, he beheld the city and wept over it, [42] saying, 'If thou hadst known, even thou, at least in this thy day, the things which belong unto thy peace! but now they are hid from thine eyes. [43] For the days shall come upon thee, that thine enemies shall cast a trench about thee, and compass thee round, and keep thee in on every side, [44] and shall lay thee even with the ground, and thy children within thee: and they shall not leave in thee one stone upon another, because thou knewest not the time of thy visitation.'

[45] And he went into the Temple, and began to cast out them that sold therein, and them that bought, [46] saying unto them, 'It is written, "My house is the house of prayer": but ye have made it a den of thieves'.

[47] And he taught daily in the Temple. But the chief priests and the scribes, and the chief of the people sought to destroy him, [48] and could not find what they might do: for all the people were very attentive to hear him.

Chapter 20

1 Christ avoucheth his authority by a question of John's baptism. 9 The parable of the vineyard. 19 Of giving tribute to Caesar. 27 He convinceth the Sadducees that denied the resurrection. 41 How Christ is the Son of David. 45 He warneth his disciples to beware of the scribes.

A<small>ND</small> it came to pass, that on one of those days, as he taught the people in the Temple, and preached the gospel, the chief priests and the scribes came upon him, with the elders, ² and spake unto him, saying, 'Tell us, by what authority doest thou these things? or who is he that gave thee this authority?' ³ And he answered, and said unto them, 'I will also ask you one thing, and answer me. ⁴ The baptism of John, was it from heaven, or of men?' ⁵ And they reasoned with themselves, saying, 'If we shall say, "From heaven", he will say, "Why then believed ye him not?" ⁶ But and if we say, "Of men", all the people will stone us: for they be persuaded that John was a prophet.' ⁷ And they answered, that they could not tell whence it was. ⁸ And Jesus said unto them, 'Neither tell I you by what authority I do these things'.

⁹ Then began he to speak to the people this parable: 'A certain man planted a vineyard, and let it forth to husbandmen, and went into a far country for a long time. ¹⁰ And at the season, he sent a servant to the husbandmen, that they should give him of the fruit of the vineyard, but the husbandmen beat him, and sent him away empty. ¹¹ And again he sent another servant, and they beat him also, and entreated him shamefully, and sent him away empty. ¹² And again he sent the third, and they wounded him also, and cast him out. ¹³ Then said the lord of the vineyard, "What shall I do? I will send my beloved son: it may be they will reverence him when they see him." ¹⁴ But when the husbandmen saw him, they reasoned among themselves, saying, "This is the heir, come, let us kill him, that the inheritance may be ours". ¹⁵ So they cast him out of the vineyard, and killed him. What therefore shall the lord of the vineyard do unto them? ¹⁶ He shall come and destroy these husbandmen, and shall give the vineyard to others.' And when they heard it, they said, 'God forbid'. ¹⁷ And he beheld them, and said, 'What is this then that is written, "The stone which the builders rejected, the same is become the head of the corner"? ¹⁸ Whosoever shall fall upon that stone, shall be broken: but on whomsoever it shall fall, it will grind him to powder.'

¹⁹ And the chief priests and the scribes the same hour sought to lay hands on him, and they feared the people: for they perceived that he had spoken this parable against them. ²⁰ And they watched him, and sent forth spies, which should feign themselves just men, that they might take hold of his words, that so they might deliver him unto the power and authority of the governor. ²¹ And they asked him, saying, 'Master, we know that thou sayest and teachest rightly, neither acceptest thou the person of any, but teachest the way of God truly. ²² Is it lawful for us to give tribute unto Caesar, or no?' ²³ But he perceived their craftiness, and said unto them, 'Why tempt ye me? ²⁴ Show me a penny: whose image and superscription hath it?' They answered, and said, 'Caesar's'. ²⁵ And he said unto them, 'Render therefore unto Caesar the things which be Caesar's, and unto God the things which be God's'. ²⁶ And they could not take hold of his words before the people, and they marvelled at his answer, and held their peace.

²⁷ Then came to him certain of the Sadducees (which deny that there is any resurrection) and they asked him, ²⁸ saying, 'Master, Moses wrote unto us, "If any man's brother die, having a wife, and he die without children, that his brother should take his wife, and raise up seed unto his brother". ²⁹ There were therefore seven brethren, and the first took a wife, and died without children. ³⁰ And the second took her to wife, and he died childless. ³¹ And the third took her, and in like manner the seven also. And they left no children, and died. ³² Last of all the woman died also. ³³ Therefore in the resurrection, whose wife of them is she? for seven had her to wife.'

³⁴ And Jesus answering, said unto them, 'The children of this world, marry, and are given in marriage: ³⁵ but they which shall be accompted worthy to obtain that world, and the resurrection from the dead, neither marry, nor are given in marriage. ³⁶ Neither can they die any more; for they are equal unto the angels, and are the children of God, being the children of the resurrection. ³⁷ Now that the dead are raised, even Moses showed at the bush, when he calleth the Lord, the God of Abraham, and the God of Isaac, and the God of Jacob. ³⁸ For he is not a God of the dead, but of the living; for all live unto him.' ³⁹ Then certain of the scribes answering, said, 'Master, thou hast well said'. ⁴⁰ And after that, they durst not ask him any question at all.

⁴¹ And he said unto them, 'How say they that Christ is David's son? ⁴² and David himself saith in the book of Psalms, "The Lord said to

my Lord, 'Sit thou on my right hand, [43] till I make thine enemies thy footstool' ". [44] David therefore calleth him Lord, how is he then his son?'

[45] Then in the audience of all the people, he said unto his disciples, [46] 'Beware of the scribes, which desire to walk in long robes, and love greetings in the markets, and the highest seats in the synagogues, and the chief rooms at feasts: [47] which devour widows' houses, and for a show make long prayers: the same shall receive greater damnation'.

Chapter 21

1 Christ commendeth the poor widow. 5 He foretelleth the destruction of the Temple, and of the city Jerusalem: 25 the signs also which shall be before the last day. 34 He exhorteth them to be watchful.

AND he looked up, and saw the rich men casting their gifts into the treasury. [2] And he saw also a certain poor widow, casting in thither two mites. [3] And he said, 'Of a truth, I say unto you, that this poor widow hath cast in more than they all: [4] for all these have of their abundance cast in unto the offerings of God, but she of her penury hath cast in all the living that she had'.

[5] And as some spake of the Temple, how it was adorned with goodly stones and gifts, he said, [6] 'As for these things which ye behold, the days will come, in the which there shall not be left one stone upon another, that shall not be thrown down'. [7] And they asked him, saying, 'Master, but when shall these things be? and what sign will there be, when these things shall come to pass?' [8] And he said, 'Take heed that ye be not deceived: for many shall come in my name, saying, "I am Christ", and the time draweth near: go ye not therefore after them. [9] But when ye shall hear of wars, and commotions, be not terrified: for these things must first come to pass, but the end is not by and by.'

[10] Then said he unto them, 'Nation shall rise against nation, and kingdom against kingdom: [11] and great earthquakes shall be in divers places, and famines, and pestilences: and fearful sights and great signs shall there be from heaven. [12] But before all these, they shall lay their hands on you, and persecute you, delivering you up to the synagogues, and into prisons, being brought before kings and rulers for my name's sake. [13] And it shall turn to you for a testimony. [14] Settle it therefore in your hearts, not to meditate before what ye shall answer.

[15] For I will give you a mouth and wisdom, which all your adversaries shall not be able to gainsay, nor resist. [16] And ye shall be betrayed both by parents and brethren, and kinsfolks and friends, and some of you shall they cause to be put to death. [17] And ye shall be hated of all men for my name's sake. [18] But there shall not a hair of your head perish. [19] In your patience possess ye your souls.

[20] 'And when ye shall see Jerusalem compassed with armies, then know that the desolation thereof is nigh. [21] Then let them which are in Judea, flee to the mountains, and let them which are in the midst of it, depart out, and let not them that are in the countries, enter thereinto. [22] For these be the days of vengeance, that all things which are written may be fulfilled. [23] But woe unto them that are with child, and to them that give suck in those days, for there shall be great distress in the land, and wrath upon this people. [24] And they shall fall by the edge of the sword, and shall be led away captive into all nations, and Jerusalem shall be trodden down of the Gentiles, until the times of the Gentiles be fulfilled. [25] And there shall be signs in the sun, and in the moon, and in the stars, and upon the earth distress of nations, with perplexity, the sea and the waves roaring, [26] men's hearts failing them for fear, and for looking after those things which are coming on the earth; for the powers of heaven shall be shaken. [27] And then shall they see the Son of Man coming in a cloud with power and great glory. [28] And when these things begin to come to pass, then look up, and lift up your heads, for your redemption draweth nigh.'

[29] And he spake to them a parable, 'Behold the fig tree, and all the trees, [30]when they now shoot forth, ye see and know of your own selves, that summer is now nigh at hand. [31] So likewise ye, when ye see these things come to pass, know ye that the kingdom of God is nigh at hand. [32] Verily I say unto you, this generation shall not pass away, till all be fulfilled. [33] Heaven and earth shall pass away, but my words shall not pass away.

[34] 'And take heed to yourselves, lest at any time your hearts be overcharged with surfeiting, and drunkenness, and cares of this life, and so that day come upon you unawares. [35] For as a snare shall it come on all them that dwell on the face of the whole earth. [36] Watch ye therefore, and pray always, that ye may be accompted worthy to escape all these things that shall come to pass, and to stand before the Son of Man.'

³⁷ And in the day time he was teaching in the Temple, and at night he went out, and abode in the mount that is called the Mount of Olives. ³⁸ And all the people came early in the morning to him in the Temple, for to hear him.

Chapter 22

1 The Jews conspire against Christ. 3 Satan prepareth Judas to betray him. 7 The apostles prepare the Passover. 19 Christ instituteth his holy supper, 21 covertly foretelleth of the traitor, 24 dehorteth the rest of his apostles from ambition, 31 assureth Peter his faith should not fail: 34 and yet he should deny him thrice. 39 He prayeth in the mount, and sweateth blood, 47 is betrayed with a kiss: 50 he healeth Malchus's ear, 54 he is thrice denied of Peter, 63 shamefully abused, 66 and confesseth himself to be the Son of God.

Now the Feast of Unleavened Bread drew nigh, which is called the Passover. ² And the chief priests and scribes sought how they might kill him; for they feared the people.

³ Then entered Satan into Judas surnamed Iscariot, being of the number of the twelve. ⁴ And he went his way, and communed with the chief priests and captains, how he might betray him unto them. ⁵ And they were glad, and covenanted to give him money. ⁶ And he promised, and sought opportunity to betray him unto them in the absence of the multitude.

⁷ Then came the day of Unleavened Bread, when the Passover must be killed. ⁸ And he sent Peter and John, saying, 'Go and prepare us the Passover, that we may eat'. ⁹ And they said unto him, 'Where wilt thou that we prepare?' ¹⁰ And he said unto them, 'Behold, when ye are entered into the city, there shall a man meet you, bearing a pitcher of water, follow him into the house where he entereth in. ¹¹ And ye shall say unto the goodman of the house, "The Master saith unto thee, 'Where is the guest-chamber where I shall eat the Passover with my disciples?' " ¹² And he shall show you a large upper room furnished, there make ready.' ¹³ And they went, and found as he had said unto them, and they made ready the Passover.

¹⁴ And when the hour was come, he sat down, and the twelve apostles with him. ¹⁵ And he said unto them, 'With desire I have desired to eat this Passover with you before I suffer. ¹⁶ For I say unto you,

I will not any more eat thereof, until it be fulfilled in the kingdom of God.' ¹⁷ And he took the cup, and gave thanks, and said, 'Take this, and divide it among yourselves. ¹⁸ For I say unto you, I will not drink of the fruit of the vine, until the kingdom of God shall come.' ¹⁹ And he took bread, and gave thanks, and brake it, and gave unto them, saying, 'This is my body which is given for you, this do in remembrance of me'. ²⁰ Likewise also the cup after supper, saying, 'This cup is the new testament in my blood, which is shed for you. ²¹ But behold, the hand of him that betrayeth me, is with me on the table. ²² And truly the Son of Man goeth as it was determined, but woe unto that man by whom he is betrayed.' ²³ And they began to enquire among themselves, which of them it was that should do this thing.

²⁴ And there was also a strife among them, which of them should be accompted the greatest. ²⁵ And he said unto them, 'The kings of the Gentiles exercise lordship over them, and they that exercise authority upon them, are called benefactors. ²⁶ But ye shall not be so; but he that is greatest among you, let him be as the younger, and he that is chief, as he that doth serve. ²⁷ For whether is greater, he that sitteth at meat, or he that serveth? Is not he that sitteth at meat? But I am among you as he that serveth. ²⁸ Ye are they which have continued with me in my temptations. ²⁹ And I appoint unto you a kingdom, as my Father hath appointed unto me, ³⁰ that ye may eat and drink at my table in my kingdom, and sit on thrones judging the twelve tribes of Israel.'

³¹ And the Lord said, 'Simon, Simon, behold, Satan hath desired to have you, that he may sift you as wheat: ³² but I have prayed for thee, that thy faith fail not; and when thou art converted, strengthen thy brethren'. ³³ And he said unto him, 'Lord, I am ready to go with thee both into prison, and to death'. ³⁴ And he said, 'I tell thee Peter, the cock shall not crow this day, before that thou shalt thrice deny that thou knowest me'.

³⁵ And he said unto them, 'When I sent you without purse, and scrip, and shoes, lacked ye any thing?' And they said, 'Nothing'. ³⁶ Then said he unto them, 'But now, he that hath a purse, let him take it, and likewise his scrip: and he that hath no sword, let him sell his garment, and buy one. ³⁷ For I say unto you, that this that is written, must yet be accomplished in me, "And he was reckoned among the transgressors": for the things concerning me have an end.' ³⁸ And they said, 'Lord, behold, here are two swords'. And he said unto them, 'It is enough'.

[39] And he came out, and went, as he was wont, to the Mount of Olives, and his disciples also followed him. [40] And when he was at the place, he said unto them, 'Pray, that ye enter not into temptation'. [41] And he was withdrawn from them about a stone's cast, and kneeled down, and prayed, [42] saying, 'Father, if thou be willing, remove this cup from me: nevertheless, not my will, but thine be done'. [43] And there appeared an angel unto him from heaven, strengthening him. [44] And being in an agony, he prayed more earnestly, and his sweat was as it were great drops of blood falling down to the ground. [45] And when he rose up from prayer, and was come to his disciples, he found them sleeping for sorrow, [46] and said unto them, 'Why sleep ye? Rise, and pray, lest ye enter into temptation.'

[47] And while he yet spake, behold, a multitude, and he that was called Judas, one of the twelve, went before them, and drew near unto Jesus, to kiss him. [48] But Jesus said unto him, 'Judas, betrayest thou the Son of Man with a kiss?' [49] When they which were about him, saw what would follow, they said unto him, 'Lord, shall we smite with the sword?' [50] And one of them smote the servant of the High Priest, and cut off his right ear. [51] And Jesus answered, and said, 'Suffer ye thus far'. And he touched his ear, and healed him. [52] Then Jesus said unto the chief priests, and captains of the Temple, and the elders which were come to him, 'Be ye come out as against a thief, with swords and staves? [53] When I was daily with you in the Temple, ye stretched forth no hands against me: but this is your hour, and the power of darkness.'

[54] Then took they him, and led him, and brought him into the High Priest's house, and Peter followed afar off. [55] And when they had kindled a fire in the mids of the hall, and were set down together, Peter sat down among them. [56] But a certain maid beheld him as he sat by the fire, and earnestly looked upon him, and said, 'This man was also with him'. [57] And he denied him, saying, 'Woman, I know him not'. [58] And after a little while another saw him, and said, 'Thou art also of them'. And Peter said, 'Man, I am not'. [59] And about the space of one hour after, another confidently affirmed, saying, 'Of a truth this fellow also was with him; for he is a Galilean'. [60] And Peter said, 'Man, I know not what thou sayest'. And immediately, while he yet spake, the cock crew. [61] And the Lord turned, and looked upon Peter; and Peter remembered the word of the Lord, how he had said unto him, 'Before the cock crow, thou shalt deny me thrice'. [62] And Peter went out, and wept bitterly.

⁶³ And the men that held Jesus, mocked him, and smote him. ⁶⁴ And when they had blindfolded him, they struck him on the face, and asked him, saying, 'Prophesy, who is it that smote thee?' ⁶⁵ And many other things blasphemously spake they against him.

⁶⁶ And as soon as it was day, the elders of the people, and the chief priests and the scribes came together, and led him into their council, saying, ⁶⁷ 'Art thou the Christ? Tell us.' And he said unto them, 'If I tell you, you will not believe. ⁶⁸ And if I also ask you, you will not answer me, nor let me go. ⁶⁹ Hereafter shall the Son of Man sit on the right hand of the power of God.' ⁷⁰ Then said they all, 'Art thou then the Son of God?' And he said unto them, 'Ye say that I am'. ⁷¹ And they said, 'What need we any further witness? for we our selves have heard of his own mouth.'

Chapter 23

1 *Jesus is accused before Pilate, and sent to Herod.* 8 *Herod mocketh him.* 12 *Herod and Pilate are made friends.* 13 *Barabbas is desired of the people, and is loosed by Pilate, and Jesus is given to be crucified.* 27 *He telleth the women that lament him, the destruction of Jerusalem:* 34 *prayeth for his enemies.* 39 *Two evil doers are crucified with him.* 46 *His death.* 50 *His burial.*

AND the whole multitude of them arose, and led him unto Pilate. ² And they began to accuse him, saying, 'We found this fellow perverting the nation, and forbidding to give tribute to Caesar, saying, that he himself is Christ a King'. ³ And Pilate asked him, saying, 'Art thou the King of the Jews?' And he answered him, and said, 'Thou sayest it'. ⁴ Then said Pilate to the chief priests, and to the people, 'I find no fault in this man'. ⁵ And they were the more fierce, saying, 'He stirreth up the people, teaching throughout all Jewry, beginning from Galilee to this place'.

⁶ When Pilate heard of Galilee, he asked whether the man were a Galilean. ⁷ And as soon as he knew that he belonged unto Herod's jurisdiction, he sent him to Herod, who himself also was at Jerusalem at that time. ⁸ And when Herod saw Jesus, he was exceeding glad, for he was desirous to see him of a long season, because he had heard many things of him, and he hoped to have seen some miracle done by him. ⁹Then he questioned with him in many words, but he

answered him nothing. [10] And the chief priests and scribes stood, and vehemently accused him. [11] And Herod with his men of war set him at naught, and mocked him, and arrayed him in a gorgeous robe, and sent him again to Pilate. [12] And the same day Pilate and Herod were made friends together; for before, they were at enmity between themselves.

[13] And Pilate, when he had called together the chief priests, and the rulers, and the people, [14] said unto them, 'Ye have brought this man unto me, as one that perverteth the people, and behold, I having examined him before you, have found no fault in this man, touching those things whereof ye accuse him. [15] No, nor yet Herod: for I sent you to him, and lo, nothing worthy of death is done unto him. [16] I will therefore chastise him, and release him.' [17] For of necessity he must release one unto them at the feast.

[18] And they cried out all at once, saying, 'Away with this man, and release unto us Barabbas', [19] who for a certain sedition made in the city, and for murder, was cast in prison. [20] Pilate therefore willing to release Jesus, spake again to them: [21] but they cried, saying, 'Crucify him, crucify him'. [22] And he said unto them the third time, 'Why, what evil hath he done? I have found no cause of death in him, I will therefore chastise him, and let him go.' [23] And they were instant with loud voices, requiring that he might be crucified: and the voices of them, and of the chief priests prevailed. [24] And Pilate gave sentence that it should be as they required. [25] And he released unto them, him that for sedition and murder was cast into prison, whom they had desired, but he delivered Jesus to their will.

[26] And as they led him away, they laid hold upon one Simon a Cyrenian, coming out of the country, and on him they laid the cross, that he might bear it after Jesus. [27] And there followed him a great company of people, and of women, which also bewailed and lamented him. [28] But Jesus turning unto them, said, 'Daughters of Jerusalem, weep not for me, but weep for yourselves, and for your children. [29] For behold, the days are coming, in the which they shall say, "Blessed are the barren, and the wombs that never bare, and the paps which never gave suck". [30] Then shall they begin to say to the mountains, "Fall on us"; and to the hills, "Cover us". [31] For if they do these things in a green tree, what shall be done in the dry?'

[32] And there were also two other malefactors led with him, to be put to death. [33] And when they were come to the place which is called

Calvary, there they crucified him, and the malefactors, one on the right hand, and the other on the left.

[34] Then said Jesus, 'Father, forgive them, for they know not what they do'. And they parted his raiment, and cast lots. [35] And the people stood beholding, and the rulers also with them derided him, saying, 'He saved others, let him save himself, if he be Christ, the chosen of God'. [36] And the soldiers also mocked him, coming to him, and offering him vinegar, [37] and saying, 'If thou be the King of the Jews, save thyself'. [38] And a superscription also was written over him in letters of Greek, and Latin, and Hebrew, '*THIS IS THE KING OF THE JEWS*'.

[39] And one of the malefactors which were hanged, railed on him, saying, 'If thou be Christ, save thyself and us'. [40] But the other answering, rebuked him, saying, 'Dost not thou fear God, seeing thou art in the same condemnation? [41] And we indeed justly; for we receive the due reward of our deeds, but this man hath done nothing amiss.' [42] And he said unto Jesus, 'Lord, remember me when thou comest into thy kingdom'. [43] And Jesus said unto him, 'Verily, I say unto thee, today shalt thou be with me in paradise'.

[44] And it was about the sixth hour, and there was a darkness over all the earth, until the ninth hour. [45] And the sun was darkened, and the veil of the Temple was rent in the mids. [46] And when Jesus had cried with a loud voice, he said, 'Father, into thy hands I commend my spirit': and having said thus, he gave up the ghost. [47] Now when the centurion saw what was done, he glorified God, saying, 'Certainly this was a righteous man'. [48] And all the people that came together to that sight, beholding the things which were done, smote their breasts, and returned. [49] And all his acquaintance, and the women that followed him from Galilee, stood a far off, beholding these things.

[50] And behold, there was a man named Joseph, a councillor; and he was a good man, and a just [51] (the same had not consented to the counsel and deed of them): he was of Arimathea, a city of the Jews (who also himself waited for the kingdom of God). [52] This man went unto Pilate, and begged the body of Jesus. [53] And he took it down, and wrapped it in linen, and laid it in a sepulchre that was hewn in stone, wherein never man before was laid. [54] And that day was the Preparation, and the Sabbath drew on. [55] And the women also which came with him from Galilee, followed after, and beheld the sepulchre, and how his body was laid. [56] And they returned, and prepared

spices and ointments, and rested the Sabbath day, according to the commandment.

Chapter 24

1 Christ's resurrection is declared by two angels, to the women that come to the sepulchre. 9 These report it to others. 13 Christ himself appeareth to the two disciples that went to Emmaus: 36 afterwards he appeareth to the apostles, and reproveth their unbelief: 47 giveth them a charge: 49 promiseth the Holy Ghost: 51 and so ascendeth into heaven.

N OW upon the first day of the week, very early in the morning, they came unto the sepulchre, bringing the spices which they had prepared, and certain others with them. ² And they found the stone rolled away from the sepulchre. ³ And they entered in, and found not the body of the Lord Jesus. ⁴ And it came to pass, as they were much perplexed thereabout, behold, two men stood by them in shining garments. ⁵ And as they were afraid, and bowed down their faces to the earth, they said unto them, 'Why seek ye the living among the dead? ⁶ He is not here, but is risen: remember how he spake unto you when he was yet in Galilee, ⁷ saying, "The Son of Man must be delivered into the hands of sinful men, and be crucified, and the third day rise again".' ⁸ And they remembered his words, ⁹ and returned from the sepulchre, and told all these things unto the eleven, and to all the rest. ¹⁰ It was Mary Magdalene, and Joanna, and Mary the mother of James, and other women that were with them, which told these things unto the apostles. ¹¹ And their words seemed to them as idle tales, and they believed them not. ¹² Then arose Peter, and ran unto the sepulchre, and stooping down, he beheld the linen clothes laid by themselves, and departed, wondering in himself at that which was come to pass.

¹³ And behold, two of them went that same day to a village called Emmaus, which was from Jerusalem about threescore furlongs. ¹⁴ And they talked together of all these things which had happened. ¹⁵ And it came to pass, that while they communed together, and reasoned, Jesus himself drew near, and went with them. ¹⁶ But their eyes were holden, that they should not know him. ¹⁷ And he said unto them, 'What manner of communications are these that ye have one to another as ye walk, and are sad?' ¹⁸ And the one of them, whose name was Cleopas,

answering, said unto him, 'Art thou only a stranger in Jerusalem, and hast not known the things which are come to pass there in these days?' ¹⁹ And he said unto them, 'What things?' And they said unto him, 'Concerning Jesus of Nazareth, which was a prophet, mighty in deed and word before God, and all the people. ²⁰ And how the chief priests and our rulers delivered him to be condemned to death, and have crucified him. ²¹ But we trusted that it had been he which should have redeemed Israel: and beside all this, today is the third day since these things were done. ²² Yea, and certain women also of our company made us astonished, which were early at the sepulchre: ²³ and when they found not his body, they came, saying, that they had also seen a vision of angels, which said that he was alive. ²⁴ And certain of them which were with us, went to the sepulchre, and found it even so as the women had said, but him they saw not.' ²⁵ Then he said unto them, 'O fools, and slow of heart to believe all that the prophets have spoken: ²⁶ ought not Christ to have suffered these things, and to enter into his glory?' ²⁷ And beginning at Moses, and all the Prophets, he expounded unto them in all the scriptures, the things concerning himself.

²⁸ And they drew nigh unto the village, whither they went, and he made as though he would have gone further. ²⁹ But they constrained him, saying, 'Abide with us, for it is towards evening, and the day is far spent': and he went in, to tarry with them. ³⁰ And it came to pass, as he sat at meat with them, he took bread, and blessed it, and brake, and gave to them. ³¹ And their eyes were opened, and they knew him, and he vanished out of their sight. ³² And they said one unto another, 'Did not our heart burn within us, while he talked with us by the way, and while he opened to us the scriptures?' ³³ And they rose up the same hour, and returned to Jerusalem, and found the eleven gathered together, and them that were with them, ³⁴ saying, 'The Lord is risen indeed, and hath appeared to Simon'. ³⁵ And they told what things were done in the way, and how he was known of them in breaking of bread.

³⁶ And as they thus spake, Jesus himself stood in the midst of them, and saith unto them, 'Peace be unto you'. ³⁷ But they were terrified, and affrighted, and supposed that they had seen a spirit. ³⁸ And he said unto them, 'Why are ye troubled? and why do thoughts arise in your hearts? ³⁹ Behold my hands and my feet, that it is I myself: handle me, and see, for a spirit hath not flesh and bones, as ye see me

have.' ⁴⁰ And when he had thus spoken, he showed them his hands and his feet. ⁴¹ And while they yet believed not for joy, and wondered, he said unto them, 'Have ye here any meat?' ⁴² And they gave him a piece of a broiled fish, and of an honeycomb. ⁴³ And he took it, and did eat before them.

⁴⁴ And he said unto them, 'These are the words which I spake unto you, while I was yet with you, that all things must be fulfilled, which were written in the Law of Moses, and in the Prophets, and in the Psalms concerning me'. ⁴⁵ Then opened he their understanding, that they might understand the scriptures, ⁴⁶ and said unto them, 'Thus it is written, and thus it behoved Christ to suffer, and to rise from the dead the third day: ⁴⁷ and that repentance and remission of sins should be preached in his name, among all nations, beginning at Jerusalem. ⁴⁸ And ye are witnesses of these things. ⁴⁹ And behold, I send the promise of my Father upon you: but tarry ye in the city of Jerusalem, until ye be endued with power from on high.'

⁵⁰ And he led them out as far as to Bethany, and he lift up his hands, and blessed them. ⁵¹ And it came to pass, while he blessed them, he was parted from them, and carried up into heaven. ⁵² And they worshipped him, and returned to Jerusalem, with great joy: ⁵³ and were continually in the Temple, praising and blessing God. Amen.

THE GOSPEL ACCORDING TO
SAINT JOHN

Chapter 1

1 *The divinity, humanity, and office of Jesus Christ.* 15 *The testimony of John.* 39 *The calling of Andrew, Peter, etc.*

I N the beginning was the Word, and the Word was with God, and the Word was God. 2 The same was in the beginning with God. 3 All things were made by him, and without him was not any thing made that was made. 4 In him was life, and the life was the light of men. 5 And the light shineth in darkness, and the darkness comprehended it not.

6 There was a man sent from God, whose name was John. 7 The same came for a witness, to bear witness of the light, that all men through him might believe. 8 He was not that light, but was sent to bear witness of that light. 9 That was the true light, which lighteth every man that cometh into the world.

10 He was in the world, and the world was made by him, and the world knew him not. 11 He came unto his own, and his own received him not. 12 But as many as received him, to them gave he power to become the sons of God, even to them that believe on his name: 13 which were born, not of blood, nor of the will of the flesh, nor of the will of man, but of God. 14 And the Word was made flesh, and dwelt among us, and we beheld his glory, the glory as of the only begotten of the Father, full of grace and truth.

15 John bare witness of him, and cried, saying, 'This was he of whom I spake, "He that cometh after me, is preferred before me", for he was before me'. 16 And of his fullness have all we received, and grace for grace. 17 For the Law was given by Moses, but grace and truth came by Jesus Christ. 18 No man hath seen God at any time: the only begotten Son, which is in the bosom of the Father, he hath declared him.

19 And this is the record of John, when the Jews sent priests and Levites from Jerusalem to ask him, 'Who art thou?' 20 And he confessed, and denied not: but confessed, 'I am not the Christ'. 21 And they asked him, 'What then? Art thou Elias?' And he saith, 'I am not'.

'Art thou that prophet?' And he answered, 'No'. [22] Then said they unto him, 'Who art thou, that we may give an answer to them that sent us? What sayest thou of thyself?' [23] He said, 'I am the voice of one crying in the wilderness: "Make straight the way of the Lord", as said the prophet Esaias'.

[24] And they which were sent, were of the Pharisees. [25] And they asked him, and said unto him, 'Why baptizest thou then, if thou be not that Christ, nor Elias, neither that prophet?' [26] John answered them, saying, 'I baptize with water, but there standeth one among you, whom ye know not, [27] he it is, who coming after me, is preferred before me, whose shoe's latchet I am not worthy to unloose'. [28] These things were done in Bethabara beyond Jordan, where John was baptizing.

[29] The next day, John seeth Jesus coming unto him, and saith, 'Behold the Lamb of God, which taketh away the sin of the world. [30] This is he of whom I said, "After me cometh a man which is preferred before me": for he was before me. [31] And I knew him not: but that he should be made manifest to Israel, therefore am I come baptizing with water.' [32] And John bare record saying, 'I saw the Spirit descending from heaven, like a dove, and it abode upon him. [33] And I knew him not: but he that sent me to baptize with water, the same said unto me, "Upon whom thou shalt see the Spirit descending, and remaining on him, the same is he which baptizeth with the Holy Ghost". [34] And I saw, and bare record, that this is the Son of God.'

[35] Again the next day after, John stood, and two of his disciples. [36] And looking upon Jesus as he walked, he saith, 'Behold the Lamb of God'. [37] And the two disciples heard him speak, and they followed Jesus. [38] Then Jesus turned, and saw them following, and saith unto them, 'What seek ye?' They said unto him, 'Rabbi' (which is to say being interpreted, Master), 'where dwellest thou?' [39] He saith unto them, 'Come and see'. They came and saw where he dwelt, and abode with him that day: for it was about the tenth hour. [40] One of the two which heard John speak, and followed him, was Andrew, Simon Peter's brother. [41] He first findeth his own brother Simon, and saith unto him, 'We have found the Messiah', which is, being interpreted, the Christ. [42] And he brought him to Jesus. And when Jesus beheld him, he said, 'Thou art Simon the son of Jona: thou shalt be called Cephas', which is, by interpretation, a stone.

[43] The day following, Jesus would go forth into Galilee, and findeth Philip, and saith unto him, 'Follow me'. [44] Now Philip was of

Bethsaida, the city of Andrew and Peter. [45] Philip findeth Nathanael, and saith unto him, 'We have found him of whom Moses in the Law, and the Prophets did write, Jesus of Nazareth the son of Joseph'. [46] And Nathanael said unto him, 'Can there any good thing come out of Nazareth?' Philip saith unto him, 'Come and see'. [47] Jesus saw Nathanael coming to him, and saith of him, 'Behold an Israelite indeed in whom is no guile'. [48] Nathanael saith unto him, 'Whence knowest thou me?' Jesus answered, and said unto him, 'Before that Philip called thee, when thou wast under the fig tree, I saw thee'. [49] Nathanael answered, and saith unto him, 'Rabbi, thou art the Son of God, thou art the King of Israel'. [50] Jesus answered, and said unto him, 'Because I said unto thee, I saw thee under the fig tree, believest thou? thou shalt see greater things than these'. [51] And he saith unto him, 'Verily, verily I say unto you, hereafter ye shall see heaven open, and the angels of God ascending and descending upon the Son of Man'.

Chapter 2

1 *Christ turneth water into wine,* 12 *departeth into Capernaum, and to Jerusalem,* 14 *where he purgeth the Temple of buyers and sellers.* 19 *He foretelleth his death and resurrection.* 23 *Many believed because of his miracles, but he would not trust himself with them.*

AND the third day there was a marriage in Cana of Galilee, and the mother of Jesus was there. [2] And both Jesus was called, and his disciples, to the marriage. [3] And when they wanted wine, the mother of Jesus saith unto him, 'They have no wine'. [4] Jesus saith unto her, 'Woman, what have I to do with thee? mine hour is not yet come'. [5] His mother saith unto the servants, 'Whatsoever he saith unto you, do it'. [6] And there were set there six water pots of stone, after the manner of the purifying of the Jews, containing two or three firkins apiece. [7] Jesus saith unto them, 'Fill the water pots with water'. And they filled them up to the brim. [8] And he saith unto them, 'Draw out now, and bear unto the governor of the feast'. And they bare it. [9] When the ruler of the feast had tasted the water that was made wine, and knew not whence it was (but the servants which drew the water knew), the governor of the feast called the bridegroom, [10] and saith unto him, 'Every man at the beginning doth set forth good wine, and when men have well drunk, then that which is worse: but thou hast kept the good wine until now'. [11] This beginning of miracles did Jesus in Cana of Galilee, and manifested forth his glory, and his disciples believed on him.

[12] After this he went down to Capernaum, he and his mother, and his brethren, and his disciples, and they continued there not many days.

[13] And the Jews' Passover was at hand, and Jesus went up to Jerusalem, [14] and found in the Temple those that sold oxen, and sheep, and doves, and the changers of money, sitting. [15] And when he had made a scourge of small cords, he drove them all out of the Temple, and the sheep and the oxen; and poured out the changers' money, and overthrew the tables, [16] and said unto them that sold doves, 'Take these things hence, make not my Father's house an house of merchandise'. [17] And his disciples remembered that it was written, 'The zeal of thine house hath eaten me up'. [18] Then answered the Jews, and said unto him, 'What sign showest thou unto us, seeing that thou doest these things?' [19] Jesus answered, and said unto them, 'Destroy this temple, and in three days I will raise it up'. [20] Then said the Jews, 'Forty and six years was this Temple in building, and wilt thou rear it up in three days?' [21] But he spake of the temple of his body. [22] When therefore he was risen from the dead, his disciples remembered that he had said this unto them: and they believed the scripture, and the word which Jesus had said.

[23] Now when he was in Jerusalem at the Passover, in the feast day, many believed in his name, when they saw the miracles which he did. [24] But Jesus did not commit himself unto them, because he knew all men, [25] and needed not that any should testify of man: for he knew what was in man.

Chapter 3

[1] Christ teacheth Nicodemus the necessity of regeneration. [14] Of faith in his death. [16] The great love of God towards the world. [18] Condemnation for unbelief. [23] The baptism, witness and doctrine of John concerning Christ.

THERE was a man of the Pharisees, named Nicodemus, a ruler of the Jews: [2] the same came to Jesus by night, and said unto him,

'Rabbi, we know that thou art a teacher come from God: for no man can do these miracles that thou doest, except God be with him'. ³ Jesus answered, and said unto him, 'Verily, verily I say unto thee, except a man be born again, he cannot see the kingdom of God'. ⁴ Nicodemus saith unto him, 'How can a man be born when he is old? Can he enter the second time into his mother's womb, and be born?' ⁵ Jesus answered, 'Verily, verily I say unto thee, except a man be born of water and of the Spirit, he cannot enter into the kingdom of God. ⁶ That which is born of the flesh, is flesh, and that which is born of the Spirit, is spirit. ⁷ Marvel not that I said unto thee, "Ye must be born again". ⁸ The wind bloweth where it listeth, and thou hearest the sound thereof, but canst not tell whence it cometh, and whither it goeth: so is every one that is born of the Spirit.' ⁹ Nicodemus answered, and said unto him, 'How can these things be?' ¹⁰Jesus answered, and said unto him, 'Art thou a master of Israel, and knowest not these things?

¹¹ 'Verily, verily I say unto thee, we speak that we do know, and testify that we have seen; and ye receive not our witness. ¹² If I have told you earthly things, and ye believe not: how shall ye believe if I tell you of heavenly things? ¹³ And no man hath ascended up to heaven, but he that came down from heaven, even the Son of Man which is in heaven. ¹⁴ And as Moses lifted up the serpent in the wilderness: even so must the Son of Man be lifted up: ¹⁵ that whosoever believeth in him should not perish, but have eternal life. ¹⁶ For God so loved the world, that he gave his only begotten Son: that whosoever believeth in him, should not perish, but have everlasting life. ¹⁷ For God sent not his Son into the world to condemn the world: but that the world through him might be saved. ¹⁸ He that believeth on him, is not condemned: but he that believeth not, is condemned already, because he hath not believed in the name of the only begotten Son of God. ¹⁹ And this is the condemnation, that light is come into the world, and men loved darkness rather than light, because their deeds were evil. ²⁰ For every one that doeth evil, hateth the light, neither cometh to the light, lest his deeds should be reproved. ²¹ But he that doeth truth cometh to the light, that his deeds may be made manifest, that they are wrought in God.'

²² After these things, came Jesus and his disciples into the land of Judea, and there he tarried with them, and baptized. ²³ And John also was baptizing in Aenon, near to Salim, because there was much water there: and they came, and were baptized. ²⁴ For John was not yet cast into prison.

²⁵ Then there arose a question between some of John's disciples and the Jews, about purifying. ²⁶ And they came unto John, and said unto him, 'Rabbi, he that was with thee beyond Jordan, to whom thou barest witness, behold, the same baptizeth, and all men come to him'. ²⁷ John answered, and said, 'A man can receive nothing, except it be given him from heaven. ²⁸ Ye yourselves bear me witness, that I said I am not the Christ, but that I am sent before him. ²⁹ He that hath the bride, is the bridegroom: but the friend of the bridegroom, which standeth and heareth him, rejoiceth greatly because of the bridegroom's voice: this my joy therefore is fulfilled. ³⁰ He must increase, but I must decrease.

³¹ 'He that cometh from above, is above all: he that is of the earth, is earthly, and speaketh of the earth: he that cometh from heaven is above all: ³² and what he hath seen and heard, that he testifieth, and no man receiveth his testimony: ³³ he that hath received his testimony, hath set to his seal, that God is true. ³⁴ For he whom God hath sent, speaketh the words of God: for God giveth not the Spirit by measure unto him. ³⁵ The Father loveth the Son, and hath given all things into his hand. ³⁶ He that believeth on the Son, hath everlasting life: and he that believeth not the Son, shall not see life: but the wrath of God abideth on him.'

Chapter 4

1 *Christ talketh with a woman of Samaria, and revealeth himself unto her.* 27 *His disciples marvel.* 31 *He declareth to them his zeal to God's glory.* 39 *Many Samaritans believe on him.* 43 *He departeth into Galilee, and healeth the ruler's son that lay sick at Capernaum.*

WHEN therefore the Lord knew how the Pharisees had heard that Jesus made and baptized moe disciples than John ² (though Jesus himself baptized not, but his disciples): ³ he left Judea, and departed again into Galilee. ⁴ And he must needs go through Samaria. ⁵ Then cometh he to a city of Samaria, which is called Sychar, near to the parcel of ground that Jacob gave to his son Joseph. ⁶ Now Jacob's well was there. Jesus therefore being wearied with his journey, sat thus on the well: and it was about the sixth hour.

⁷ There cometh a woman of Samaria to draw water: Jesus saith unto her, 'Give me to drink'. ⁸ For his disciples were gone away

unto the city to buy meat. ⁹ Then saith the woman of Samaria unto him, 'How is it that thou, being a Jew, askest drink of me, which am a woman of Samaria?' For the Jews have no dealings with the Samaritans. ¹⁰ Jesus answered, and said unto her, 'If thou knewest the gift of God, and who it is that saith to thee, "Give me to drink"; thou wouldst have asked of him, and he would have given thee living water'. ¹¹ The woman saith unto him, 'Sir, thou hast nothing to draw with, and the well is deep: from whence then hast thou that living water? ¹² Art thou greater than our father Jacob, which gave us the well, and drank thereof himself, and his children, and his cattle?' ¹³ Jesus answered, and said unto her, 'Whosoever drinketh of this water, shall thirst again: ¹⁴ but whosoever drinketh of the water that I shall give him, shall never thirst: but the water that I shall give him, shall be in him a well of water springing up into everlasting life'. ¹⁵ The woman saith unto him, 'Sir, give me this water, that I thirst not, neither come hither to draw'.

¹⁶ Jesus saith unto her, 'Go, call thy husband, and come hither'. ¹⁷ The woman answered, and said, 'I have no husband'. Jesus said unto her, 'Thou hast well said, "I have no husband": ¹⁸ for thou hast had five husbands, and he whom thou now hast is not thy husband: in that saidst thou truly'. ¹⁹ The woman saith unto him, 'Sir, I perceive that thou art a prophet. ²⁰ Our fathers worshipped in this mountain, and ye say, that in Jerusalem is the place where men ought to worship.' ²¹ Jesus saith unto her, 'Woman, believe me, the hour cometh when ye shall neither in this mountain, nor yet at Jerusalem, worship the Father. ²² Ye worship ye know not what: we know what we worship: for salvation is of the Jews. ²³ But the hour cometh, and now is, when the true worshippers shall worship the Father in spirit, and in truth: for the Father seeketh such to worship him. ²⁴ God is a Spirit, and they that worship him, must worship him in spirit and in truth.' ²⁵ The woman saith unto him, 'I know that Messiah cometh, which is called Christ: when he is come, he will tell us all things'. ²⁶ Jesus saith unto her, 'I that speak unto thee, am he'.

²⁷ And upon this came his disciples, and marvelled that he talked with the woman: yet no man said, 'What seekest thou?' or, 'Why talkest thou with her?' ²⁸ The woman then left her water pot, and went her way into the city, and saith to the men, ²⁹ 'Come, see a man, which told me all things that ever I did: is not this the Christ?' ³⁰ Then they went out of the city, and came unto him.

³¹ In the mean while his disciples prayed him, saying, 'Master, eat'.
³² But he said unto them, 'I have meat to eat that ye know not of'.
³³ Therefore said the disciples one to another, 'Hath any man brought him ought to eat?' ³⁴ Jesus saith unto them, 'My meat is, to do the will of him that sent me, and to finish his work. ³⁵ Say not ye, "There are yet four months, and then cometh harvest"? Behold, I say unto you, lift up your eyes, and look on the fields: for they are white already to harvest. ³⁶ And he that reapeth receiveth wages, and gathereth fruit unto life eternal: that both he that soweth, and he that reapeth, may rejoice together. ³⁷ And herein is that saying true, "One soweth, and another reapeth". ³⁸ I sent you to reap that whereon ye bestowed no labour: other men laboured, and ye are entered into their labours.'

³⁹ And many of the Samaritans of that city believed on him, for the saying of the woman, which testified, 'He told me all that ever I did'. ⁴⁰ So when the Samaritans were come unto him, they besought him that he would tarry with them, and he abode there two days. ⁴¹ And many moe believed, because of his own word: ⁴² and said unto the woman, 'Now we believe, not because of thy saying, for we have heard him ourselves, and know that this is indeed the Christ, the saviour of the world'.

⁴³ Now after two days he departed thence, and went into Galilee: ⁴⁴ for Jesus himself testified, that a prophet hath no honour in his own country. ⁴⁵ Then when he was come into Galilee, the Galileans received him, having seen all the things that he did at Jerusalem at the feast, for they also went unto the feast.

⁴⁶ So Jesus came again into Cana of Galilee, where he made the water wine. And there was a certain nobleman, whose son was sick at Capernaum. ⁴⁷ When he heard that Jesus was come out of Judea into Galilee, he went unto him, and besought him that he would come down, and heal his son: for he was at the point of death. ⁴⁸ Then said Jesus unto him, 'Except ye see signs and wonders, ye will not believe'. ⁴⁹ The nobleman saith unto him, 'Sir, come down ere my child die'. ⁵⁰ Jesus saith unto him, 'Go thy way, thy son liveth'. And the man believed the word that Jesus had spoken unto him, and he went his way. ⁵¹ And as he was now going down, his servants met him, and told him, saying, 'Thy son liveth'. ⁵² Then enquired he of them the hour when he began to amend: and they said unto him, 'Yesterday at the seventh hour the fever left him'. ⁵³ So the father knew that it was at the same hour, in the which Jesus said unto him, 'Thy son liveth',

and himself believed, and his whole house. ⁵⁴ This is again the second miracle that Jesus did, when he was come out of Judea into Galilee.

Chapter 5

1 Jesus on the Sabbath day cureth him that was diseased eight and thirty years. 10 The Jews therefore cavil, and persecute him for it. 17 He answereth for himself, and reproveth them, showing by the testimony of his Father, 32 of John, 36 of his works, 39 and of the scriptures, who he is.

AFTER this there was a feast of the Jews, and Jesus went up to Jerusalem. ² Now there is at Jerusalem by the Sheep Market, a pool, which is called in the Hebrew tongue Bethesda, having five porches. ³ In these lay a great multitude of impotent folk, of blind, halt, withered, waiting for the moving of the water. ⁴ For an angel went down at a certain season into the pool, and troubled the water: whosoever then first after the troubling of the water stepped in, was made whole of whatsoever disease he had. ⁵ And a certain man was there, which had an infirmity thirty and eight years. ⁶ When Jesus saw him lie, and knew that he had been now a long time in that case, he saith unto him, 'Wilt thou be made whole?' ⁷ The impotent man answered him, 'Sir, I have no man when the water is troubled, to put me into the pool: but while I am coming, another steppeth down before me'. ⁸ Jesus saith unto him, 'Rise, take up thy bed, and walk'. ⁹ And immediately the man was made whole, and took up his bed, and walked: and on the same day was the Sabbath.

¹⁰ The Jews therefore said unto him that was cured, 'It is the Sabbath day, it is not lawful for thee to carry thy bed'. ¹¹ He answered them, 'He that made me whole, the same said unto me, "Take up thy bed, and walk" '. ¹² Then asked they him, 'What man is that which said unto thee, "Take up thy bed, and walk"?' ¹³ And he that was healed wist not who it was: for Jesus had conveyed himself away, a multitude being in that place. ¹⁴ Afterward Jesus findeth him in the Temple, and said unto him, 'Behold, thou art made whole: sin no more, lest a worse thing come unto thee'. ¹⁵ The man departed, and told the Jews that it was Jesus which had made him whole. ¹⁶ And therefore did the Jews persecute Jesus, and sought to slay him, because he had done these things on the Sabbath day. ¹⁷ But Jesus answered them, 'My Father

worketh hitherto, and I work'. ¹⁸ Therefore the Jews sought the more to kill him, not only because he had broken the Sabbath, but said also, that God was his Father, making himself equal with God.

¹⁹ Then answered Jesus and said unto them, 'Verily, verily I say unto you, the Son can do nothing of himself, but what he seeth the Father do: for what things soever he doeth, these also doeth the Son likewise. ²⁰ For the Father loveth the Son, and showeth him all things that himself doeth: and he will show him greater works than these, that ye may marvel. ²¹ For as the Father raiseth up the dead, and quickeneth them: even so the Son quickeneth whom he will. ²² For the Father judgeth no man: but hath committed all judgement unto the Son: ²³ that all men should honour the Son, even as they honour the Father. He that honoureth not the Son, honoureth not the Father which hath sent him. ²⁴ Verily, verily I say unto you, he that heareth my word, and believeth on him that sent me, hath everlasting life, and shall not come into condemnation: but is passed from death unto life.

²⁵ 'Verily, verily I say unto you, the hour is coming, and now is, when the dead shall hear the voice of the Son of God: and they that hear shall live. ²⁶ For as the Father hath life in himself: so hath he given to the Son to have life in himself: ²⁷ and hath given him authority to execute judgement also, because he is the Son of Man. ²⁸ Marvel not at this: for the hour is coming, in the which all that are in the graves shall hear his voice, ²⁹ and shall come forth, they that have done good, unto the resurrection of life, and they that have done evil, unto the resurrection of damnation. ³⁰ I can of mine own self do nothing: as I hear, I judge: and my judgement is just, because I seek not mine own will, but the will of the Father, which hath sent me.

³¹ 'If I bear witness of myself, my witness is not true. ³² There is another that beareth witness of me, and I know that the witness which he witnesseth of me, is true. ³³ Ye sent unto John, and he bare witness unto the truth. ³⁴ But I receive not testimony from man: but these things I say, that ye might be saved. ³⁵ He was a burning and a shining light: and ye were willing for a season to rejoice in his light. ³⁶ But I have greater witness than that of John: for the works which the Father hath given me to finish, the same works that I do, bear witness of me, that the Father hath sent me. ³⁷ And the Father himself which hath sent me, hath borne witness of me. Ye have neither heard his voice at any time, nor seen his shape. ³⁸ And ye have not his word abiding in you: for whom he hath sent, him ye believe not. ³⁹ Search the

scriptures, for in them ye think ye have eternal life, and they are they which testify of me. [40] And ye will not come to me, that ye might have life. [41] I receive not honour from men. [42] But I know you, that ye have not the love of God in you. [43] I am come in my Father's name, and ye receive me not: if another shall come in his own name, him ye will receive. [44] How can ye believe, which receive honour one of another, and seek not the honour that cometh from God only? [45] Do not think that I will accuse you to the Father: there is one that accuseth you, even Moses, in whom ye trust. [46] For had ye believed Moses, ye would have believed me: for he wrote of me. [47] But if ye believe not his writings, how shall ye believe my words?'

Chapter 6

1 *Christ feedeth five thousand men with five loaves and two fishes.* 15 *Thereupon the people would have made him king.* 16 *But withdrawing himself, he walked on the sea to his disciples:* 26 *reproveth the people flocking after him, and all the fleshly hearers of his word:* 32 *declareth himself to be the bread of life to believers.* 66 *Many disciples depart from him.* 68 *Peter confesseth him.* 70 *Judas is a devil.*

AFTER these things Jesus went over the Sea of Galilee, which is the Sea of Tiberias: [(2)] and a great multitude followed him, because they saw his miracles which he did on them that were diseased. [(3)] And Jesus went up into a mountain, and there he sat with his disciples. [(4)] And the Passover, a feast of the Jews, was nigh. [(5)] When Jesus then lift up his eyes, and saw a great company come unto him, he saith unto Philip, 'Whence shall we buy bread, that these may eat?' [(6)] And this he said to prove him: for he himself knew what he would do. [(7)] Philip answered him, 'Two hundred penny-worth of bread is not sufficient for them, that every one of them may take a little'. [(8)] One of his disciples, Andrew, Simon Peter's brother, saith unto him, [(9)] 'There is a lad here, which hath five barley loaves, and two small fishes: but what are they among so many?' [10] And Jesus said, 'Make the men sit down'. Now there was much grass in the place. So the men sat down, in number about five thousand. [11] And Jesus took the loaves, and when he had given thanks, he distributed to the disciples, and the disciples to them that were set down, and likewise of the fishes, as much as they would. [12] When they were filled, he said unto his disciples, 'Gather up the fragments that remain, that nothing be lost'. ¹³ Therefore they gathered them together, and filled twelve baskets with the fragments of the five barley loaves, which remained over and above unto them that had eaten.

¹⁴ Then those men, when they had seen the miracle that Jesus did, said, 'This is of a truth that prophet that should come into the world'. ¹⁵ When Jesus therefore perceived that they would come and take him by force, to make him a king, he departed again into a mountain him-self alone.

¹⁶ And when even was now come, his disciples went down unto the sea, ¹⁷ and entered into a ship, and went over the sea toward Capernaum: and it was now dark, and Jesus was not come to them. ¹⁸ And the sea arose, by reason of a great wind that blew. ¹⁹ So when they had rowed about five and twenty or thirty furlongs, they see Jesus walking on the sea, and drawing nigh unto the ship: and they were afraid. ²⁰ But he saith unto them, 'It is I, be not afraid'. ²¹ Then they willingly received him into the ship, and immediately the ship was at the land whither they went.

²² The day following, when the people which stood on the other side of the sea saw that there was none other boat there, save that one whereinto his disciples were entered, and that Jesus went not with his disciples into the boat, but that his disciples were gone away alone: ²³ howbeit there came other boats from Tiberias, nigh unto the place where they did eat bread, after that the Lord had given thanks: ²⁴ when the people therefore saw that Jesus was not there, neither his disciples, they also took shipping, and came to Capernaum, seeking for Jesus.

²⁵ And when they had found him on the other side of the sea, they said unto him, 'Rabbi, when camest thou hither?' ²⁶ Jesus answered them, and said, 'Verily, verily I say unto you, ye seek me, not because ye saw the miracles, but because ye did eat of the loaves, and were filled. ²⁷ Labour not for the meat which perisheth, but for that meat which endureth unto everlasting life, which the Son of Man shall give unto you: for him hath God the Father sealed.' ²⁸ Then said they unto him, 'What shall we do, that we might work the works of God?' ²⁹ Jesus answered, and said unto them, 'This is the work of God, that ye believe on him whom he hath sent'. ³⁰ They said therefore unto him, 'What sign showest thou then, that we may see, and believe thee? What dost thou work? ³¹ Our fathers did eat manna in the desert, as it is written, "He gave them bread from heaven to eat".' ³² Then

Jesus said unto them, 'Verily, verily I say unto you, Moses gave you not that bread from heaven, but my Father giveth you the true bread from heaven. ³³ For the bread of God is he which cometh down from heaven, and giveth life unto the world.' ³⁴ Then said they unto him, 'Lord, evermore give us this bread'.

³⁵ And Jesus said unto them, 'I am the bread of life: he that cometh to me, shall never hunger: and he that believeth on me, shall never thirst. ³⁶ But I said unto you, that ye also have seen me, and believe not. ³⁷ All that the Father giveth me shall come to me; and him that cometh to me, I will in no wise cast out. ³⁸ For I came down from heaven, not to do mine own will, but the will of him that sent me. ³⁹ And this is the Father's will which hath sent me, that of all which he hath given me, I should lose nothing, but should raise it up again at the last day. ⁴⁰ And this is the will of him that sent me, that every one which seeth the Son, and believeth on him, may have everlasting life: and I will raise him up at the last day.'

⁴¹ The Jews then murmured at him, because he said, 'I am the bread which came down from heaven'. ⁴² And they said, 'Is not this Jesus the son of Joseph, whose father and mother we know? How is it then that he saith, "I came down from heaven"?' ⁴³ Jesus therefore answered, and said unto them, 'Murmur not among yourselves. ⁴⁴ No man can come to me, except the Father which hath sent me, draw him: and I will raise him up at the last day. ⁴⁵ It is written in the Prophets, "And they shall be all taught of God". Every man therefore that hath heard, and hath learned of the Father, cometh unto me, ⁴⁶ not that any man hath seen the Father; save he which is of God, he hath seen the Father. ⁴⁷ Verily, verily I say unto you, he that believeth on me hath everlasting life. ⁴⁸ I am that bread of life. ⁴⁹ Your fathers did eat manna in the wilderness, and are dead. ⁵⁰ This is the bread which cometh down from heaven, that a man may eat thereof, and not die. ⁵¹ I am the living bread, which came down from heaven. If any man eat of this bread, he shall live for ever: and the bread that I will give, is my flesh, which I will give for the life of the world.'

⁵² The Jews therefore strove amongst themselves, saying, 'How can this man give us his flesh to eat?' ⁵³ Then Jesus said unto them, 'Verily, verily I say unto you, except ye eat the flesh of the Son of Man, and drink his blood, ye have no life in you. ⁵⁴ Whoso eateth my flesh, and drinketh my blood, hath eternal life, and I will raise him up at the last day. ⁵⁵ For my flesh is meat indeed, and my blood is drink indeed.

⁵⁶ He that eateth my flesh, and drinketh my blood, dwelleth in me, and I in him. ⁵⁷ As the living Father hath sent me, and I live by the Father: so, he that eateth me, even he shall live by me. ⁵⁸ This is that bread which came down from heaven: not as your fathers did eat manna, and are dead: he that eateth of this bread, shall live for ever.' ⁵⁹ These things said he in the synagogue, as he taught in Capernaum.

⁶⁰ Many therefore of his disciples, when they had heard this, said, 'This is an hard saying, who can hear it?' ⁶¹ When Jesus knew in himself, that his disciples murmured at it, he said unto them, 'Doth this offend you? ⁶² What and if ye shall see the Son of Man ascend up where he was before? ⁶³ It is the spirit that quickeneth, the flesh profiteth nothing: the words that I speak unto you, they are spirit, and they are life. ⁶⁴ But there are some of you that believe not.' For Jesus knew from the beginning, who they were that believed not, and who should betray him. ⁶⁵ And he said, 'Therefore said I unto you, that no man can come unto me, except it were given unto him of my Father'.

⁶⁶ From that time many of his disciples went back, and walked no more with him. ⁶⁷ Then said Jesus unto the twelve, 'Will ye also go away?' ⁶⁸ Then Simon Peter answered him, 'Lord, to whom shall we go? Thou hast the words of eternal life. ⁶⁹ And we believe and are sure that thou art that Christ, the Son of the living God.' ⁷⁰ Jesus answered them, 'Have not I chosen you twelve, and one of you is a devil?' ⁷¹ He spake of Judas Iscariot the son of Simon: for he it was that should betray him, being one of the twelve.

Chapter 7

1 *Jesus reproveth the ambition and boldness of his kinsmen:* 10 *goeth up from Galilee to the Feast of Tabernacles,* 14 *teacheth in the Temple.* 40 *Divers opinions of him among the people.* 45 *The Pharisees are angry that their officers took him not, and chide with Nicodemus for taking his part.*

AFTER these things Jesus walked in Galilee: for he would not walk in Jewry, because the Jews sought to kill him. ² Now the Jews' Feast of Tabernacles was at hand. ³ His brethren therefore said unto him, 'Depart hence, and go into Judea, that thy disciples also may see the works that thou doest. ⁴ For there is no man that doeth any thing in secret, and he himself seeketh to be known openly: if thou do these things, show thyself to the world.' ⁵ For neither did his brethren believe in him. ⁶ Then Jesus said unto them, 'My time is not yet come: but your time is always ready. ⁷ The world cannot hate you, but me it hateth, because I testify of it, that the works thereof are evil. ⁸ Go ye up unto this feast: I go not up yet unto this feast, for my time is not yet full come.' ⁹ When he had said these words unto them, he abode still in Galilee.

¹⁰ But when his brethren were gone up, then went he also up unto the feast, not openly, but as it were in secret. ¹¹ Then the Jews sought him at the feast, and said, 'Where is he?' ¹² And there was much murmuring among the people, concerning him: for some said, 'He is a good man': others said, 'Nay, but he deceiveth the people'. ¹³ Howbeit, no man spake openly of him, for fear of the Jews.

¹⁴ Now about the midst of the feast, Jesus went up into the Temple, and taught. ¹⁵ And the Jews marvelled, saying, 'How knoweth this man letters, having never learned?' ¹⁶ Jesus answered them, 'My doctrine is not mine, but his that sent me. ¹⁷ If any man will do his will, he shall know of the doctrine, whether it be of God, or whether I speak of myself. ¹⁸ He that speaketh of himself, seeketh his own glory: but he that seeketh his glory that sent him, the same is true, and no unrighteousness is in him.

¹⁹ 'Did not Moses give you the Law, and yet none of you keepeth the Law? Why go ye about to kill me?' ²⁰ The people answered, and said, 'Thou hast a devil: who goeth about to kill thee?' ²¹ Jesus answered, and said unto them, 'I have done one work, and ye all marvel. ²² Moses therefore gave unto you circumcision (not because it is of Moses, but of the fathers), and ye on the Sabbath day circumcise a man. ²³ If a man on the Sabbath day receive circumcision, that the Law of Moses should not be broken; are ye angry at me, because I have made a man every whit whole on the Sabbath day? ²⁴ Judge not according to the appearance, but judge righteous judgement.'

²⁵ Then said some of them of Jerusalem, 'Is not this he, whom they seek to kill? ²⁶ But lo, he speaketh boldly, and they say nothing unto him. Do the rulers know indeed that this is the very Christ? ²⁷ Howbeit we know this man whence he is: but when Christ cometh, no man knoweth whence he is.' ²⁸ Then cried Jesus in the Temple as he taught, saying, 'Ye both know me, and ye know whence I am, and I am not come of myself, but he that sent me is true, whom ye know not.

[29] But I know him, for I am from him, and he hath sent me.' [30] Then they sought to take him: but no man laid hands on him, because his hour was not yet come. [31] And many of the people believed on him, and said, 'When Christ cometh, will he do moe miracles than these which this man hath done?'

[32] The Pharisees heard that the people murmured such things concerning him: and the Pharisees and the chief priests sent officers to take him. [33] Then said Jesus unto them, 'Yet a little while am I with you, and then I go unto him that sent me. [34] Ye shall seek me, and shall not find me: and where I am, thither ye cannot come.' [35] Then said the Jews among themselves, 'Whither will he go, that we shall not find him? Will he go unto the dispersed among the Gentiles, and teach the Gentiles? [36] What manner of saying is this that he said, "Ye shall seek me, and shall not find me? and where I am, thither ye cannot come"?'

[37] In the last day, that great day of the feast, Jesus stood, and cried, saying, 'If any man thirst, let him come unto me, and drink. [38] He that believeth on me, as the scripture hath said, out of his belly shall flow rivers of living water.' [39] (But this spake he of the Spirit, which they that believe on him, should receive. For the Holy Ghost was not yet given, because that Jesus was not yet glorified.)

[40] Many of the people therefore, when they heard this saying, said, 'Of a truth this is the Prophet'. [41] Others said, 'This is the Christ'. But some said, 'Shall Christ come out of Galilee? [42] Hath not the scripture said, that Christ cometh of the seed of David, and out of the town of Bethlehem, where David was?' [43] So there was a division among the people because of him. [44] And some of them would have taken him, but no man laid hands on him.

[45] Then came the officers to the chief priests and Pharisees, and they said unto them, 'Why have ye not brought him?' [46] The officers answered, 'Never man spake like this man'. [47] Then answered them the Pharisees, 'Are ye also deceived? [48] Have any of the rulers, or of the Pharisees believed on him? [49] But this people who knoweth not the Law, are cursed.' [50] Nicodemus saith unto them (he that came to Jesus by night, being one of them), [51] 'Doth our law judge any man before it hear him, and know what he doeth?' [52] They answered, and said unto him, 'Art thou also of Galilee? Search, and look: for out of Galilee ariseth no prophet.' [53] And every man went unto his own house.

Chapter 8

1 *Christ delivereth the woman taken in adultery.* 12 *He preacheth himself
the light of the world, and justifieth his doctrine:* 33 *answereth the Jews
that boasted of Abraham,* 59 *and conveyeth himself from their cruelty.*

JESUS went unto the Mount of Olives: ² and early in the morning
he came again into the Temple, and all the people came unto him,
and he sat down, and taught them. ³ And the scribes and Pharisees
brought unto him a woman taken in adultery, and when they had set
her in the mids, ⁴ they say unto him, 'Master, this woman was taken
in adultery, in the very act. ⁵ Now Moses in the Law commanded us,
that such should be stoned: but what sayest thou?' ⁶ This they said,
tempting him, that they might have to accuse him. But Jesus stooped
down, and with his finger wrote on the ground as though he heard
them not. ⁷ So when they continued asking him, he lift up himself,
and said unto them, 'He that is without sin among you, let him first
cast a stone at her'. ⁸ And again, he stooped down, and wrote on the
ground. ⁹ And they which heard it, being convicted by their own con-
science, went out one by one, beginning at the eldest, even unto the
last: and Jesus was left alone, and the woman standing in the midst.
¹⁰ When Jesus had lift up himself, and saw none but the woman, he
said unto her, 'Woman, where are those thine accusers? Hath no man
condemned thee?' ¹¹ She said, 'No man, Lord'. And Jesus said unto
her, 'Neither do I condemn thee: go, and sin no more'.

¹² Then spake Jesus again unto them, saying, 'I am the light of the
world: he that followeth me, shall not walk in darkness, but shall have
the light of life'. ¹³ The Pharisees therefore said unto him, 'Thou bear-
est record of thyself, thy record is not true'. ¹⁴ Jesus answered, and said
unto them, 'Though I bear record of myself, yet my record is true: for
I know whence I came, and whither I go: but ye cannot tell whence I
come, and whither I go. ¹⁵ Ye judge after the flesh, I judge no man.
¹⁶ And yet if I judge, my judgement is true: for I am not alone, but I
and the Father that sent me. ¹⁷ It is also written in your Law, that the
testimony of two men is true. ¹⁸ I am one that bear witness of myself,
and the Father that sent me, beareth witness of me.' ¹⁹ Then said they
unto him, 'Where is thy Father?' Jesus answered, 'Ye neither know
me, nor my Father: if ye had known me, ye should have known my
Father also'. ²⁰ These words spake Jesus in the treasury, as he taught

in the Temple: and no man laid hands on him, for his hour was not yet come.

²¹ Then said Jesus again unto them, 'I go my way, and ye shall seek me, and shall die in your sins: whither I go, ye cannot come'. ²² Then said the Jews, 'Will he kill himself? because he saith, "Whither I go, ye cannot come" '. ²³ And he said unto them, 'Ye are from beneath, I am from above: ye are of this world, I am not of this world. ²⁴ I said therefore unto you, that ye shall die in your sins. For if ye believe not that I am he, ye shall die in your sins.' ²⁵ Then said they unto him, 'Who art thou?' And Jesus saith unto them, 'Even the same that I said unto you from the beginning. ²⁶ I have many things to say, and to judge of you: but he that sent me is true, and I speak to the world, those things which I have heard of him.' ²⁷ They understood not that he spake to them of the Father. ²⁸ Then said Jesus unto them, 'When ye have lift up the Son of Man, then shall ye know that I am he, and that I do nothing of myself: but as my Father hath taught me, I speak these things. ²⁹ And he that sent me, is with me: the Father hath not left me alone: for I do always those things that please him.' ³⁰ As he spake these words, many believed on him.

³¹ Then said Jesus to those Jews which believed on him, 'If ye continue in my word, then are ye my disciples indeed. ³² And ye shall know the truth, and the truth shall make you free.' ³³ They answered him, 'We be Abraham's seed, and were never in bondage to any man: how sayest thou, "Ye shall be made free"?'

³⁴ Jesus answered them, 'Verily, verily I say unto you, whosoever committeth sin, is the servant of sin. ³⁵ And the servant abideth not in the house for ever: but the Son abideth ever. ³⁶ If the Son therefore shall make you free, ye shall be free indeed. ³⁷ I know that ye are Abraham's seed, but ye seek to kill me, because my word hath no place in you. ³⁸ I speak that which I have seen with my Father: and ye do that which ye have seen with your father.'

³⁹ They answered, and said unto him, 'Abraham is our father'. Jesus saith unto them, 'If ye were Abraham's children, ye would do the works of Abraham. ⁴⁰ But now ye seek to kill me, a man that hath told you the truth, which I have heard of God: this did not Abraham. ⁴¹ Ye do the deeds of your father.' Then said they to him, 'We be not born of fornication, we have one Father, even God'. ⁴² Jesus said unto them, 'If God were your Father, ye would love me: for I proceeded forth, and came from God: neither came I of myself, but he sent me.

⁴³ Why do ye not understand my speech? even because ye cannot hear my word. ⁴⁴ Ye are of your father the devil, and the lusts of your father ye will do: he was a murderer from the beginning, and abode not in the truth, because there is no truth in him. When he speaketh a lie, he speaketh of his own: for he is a liar, and the father of it. ⁴⁵ And because I tell you the truth, ye believe me not. ⁴⁶ Which of you convinceth me of sin? And if I say the truth, why do ye not believe me? ⁴⁷ He that is of God, heareth God's words: ye therefore hear them not, because ye are not of God.'

⁴⁸ Then answered the Jews, and said unto him, 'Say we not well that thou art a Samaritan, and hast a devil?' ⁴⁹ Jesus answered, 'I have not a devil: but I honour my Father, and ye do dishonour me. ⁵⁰ And I seek not mine own glory, there is one that seeketh and judgeth. ⁵¹ Verily, verily I say unto you, if a man keep my saying, he shall never see death.' ⁵² Then said the Jews unto him, 'Now we know that thou hast a devil. Abraham is dead, and the prophets: and thou sayest, "If a man keep my saying, he shall never taste of death". ⁵³ Art thou greater than our father Abraham, which is dead? and the prophets are dead: whom makest thou thyself?' ⁵⁴ Jesus answered, 'If I honour myself, my honour is nothing: it is my Father that honoureth me, of whom ye say, that he is your God: ⁵⁵ yet ye have not known him, but I know him: and if I should say, "I know him not", I shall be a liar like unto you: but I know him, and keep his saying. ⁵⁶ Your father Abraham rejoiced to see my day: and he saw it, and was glad.' ⁵⁷ Then said the Jews unto him, 'Thou art not yet fifty years old, and hast thou seen Abraham?' ⁵⁸ Jesus said unto them, 'Verily, verily I say unto you, before Abraham was, I am'. ⁵⁹ Then took they up stones to cast at him: but Jesus hid himself, and went out of the Temple, going through the midst of them, and so passed by.

Chapter 9

1 *The man that was born blind restored to sight.* 8 *He is brought to the Pharisees.* 13 *They are offended at it, and excommunicate him:* 35 *but he is received of Jesus, and confesseth him.* 39 *Who they are whom Christ enlighteneth.*

AND as Jesus passed by, he saw a man which was blind from his birth. ² And his disciples asked him, saying, 'Master, who did sin, this man, or his parents, that he was born blind?' ³ Jesus answered, 'Neither hath this man sinned, nor his parents: but that the works of God should be made manifest in him. ⁴ I must work the works of him that sent me, while it is day: the night cometh, when no man can work. ⁵ As long as I am in the world, I am the light of the world.' ⁶ When he had thus spoken, he spat on the ground, and made clay of the spittle, and he anointed the eyes of the blind man with the clay, ⁷ and said unto him, 'Go, wash in the pool of Siloam' (which is by interpretation, Sent). He went his way therefore, and washed, and came seeing. ⁸ The neighbours therefore, and they which before had seen him, that he was blind, said, 'Is not this he that sat and begged?' ⁹ Some said, 'This is he': others said, 'He is like him': but he said, 'I am he'. ¹⁰ Therefore said they unto him, 'How were thine eyes opened?' ¹¹ He answered and said, 'A man that is called Jesus, made clay, and anointed mine eyes, and said unto me, "Go to the pool of Siloam, and wash": and I went and washed, and I received sight'. ¹² Then said they unto him, 'Where is he?' He said, 'I know not'.

¹³ They brought to the Pharisees him that aforetime was blind. ¹⁴ And it was the Sabbath day when Jesus made the clay, and opened his eyes. ¹⁵ Then again the Pharisees also asked him how he had received his sight. He said unto them, 'He put clay upon mine eyes, and I washed, and do see'. ¹⁶ Therefore said some of the Pharisees, 'This man is not of God, because he keepeth not the Sabbath day'. Others said, 'How can a man that is a sinner do such miracles?' And there was a division among them. ¹⁷ They say unto the blind man again, 'What sayest thou of him, that he hath opened thine eyes?' He said, 'He is a prophet'.

¹⁸ But the Jews did not believe concerning him, that he had been blind, and received his sight, until they called the parents of him that had received his sight. ¹⁹ And they asked them, saying, 'Is this your son, who ye say was born blind? How then doth he now see?' ²⁰ His parents answered them, and said, 'We know that this is our son, and that he was born blind: ²¹ but by what means he now seeth, we know not, or who hath opened his eyes we know not: he is of age, ask him, he shall speak for himself'. ²² These words spake his parents, because they feared the Jews: for the Jews had agreed already, that if any man did confess that he was Christ, he should be put out of the synagogue. ²³ Therefore said his parents, 'He is of age, ask him'.

²⁴ Then again called they the man that was blind, and said unto him, 'Give God the praise, we know that this man is a sinner'. ²⁵ He

answered, and said, 'Whether he be a sinner or no, I know not: one thing I know, that whereas I was blind, now I see'. ²⁶ Then said they to him again, 'What did he to thee? how opened he thine eyes?' ²⁷ He answered them, 'I have told you already, and ye did not hear: wherefore would ye hear it again? Will ye also be his disciples?' ²⁸ Then they reviled him, and said, 'Thou art his disciple, but we are Moses' disciples. ²⁹ We know that God spake unto Moses: as for this fellow, we know not from whence he is.' ³⁰ The man answered, and said unto them, 'Why herein is a marvellous thing, that ye know not from whence he is, and yet he hath opened mine eyes. ³¹ Now we know that God heareth not sinners: but if any man be a worshipper of God, and doeth his will, him he heareth. ³² Since the world began was it not heard that any man opened the eyes of one that was born blind: ³³ if this man were not of God, he could do nothing.' ³⁴ They answered, and said unto him, 'Thou wast altogether born in sins, and dost thou teach us?' And they cast him out.

³⁵ Jesus heard that they had cast him out; and when he had found him, he said unto him, 'Dost thou believe on the Son of God?' ³⁶ He answered and said, 'Who is he, Lord, that I might believe on him?' ³⁷ And Jesus said unto him, 'Thou hast both seen him, and it is he that talketh with thee'. ³⁸ And he said, 'Lord, I believe'. And he worshipped him. ³⁹ And Jesus said, 'For judgement I am come into this world, that they which see not might see, and that they which see, might be made blind'. ⁴⁰ And some of the Pharisees which were with him, heard these words, and said unto him, 'Are we blind also?' ⁴¹ Jesus said unto them, 'If ye were blind, ye should have no sin: but now ye say, "We see"; therefore your sin remaineth'.

Chapter 10

1 *Christ is the door and the good shepherd.* 19 *Divers opinions of him.* 24 *He proveth by his works, that he is Christ the Son of God,* 39 *escapeth the Jews,* 40 *and went again beyond Jordan, where many believed on him.*

'VERILY, verily I say unto you, he that entereth not by the door into the sheepfold, but climbeth up some other way, the same is a thief, and a robber. ² But he that entereth in by the door, is the shepherd of the sheep. ³ To him the porter openeth, and the sheep hear his voice, and he calleth his own sheep by name, and leadeth them out. [4] And when he putteth forth his own sheep, he goeth before them, and the sheep follow him: for they know his voice. [5] And a stranger will they not follow, but will flee from him, for they know not the voice of strangers.' [6] This parable spake Jesus unto them: but they understood not what things they were which he spake unto them.

[7] Then said Jesus unto them again, 'Verily, verily I say unto you, I am the door of the sheep. [8] All that ever came before me are thieves and robbers: but the sheep did not hear them. [9] I am the door: by me if any man enter in, he shall be saved, and shall go in and out, and find pasture. [10] The thief cometh not, but for to steal and to kill, and to destroy: I am come that they might have life, and that they might have it more abundantly.

[11] I am the good shepherd: the good shepherd giveth his life for the sheep. [12] But he that is an hireling and not the shepherd, whose own the sheep are not, seeth the wolf coming, and leaveth the sheep, and fleeth: and the wolf catcheth them, and scattereth the sheep. [13] The hireling fleeth, because he is an hireling, and careth not for the sheep. [14] I am the good shepherd, and know my sheep, and am known of mine. [15] As the Father knoweth me, even so know I the Father: and I lay down my life for the sheep. [16] And other sheep I have, which are not of this fold: them also I must bring, and they shall hear my voice; and there shall be one fold, and one shepherd. [17] Therefore doth my Father love me, because I lay down my life that I might take it again. [18] No man taketh it from me, but I lay it down of myself: I have power to lay it down, and I have power to take it again. This commandment have I received of my Father.'

[19] There was a division therefore again among the Jews for these sayings. [20] And many of them said, 'He hath a devil, and is mad, why hear ye him?' [21] Others said, 'These are not the words of him that hath a devil. Can a devil open the eyes of the blind?'

[22] And it was at Jerusalem the Feast of the Dedication, and it was winter. [23] And Jesus walked in the Temple in Solomon's Porch. [24] Then came the Jews round about him, and said unto him, 'How long dost thou make us to doubt? If thou be the Christ, tell us plainly.' [25] Jesus answered them, 'I told you, and ye believed not: the works that I do in my Father's name, they bear witness of me. [26] But ye believe not, because ye are not of my sheep, as I said unto you. [27] My sheep hear my voice, and I know them, and they follow me. [28] And I give unto

them eternal life, and they shall never perish, neither shall any man pluck them out of my hand. [29] My Father which gave them me, is greater than all: and no man is able to pluck them out of my Father's hand. [30] I and my Father are one.'

[31] Then the Jews took up stones again to stone him. [32] Jesus answered them, 'Many good works have I showed you from my Father; for which of those works do ye stone me?' [33] The Jews answered him, saying, 'For a good work we stone thee not, but for blasphemy, and because that thou, being a man, makest thyself God'. [34] Jesus answered them, 'Is it not written in your Law, "I said, 'Ye are gods' "? [35] If he called them gods, unto whom the word of God came, and the scripture cannot be broken: [36] say ye of him, whom the Father hath sanctified and sent into the world, "Thou blasphemest"; because I said, "I am the Son of God"? [37] If I do not the works of my Father, believe me not. [38] But if I do, though ye believe not me, believe the works: that ye may know and believe that the Father is in me, and I in him.'

[39] Therefore they sought again to take him: but he escaped out of their hand, [40] and went away again beyond Jordan, into the place where John at first baptized: and there he abode. [41] And many resorted unto him, and said, 'John did no miracle: but all things that John spake of this man were true'. [42] And many believed on him there.

Chapter 11

1 Christ raiseth Lazarus, four days buried. 45 Many Jews believe. 47 The high priests and Pharisees gather a council against Christ. 49 Caiaphas prophesieth. 54 Jesus hid himself. 55 At the Passover they enquire after him, and lay wait for him.

NOW a certain man was sick, named Lazarus of Bethany, the town of Mary, and her sister Martha. [2] (It was that Mary which anointed the Lord with ointment, and wiped his feet with her hair, whose brother Lazarus was sick.) [3] Therefore his sister sent unto him, saying, 'Lord, behold, he whom thou lovest, is sick'. [4] When Jesus heard that, he said, 'This sickness is not unto death, but for the glory of God, that the Son of God might be glorified thereby'. [5] Now Jesus loved Martha, and her sister, and Lazarus. [6] When he had heard therefore that he was sick, he abode two days still in the same place where he was.

⁷ Then after that saith he to his disciples, 'Let us go into Judea again'. ⁸ His disciples say unto him, 'Master, the Jews of late sought to stone thee, and goest thou thither again?' ⁹ Jesus answered, 'Are there not twelve hours in the day? If any man walk in the day, he stumbleth not, because he seeth the light of this world. ¹⁰ But if a man walk in the night, he stumbleth, because there is no light in him.' ¹¹ These things said he, and after that he saith unto them, 'Our friend Lazarus sleepeth, but I go, that I may awake him out of sleep'. ¹² Then said his disciples, 'Lord, if he sleep, he shall do well'. ¹³ Howbeit Jesus spake of his death: but they thought that he had spoken of taking of rest in sleep. ¹⁴ Then said Jesus unto them plainly, 'Lazarus is dead: ¹⁵ and I am glad for your sakes, that I was not there (to the intent ye may believe): nevertheless, let us go unto him'. ¹⁶ Then said Thomas, which is called Didymus, unto his fellow disciples, 'Let us also go, that we may die with him'.

¹⁷ Then when Jesus came, he found that he had lain in the grave four days already. ¹⁸ Now Bethany was nigh unto Jerusalem, about fifteen furlongs off: ¹⁹ and many of the Jews came to Martha and Mary, to comfort them concerning their brother. ²⁰ Then Martha, as soon as she heard that Jesus was coming, went and met him: but Mary sat still in the house. ²¹ Then said Martha unto Jesus, 'Lord, if thou hadst been here, my brother had not died. ²² But I know, that even now, whatsoever thou wilt ask of God, God will give it thee.' ²³ Jesus saith unto her, 'Thy brother shall rise again'. ²⁴ Martha saith unto him, 'I know that he shall rise again in the resurrection at the last day'. ²⁵ Jesus said unto her, 'I am the resurrection, and the life: he that believeth in me, though he were dead, yet shall he live. ²⁶ And whosoever liveth, and believeth in me, shall never die. Believest thou this?' ²⁷ She saith unto him, 'Yea Lord, I believe that thou art the Christ the Son of God, which should come into the world'.

²⁸ And when she had so said, she went her way, and called Mary her sister secretly, saying, 'The Master is come, and calleth for thee'. ²⁹ As soon as she heard that, she arose quickly, and came unto him. ³⁰ Now Jesus was not yet come into the town, but was in that place where Martha met him. ³¹ The Jews then which were with her in the house, and comforted her, when they saw Mary that she rose up hastily, and went out, followed her, saying, 'She goeth unto the grave, to weep there'. ³² Then when Mary was come where Jesus was, and saw him, she fell down at his feet, saying unto him, 'Lord, if thou

hadst been here, my brother had not died'. ³³ When Jesus therefore saw her weeping, and the Jews also weeping which came with her, he groaned in the spirit, and was troubled, ³⁴ and said, 'Where have ye laid him?' They say unto him, 'Lord, come and see'. ³⁵ Jesus wept. ³⁶ Then said the Jews, 'Behold, how he loved him'. ³⁷ And some of them said, 'Could not this man, which opened the eyes of the blind, have caused that even this man should not have died?'

³⁸ Jesus therefore again groaning in himself, cometh to the grave. It was a cave, and a stone lay upon it. ³⁹ Jesus said, 'Take ye away the stone'. Martha, the sister of him that was dead, saith unto him, 'Lord, by this time he stinketh: for he hath been dead four days'. ⁴⁰ Jesus saith unto her, 'Said I not unto thee, that if thou wouldst believe, thou shouldst see the glory of God?' ⁴¹ Then they took away the stone from the place where the dead was laid. And Jesus lift up his eyes, and said, 'Father, I thank thee, that thou hast heard me. ⁴² And I knew that thou hearest me always: but because of the people which stand by, I said it, that they may believe that thou hast sent me.' ⁴³ And when he thus had spoken, he cried with a loud voice, 'Lazarus, come forth'. ⁴⁴ And he that was dead, came forth, bound hand and foot with grave-clothes: and his face was bound about with a napkin. Jesus saith unto them, 'Loose him, and let him go'.

⁴⁵ Then many of the Jews which came to Mary, and had seen the things which Jesus did, believed on him. ⁴⁶ But some of them went their ways to the Pharisees, and told them what things Jesus had done. ⁴⁷ Then gathered the chief priests and the Pharisees a council, and said, 'What do we? for this man doeth many miracles. ⁴⁸ If we let him thus alone, all men will believe on him, and the Romans shall come, and take away both our place and nation.' ⁴⁹ And one of them named Caiaphas, being the High Priest that same year, said unto them, 'Ye know nothing at all, ⁵⁰ nor consider that it is expedient for us, that one man should die for the people, and that the whole nation perish not'. ⁵¹ And this spake he not of himself: but being High Priest that year, he prophesied that Jesus should die for that nation: ⁵² and not for that nation only, but that also he should gather together in one, the children of God that were scattered abroad. ⁵³ Then from that day forth, they took counsel together for to put him to death.

⁵⁴ Jesus therefore walked no more openly among the Jews: but went thence unto a country near to the wilderness, into a city called Ephraim, and there continued with his disciples.

⁵⁵ And the Jews' Passover was nigh at hand: and many went out of the country up to Jerusalem before the Passover to purify themselves. ⁵⁶ Then sought they for Jesus, and spake among themselves, as they stood in the Temple, 'What think ye, that he will not come to the feast?' ⁵⁷ Now both the chief priests and the Pharisees had given a commandment, that if any man knew where he were, he should show it, that they might take him.

Chapter 12

1 *Jesus excuseth Mary anointing his feet.* 9 *The people flock to see Lazarus.* 10 *The high priests consult to kill him.* 12 *Christ rideth into Jerusalem.* 20 *Greeks desire to see Jesus.* 23 *He foretelleth his death.* 37 *The Jews are generally blinded:* 42 *yet many chief rulers believe, but do not confess him:* 44 *therefore Jesus calleth earnestly for confession of faith.*

THEN Jesus, six days before the Passover, came to Bethany, where Lazarus was, which had been dead, whom he raised from the dead. ² There they made him a supper, and Martha served: but Lazarus was one of them that sat at the table with him. ³ Then took Mary a pound of ointment of spikenard, very costly, and anointed the feet of Jesus, and wiped his feet with her hair: and the house was filled with the odour of the ointment. ⁴ Then saith one of his disciples, Judas Iscariot, Simon's son, which should betray him, ⁵ 'Why was not this ointment sold for three hundred pence, and given to the poor?' ⁶ This he said, not that he cared for the poor: but because he was a thief, and had the bag, and bare what was put therein. ⁷ Then said Jesus, 'Let her alone, against the day of my burying hath she kept this. ⁸ For the poor always ye have with you: but me ye have not always.'

⁹ Much people of the Jews therefore knew that he was there: and they came, not for Jesus's sake only, but that they might see Lazarus also, whom he had raised from the dead. ¹⁰ But the chief priests consulted, that they might put Lazarus also to death, ¹¹ because that by reason of him many of the Jews went away and believed on Jesus.

¹² On the next day, much people that were come to the feast, when they heard that Jesus was coming to Jerusalem, ¹³ took branches of palm trees, and went forth to meet him, and cried, 'Hosanna: blessed is the King of Israel that cometh in the name of the Lord'. ¹⁴ And Jesus,

when he had found a young ass, sat thereon, as ⌐
not, daughter of Sion, behold, thy King cometh, si⌐
colt'. [16] These things understood not his disciples at ⌐
when Jesus was glorified, then remembered they that these th⌐
written of him, and that they had done these things unto him. ⌐
people therefore that was with him, when he called Lazarus out of h⌐
grave, and raised him from the dead, bare record. [18] For this cause the
people also met him, for that they heard that he had done this miracle.
[19] The Pharisees therefore said among themselves, 'Perceive ye how ye
prevail nothing? Behold, the world is gone after him.'

[20] And there were certain Greeks among them, that came up to
worship at the feast: [21] the same came therefore to Philip, which was
of Bethsaida of Galilee, and desired him, saying, 'Sir, we would see
Jesus'. [22] Philip cometh and telleth Andrew: and again Andrew and
Philip told Jesus. [23] And Jesus answered them, saying, 'The hour is
come, that the Son of Man should be glorified. [24] Verily, verily, I say
unto you, except a corn of wheat fall into the ground, and die, it abideth alone: but if it die, it bringeth forth much fruit. [25] He that loveth
his life, shall lose it: and he that hateth his life in this world, shall keep
it unto life eternal. [26] If any man serve me, let him follow me, and
where I am, there shall also my servant be: if any man serve me, him
will my Father honour.

[27] 'Now is my soul troubled, and what shall I say? "Father, save me
from this hour", but for this cause came I unto this hour. [28] Father,
glorify thy name.' Then came there a voice from heaven, saying, 'I
have both glorified it, and will glorify it again'. [29] The people therefore that stood by, and heard it, said that it thundered: others said,
'An angel spake to him'. [30] Jesus answered, and said, 'This voice came
not because of me, but for your sakes. [31] Now is the judgement of this
world: now shall the prince of this world be cast out. [32] And I, if I be
lifted up from the earth, will draw all men unto me.' [33] (This he said,
signifying what death he should die.) [34] The people answered him, 'We
have heard out of the Law, that Christ abideth for ever: and how sayest
thou, "The Son of Man must be lift up"? Who is this Son of Man?'
[35] Then Jesus said unto them, 'Yet a little while is the light with you:
walk while ye have the light, lest darkness come upon you: for he that
walketh in darkness, knoweth not whither he goeth. [36] While ye have
light, believe in the light, that ye may be the children of light.' These
things spake Jesus, and departed, and did hide himself from them.

But though he had done so many miracles before them, yet they believed not on him: [38] that the saying of Esaias the prophet might be fulfilled, which he spake, 'Lord, who hath believed our report? and to whom hath the arm of the Lord been revealed?' [39] Therefore they could not believe, because that Esaias said again, [40] 'He hath blinded their eyes, and hardened their heart, that they should not see with their eyes, nor understand with their heart, and be converted, and I should heal them'. [41] These things said Esaias, when he saw his glory, and spake of him. [42] Nevertheless, among the chief rulers also, many believed on him; but because of the Pharisees they did not confess him, lest they should be put out of the synagogue. [43] For they loved the praise of men, more than the praise of God.

[44] Jesus cried, and said, 'He that believeth on me, believeth not on me, but on him that sent me. [45] And he that seeth me, seeth him that sent me. [46] I am come a light into the world, that whosoever believeth on me, should not abide in darkness. [47] And if any man hear my words, and believe not, I judge him not; for I came not to judge the world, but to save the world. [48] He that rejecteth me, and receiveth not my words, hath one that judgeth him: the word that I have spoken, the same shall judge him in the last day. [49] For I have not spoken of myself; but the Father which sent me, he gave me a commandment what I should say, and what I should speak. [50] And I know that his commandment is life everlasting: whatsoever I speak therefore, even as the Father said unto me, so I speak.'

Chapter 13

1 Jesus washeth the disciples' feet: exhorteth them to humility and charity. 18 He foretelleth, and discovereth to John by a token that Judas should betray him: 31 commandeth them to love one another, 36 and forewarneth Peter of his denial.

Now before the Feast of the Passover, when Jesus knew that his hour was come, that he should depart out of this world unto the Father, having loved his own which were in the world, he loved them unto the end. [2] And supper being ended, the devil having now put into the heart of Judas Iscariot, Simon's son, to betray him, [3] Jesus knowing that the Father had given all things into his hands, and that he was come from God, and went to God: [4] he riseth from supper,

and laid aside his garments; and took a towel, and girded himself.
⁵ After that, he poureth water into a basin, and began to wash the disciples' feet, and to wipe them with the towel wherewith he was girded.
⁶ Then cometh he to Simon Peter: and Peter saith unto him, 'Lord, dost thou wash my feet?' ⁷ Jesus answered, and said unto him, 'What I do, thou knowest not now: but thou shalt know hereafter'. ⁸ Peter saith unto him, 'Thou shalt never wash my feet'. Jesus answered him, 'If I wash thee not, thou hast no part with me'. ⁹ Simon Peter saith unto him, 'Lord, not my feet only, but also my hands and my head'. ¹⁰ Jesus saith to him, 'He that is washed, needeth not, save to wash his feet, but is clean every whit: and ye are clean, but not all'. ¹¹ For he knew who should betray him, therefore said he, 'Ye are not all clean'.

¹² So after he had washed their feet, and had taken his garments, and was set down again, he said unto them, 'Know ye what I have done to you? ¹³ Ye call me Master and Lord, and ye say well: for so I am. ¹⁴ If I then your Lord and Master, have washed your feet, ye also ought to wash one another's feet. ¹⁵ For I have given you an example, that ye should do as I have done to you. ¹⁶ Verily, verily I say unto you, the servant is not greater than his lord, neither he that is sent, greater than he that sent him. ¹⁷ If ye know these things, happy are ye if ye do them. ¹⁸ 'I speak not of you all: I know whom I have chosen: but that the scripture may be fulfilled, "He that eateth bread with me, hath lift up his heel against me". ¹⁹ Now I tell you before it come, that when it is come to pass, ye may believe that I am he. ²⁰ Verily, verily I say unto you, he that receiveth whomsoever I send, receiveth me: and he that receiveth me, receiveth him that sent me.'

²¹ When Jesus had thus said, he was troubled in spirit, and testified, and said, 'Verily, verily I say unto you, that one of you shall betray me'. ²² Then the disciples looked one on another, doubting of whom he spake. ²³ Now there was leaning on Jesus's bosom one of his disciples, whom Jesus loved. ²⁴ Simon Peter therefore beckoned to him, that he should ask who it should be of whom he spake. ²⁵ He then lying on Jesus's breast, saith unto him, 'Lord, who is it?' ²⁶ Jesus answered, 'He it is to whom I shall give a sop, when I have dipped it'. And when he had dipped the sop, he gave it to Judas Iscariot the son of Simon. ²⁷ And after the sop, Satan entered into him. Then said Jesus unto him, 'That thou doest, do quickly'. ²⁸ Now no man at the table knew for what intent he spake this unto him. ²⁹ For some of them thought, because Judas had the bag, that Jesus had said unto him, 'Buy those

things that we have need of against the feast': or that he should give something to the poor. ³⁰ He then having received the sop, went immediately out: and it was night.

³¹ Therefore when he was gone out, Jesus said, 'Now is the Son of Man glorified: and God is glorified in him. ³² If God be glorified in him, God shall also glorify him in himself, and shall straightway glorify him. ³³ Little children, yet a little while I am with you. Ye shall seek me, and as I said unto the Jews, "Whither I go, ye cannot come": so now I say to you. ³⁴ A new commandment I give unto you, that ye love one another; as I have loved you, that ye also love one another. ³⁵ By this shall all men know that ye are my disciples, if ye have love one to another.'

³⁶ Simon Peter said unto him, 'Lord, whither goest thou?' Jesus answered him, 'Whither I go, thou canst not follow me now: but thou shalt follow me afterwards'. ³⁷ Peter said unto him, 'Lord, why can not I follow thee now? I will lay down my life for thy sake.' ³⁸ Jesus answered him, 'Wilt thou lay down thy life for my sake? Verily, verily I say unto thee, the cock shall not crow, till thou hast denied me thrice.'

Chapter 14

1 Christ comforteth his disciples with the hope of heaven: 6 professeth himself the way, the truth, and the life, and one with the Father: 13 assureth their prayers in his name to be effectual: 15 requesteth love and obedience, 16 promiseth the Holy Ghost the comforter, 27 and leaveth his peace with them.

'LET not your heart be troubled: ye believe in God, believe also in me. ² In my Father's house are many mansions; if it were not so, I would have told you: I go to prepare a place for you. ³ And if I go and prepare a place for you, I will come again, and receive you unto myself, that where I am, there ye may be also. ⁴ And whither I go ye know, and the way ye know.'

⁵ Thomas saith unto him, 'Lord, we know not whither thou goest: and how can we know the way?' ⁶ Jesus saith unto him, 'I am the way, the truth, and the life: no man cometh unto the Father but by me. ⁷ If ye had known me, ye should have known my Father also: and from henceforth ye know him, and have seen him.'

⁸ Philip saith unto him, 'Lord, show us the Father, and it sufficeth us'. ⁹ Jesus saith unto him, 'Have I been so long time with you, and yet hast thou not known me, Philip? He that hath seen me, hath seen the Father, and how sayest thou then, "Show us the Father?" ¹⁰ Believest thou not that I am in the Father, and the Father in me? The words that I speak unto you, I speak not of myself: but the Father that dwelleth in me, he doeth the works. ¹¹ Believe me that I am in the Father, and the Father in me: or else believe me for the very works' sake. ¹² Verily, verily I say unto you, he that believeth on me, the works that I do, shall he do also, and greater works than these shall he do, because I go unto my Father. ¹³ And whatsoever ye shall ask in my name, that will I do, that the Father may be glorified in the Son. ¹⁴ If ye shall ask any thing in my name, I will do it.

¹⁵ 'If ye love me, keep my commandments. ¹⁶ And I will pray the Father, and he shall give you another Comforter, that he may abide with you for ever, ¹⁷ even the Spirit of truth, whom the world cannot receive, because it seeth him not, neither knoweth him: but ye know him, for he dwelleth with you, and shall be in you. ¹⁸ I will not leave you comfortless, I will come to you. ¹⁹ Yet a little while, and the world seeth me no more, but ye see me: because I live, ye shall live also. ²⁰ At that day ye shall know that I am in my Father, and you in me, and I in you. ²¹ He that hath my commandments, and keepeth them, he it is that loveth me: and he that loveth me shall be loved of my Father, and I will love him, and will manifest myself to him.'

²² Judas saith unto him, not Iscariot, 'Lord, how is it that thou wilt manifest thyself unto us, and not unto the world?' ²³ Jesus answered, and said unto him, 'If a man love me, he will keep my words: and my Father will love him, and we will come unto him, and make our abode with him. ²⁴ He that loveth me not, keepeth not my sayings, and the word which you hear, is not mine, but the Father's which sent me. ²⁵ These things have I spoken unto you, being yet present with you. ²⁶ But the Comforter, which is the Holy Ghost, whom the Father will send in my name, he shall teach you all things, and bring all things to your remembrance, whatsoever I have said unto you.

²⁷ 'Peace I leave with you, my peace I give unto you: not as the world giveth, give I unto you: let not your heart be troubled, neither let it be afraid. ²⁸ Ye have heard how I said unto you, "I go away, and come again unto you". If ye loved me, ye would rejoice, because I said, "I go unto the Father": for my Father is greater than I. ²⁹ And now

I have told you before it come to pass, that when it is come to pass, ye might believe. ³⁰ Hereafter I will not talk much with you: for the prince of this world cometh, and hath nothing in me. ³¹ But that the world may know that I love the Father: and as the Father gave me commandment, even so I do. Arise, let us go hence.'

Chapter 15

1 *The consolation and mutual love between Christ and his members,*
under the parable of the vine. 18 *A comfort in the hatred and persecution*
of the world. 26 *The office of the Holy Ghost, and of the apostles.*

'I AM the true vine, and my Father is the husbandman. ²Every branch in me that beareth not fruit, he taketh away: and every branch that beareth fruit, he purgeth it, that it may bring forth more fruit. ³Now ye are clean through the word which I have spoken unto you. ⁴Abide in me, and I in you: as the branch cannot bear fruit of itself, except it abide in the vine: no more can ye, except ye abide in me. ⁵I am the vine, ye are the branches: he that abideth in me, and I in him, the same bringeth forth much fruit: for without me ye can do nothing. ⁶If a man abide not in me, he is cast forth as a branch, and is withered, and men gather them, and cast them into the fire, and they are burned. ⁷If ye abide in me, and my words abide in you, ye shall ask what ye will, and it shall be done unto you. ⁸Herein is my Father glorified, that ye bear much fruit; so shall ye be my disciples. ⁹As the Father hath loved me, so have I loved you: continue ye in my love. ¹⁰ If ye keep my commandments, ye shall abide in my love, even as I have kept my Father's commandments, and abide in his love. ¹¹ These things have I spoken unto you, that my joy might remain in you, and that your joy might be full.

¹² 'This is my commandment, that ye love one another, as I have loved you. ¹³ Greater love hath no man than this, that a man lay down his life for his friends. ¹⁴ Ye are my friends, if ye do whatsoever I command you. ¹⁵ Henceforth I call you not servants, for the servant knoweth not what his lord doeth, but I have called you friends: for all things that I have heard of my Father, I have made known unto you. ¹⁶ Ye have not chosen me, but I have chosen you, and ordained you, that ye should go and bring forth fruit, and that your fruit should remain: that whatsoever ye shall ask of the Father in my name,

he may give it you. ¹⁷ These things I command you, that ye love one another.

¹⁸ 'If the world hate you, ye know that it hated me before it hated you. ¹⁹ If ye were of the world, the world would love his own: but because ye are not of the world, but I have chosen you out of the world, therefore the world hateth you. ²⁰ Remember the word that I said unto you, "The servant is not greater than the lord". If they have persecuted me, they will also persecute you; if they have kept my saying, they will keep yours also. ²¹ But all these things will they do unto you for my name's sake, because they know not him that sent me. ²² If I had not come, and spoken unto them, they had not had sin: but now they have no cloak for their sin. ²³ He that hateth me, hateth my Father also. ²⁴ If I had not done among them the works which none other man did, they had not had sin: but now have they both seen and hated both me and my Father. ²⁵ But this cometh to pass, that the word might be fulfilled that is written in their Law, "They hated me without a cause".

²⁶ 'But when the Comforter is come, whom I will send unto you from the Father, even the Spirit of truth, which proceedeth from the Father, he shall testify of me. ²⁷ And ye also shall bear witness, because ye have been with me from the beginning.'

Chapter 16

1 *Christ comforteth his disciples against tribulation by the promise of the Holy Ghost, and by his resurrection and ascension:* 23 *assureth their prayers made in his name to be acceptable to his Father.* 33 *Peace in Christ, and in the world affliction.*

'THESE things have I spoken unto you, that ye should not be offended. ² They shall put you out of the synagogues: yea, the time cometh, that whosoever killeth you, will think that he doeth God service. ³ And these things will they do unto you, because they have not known the Father, nor me. ⁴ But these things have I told you, that when the time shall come, ye may remember that I told you of them. And these things I said not unto you at the beginning, because I was with you. ⁵ But now I go my way to him that sent me, and none of you asketh me, "Whither goest thou?" ⁶ But because I have said these things unto you, sorrow hath filled your heart. ⁷ Nevertheless, I tell you the truth, it is expedient for you that I go away: for if I go not away, the Comforter will not come unto you: but if I depart, I will send him unto you. [8] And when he is come, he will reprove the world of sin, and of righteousness, and of judgement. [9] Of sin, because they believe not on me. [10] Of righteousness, because I go to my Father, and ye see me no more. [11] Of judgement, because the prince of this world is judged.

[12] 'I have yet many things to say unto you, but ye cannot bear them now. [13] Howbeit, when he the Spirit of truth is come, he will guide you into all truth: for he shall not speak of himself: but whatsoever he shall hear, that shall he speak, and he will show you things to come. [14] He shall glorify me, for he shall receive of mine, and shall show it unto you. [15] All things that the Father hath, are mine: therefore said I that he shall take of mine, and shall show it unto you.

[16] 'A little while, and ye shall not see me: and again a little while, and ye shall see me: because I go to the Father.' [17] Then said some of his disciples among themselves, 'What is this that he saith unto us, "A little while, and ye shall not see me": and again, "A little while, and ye shall see me": and, "Because I go to the Father"?' [18] They said therefore, 'What is this that he saith, "A little while"? We cannot tell what he saith.' [19] Now Jesus knew that they were desirous to ask him, and said unto them, 'Do ye enquire among yourselves of that I said, "A little while, and ye shall not see me": and again, "A little while, and ye shall see me"? [20] Verily, verily I say unto you, that ye shall weep and lament, but the world shall rejoice: and ye shall be sorrowful, but your sorrow shall be turned into joy. [21] A woman, when she is in travail, hath sorrow, because her hour is come: but as soon as she is delivered of the child, she remembereth no more the anguish, for joy that a man is born into the world. [22] And ye now therefore have sorrow: but I will see you again, and your heart shall rejoice, and your joy no man taketh from you. [23] And in that day ye shall ask me nothing. Verily, verily I say unto you, whatsoever ye shall ask the Father in my name, he will give it you. [24] Hitherto have ye asked nothing in my name: ask, and ye shall receive, that your joy may be full.

[25] 'These things have I spoken unto you in proverbs: the time cometh when I shall no more speak unto you in proverbs, but I shall show you plainly of the Father. [26] At that day ye shall ask in my name: and I say not unto you that I will pray the Father for you: [27] for the Father himself loveth you, because ye have loved me, and have believed that

I came out from God. [28] I came forth from the Father, and am come into the world: again, I leave the world, and go to the Father.'

[29] His disciples said unto him, 'Lo, now speakest thou plainly, and speakest no proverb. [30] Now are we sure that thou knowest all things, and needest not that any man should ask thee: by this we believe that thou camest forth from God.' [31] Jesus answered them, 'Do ye now believe? [32] Behold, the hour cometh, yea is now come, that ye shall be scattered, every man to his own, and shall leave me alone: and yet I am not alone, because the Father is with me. [33] These things I have spoken unto you, that in me ye might have peace. In the world ye shall have tribulation: but be of good cheer, I have overcome the world.'

Chapter 17

1 Christ prayeth to his Father to glorify him, 6 to preserve his apostles 11 in unity, 17 and truth, 20 to glorify them, and all other believers with him in heaven.

THESE words spake Jesus, and lift up his eyes to heaven, and said, 'Father, the hour is come, glorify thy Son, that thy Son also may glorify thee: [2] as thou hast given him power over all flesh, that he should give eternal life to as many as thou hast given him. [3] And this is life eternal, that they might know thee the only true God, and Jesus Christ, whom thou hast sent. [4] I have glorified thee on the earth: I have finished the work which thou gavest me to do. [5] And now O Father, glorify thou me, with thine own self, with the glory which I had with thee before the world was.

[6] 'I have manifested thy name unto the men which thou gavest me out of the world: thine they were, and thou gavest them me, and they have kept thy word. [7] Now they have known that all things whatsoever thou hast given me, are of thee. [8] For I have given unto them the words which thou gavest me, and they have received them, and have known surely that I came out from thee, and they have believed that thou didst send me. [9] I pray for them, I pray not for the world: but for them which thou hast given me, for they are thine. [10] And all mine are thine, and thine are mine: and I am glorified in them. [11] And now I am no more in the world, but these are in the world, and I come to thee. Holy Father, keep through thine own name, those whom thou hast

given me, that they may be one, as we are. ¹² While I was with them in the world, I kept them in thy name: those that thou gavest me, I have kept, and none of them is lost, but the son of perdition: that the scripture might be fulfilled. ¹³ And now come I to thee, and these things I speak in the world, that they might have my joy fulfilled in themselves. ¹⁴ I have given them thy word, and the world hath hated them, because they are not of the world, even as I am not of the world. ¹⁵ I pray not that thou shouldst take them out of the world, but that thou shouldst keep them from the evil. ¹⁶ They are not of the world, even as I am not of the world. ¹⁷ Sanctify them through thy truth: thy word is truth. ¹⁸ As thou hast sent me into the world, even so have I also sent them into the world. ¹⁹ And for their sakes I sanctify myself, that they also might be sanctified through the truth.

²⁰ 'Neither pray I for these alone; but for them also which shall believe on me through their word: ²¹ that they all may be one, as thou Father art in me, and I in thee, that they also may be one in us: that the world may believe that thou hast sent me. ²² And the glory which thou gavest me, I have given them: that they may be one, even as we are one: ²³ I in them, and thou in me, that they may be made perfect in one, and that the world may know that thou hast sent me, and hast loved them, as thou hast loved me. ²⁴ Father, I will that they also whom thou hast given me, be with me where I am, that they may behold my glory which thou hast given me: for thou lovedst me before the foundation of the world.

²⁵ 'O righteous Father, the world hath not known thee: but I have known thee, and these have known that thou hast sent me. ²⁶ And I have declared unto them thy name, and will declare it: that the love wherewith thou hast loved me, may be in them, and I in them.'

Chapter 18

WHEN Jesus had spoken these words, he went forth with his disciples over the brook Cedron, where was a garden, into the which he entered, and his disciples. [2] And Judas also which betrayed him, knew the place: for Jesus oft times resorted thither with his disciples. [3] Judas then having received a band of men, and officers from the chief priests and Pharisees, cometh thither with lanterns and torches, and weapons. [4] Jesus therefore knowing all things that should come upon him, went forth, and said unto them, 'Whom seek ye?' [5] They answered him, 'Jesus of Nazareth'. Jesus saith unto them, 'I am he'. And Judas also which betrayed him, stood with them. [6] As soon then as he had said unto them, 'I am he', they went backward, and fell to the ground. [7] Then asked he them again, 'Whom seek ye?' And they said, 'Jesus of Nazareth'. [8] Jesus answered, 'I have told you that I am he: if therefore ye seek me, let these go their way': [9] that the saying might be fulfilled which he spake, 'Of them which thou gavest me, have I lost none'. [10] Then Simon Peter having a sword, drew it, and smote the High Priest's servant, and cut off his right ear: the servant's name was Malchus. [11] Then said Jesus unto Peter, 'Put up thy sword into the sheath: the cup which my Father hath given me, shall I not drink it?'

[12] Then the band and the captain, and officers of the Jews, took Jesus, and bound him, [13] and led him away to Annas first, for he was father-in-law to Caiaphas, which was the High Priest that same year. [14] Now Caiaphas was he which gave counsel to the Jews, that it was expedient that one man should die for the people.

[15] And Simon Peter followed Jesus, and so did another disciple: that disciple was known unto the High Priest, and went in with Jesus into the palace of the High Priest. [16] But Peter stood at the door without. Then went out that other disciple, which was known unto the High Priest, and spake unto her that kept the door, and brought in Peter. [17] Then saith the damsel that kept the door unto Peter, 'Art not thou also one of this man's disciples?' He saith, 'I am not'. [18] And the servants and officers stood there, who had made a fire of coals (for it was cold), and they warmed themselves: and Peter stood with them, and warmed himself.

[19] The High Priest then asked Jesus of his disciples, and of his doctrine. [20] Jesus answered him, 'I spake openly to the world, I ever taught in the synagogue, and in the Temple, whither the Jews always resort, and in secret have I said nothing: [21] why askest thou me? Ask them which heard me, what I have said unto them: behold, they know what I said.' [22] And when he had thus spoken, one of the officers which

stood by, struck Jesus with the palm of his hand, saying, 'Answerest thou the High Priest so?' [23] Jesus answered him, 'If I have spoken evil, bear witness of the evil: but if well, why smitest thou me?' [24] Now Annas had sent him bound unto Caiaphas the High Priest.

[25] And Simon Peter stood and warmed himself. They said therefore unto him, 'Art not thou also one of his disciples?' He denied it, and said, 'I am not'. [26] One of the servants of the High Priest, being his kinsman whose ear Peter cut off, saith, 'Did not I see thee in the garden with him?' [27] Peter then denied again, and immediately the cock crew.

[28] Then led they Jesus from Caiaphas unto the hall of judgement: and it was early, and they themselves went not into the judgement hall, lest they should be defiled: but that they might eat the Passover. [29] Pilate then went out unto them, and said, 'What accusation bring you against this man?' [30] They answered, and said unto him, 'If he were not a malefactor, we would not have delivered him up unto thee'. [31] Then said Pilate unto them, 'Take ye him, and judge him according to your law'. The Jews therefore said unto him, 'It is not lawful for us to put any man to death': [32] that the saying of Jesus might be fulfilled, which he spake, signifying what death he should die.

[33] Then Pilate entered into the judgement hall again, and called Jesus, and said unto him, 'Art thou the King of the Jews?' [34] Jesus answered him, 'Sayest thou this thing of thyself, or did others tell it thee of me?' [35] Pilate answered, 'Am I a Jew? Thine own nation, and the chief priests have delivered thee unto me: what hast thou done?' [36] Jesus answered, 'My kingdom is not of this world: if my kingdom were of this world, then would my servants fight, that I should not be delivered to the Jews: but now is my kingdom not from hence'. [37] Pilate therefore said unto him, 'Art thou a king then?' Jesus answered, 'Thou sayest that I am a king. To this end was I born, and for this cause came I into the world, that I should bear witness unto the truth: every one that is of the truth heareth my voice.' [38] Pilate saith unto him, 'What is truth?'

And when he had said this, he went out again unto the Jews, and saith unto them, 'I find in him no fault at all. [39] But ye have a custom that I should release unto you one at the Passover: will ye therefore that I release unto you the King of the Jews?' [40] Then cried they all again, saying, 'Not this man, but Barabbas'. Now Barabbas was a robber.

Chapter 19

1 *Christ is scourged, crowned with thorns, and beaten.* 4 *Pilate is desir-*
ous to release him, but being overcome with the outrage of the Jews, he
delivered him to be crucified. 23 *They cast lots for his garments.* 26 *He*
commendeth his mother to John. 28 *He dieth.* 31 *His side is pierced.*
38 *He is buried by Joseph and Nicodemus.*

THEN Pilate therefore took Jesus, and scourged him. ² And the soldiers plaited a crown of thorns, and put it on his head, and they
put on him a purple robe, ³ and said, 'Hail King of the Jews': and
they smote him with their hands. ⁴ Pilate therefore went forth again,
and saith unto them, 'Behold, I bring him forth to you, that ye may
know that I find no fault in him'. ⁵ Then came Jesus forth, wearing
the crown of thorns, and the purple robe: and Pilate saith unto them,
'Behold the man'. ⁶ When the chief priests therefore and officers saw
him, they cried out, saying, 'Crucify him, crucify him'. Pilate saith
unto them, 'Take ye him, and crucify him: for I find no fault in him'.
⁷ The Jews answered him, 'We have a law, and by our law he ought to
die, because he made himself the Son of God'.

⁸ When Pilate therefore heard that saying, he was the more afraid,
⁹ and went again into the judgement hall, and saith unto Jesus,
'Whence art thou?' But Jesus gave him no answer. ¹⁰ Then saith
Pilate unto him, 'Speakest thou not unto me? Knowest thou not, that
I have power to crucify thee, and have power to release thee?' ¹¹ Jesus
answered, 'Thou couldst have no power at all against me, except it
were given thee from above: therefore he that delivered me unto thee,
hath the greater sin'. ¹² And from thenceforth Pilate sought to release
him: but the Jews cried out, saying, 'If thou let this man go, thou
art not Caesar's friend: whosoever maketh himself a king, speaketh
against Caesar'.

¹³ When Pilate therefore heard that saying, he brought Jesus forth,
and sat down in the judgement seat, in a place that is called the
Pavement, but in the Hebrew, Gabbatha. ¹⁴ And it was the Preparation
of the Passover, and about the sixth hour: and he saith unto the Jews,
'Behold your King'. ¹⁵ But they cried out, 'Away with him, away with
him, crucify him'. Pilate saith unto them, 'Shall I crucify your King?'
The chief priests answered, 'We have no king but Caesar'. ¹⁶ Then
delivered he him therefore unto them to be crucified: and they took

Jesus, and led him away. [17] And he bearing his cross, went forth into a place called The Place of a Skull, which is called in the Hebrew, Golgotha: [18] where they crucified him, and two other with him, on either side one, and Jesus in the midst. [19] And Pilate wrote a title, and put it on the cross. And the writing was, '*JESUS OF NAZARETH, THE KING OF THE JEWS*'. [20] This title then read many of the Jews: for the place where Jesus was crucified was nigh to the city, and it was written in Hebrew, and Greek, and Latin. [21] Then said the chief priests of the Jews to Pilate, 'Write not, "The King of the Jews": but that he said, "I am King of the Jews" '. [22] Pilate answered, 'What I have written, I have written'.

[23] Then the soldiers, when they had crucified Jesus, took his garments, and made four parts, to every soldier a part, and also his coat: now the coat was without seam, woven from the top throughout. [24] They said therefore among themselves, 'Let us not rend it, but cast lots for it, whose it shall be': that the scripture might be fulfilled, which saith, 'They parted my raiment among them, and for my vesture they did cast lots'. These things therefore the soldiers did.

[25] Now there stood by the cross of Jesus, his mother, and his mother's sister, Mary the wife of Cleophas, and Mary Magdalene. [26] When Jesus therefore saw his mother, and the disciple standing by, whom he loved, he saith unto his mother, 'Woman, behold thy son'. [27] Then saith he to the disciple, 'Behold thy mother'. And from that hour that disciple took her unto his own home.

[28] After this, Jesus knowing that all things were now accomplished, that the scripture might be fulfilled, saith, 'I thirst'. [29] Now there was set a vessel, full of vinegar: and they filled a sponge with vinegar, and put it upon hyssop, and put it to his mouth. [30] When Jesus therefore had received the vinegar, he said, 'It is finished', and he bowed his head, and gave up the ghost.

[31] The Jews therefore, because it was the Preparation, that the bodies should not remain upon the cross on the Sabbath day (for that Sabbath day was an high day), besought Pilate that their legs might be broken, and that they might be taken away. [32] Then came the soldiers, and brake the legs of the first, and of the other, which was crucified with him. [33] But when they came to Jesus, and saw that he was dead already, they brake not his legs. [34] But one of the soldiers with a spear pierced his side, and forthwith came there out blood and water. [35] And he that saw it bare record, and his record is true, and he knoweth that

he saith true, that ye might believe. ³⁶ For these things were done, that the scripture should be fulfilled, 'A bone of him shall not be broken'. ³⁷ And again another scripture saith, 'They shall look on him whom they pierced'.

³⁸ And after this, Joseph of Arimathea (being a disciple of Jesus, but secretly for fear of the Jews), besought Pilate that he might take away the body of Jesus, and Pilate gave him leave: he came therefore, and took the body of Jesus. ³⁹ And there came also Nicodemus, which at the first came to Jesus by night, and brought a mixture of myrrh and aloes, about an hundred pound weight. ⁴⁰ Then took they the body of Jesus, and wound it in linen clothes, with the spices, as the manner of the Jews is to bury. ⁴¹ Now in the place where he was crucified, there was a garden, and in the garden a new sepulchre, wherein was never man yet laid. ⁴² There laid they Jesus therefore, because of the Jews' Preparation day, for the sepulchre was nigh at hand.

Chapter 20

1 Mary cometh to the sepulchre. 3 So do Peter and John ignorant of the resurrection. 11 Jesus appeareth to Mary Magdalene, 19 and to his disciples. 24 The incredulity, and confession of Thomas. 30 The scripture is sufficient to salvation.

THE first day of the week, cometh Mary Magdalene early when it was yet dark, unto the sepulchre, and seeth the stone taken away from the sepulchre. ² Then she runneth and cometh to Simon Peter, and to the other disciple whom Jesus loved, and saith unto them, 'They have taken away the Lord out of the sepulchre, and we know not where they have laid him'. ³ Peter therefore went forth, and that other disciple, and came to the sepulchre. ⁴ So they ran both together, and the other disciple did outrun Peter, and came first to the sepulchre. ⁵ And he stooping down and looking in, saw the linen clothes lying, yet went he not in. ⁶ Then cometh Simon Peter following him, and went into the sepulchre, and seeth the linen clothes lie, ⁷ and the napkin that was about his head, not lying with the linen clothes, but wrapped together in a place by itself. ⁸ Then went in also that other disciple which came first to the sepulchre, and he saw, and believed. ⁹ For as yet they knew not the scripture, that he must rise again from the dead. ¹⁰ Then the disciples went away again unto their own home.

[11] But Mary stood without at the sepulchre, weeping: and as she wept, she stooped down, and looked into the sepulchre, [12] and seeth two angels in white, sitting, the one at the head, and the other at the feet, where the body of Jesus had lain. [13] And they say unto her, 'Woman, why weepest thou?' She saith unto them, 'Because they have taken away my Lord, and I know not where they have laid him'. [14] And when she had thus said, she turned herself back, and saw Jesus standing, and knew not that it was Jesus. [15] Jesus saith unto her, 'Woman, why weepest thou? whom seekest thou?' She, supposing him to be the gardener, saith unto him, 'Sir, if thou have borne him hence, tell me where thou hast laid him, and I will take him away'. [16] Jesus saith unto her, 'Mary'. She turned herself, and saith unto him, 'Rabboni', which is to say, 'Master'. [17] Jesus saith unto her, 'Touch me not: for I am not yet ascended to my Father: but go to my brethren, and say unto them, I ascend unto my Father, and your Father, and to my God, and your God'. [18] Mary Magdalene came and told the disciples that she had seen the Lord, and that he had spoken these things unto her.

[19] Then the same day at evening, being the first day of the week, when the doors were shut where the disciples were assembled for fear of the Jews, came Jesus, and stood in the midst, and saith unto them, 'Peace be unto you'. [20] And when he had so said, he showed unto them his hands and his side. Then were the disciples glad, when they saw the Lord. [21] Then said Jesus to them again, 'Peace be unto you: as my Father hath sent me, even so send I you'. [22] And when he had said this, he breathed on them, and saith unto them, 'Receive ye the Holy Ghost. [23] Whose soever sins ye remit, they are remitted unto them, and whose soever sins ye retain, they are retained.'

[24] But Thomas, one of the twelve, called Didymus, was not with them when Jesus came. [25] The other disciples therefore said unto him, 'We have seen the Lord'. But he said unto them, 'Except I shall see in his hands the print of the nails, and put my finger into the print of the nails, and thrust my hand into his side, I will not believe'.

[26] And after eight days, again his disciples were within, and Thomas with them: then came Jesus, the doors being shut, and stood in the midst, and said, 'Peace be unto you'. [27] Then saith he to Thomas, 'Reach hither thy finger, and behold my hands, and reach hither thy hand, and thrust it into my side, and be not faithless, but believing'. [28] And Thomas answered, and said unto him, 'My Lord, and my God'. [29] Jesus saith unto him, 'Thomas, because thou hast seen me,

thou hast believed: blessed are they that have not seen, and yet have believed'.

[30] And many other signs truly did Jesus in the presence of his disciples, which are not written in this book: [31] but these are written, that ye might believe that Jesus is the Christ, the Son of God, and that believing ye might have life through his name.

Chapter 21

[1] *Christ appearing again to his disciples was known of them by the great draught of fishes.* 12 *He dineth with them:* 15 *earnestly command-eth Peter to feed his lambs and sheep:* 18 *foretelleth him of his death:* 22 *rebuketh his curiosity touching John.* 25 *The conclusion.*

AFTER these things Jesus showed himself again to the disciples at the sea of Tiberias, and on this wise showed he himself. [2] There were together Simon Peter, and Thomas called Didymus, and Nathanael of Cana in Galilee, and the sons of Zebedee, and two other of his disciples. [3] Simon Peter saith unto them, 'I go a fishing'. They say unto him, 'We also go with thee'. They went forth, and entered into a ship immediately, and that night they caught nothing.

[4] But when the morning was now come, Jesus stood on the shore: but the disciples knew not that it was Jesus. [5] Then Jesus saith unto them, 'Children, have ye any meat?' They answered him, 'No'. [6] And he said unto them, 'Cast the net on the right side of the ship, and ye shall find'. They cast therefore, and now they were not able to draw it, for the multitude of fishes. [7] Therefore that disciple whom Jesus loved, saith unto Peter, 'It is the Lord'. Now when Simon Peter heard that it was the Lord, he girt his fisher's coat unto him (for he was naked), and did cast himself into the sea. [8] And the other disciples came in a little ship (for they were not far from land, but as it were two hundred cubits), dragging the net with fishes. [9] As soon then as they were come to land, they saw a fire of coals there, and fish laid thereon, and bread. [10] Jesus saith unto them, 'Bring of the fish which ye have now caught'. [11] Simon Peter went up, and drew the net to land full of great fishes, an hundred and fifty and three: and for all there were so many, yet was not the net broken. [12] Jesus saith unto them, 'Come, and dine'. And none of the disciples durst ask him, 'Who art thou?' knowing that it was the Lord. [13] Jesus then cometh, and taketh bread, and giveth

them, and fish likewise. [14] This is now the third time that Jesus showed himself to his disciples, after that he was risen from the dead.

[15] So when they had dined, Jesus saith to Simon Peter, 'Simon, son of Jonas, lovest thou me more than these?' He saith unto him, 'Yea, Lord, thou knowest that I love thee'. He saith unto him, 'Feed my lambs'. [16] He saith to him again the second time, 'Simon, son of Jonas, lovest thou me?' He saith unto him, 'Yea Lord, thou knowest that I love thee'. He saith unto him, 'Feed my sheep'. [17] He said unto him the third time, 'Simon, son of Jonas, lovest thou me?' Peter was grieved because he said unto him the third time, 'Lovest thou me?' And he said unto him, 'Lord, thou knowest all things, thou knowest that I love thee'. Jesus saith unto him, 'Feed my sheep. [18] Verily, verily I say unto thee, when thou wast young, thou girdedst thyself, and walkedst whither thou wouldst: but when thou shalt be old, thou shalt stretch forth thy hands, and another shall gird thee, and carry thee whither thou wouldst not.' [19] This spake he, signifying by what death he should glorify God. And when he had spoken this, he saith unto him, 'Follow me'.

[20] Then Peter turning about, seeth the disciple whom Jesus loved, following, which also leaned on his breast at supper, and said, 'Lord, which is he that betrayeth thee?' [21] Peter seeing him, saith to Jesus, 'Lord, and what shall this man do?' [22] Jesus saith unto him, 'If I will that he tarry till I come, what is that to thee? Follow thou me.' [23] Then went this saying abroad among the brethren, that that disciple should not die: yet Jesus said not unto him, 'He shall not die': but, 'If I will that he tarry till I come, what is that to thee?'

[24] This is the disciple which testifieth of these things, and wrote these things: and we know that his testimony is true. [25] And there are also many other things which Jesus did, the which if they should be written every one, I suppose that even the world itself could not contain the books that should be written. Amen.

EXPLANATORY NOTES

Books of the Bible (not including books in the Apocrypha, whose titles are given in full)

Acts	Acts of the Apostles	Lev.	Leviticus
Amos	Amos	Luke	Gospel of Luke
1 Chron.	1 Chronicles	Mal.	Malachi
2 Chron.	2 Chronicles	Mark	Gospel of Mark
Col.	Colossians	Matt.	Gospel of Matthew
1 Cor.	1 Corinthians	Mic.	Micah
Dan.	Daniel	Neh.	Nehemiah
Deut.	Deuteronomy	Num.	Numbers
Eccl.	Ecclesiastes	1 Pet.	1 Peter
Eph.	Ephesians	2 Pet.	2 Peter
Exod.	Exodus	Philem.	Philemon
Ezek.	Ezekiel	Prov.	Proverbs
Gal.	Galatians	Ps(s).	Psalm(s)
Gen.	Genesis	Prov.	Proverbs
Heb.	Hebrews	Rev.	Revelation
Hos.	Hosea	Rom.	Romans
Isa.	Isaiah	Ruth	Ruth
James	James	1 Sam.	1 Samuel
Jer.	Jeremiah	2 Sam.	2 Samuel
Job	Job	Song of Sol.	Song of Solomon
Joel	Joel	1 Thess.	1 Thessalonians
John	Gospel of John	2 Thess.	2 Thessalonians
Jon.	Jonah	1 Tim.	1 Timothy
Josh.	Joshua	2 Tim.	2 Timothy
Judg.	Judges	Titus	Titus
1 Kings	1 Kings	Zech.	Zechariah
2 Kings	2 Kings	Zeph.	Zephaniah
Lam.	Lamentations		

Other works:

Josephus *Ant.* Flavius Josephus, *Jewish Antiquities* (93–4 CE), trans. William Whiston, ed. Brian McGing (London, 2006).

Josephus *War* Flavius Josephus, *The Jewish War* (77–8 CE), trans. G. A. Williamson, rev. E. Mary Smallwood (London, 1981).

The Gospels are quoted from the present edition. All other quotations from the Bible are from *The Bible: Authorized King James Bible*, ed. Robert Carroll

and Stephen Prickett (Oxford, 1997), abbreviated as 'AV'. Reference is also
made to the New Revised Standard Version of the Bible (1989), abbreviated
as 'NRSV', as presented in *The New Oxford Annotated Bible*, augmented
3rd edn., ed. Michael D. Coogan, with Marc Z. Brettler, Carol A. Newsom,
and Pheme Perkins (Oxford, 2007). The Old Testament is referred to as the
'Hebrew Bible'. The New Testament is abbreviated as 'NT'.

In the notes and glossaries that follow, information has been taken from the
following sources: *The Anchor Bible Dictionary*, ed. David Noel Freedman
and others, 6 vols. (New York, 1992); *The Cambridge Companion to the Bible*,
2nd edn., gen. ed. Bruce Chilton (Cambridge, 2008); *The HarperCollins Study
Bible*, rev. edn., gen. ed. Harold W. Attridge (New York, 2006); *The New Oxford
Annotated Bible*, augmented 3rd edn., ed. Michael D. Coogan, with Marc Z.
Brettler, Carol A. Newsom, and Pheme Perkins (Oxford, 2007); *The Oxford
Bible Commentary*, ed. John Barton and John Muddiman (Oxford, 2001);
The Oxford Companion to the Bible, ed. Bruce M. Metzger and Michael D.
Coogan (Oxford, 1993); *The Oxford Dictionary of the Christian Church*, 3rd
edn., ed. F. L. Cross and E. A. Livingstone (Oxford, 1997); *The Oxford English
Dictionary*, 2nd edn. (Oxford, 1989); Geza Vermes, *Who's Who in the Age of
Jesus* (London, 2005).

MATTHEW

CHAPTER I

1 *The book of the generation*: 'an account of the genealogy' (NRSV).

   Jesus Christ . . . David . . . Abraham: on the name 'Jesus Christ' and the
   significance of the link with David and Abraham, see Introduction, pp.
   xvii–xviii. Matthew divides his genealogy into three ages: (1) from Abraham
   to David, vv. 2–6; (2) from David to the exile of the Jews to Babylon, vv.
   6–11; (3) from the exile to the time of Jesus, vv. 12–16.

2–11 *Isaac . . . Jechonias* [Jechoniah]: for the sources of these names, see (in
   sequence) Gen. 21:3, 25:26, 29:35, 38:24–30; 1 Chron. 2:5; Ruth 4:18–22;
   1 Sam. 17:12; 2 Sam. 12:24, 11:2–17; 1 Chron. 3:10–15.

   carried away to Babylon: a reference to the deportation of the Jewish people
   to Babylon in the sixth century BCE, following the conquest of Jerusalem by
   Nebuchadnezzar, and the destruction of Solomon's Temple. See 2 Kings
   24, 25.

12 *Salatheil . . . Zorobabel* [Zerubbabel]: see 1 Chron. 3:17–19.

13–15 *Abiud . . . Jacob*: no source is known for these names.

16 *Joseph*: the genealogy of Jesus here is traced back from his legal father,
   Joseph.

17 *fourteen generations*: some names have been left out (compare vv. 8 and 9
   with 1 Chron. 3:10–13) in order to achieve the symmetry of fourteen–

fourteen–fourteen (though in fact there are only thirteen generations in the third series). The triadic structure is a favourite literary device of Matthew.

18 *was on this wise*: 'took place in this way' (NRSV).

the Holy Ghost: an alternative title, often used in the AV, for the Holy Spirit (in Christian theology the Third Person of the Trinity).

19 *put her away privily*: divorce her discreetly. (Joseph would have felt himself obliged to divorce Mary under Jewish Law, on grounds of her apparent sexual unfaithfulness within marriage.)

20 *that*: i.e. the child.

23 *Behold . . . Emmanuel*: quoted from Isa. 7:14. See Introduction, p. xviii, n. 21.

25 *knew her not*: 'had no marital relations with her' (NRSV).

he called his name Jesus: Jewish boys received their names when they were circumcised, eight days after birth (see Gen. 17:12; Lev. 12:3; Luke 1:59, 2:21). The right of choosing the name of a son belonged to his father. As well as his given name, a Jewish man also bore his father's name: he was 'son of' so-and-so. The word for 'son' in Aramaic is 'bar', and Jesus would thus have been known as 'Joshua bar Joseph'.

CHAPTER 2

1 *wise men from the east*: usually known as the 'magi', from a Greek word meaning 'skilled in magical arts and astrology'. In later Western Christian tradition it was assumed that there were three of them (because three gifts are mentioned), and that they were kings (because they were wealthy and conversed with King Herod). They were also then furnished with names: Balthasar, Melchior, and Caspar.

2 *his star*: it was widely believed in the ancient world that important births would be announced by the appearance of a star. Matthew would have regarded this star as another fulfilment of prophecy: 'there shall come a Star out of Jacob, and a Sceptre shall rise out of Israel' (Num. 24:17).

4 *all the chief priests and scribes*: i.e. the members of the Sanhedrin, the Jewish supreme council and judicial court, which was presided over by the High Priest. (For the scribes, see note to 5:20, below.)

Christ: or, more properly, the Christ (i.e. the Messiah).

should be: 'was to be' (NRSV).

6 *thou Bethlehem . . . my people Israel*: see Mic. 5:2. The birth of Jesus is taken by Matthew to be a fulfilment of this prophecy. (It is also alluded to in John 7:42.)

11 *gold . . . frankincense . . . myrrh*: gifts suitable for a king; see Ps. 72:15; Isa. 60:6; Ps. 45:8; Song of Sol. 3:6, etc.

15 *Out of Egypt have I called my son*: quoting from Hos. 11:1. The 'son' referred to by Hosea is Moses (see Exod. 4:22–3), and Matthew is thus making a link between Jesus and Moses, the great deliverer of the Jewish people.

16 *slew all the children*: Josephus records many instances of atrocities ordered by Herod, including the murder of close relatives, so this story is not altogether implausible. Matthew, however, may have included it because Moses was likewise threatened by Pharaoh's order that the sons of the Hebrew slaves be killed (Exod. 1:16, 22).

17 *Jeremy*: i.e. Jeremiah. The quoted passage is Jer. 31:15. Rachel, the wife of Jacob (Gen. 35:16–20), is imagined as weeping from her tomb in Ramah over the Jewish captives following the conquest of Jerusalem by the Babylonians in the sixth century BCE.

20 *go into . . . young child's life*: alluding to Exod. 4:19, where Moses is told by God to return to Egypt, 'for all the men are dead which sought thy life'.

23 *He shall be called a Nazarene*: no specific source for this quotation is known. A 'Nazarene' (or 'Nazirite') was an individual specially set apart for sacred service, and who had to fulfil certain conditions in order to remain consecrated, such as not having contact with a dead body, or allowing a razor to cut his hair (see Num. 6). In Acts (24:5), the early Christians are referred to as 'Nazarenes' (i.e. followers of Jesus of Nazareth).

CHAPTER 3

1 *the wilderness of Judea*: the part of Judea near Jericho, where the Jordan empties into the Dead Sea.

2 *Repent*: the literal meaning of the Greek word is 'change one's mind', but as used here and elsewhere in NT it has the stronger sense of 'turning back' or 'turning away', or 'conversion' from one's sinful past to God's way, with a consequent change in conduct.

the kingdom of heaven: Matthew uses this phrase (in all but four places) rather than 'kingdom of God', which is the usual formulation in the other Synoptic Gospels. 'Kingdom' here is not a place; the phrase refers, rather, to the 'king*ship*' (or 'rule') of God.

3 *Esaias . . . paths straight*: see Isa. 40:3.

4 *raiment of camel's hair . . . wild honey*: John's ascetic style of clothing recalls the description of the prophet Elijah in 2 Kings 1:8. Locusts were among the permitted foods in Jewish dietary law (see Lev. 11:22), and were indeed eaten by the poor. By 'wild honey' is meant honey from wild bees.

7 *Pharisees and Sadducees*: see Introduction, pp. xx–xxi.

9 *We have Abraham to our father*: 'We have Abraham as our ancestor' (NRSV).

11 *Holy Ghost, and with fire*: for 'Holy Ghost' see note to 1:18. 'Fire' here represents purification.

12 *purge his floor*: 'clear his threshing floor' (NRSV).

15 *fulfil all righteousness*: i.e. fulfil all God's commandments.

Then he suffered him: i.e. John allowed Jesus to have his way.

16 *went up*: i.e. came up (having been immersed).

dove: the dove was one of the most widely used symbols of the Holy Spirit in early Christianity, no doubt because of its inclusion in the Gospel accounts of Jesus's baptism. It was also often linked with the Spirit which 'moved upon' or 'hovered over' the face of the waters in Gen. 1:2, and with Noah's dove, which brought news of deliverance from the Flood (see Gen. 8:8–12).

17 *This is my . . . well pleased*: the words here echo those of Ps. 2:7, 'Thou art my Son; this day have I begotten thee', and Isa. 42:1, 'Behold my servant . . . in whom my soul delighteth'.

CHAPTER 4

1 *the devil*: i.e. Satan, the arch-enemy of God, also given the name Beelzebub, 'the prince of the devils' (see note to 9:34, below).

2 *forty*: not to be understood literally, but as a conventional number for a lengthy period. Thus Israel spent forty years in the wilderness (Deut. 8:2); Moses was 'forty days and forty nights' on Mount Sinai (Exod. 24:18, 34:28); and Elijah journeyed for 'forty days and forty nights' without food (1 Kings 19:8).

an hungered: i.e. overcome with hunger. The AV usage of this archaic form is the last recorded in *OED* (except in the Revised Version of the New Testament, published in 1881).

3 *Son of God*: the Davidic kings of Israel were called 'sons' of God, a title indicating not deification, but that they held their kingship from God and had a special relationship with him (see e.g. 2 Sam. 7:14; Pss 2:7, 89:26–9). The title was also used of the Jewish people as a whole, who would be described as 'sons' or 'daughters' of God (see e.g. Deut. 32:19). For early Christians, however, the term signified Jesus's unique relationship to God.

4 *It is written*: in Deut. 8:3.

5 *the holy city*: i.e. Jerusalem.

6 *it is written*: in Ps. 91:11–12.

7 *It is written*: in Deut. 6:16.

10 *it is written*: in Deut. 6:13, 10:20.

11 *angels came*: the prophet Elijah was also fed by angels (see 1 Kings 19:5–8).

15–16 *The land . . . sprung up*: quoted from Isa. 9:1–2. The districts of Zabulon [Zebulun] and Nephthali [Naphtali] made up the province of Galilee when it was under Assyrian rule. Galilee is therefore said to be 'of the Gentiles' in the sense that it was ruled by non-Israelites.

23 *synagogues*: these were public meeting-places, used primarily for prayer, together with reading and interpretation of the Law, but also for local administrative and judicial business.

gospel of the kingdom: i.e. the good news of the advent of the rule of God on earth.

CHAPTER 5

1 *a mountain*: in having Jesus ascend a mountain to begin his teaching, Matthew may again be associating him with Moses, who received the Law from God on Mount Sinai (Exod. 19–24). The 'Sermon on the Mount' is the first of five major discourses by Jesus in Matthew (see Introduction, p. xix).

3 *Blessed*: i.e. 'happy', 'fortunate'. The sequence of verses in the form 'Blessed are . . . for . . .' are known as the Beatitudes ('blessings'). There are analogies for the form in the Hebrew Bible; see e.g. Ps. 1:1; Isa. 32:20.

    the poor in spirit: probably meaning 'humble', in the moral sense, though it should be noted that the Greek word translated as 'poor' has the meaning 'reduced to beggary' or 'destitute', and the parallel in Luke (6:20) is simply 'Blessed be ye [are the] poor'.

5 *Blessed . . . the earth*: compare Ps. 37:11. 'Meek' here is to be understood as patient and without resentment under injury or reproach.

8 *the pure in heart*: a phrase from the Hebrew Bible (see e.g. Ps. 24:3–4) meaning sincere, or single-minded in carrying out God's will.

10 *for righteousness' sake*: i.e. for their obedience to the will of God.

12 *so persecuted they the prophets*: for slaying of prophets in the Hebrew Bible, see e.g. 1 Kings 18:13, 19:14; Neh. 9:26.

15 *candle*: 'lamp' (NRSV). Oil lamps, not candles, were used for light in first-century Palestine.

17 *the Law . . . the Prophets*: two of the three parts making up the Hebrew Bible (see Introduction, p. xvi). By 'fulfil' Jesus here means 'complete'.

20 *scribes*: scholars devoted to the study and interpretation of the Law, and to drawing out its implications for daily living. They taught in the courts of the Temple and in synagogues, and were highly esteemed, being addressed as 'Rabbi' or 'doctor of the Law'. Their accumulated oral teachings, known as the Talmud, were committed to writing between the second and sixth centuries CE.

21 *Thou shalt . . . the judgement*: see Exod. 20:13, 21:12; Deut. 5:17. By 'in danger of the judgement' is meant 'liable to be sentenced by a court'; see Deut. 17:8–13.

22 *Raca*: an Aramaic term of abuse or insult, meaning something like 'worthless', 'good for nothing'.

    the council: i.e. the Sanhedrin, the supreme court of the Jews (and thus higher than the local court that would pass 'the judgement').

    hell: the word used to translate the Greek *geenna* (Latin *Gehenna*), a place-name meaning 'Valley of Hinnom' (the modern Wadi er-Rababeh, a deep ravine which curves round the west and south sides of Jerusalem). It was said to have been the ancient site of Canaanite rites of child sacrifice (see 2 Kings 23:10; Jer. 19:4–6), but by the time of Jesus was used as a dump where rubbish was kept burning continually. The word 'Gehenna' came to represent metaphorically the place of fiery punishment for the wicked after death, which is how it is used in the NT. Somewhat confusingly, the word 'hell' is also used in the AV to translate 'Hades'; see note to 11:23, below.

23 *gift to the altar*: a reference to the bringing of animals or birds to the Temple at Jerusalem for sacrifice.

25 *in the way*: 'on the way to court' (NRSV).

27 *Thou shalt not commit adultery*: see Exod. 20:14; Deut. 5:18.

30 *And if thy . . . into hell*: cf. 18:8–9.

31 *Whosoever . . . divorcement*: see Deut. 24:1–4. By 'put away' is meant 'divorce'. Jewish practice was that the man initiates divorce by issuing his wife with a 'bill of divorcement'.

32 *saving for the cause of fornication*: this 'exception clause' (also in 19:9) which opens up the legitimacy of divorce in some limited circumstances (i.e. due to unchastity in the wife) is not present in the parallel passages in Mark 10:11, and Luke 16:18, where divorce is apparently ruled out completely (though it is possible that adultery by the wife would have been assumed to be included as (the only) reason for divorce).

33 *Thou shalt not . . . thine oaths*: see Exod. 20:7; Lev. 19:12; Num. 30:2–15; Deut. 23:21.

34 *swear not at all*: according to Josephus (*War*, pp. 134–5), the Essenes (a Jewish sect at the time of Jesus notable for their austerity of life) also rejected the taking of oaths and vows.

35 *earth . . . King*: quoted from Isa. 66:1; Ps. 48:2.

38 *An eye . . . a tooth*: see Exod. 21:24; Lev. 24:20; Deut. 19:21. It should be noted that the law of retaliation (*lex talionis*) was designed to limit the taking of excessive revenge, laying down that punishment be proportionate to the injury. By the time of Jesus, financial compensation for injury had replaced literal retaliation.

39 *smite thee on thy right cheek*: cf. Lam. 3:30. Reference to the 'right' cheek may suggest that the blow was a back-handed one, which would have been regarded as especially insulting.

40 *coat . . . cloak*: a 'coat' was a long tunic worn next to the skin; a 'cloak' was an outer garment, or robe. The Law stipulated that a creditor who had taken his debtor's cloak as a pledge had to return it to him at nightfall, so that he would have something to sleep in (Exod. 22:26–7; Deut. 24:12–13).

41 *compel thee to go a mile*: this may refer to the right of Roman soldiers to force civilians to carry goods. (Cf. 27:32, where Simon of Cyrene is 'compelled' to carry Jesus's cross.)

42 *Give to him . . . not thou away*: cf. Deut. 15:7–8.

43 *Thou shalt . . . thine enemy*: the command to 'love thy neighbour' is quoted from Lev. 19:18. The words 'and hate thine enemy' are not found in the

Hebrew Bible, though the idea of hating the wicked and the enemies of God is present; see Ps. 139:19–22, 'I hate them with perfect hatred: I count them mine enemies'.

46 *publicans*: i.e. tax collectors. The English word is derived from the Latin *publicani*, but these were in fact the higher-up revenue officials who farmed out the collection of taxes. The people described as 'publicans' in the AV were the minor officials who actually collected the taxes. They were much disliked, not only because often dishonest, but because they served the Roman authorities.

48 *perfect*: i.e. perfect in love (not perfect in the sense of sinless). There may be an echo of Deut. 18:13, 'Thou shalt be perfect with the LORD thy God'.

CHAPTER 6

1 *do not your alms*: i.e. 'do not carry out your almsgiving'. Alms (charitable gifts) were given to the poor at synagogues on the Sabbath.

5 *hypocrites*: part of the religious observance expected of Jewish males was that they pray morning and evening, facing in the direction of Jerusalem, either bowing down or, as here, standing. Hypocrisy is a charge often levelled against the Pharisees in the Gospels.

9–13 *Our Father . . . Amen*: see Isa. 63:16, 64:8, for references to God as 'our father'. A shorter version of the Lord's Prayer is given in Luke 11:2–4.

12 *debts*: here used as a metaphor for 'sins' (cf. Luke 11:4).

13 *lead us not into temptation*: 'do not bring us to the time of trial' (NRSV). Some scholars interpret this as referring to an apocalyptic 'time of trial', or persecution, before God's kingdom would be established. The prayer is asking for this time to be shortened.

for thine . . . Amen: these words, the doxology, do not appear in all the ancient texts, and are almost certainly a later scribal addition. (They are not included in Luke.) However, some such formula would have been used to end a prayer, and it may have been expected that these or similar words would be added by anyone using this prayer.

16 *fast*: fasting was obligatory for Jews on certain days, most particularly the Day of Atonement (Yom Kippur), but could also be adopted more generally as a mark of piety.

disfigure their faces: i.e. cover their heads with ashes.

23 *if thine eye be evil*: i.e. if you are envious (if you have an 'evil eye'). See also 20:15.

24 *mammon*: an Aramaic word, meaning 'wealth', 'possessions'; here personified as an evil master.

26 *much better than*: 'of more value than' (NRSV).

29 *Solomon in all his glory*: for Solomon's splendour, see 1 Kings 10.

34 *Take . . . no thought*: 'do not worry' (NRSV).

CHAPTER 7

6   *that which is holy*: i.e. meat from sacrificial animals.

   rend you: i.e. (of the dogs) attack you, tear you to pieces.

12   *all things whatsoever . . . so to them*: this saying (usually shortened to 'do as you would be done by') has become known as the 'Golden Rule'. Versions of it are found in Jewish, Greek, and Roman writings.

   the Law and the Prophets: see note to 5:17.

23   *depart . . . iniquity*: quoting Ps. 6:8.

CHAPTER 8

2   *Leper . . . clean*: leprosy is a skin disease which eats away the tissues of the limbs and face, leading to disfigurement and the loss of fingers and toes. Under the Law, lepers were made to live away from the community and they had to announce their presence by calling out 'Unclean, unclean'. See Lev. 13:1–45; Num. 5:1–4.

4   *gift that Moses commanded*: see Lev. 14:2–32, where the sacrifices to be offered by anyone cured of leprosy are set out.

11   *from the east and west*: i.e. from outside Israelite territories, thus including Gentiles.

   sit down . . . kingdom of heaven: the meaning seems to be that Gentiles will take part in the messianic banquet at the end of the world (for references to which, see e.g. Isa. 25:6–8; Rev. 19:9).

12   *the children of the kingdom*: i.e. the Jews, or perhaps more specifically the Pharisees (see 23:29–33).

   weeping and gnashing of teeth: a favourite phrase in Matthew to describe the torments of the damned. It occurs once in Luke (13:28).

17   *Himself took . . . our sicknesses*: see Isa. 53:4.

18   *the other side*: i.e. to the eastern side of the Sea of Galilee.

19   *Master*: i.e. 'teacher' (Rabbi). In this Gospel the term is usually only given to Jesus by his enemies.

20   *Son of Man*: this is the most frequent self-designation by Jesus in the Gospels, and its meaning has been much debated. As used in the earlier parts of the Hebrew Bible, the phrase often referred simply to humankind (see e.g. Num. 23:19; Ps. 8:4), but it could also refer to an individual, as when Ezekiel is addressed by God as 'Son of Man' (e.g. 2:1). Later, especially in Daniel (7:13–14), it took on a more apocalyptic significance, referring to a transcendent heavenly being, one who would be revealed by God at the end of time as redeemer and judge. It seems to be applied by Jesus to himself in a number of different ways. In the present instance it seems simply to refer to himself as a person (as also in 9:6, 11:19, 12:8, etc.). In other places in the Gospels (e.g. Mark 10:45) it seems to be associated with the 'suffering servant' figure of Isaiah 53, and in this sense figures prominently in predictions of Jesus's Passion

(see e.g. Matt. 20:28, Mark 8:31). Elsewhere it seems to draw on some of the apocalyptic overtones of Daniel (see e.g. Matt. 16:27–8, 19:28, 24:30, 25:31; Luke 12:8–10, 18:8). Some scholars have argued that Jesus was giving the term a new significance, and that the term emphasized his humility, by contrast with titles such as 'Son of God', or 'Son of David'.

22 *let the dead bury their dead*: taken literally, this would have been regarded by Jews as a shocking challenge to the religious duty of burying the dead. The meaning may be 'let the [spiritually] dead' look after burials; his disciples must follow Jesus now, and nothing can be more important than discipleship.

28 *Gergesenes*: 'Gadarenes' (NRSV, following a variant manuscript reading). See also Mark 5:1 and Luke 8:26, where the place is given as the 'country of the Gadarenes', i.e. near Gadara.

tombs: these were believed to be one of the habitations of demons. In Palestine tombs were often vaults cut into cliffs.

33 *the city*: i.e. of Gadara.

CHAPTER 9

1 *his own city*: i.e. Capernaum (not Nazareth; see 4:13).

3 *blasphemeth*: i.e. dishonours the name of God.

9 *receipt of custom*: the receiving-place for taxes.

13 *I will . . . not sacrifice*: quoted from Hos. 6:6.

14 *John*: i.e. John the Baptist.

15 *children of the bride-chamber*: by 'children' here is meant the young men who attended the bridegroom, and by 'bride-chamber' the room in which the wedding is to be held.

16 *taketh from*: i.e. pulls away from (presumably once the new material shrinks).

17 *bottles*: i.e. wineskins. Old ones would become brittle, and would burst under the pressure of the fermentation of fresh grape juice. (The point of the parable is that the 'new' gospel cannot be contained within the 'old' Law.)

18 *ruler*: in Mark (5:22) this is given as 'one of the rulers of the synagogue', i.e. an official of the synagogue.

20 *an issue of blood*: a continuous haemorrhage, possibly menstrual. This would have made the woman ritually unclean under the Law, and anything she touched would also be unclean (see Lev. 15:19–30).

hem: i.e. the fringes, or tassels, attached by a blue cord, which were worn on the four corners of a Jewish man's outer garment, as a reminder to keep the commandments (see Num. 15:38–40).

23 *minstrels*: i.e. the flute players who were part of Jewish funeral ceremonies, accompanying the dirges sung by professional mourners.

27 *Son of David*: a title frequently given to Jesus in Matthew (see 1:1, 12:23, etc.). It referred back to the messianic expectation of a Son of David in the Hebrew Bible (see e.g. 2 Sam. 7:12–13; Ps. 89).

34 *the prince of the devils*: i.e. Satan, also called Beelzebub (or Baal-zebub), meaning, in Hebrew, 'Lord of the Flies', a derogatory reference to Baal, the most important of the Canaanite gods (see 2 Kings 1:2).

36 *as sheep having no shepherd*: often said of Israel in the Hebrew Bible (see e.g. Num. 27:17; 1 Kings 22:17; Ezek. 34:8; Zech. 10:2).

CHAPTER 10

1 *twelve*: this was also the number of the tribes of Israel, and thus symbolizes the idea that the disciples are to be the leaders of the new Israel.

2 *apostles*: a term (literally meaning 'those who are sent') used only once in Matthew and in Mark, but more frequently in Luke.

5 *the way of the Gentiles*: i.e. Gentile territory.

Samaritans: see Introduction, p. xxx.

12 *salute it*: i.e. utter the greeting 'Peace be to this house'.

17 *councils*: local Jewish courts, attached to synagogues.

18 *governors and kings*: the Romans ruled Palestine through governors such as Pontius Pilate (see 27:2) and titular kings (the Herods).

22 *the end*: i.e. the end of the age before Jesus would return.

25 *Beelzebub*: see note to 9:34, above.

28 *him*: i.e. God.

29 *two sparrows*: sparrows were the cheapest living things sold for food.

35–6 *For I am come . . . own household*: alluding to Mic. 7:6, a passage understood by Jews as prophesying the woes that would be experienced before the coming of the messianic age.

38 *cross*: the wooden structure used by the Romans for crucifixion, here used figuratively.

42 *little ones*: i.e. the disciples.

CHAPTER 11

2 *John*: i.e. John the Baptist (his arrest is mentioned in 4:12; see also 14:3–12).

3 *he that should come*: i.e. the Messiah.

5 *The blind . . . preached to them*: these words recall messianic passages in Isaiah; see Isa. 29:18–19, 35:5–6, 61:1.

6 *not be offended in me*: 'takes no offence at me' (NRSV).

8 *are in kings' houses*: i.e. are courtiers, live in royal palaces.

9 *more than a prophet*: in the sense that John is the prophet in whom prophecy begins to be fulfilled (see next verse).

10 *it is written*: in Mal. 3:1 (of Elijah) and Exod. 23:20 (of Moses); cf. Isa. 40:3, quoted in 3:3.

13 *the Prophets and the Law*: see note to 5:17.

14 *Elias*: i.e. Elijah. See Mal. 4:5, and note to 3:4.

16 *this generation*: a phrase used frequently in the Gospels, usually to indicate that contemporary Jews are faithless and corrupt.

19 *wisdom is justified of her children*: perhaps meaning 'wisdom [i.e. God] will be proved righteous [or be vindicated] through the ministry of John and Jesus'.

21 *sackcloth and ashes*: sackcloth was a coarsely woven fabric, sometimes made from camels' hair, worn as a loincloth next to the skin. To sit in ashes and sprinkle ashes over one's head while wearing sackcloth was a sign of repentance, or of lamentation.

23 *exalted . . . hell*: echoing Isa. 14:13–15. The Greek word translated here as 'hell' is more properly translated by 'Hades' (as in NRSV), which (like the Hebrew word Sheol) referred to the dwelling-place of souls after death, the underworld.

25 *answered, and said*: an archaic construction, of which the AV provides the last examples recorded in *OED*.

29 *ye shall find rest unto your souls*: cf. Jer. 6:16.

CHAPTER 12

2 *not lawful . . . upon the Sabbath day*: see Exod. 20:8–11.

3 *what David did*: see 1 Sam. 21:1–6.

4 *shewbread*: the Hebrew term means 'Bread of the Presence', the name given to the twelve consecrated loaves displayed in the Temple sanctuary every Sabbath (see Lev. 24:5–9).

5 *priests . . . are blameless*: the priests have to perform certain duties even on the Sabbath, but because they are commanded to do so, they are blameless.

6 *one*: i.e. Jesus himself (see v. 8).

7 *I will . . . not sacrifice*: quoting Hos. 6:6 (also quoted at 9:13, above).

9 *their*: i.e. the Pharisees'.

18–21 *Behold . . . Gentiles trust*: quoting (freely) Isa. 42:1–4.

27 *your children*: i.e. Jewish exorcists.

29 *the strong man*: i.e. Satan, whose 'goods' are those possessed by devils, but who is 'bound' by Jesus and his house 'spoiled', or plundered.

31 *blasphemy against the Holy Ghost*: i.e. the Pharisees' attribution to Satan of Jesus's power (v. 24).

32 *speaketh a word . . . the world to come*: the meaning seems to be that to speak against Jesus as man may be forgiven, but to speak against the work of God by calling it the work of Satan will not be forgiven. (This has become known as the 'unpardonable sin'.)

39 *adulterous*: here used in a metaphorical sense of unfaithfulness to God (and often used as such in the Hebrew Bible; see e.g. Jer. 3:8; Hos. 2:2–10).

40 *Jonas* [Jonah] . . . *of the earth*: see Jon. 1:17. Jesus is here drawing a comparison between Jonah's three days and nights in the whale and his own stay in the tomb before his resurrection.

41 *Nineveh . . . preaching of Jonas* [Jonah]: see Jon. 3:5.

42 *queen of the south*: i.e. the Queen of Sheba. The story of her visit to Solomon is recounted in 1 Kings 10:1–10. She will condemn the present generation because they have not come to (i.e. come to believe in) Jesus, a 'greater than Solomon'.

43 *unclean spirit*: a demon. Demons were believed to inhabit deserts.

44 *he*: i.e. the demon, who returns to his 'house', i.e. the man who was possessed. (The house is 'empty' because no good spirit has come in to take the place of the evil one.)

CHAPTER 13

1 *the sea side*: i.e. the Sea of Galilee.

3 *parables*: a term (from the Greek *parabolē*) specifically used to designate some thirty different sayings or stories of Jesus in the Gospels, though there are many other examples in which the term is not explicitly used. See Introduction, pp. xxix–xxx.

12 *whosoever hath*: i.e. whoever has knowledge of the kingdom of heaven (or God). The point of this paradoxical saying is perhaps to be understood as residing in its first part, with its stress on the need for receptivity to the truth. See also 25:29; Mark 4:25; Luke 8:18.

14–15 *By hearing . . . heal them*: quoted from Isa. 6:9–10. This passage from Isaiah was understood by early Christians as referring to the rejection of the Messiah by the Jews.

19 *the wicked one*: Satan, or the devil.

21 *dureth for a while*: 'endures only for a while' (NRSV).

25 *tares*: probably darnel, a species of vetch that grows among corn and whose kernels have to be laboriously separated from those of the corn after harvesting, because if ground into the meal they cause sickness.

27 *servants*: the Greek word here and elsewhere in the Gospels has the stronger meaning of 'bondmen' or 'slaves' (which is how it is usually rendered in modern translations).

32 *the least . . . greatest among herbs*: there is some exaggeration here, to make the point that great things come from small beginnings. The mustard seed was proverbially tiny; a mustard plant would grow to about 8 or 10 feet.

33 *hid in*: 'mixed in with' (NRSV). Three measures of meal was a large amount, enough for a hundred loaves.

35 *I will open . . . the world*: quoted from Ps. 78:2. This Psalm is attributed to Asaph, described as 'the seer' in 2 Chron. 29:30.

39 *end of the world*: i.e. at the Day of Judgement (see also v. 49, 24:3, 28:20). Cf. Joel 3:13.

43 *righteous shine forth as the sun*: Cf. Dan. 12:3.

47 *of every kind*: i.e. fish of every kind, perhaps meaning clean and unclean, or edible and inedible, as specified in Lev. 11:9–12.

52 *every scribe*: i.e. every disciple (cf. 23:34).

instructed . . . new and old: the meaning seems to be that trained disciples will teach about the *old* Law and its *new* fulfilment in the teachings of Jesus.

54 *his own country*: in Luke 4:16 this is specified as Nazareth. Jesus's rejection in his own town is a pivotal event in all the Gospels (see Mark 6:1–6; Luke 4:16–30; John 4:44).

55 *carpenter's son*: meant as an insult.

57 *were offended in him*: 'took offence at him' (NRSV).

A prophet . . . in his own house: a well-known proverb. See also Luke 4:24; John 4:44.

CHAPTER 14

1 *Herod the Tetrarch*: i.e. Herod Antipas.

4 *not lawful for thee to have her*: marriage between a man and his brother's wife was not permitted under Mosaic Law (see Lev. 18:16, 20:21).

5 *feared the multitude*: according to Josephus (*Ant.*, 18:116–19), Herod ordered John's execution because he feared he might 'raise a rebellion' against him.

6 *the daughter*: Salome (see Josephus *Ant.*, 18:136).

15 *the time is now past*: 'the hour is now late' (NRSV).

19 *blessed*: i.e. blessed God, offering his thanks for the food.

20 *twelve baskets full*: cf. the miraculous feeding of 100 men by the prophet Elisha, 2 Kings 4:42–4.

22 *the other side*: i.e. to Bethsaida, on the other side of Galilee (see Mark 6:45).

25 *the fourth watch of the night*: i.e. between 3 and 6 a.m. (The Romans divided the time between 6 p.m. and 6 a.m. into four equal periods called watches.)

36 *hem of his garment*: see note to 9:20.

CHAPTER 15

2 *the tradition of the elders*: i.e. the oral Law, which contained regulations (such as the requirement to wash hands before eating) not included in the written Law (Torah). See Introduction, p. xx.

4 *Honour . . . die the death*: see Exod. 20:12, 21:17; Deut. 5:16; Lev. 20:9; cf. Prov. 20:20.

5–6 *It is a gift . . . shall be free*: Jesus is accusing the Pharisees of giving precedence to a 'Corban' vow (a vow which required the person taking it to give some possession to the Temple rather than to his parents, who might be thought to have a stronger right to it), and thus giving their own tradition more importance than the commandments of the written Law. (See also Mark 7:11 and note.)

7 *Esaias*: the quotation is from Isa. 29:13.

11 *into the mouth defileth*: Jesus now returns to the question asked in v. 2, declaring that it is not what is eaten that defiles, but what goes out from the mouth (evil words and actions, as he explains in v. 19).

19 *out of the heart proceed evil thoughts*: cf. Gen. 6:5, 8:21.

22 *woman of Canaan*: here meaning perhaps simply a Gentile woman. See Mark 7:26.

   vexed with a devil: 'tormented by a demon' (NRSV).

24 *lost sheep of . . . Israel*: cf. 10:6.

26 *children's . . . dogs*: the 'children' here are the Jews; 'dogs' was an insulting term for Gentiles (though it seems unlikely that Jesus meant it in this harsh sense, and was merely meaning that there must be *some* priorities).

27 *Truth*: i.e. 'yes, this is true'.

30 *cast them down*: 'put them' (NRSV).

32–8 *Then Jesus . . . women and children*: it is unclear whether this is a reiteration of the story (in 14:13–21) of the Feeding of the Five Thousand, or whether they are separate events (as Jesus seems to imply in 16:9–10). To explain the inclusion of two accounts, commentators have suggested that the Feeding of the Five Thousand was intended to symbolize the giving of the Bread of Life to the Jews (the twelve baskets representing the twelve tribes of Israel), and the Feeding of the Four Thousand the giving the Bread of Life to the Gentiles (the seven baskets representing the seventy nations into which the Gentile world was traditionally divided, as in Gen. 10).

CHAPTER 16

1 *Sadducees*: it seems strange that Sadducees would be encountered in Galilee, far from Jerusalem, because they were mainly associated with the Temple. They are not mentioned in Mark 8:11, the parallel verse.

4 *Jonas*: i.e. Jonah. See 12:38–41 (which makes it clear that by the 'sign' of Jonah, Jesus means his own resurrection).

5 *other side*: the eastern side of the Sea of Galilee.

6 *leaven*: under Jewish Law, sacrifices containing leaven (i.e. yeast, or sour and fermenting dough) were forbidden (see e.g. Exod. 23:18; Lev. 2:11), and leaven was generally regarded as representing hidden corruption or evil, an idea carried over into early Christianity (see e.g. 1 Cor. 5:8). Here it represents the teaching of the Pharisees and the Sadducees (as Jesus has to explain, v. 12).

14 *Some say . . . John the Baptist*: Herod Antipas has said this; see 14:2.

   Elias: i.e. Elijah. John the Baptist was believed to be Elijah returned from heaven; see 11:14.

17 *Simon bar Jona*: i.e. 'Simon son of Jonah' (NRSV), 'bar' being the Aramaic form of the Hebrew 'ben'.

   flesh and blood: i.e. mere men, as opposed to God.

18 *Peter, and upon this rock*: a play on words in both Greek and Aramaic: *Petros* (Peter), *petra* (rock), *Cephas* (or *kepha*) for both in Aramaic. See John 1:42.

   church: Matthew is the only Gospel writer to use the word 'church', and it is only used twice by Jesus (see 18:17). The Greek word translated thus meant an 'assembly'.

   hell: i.e. Hades (see note to 11:23, above).

19 *keys*: symbolizing authority (see Isa. 22:22).

   bind . . . loose: used here as legal terms, meaning to 'forbid' and 'allow', or 'condemn' and 'acquit'. The same authority is given elsewhere to all twelve apostles; see 18:18; John 20:23.

22 *took him*: 'took him aside' (NRSV).

23 *Get thee . . . Satan*: the same expression is used at the end of the temptation of Jesus by Satan (4:10).

24 *come after me*: i.e. 'become my follower'.

26 *lose his own soul*: i.e. forfeit his life.

27 *reward . . . works*: cf. Ps. 62:12.

28 *shall not taste of death*: one of several predictions that the coming of the Son of Man would happen within the lifetime of that generation (see 10:23, 24:34).

CHAPTER 17

1 *six days*: the exact note of time is unusual in the Gospels, and may be an allusion to the 'six days' of Exod. 24:16.

   an high mountain: mountains were the traditional settings for theophanies and supernatural revelations in the Hebrew Bible (see e.g. Exod. 24 and 34; 1 Kings 19:8–12).

2 *transfigured*: i.e. changed or transformed into a being with a divine appearance. (The Greek word means, literally, metamorphosed.)

   face did shine as the sun: when Moses descended from Sinai with the tablets of the Law, 'the skin of his face shone' (Exod. 34:29). Cf. 13:43, and Rev. 1:16.

   raiment . . . the light: cf. 28:3; Dan. 7:9; Rev. 3:4–5.

3 *Moses and Elias*: they perhaps represent the Law and the Prophets, whose teachings Jesus said he had come to fulfil (see 5:17).

4 *tabernacles*: i.e. 'dwellings' or 'tents', or 'booths' (as in Lev. 23:34–44). Peter's suggestion may mean that he wishes to prolong their vision.

5 *bright cloud*: representing the presence of God (see Exod. 24:15–16, 40:34–5).

This is . . . well pleased: see note to 3:17.

10 *Elias must first come*: see Mal. 4:5–6, where it is prophesied that Elijah would be sent before the Messiah. Jesus goes on to explain that John the Baptist is thus Elijah.

12 *done unto . . . they listed*: i.e. they have killed John the Baptist (14:1–12), a fate the Messiah (Jesus) will also suffer.

15 *he is lunatic*: this is a literal rendering of the Greek (also used by Matthew at 4:24). The boy's symptoms are described more fully in Mark 9:18–22, from which it is clear that he is suffering from epilepsy.

17 *O faithless . . . generation*: similar words are used by Moses of the Israelites; see Deut. 32:5.

20 *this mountain . . . shall remove*: a proverbial Jewish saying (also used by Paul, 1 Cor. 13:2).

23 *exceeding sorry*: 'greatly distressed' (NRSV).

24 *received tribute money*: i.e. collected Temple tax. Under Jewish Law (Exod. 30:11–16), each adult Jewish male was required to pay half a shekel (Greek *didrachma*) each year to support the Temple in Jerusalem.

27 *a piece of money*: the Greek word specifies a stater, a coin worth two didrachmas.

CHAPTER 18

10 *their angels*: i.e. their guardian angels, who would represent them in heaven. This was a Jewish belief; see e.g. Gen. 48:16, and Tobit (Apocrypha) 5:21.

15 *thou has gained thy brother*: i.e. regained him and restored him to the family or church. Lying behind this is a passage in Lev. 19:17–18, quoted by Matthew in 5:43, and again in 19:19 and 22:39.

16 *two or three witnesses*: a requirement of the Law; see Deut. 19:15.

17 *church*: see note to 16:18.

let him be . . . a publican: 'let such a one be to you as a Gentile and a tax collector' (NRSV).

22 *seven . . . seventy times seven*: cf. Gen. 4:24, where these numbers are used of vengeance. Seven is a number suggesting completeness (see e.g. Lev. 26:18); seventy times seven suggests an unlimited amount.

23 *take accompt of his servants*: 'settle accounts with his slaves' (NRSV).

24 *ten thousand talents*: an unimaginably large sum, a talent being the largest unit of currency, of which one would be worth 6,000 denarii, or more than fifteen years' wages for a labourer.

28 *an hundred pence*: a relatively small sum, a 'penny', or denarius, being the equivalent of a day's wages for a labourer.

31 *very sorry*: see note to 17:23.

34 *to the tormentors*: 'to be tortured' (NRSV).

pay all that was due: an impossibility, given the vastness of the sum, and so his imprisonment would be for ever.

CHAPTER 19

1 *the coasts of Judea, beyond Jordan*: i.e. the district called Perea.

3 *for every cause*: 'for any cause' (NRSV). The question of permissible grounds for divorce was disputed because although permitted by the Law (Deut. 24:1), the grounds are not specified. (See also notes to 5:31–2.)

4 *male and female*: quoting from Gen. 1:27.

5 *For this cause . . . one flesh*: quoting from Gen. 2:24.

7 *Moses . . . her away*: Deut. 24:1–4 (and see note to 5:31, above).

9 *except it be for fornication*: see note to 5:32.

10 *not good to marry*: marriage and procreation was regarded by Jews as an obligation (see Gen. 1:28).

12 *eunuchs*: i.e. castrated males, who were excluded from the community in ancient Israel (see Deut. 23:1). Jesus is saying that some males are born impotent; others are made impotent by castration; and others practise celibacy voluntarily.

13 *put his hands on them*: laying on of hands was a traditional part of giving a blessing (see e.g. Gen. 48:13–20).

18–19 *Thou shalt . . . as thy self*: Jesus cites here five of the Ten Commandments (see Exod. 20:12–16; Deut. 5:16–20) and adds another taken from Lev. 19:18.

28 *in the regeneration*: 'at the renewal of all things' (NRSV), following the final judgement, when God's will will be done on earth.

twelve thrones . . . of Israel: see note to 10:1.

CHAPTER 20

1 *kingdom of heaven is like . . . an householder*: this formulaic opening to the parable is not to be taken as meaning that the kingdom is like a householder (or landowner); rather it is like the reckoning the householder makes with his labourers at the end of the day, i.e. that 'the last shall be first' (v. 16).

early: i.e. about 6 a.m.

2 *penny*: the AV translation for the Roman denarius, a coin roughly equivalent in value to the Greek drachma. It represented an average daily wage for a labourer.

the third hour: i.e. about 9 a.m.

market place: day-labourers would gather here hoping to be hired.

5 *the sixth and ninth hour*: i.e. about noon, and about 3 p.m.

6 *the eleventh hour*: i.e. about 5 p.m.

8 *when even was come*: according to Jewish Law, day-labourers had to be paid before sunset on the same day (see Lev. 19:13; Deut. 24:15).

15 *Is thine eye evil*: i.e. are you envious. (Having an 'evil eye' was a metaphor for being envious. See 6:23; Mark 7:22.)

19 *Gentiles*: here referring to the Romans, who had authority to execute criminals.

20 *mother of Zebedee's children*: i.e. Salome, the mother of the disciples James and John.

21 *in thy kingdom*: i.e. when you rule as King. Seats at the right hand and the left were the chief positions of honour and power (see 22:44).

22 *the cup*: in the Hebrew Bible, 'cup' is often used as a metaphor for whatever destiny is allotted by God, whether suffering (as in Isa. 51:17; Lam. 4:21), or blessing (as in Pss. 11:6, 16:5, 23:5). See also Matt. 26:39.

23 *Ye shall . . . baptized with*: according to an account in Acts 12:2, James was beheaded by Herod Agrippa I in 44 CE. There was a legend that John was also martyred, but the evidence for this is very slight.

28 *give his life . . . for many*: alluding to Isa. 53:12. 'Many' here means 'all' (there is no word for 'all' in the plural in either Hebrew or Aramaic, and 'many' is used instead). Cf. 26:28.

30 *two blind men*: in Mark's account, there is only one blind man, named Bartimaeus (Mark 10:46).

CHAPTER 21

5 *Tell ye . . . the foal of an ass*: two prophecies are here combined, from Isa. 62:11 and Zech. 9:9. In speaking of two animals, the ass and the colt, the author of Matthew has taken the poetic parallelism (repetition of the same idea in different words) in Zechariah to refer to separate animals. (See Mark 11:2–8, where only the colt is mentioned.)

8 *spread . . . in the way*: these acts of homage recall descriptions of the triumphal entry of a king or general; see 1 Kings 1:32–40; 2 Kings 9:12–13; cf. also Josephus *War*, p. 380. For the spreading of branches as part of the Festival of Booths, and at the Feast of the Tabernacles, see Lev. 23:39–43; 1 Maccabees (Apocrypha) 13:51; 2 Maccabees (Apocrypha) 10:7.

9 *blessed . . . Lord*: from Ps. 118:26. This was one of the Hallel psalms (Pss 113–18) which were chanted at the great Jewish festivals.

the highest: 'the highest heaven' (NRSV).

12 *the Temple of God*: i.e. the Temple at Jerusalem, the centre of Jewish worship, and the only place where sacrifices could be offered.

money changers . . . doves: money changers operated within the large open area of the Temple known as the 'Court of Gentiles', offering a service to pilgrims who needed the proper coins to use for the Temple tax (for which, see note to 17:24, above). There were complaints about profiteering in the fees charged for this service. Doves were bought as sacrifices by the poor, who could not afford a lamb (see Lev. 5:7, 12:8, etc.)

13 *It is written*: in Isa. 56:7 and Jer. 7:11.

16 *have ye never read*: in Ps. 8:2.

28 *A certain man*: the first of three allegorical parables (the others are vv. 33–44, 22:2–14) whose theme is the rejection of Jesus by the religious leaders of the Jews.

33 *planted . . . tower*: a quotation from Isa. 5:1–2. By a 'tower' is meant a watchtower.

41 *They*: i.e. the chief priests and Pharisees (see vv. 23, 45).

42 *Did ye never read*: in Ps. 118:22–3. (The same text is applied to Jews in Acts 4:11 and 1 Pet. 2:7.) By the 'head of the corner' is meant the keystone, or cornerstone, the most important stone in the building. The 'stone' here is to be understood as Jesus, and the 'builders' as the Jewish religious leaders.

43 *you*: i.e. the Jewish leaders, who have rejected the 'stone'.

44 *And whosoever . . . to powder*: this verse is not found in some ancient manuscripts. It may be alluding to Isa. 8:14–15.

46 *took him for*: 'regarded him as' (NRSV).

CHAPTER 22

3 *they would not come*: to refuse a wedding invitation was regarded as an unpardonable insult.

7 *burnt up their city*: usually taken as referring (allegorically) to the destruction of Jerusalem by the Romans in 70 CE.

11 *wedding garment*: guests were expected to wear festive clothes at weddings.

12 *Friend*: intended sarcastically. (The word is always used of people who are in the wrong in this Gospel.)

16 *the Herodians*: supporters of Herod the Great and his successors.

17 *give tribute unto*: 'pay taxes to' (NRSV). The trap set for Jesus is that if he approves of the payment of the census (or poll) tax to the Romans, he would be seen as a collaborator by Jewish Zealots who were violently opposed to payment (see Josephus *War*, pp. 133, 393; *Ant.*, 18:1–10, 23–5); if he disapproves, he lays himself open to a charge of treason against Rome. (Discontent over tax did in fact lead to a rising in 6 CE, and a more serious revolt in 66 CE.)

19 *penny*: i.e. a silver denarius, which at this time would have borne the head of the emperor Tiberius (14–37 CE), and the inscription 'T[iberius] Caesar Divi Aug[usti] F[ilius] Augustus' (Tiberius Caesar, son of the divine Augustus, Augustus).

20 *image*: the making of images was forbidden to Jews; see Exod. 20:4; Deut. 5:8.

23 *Sadducees . . . no resurrection*: Sadducees did not believe in resurrection because it was not mentioned in the Torah (see Josephus *Ant.*, 18:16). Belief in resurrection was a late development in Judaism; among the (few) references in the Hebrew Bible, see Job 19:25–7; Isa. 26:19; Dan. 12:2; 2 Maccabees (Apocrypha) 7:9, 14, 23.

24 *Moses said*: the reference is to Deut. 25:5–10, which set out the rules under which the brother of a deceased man was required to marry the widow. The purpose was to preserve a deceased male's family name and line.

28 *in the resurrection*: i.e. if there be a resurrection.

30 *marry . . . marriage*: cf. St Paul's 'spiritual' account of the resurrection, 1 Cor. 15:35–54.

31–2 *that which was spoken . . . of Jacob*: quoted from Exod. 3:6.

35 *a lawyer*: i.e. a scholar of the Law as given to Moses (the Torah).

37–9 *Thou shalt . . . as thyself*: Jesus quotes from Deut. 6:5 and Lev. 19:18. The verses from Deuteronomy 6:4–9 are known as the 'Shema' (from the first word, 'Hear', in Hebrew). The Shema forms the central declaration of Jewish faith in one God, and is recited at every Jewish service, and by every observant Jew, morning and night.

42 *The Son of David*: the belief that the Messiah ('Christ') would be the son of David is based on passages in the Hebrew Bible including Isa. 9:7, 11:1, etc.

43 *in Spirit*: 'by the Spirit' (NRSV). David, traditionally believed to be the author of the Psalms, was regarded as having been inspired by God (see Acts 2:30–1, 4:25).

44 *The Lord . . . thy footstool*: quoted from Ps. 110:1.

45 *call him Lord . . . his son*: a father would not call his son 'Lord'.

CHAPTER 23

2 *sit in Moses' seat*: the presidential chair in ancient synagogues was known as the 'seat of Moses'. Here, however, the phrase is probably being used metaphorically, meaning 'have the authority to teach the Law of Moses'.

4 *heavy burdens*: i.e. the regulations of the Mosaic Law.

   they themselves . . . their fingers: 'they themselves are unwilling to lift a finger to move them' (NRSV), i.e. to help those who have broken the laws.

5 *phylacteries*: the small leather boxes containing scriptural texts on parchment that were worn tied to the forehead and the left arm by Jewish males while at prayer (in obedience to Deut. 6:6–8, 11:18).

   borders of their garments: see note to 9.20.

7 *Rabbi*: i.e. master, teacher. This was the title commonly given to a religious teacher and scholar of the Torah. The literal meaning of the Hebrew word is 'my great one'.

8 *one . . . brethren*: 'you have one teacher, and you are all students' (NRSV).

13 *woe unto you*: the first of a sequence of 'woes' pronounced against the scribes and Pharisees as representing empty religious observances.

shut up the kingdom of heaven against men: presumably by opposing the teachings of Jesus.

14 *Woe . . . damnation*: this verse is not included in many ancient manuscripts, and is omitted in NRSV. It may be an interpolation from Mark 12:40.

16 *swear by the Temple . . . is a debtor*: the reference here is to rabbinic teaching about oaths, which held that oaths 'by the Temple' were not binding ('it is nothing') but oaths 'by the gold of the Temple' were binding ('he is a debtor'). Since 'the Temple' is greater than 'the gold of the Temple', Jesus regards it as absurd to treat the lesser oath as binding. The same is true of the following example of the altar, and the sacrifice on the altar. (See 5:34–6 for Jesus's rejection of oaths.)

21 *him that dwelleth therein*: i.e. God.

23 *pay tithe of mint, and anise, and cummin*: the 'tithe' was the tenth of agricultural produce that was given to support the Temple (see Lev. 27:30–3; Deut. 14:22–9). Mint, anise (dill), and cumin were among the smallest plants grown.

weightier matters of the Law: see Mic. 6:8: 'what doth the LORD require of thee, but to do justly, and to love mercy, and to walk humbly with thy God?'

24 *gnat . . . camel*: a gnat was an 'unclean' insect (see Lev. 11:20–3), and so Jews would strain their wine before drinking it to filter out any insects such as gnats that may have fallen in. A camel was also 'unclean' (see Lev. 11:4), and was used proverbially as an example of a large animal (as also by Jesus in 19:24).

25 *ye make clean the outside of the cup*: the reference is to ceremonial washing (see Mark 7:3–4), here symbolizing the externality of the religious attitudes of the Pharisees.

extortion and excess: 'greed and self-indulgence' (NRSV).

27 *whited sepulchres*: 'whitewashed tombs' (NRSV). Tombs were regarded as unclean, because containing dead bodies, and were not to be touched (see Lev. 21:11; Num. 5:2, 19:11–20). They were whitened before Passover so that pilgrims would not accidentally touch one and thus become ritually unclean.

30 *the blood of the prophets*: see 1 Kings 19:14; 2 Chron. 24:20–2. See also Acts 7:52; 1 Thess. 2:14–15.

32 *Fill ye up . . . your fathers*: probably ironical, meaning 'Be like your fathers; complete their quota of evil'.

35 *righteous Abel*: see Gen. 4:8–10.

Zacharias, son of Barachias: the martyred Zechariah referred to here is not, in fact, the son of Barachiah (for whom see Zech. 1:1), but the son of Jehoiada; see 2 Chron. 24:20.

37 *stonest them which are sent unto thee*: cf. 2 Chron. 24:21.

would I have gathered . . . chickens under her wings: cf. 2 Esdras (Apocrypha) 1:30.

38 *your house*: i.e. the whole city of Jerusalem.

39 *Blessed is . . . the Lord*: quoted from Ps. 118:26.

CHAPTER 24

1 *buildings of the temple*: the Temple at Jerusalem at the time of Jesus had been rebuilt and lavishly adorned by Herod the Great and was one of the largest and most magnificent buildings of the ancient world. Accounts of it are given in Josephus *War*, pp. 301–5; *Ant.*, 15:380–425.

2 *there shall not be left . . . thrown down*: the destruction of the Temple by the Romans took place in 70 CE, some forty years after the death of Jesus.

8 *the beginning of sorrows*: 'the beginning of the birth pangs' (NRSV). The idea that a series of catastrophic events would precede the coming of the messianic age was widely shared.

15 *abomination of desolation . . . holy place*: the phrase 'abomination of desolation' (meaning something like 'desolating sacrilege') is used in Daniel (9:27, 11:31, 12:11) of the setting up of a statue of Zeus in the Jerusalem Temple by the Seleucid king Antiochus IV Epiphanes in 167 BCE, an act of desecration which sparked the Maccabean revolt.

understand: i.e. look more deeply into this: it is a prophecy of future events.

16 *flee into the mountains*: i.e. those in Judea, who would be at the centre of these cataclysmic events, should take refuge in the mountains. (There may be an allusion to 1 Maccabees (Apocrypha) 2:28, where Mattathias, the leader of the Maccabean revolt, and his followers are said to flee to the hills leaving their belongings behind them in the town.)

17 *on the house top . . . of his house*: i.e. don't go into the house (the staircase leading to the roof, where people spent time in the evenings, would be on the outside).

19 *woe*: here an expression of lamentation (not condemnation, as e.g. in 11:21).

20 *the Sabbath day*: travel on the Sabbath was severely restricted under Jewish Law (see Exod. 16:29) and food for travel would be unavailable.

21 *tribulation*: 'great trouble' (NRSV). The word was frequently used in apocalyptic writing; see Dan. 12:1.

22 *the elect's sake*: by 'elect' here is meant God's chosen people; the term was taken over from Judaism into early Christianity. See Deut. 7:6–8; Rom. 8:33; Col. 3:12.

25 *before*: 'beforehand' (NRSV).

26 *if they shall say unto you . . . believe it not*: see 2 Thess. 2:1–2.

27 *the coming of the Son of Man*: i.e. his second coming in judgement, marking the end of the age; see note to 8:20.

28 *wheresoever the carcass . . . gathered together*: a proverbial expression (see Job 39:30; Luke 17:37).

29 *the sun . . . be shaken*: a free paraphrasing of Isa. 13:10, 13; Ezek. 32:7; Joel 2:10, 31; Amos 8:9.

30 *the sign of the Son of Man*: see Dan. 7:13.

tribes of the earth mourn: an allusion to Zech. 12:10–12 (and see also Rev. 1:7).

clouds of heaven: a phrase from Dan. 7:13.

31 *his angels*: see 13:41, 49.

great sound of a trumpet: see Isa. 27:13.

four winds: i.e. from all four quarters of the world; see Zech. 2:6.

32 *fig tree . . . putteth forth leaves*: the fig tree is one of the few trees in Palestine that loses its leaves in winter. Its thick foliage provides shade in summer.

34 *this generation*: i.e. those alive now. (See also 10:23, 16:28.) A belief that the end was imminent was a characteristic of early Christian belief; see 1 Thess. 4:17; 2 Thess. 2:2.

35 *Heaven and earth . . . pass away*: see 5:18; cf. also Isa. 40:8.

37 *Noe*: for the story of Noah and the Flood, see Gen. 6–7. The emphasis here is on how wholly unexpected was the Flood.

40 *taken . . . left*: i.e. *taken* into the kingdom, or *left* to destruction.

43 *in what watch*: see note to 14:25.

45 *Who then . . . due season?*: i.e. he is a faithful servant (or slave) who, when left in charge of the other servants during his master's absence, provides food for them at the right time.

48 *But and if*: a phrase (obsolete since the seventeenth century) meaning simply 'but if'.

51 *appoint him his portion with*: 'put him with' (NRSV).

CHAPTER 25

1 *Then*: i.e. at the return of Jesus in glory. This event was referred to as the Parousia (from the Greek word meaning 'arrival') or the 'Second Coming'.

virgins: i.e. bridesmaids, whose task is to wait to welcome the bridegroom (and his betrothed) into his father's house on the evening before the wedding day.

lamps: these would be carried in the wedding procession.

15 *talents*: a talent was the highest denomination of currency (see note to 18:24). Five talents, equivalent to 30,000 denarii, was thus a vast sum.

16 *other five*: 'five more' (NRSV).

18 *digged in the earth*: money was often preserved by hiding it in the ground (cf. 13:44).

29 *every one that hath . . . which he hath*: see note to 13:12, above.

32 *sheep from the goats*: see Ezek. 34:17–23.

33 *right hand*: see note to 20:21.

35–6 *gave me meat . . . clothed me*: cf. Isa. 58:7; Ezek. 18:7.

41 *Depart from me . . . everlasting fire*: cf. Ps. 6:8; Rev. 20:10.

CHAPTER 26

1 *all these sayings*: i.e. the five preceding discourses (see Introduction, p. xiv).

2 *the feast of the Passover*: see Introduction, p. xxxvi.

is betrayed: 'will be handed over' (NRSV).

3 *chief priests . . . scribes . . . elders*: i.e. the local Jewish authorities (see notes to 2:4 and 5:20, above).

5 *uproar among the people*: riots were a constant source of concern to the authorities on feast days in Jerusalem (see Josephus *War*, p. 40).

7 *alabaster box*: i.e. a jar, or flask, made of alabaster, a soft, cream-coloured stone. The pouring of ointment (or oil) on the head was a part of the coronation ritual for kings (see e.g. 2 Kings 9:6), and dead bodies were anointed before burial (see v. 12).

11 *the poor always with you*: this saying may be echoing Deut. 15:11.

15 *thirty pieces of silver*: the allusion here is to Zech. 11:12–13 ('they weighed for my price thirty pieces of silver'). See also 27:9–10 where this passage is directly quoted (though wrongly attributed to Jeremiah).

17 *the first day of the Feast of Unleavened Bread*: strictly speaking, this would be 15 Nisan, the day after Passover. However, the two feasts were closely linked (see Mark 14:12; Luke 22:7; also Josephus *Ant.*, 18:29), and 'Unleavened Bread' could refer to Passover, in which case the 'first day' would be the 'day of Preparation', Thursday 14 Nisan, when Passover lambs would be slaughtered at the Temple (see Exod. 12:6).

18 *the city*: i.e. Jerusalem. The Passover feast had to be eaten there, in the evening (which would be 15 Nisan, because the Jewish day ran from sunset to sunset).

22 *Lord, is it I?*: 'Surely not I, Lord?' (NRSV).

23 *dippeth his hand*: in other meals, bread would be dipped into the dish, but at the Passover meal hands were dipped into the dish.

shall betray me: cf. Ps. 41:9.

24 *as it is written of him*: the specific text is not known, but the reference may be to Isa. 53.

25 *Master*: or Rabbi. This title is only given to Jesus by his enemies, and by Judas (see also v. 49 and note to 23:7, above).

26   *blessed it*: see also note to 14:19. The action of giving thanks to God and
     then breaking and handing round bread was the normal practice at Jewish
     meals.

27   *Drink ye all of it*: 'Drink from it, all of you' (NRSV).

28   *my blood of the new testament*: by 'testament' is here meant 'covenant', and
     Christ is using the words of Exod. 24:8, where Moses sprinkles blood as a
     symbol of the covenant God has made with the people of Israel. The word
     'new' does not appear in some of the ancient manuscripts, and may have
     been added later to align this passage more closely with 1 Cor. 11:25.

     shed for many for the remission of sins: i.e. Jesus's death will be a sacrificial
     atonement for the forgiveness of sins (the phrase 'for many' means 'for
     everybody', not just for some; see note to 20:28, above).

29   *that day*: i.e. the day of the messianic banquet (see note to 8:11, above).

30   *hymn*: the Passover feast ended with the singing of the Hallel Psalms, 115–18.

31   *be offended*: 'become deserters' (NRSV).

     it is written: in Zech. 13:7.

32   *will go before you into Galilee*: see 28:7, 16.

33   *be offended*: see note to v. 31.

34   *deny me thrice*: this prediction is fulfilled in vv. 69–75.

39   *this cup*: see note to 20:22.

41   *enter not into temptation*: see note to 6:13.

48   *kiss*: a common form of greeting; see Luke 15:20.

49   *Hail Master*: see note to v. 25.

50   *Friend*: see note to 22:12.

51   *one of them*: according to John (18:10) this was Peter.

52   *they that take . . . the sword*: Jesus's words here may be echoing Gen. 9:6
     (and see also Matt. 5:39; Rev. 13:10).

53   *legions*: a Roman legion was a body of up to 6,000 infantry, with a large
     complement of cavalry.

54   *scriptures be fulfilled*: probably referring to Zech. 13:7 (quoted earlier in v. 31).

56   *scriptures . . . be fulfilled*: the reference may again be to Zech. 13.7, but since
     Jesus has been arrested like a 'thief' (v. 55), he may also be alluding to Isa.
     53:12 ('he was numbered with the transgressors'), which is quoted in Luke
     22:37.

     forsook him and fled: see v. 31.

59   *all the council*: i.e. the Sanhedrin (see note to 5:22, above).

60   *two false witnesses*: a minimum of two witnesses was required by Jewish
     Law (see note to 18:16, above).

61   *destroy the Temple*: for Jesus's apparent prediction of the destruction of the
     Temple, see 24:2. (Cf. John 2:19–21.)

64 *power*: i.e. God, at whose right hand the Messiah would sit (see Ps. 110:1).

coming in the clouds of heaven: a quotation from Dan. 7:13.

65 *rent his clothes*: tearing of clothing was a sign of distress, such as hearing blasphemy would cause.

66 *He is guilty of death*: 'He deserves death' (NRSV). (Death was the punishment for blasphemy; see Lev. 24:10–16.)

67 *spit in his face*: cf. Isa. 50:6.

69 *without in the palace*: 'outside in the courtyard' (NRSV).

CHAPTER 27

1 *took counsel*: 'conferred together' (NRSV).

4 *innocent blood*: a curse was laid on anyone who caused the death of an innocent person for money; see Deut. 27:25.

5 *hanged himself*: Matthew's is the only reference in the Gospels to the suicide of Judas, but an account (though a somewhat different one) is also given in Acts 1:18–20.

7 *the potter's field*: alluding to Zech. 11:13.

8 *Field of Blood*: see Acts 1:19.

9 *Jeremy*: in fact the quotation is from Zechariah (11:13), not Jeremiah.

11 *Art thou the King of the Jews?*: for Jesus to have claimed to be 'King of the Jews' would have been regarded as sedition against the empire. The term would only have been used by Gentiles (such as the wise men in 2:2, or here by Pilate), because Jews did not speak of themselves as Jews, and would have said instead 'the King of Israel' (as below in v. 42).

12 *answered nothing*: cf. Isa. 53:7.

14 *to never a word*: 'no answer, not even to a single charge' (NRSV).

15 *at that feast . . . whom they would*: there is little evidence other than from the Gospels that the release of a prisoner by the governor at the feast of Passover was customary (but see Josephus *Ant.*, 20:215).

16 *Barabbas*: in some early manuscripts he is called Jesus Barabbas (which would explain Pilate's alternatives in the next verse, '[Jesus] Barabbas, or Jesus which is called Christ'). The name Barabbas means in Aramaic 'Son of Abba', i.e. 'Son of the Father'. According to Mark (15:7) and Luke (23:19, 25), Barabbas was an insurrectionary.

18 *envy*: for the envy (or jealousy) of the Jewish leaders, see 21:15.

19 *in a dream*: dreams were often regarded as conveying divine revelation, as in Joseph's dream (1:20).

20 *ask*: 'ask for' (NRSV).

21 *Whether of the twain*: 'Which of the two' (NRSV).

22 *crucified*: crucifixion was the method of execution used by the Romans for non-Romans convicted of violent crime or rebellion against the state.

The victim was nailed or tied by the hands and feet to a wooden cross or stake, and died slowly of asphyxiation.

24 *washed his hands*: washing of hands to signify innocence was a Jewish, not a Roman custom (see Deut. 21:6–7).

25 *His blood ... on our children*: this formulaic expression for taking responsibility for a death is found frequently in the Hebrew Bible. See e.g. 2 Sam. 1:16; Jer. 26:15. The phrase 'and on our children' should not be taken to refer to all subsequent generations, but to the next generation after Jesus's death.

26 *scourged*: scourging (or flogging) was regularly carried out before crucifixion, perhaps designed to weaken the victim and hasten his death. The Romans used a multi-thonged whip of knotted cord or leather, weighted with sharp bone or metal. Jesus had predicted that he would be flogged (20:19).

27 *common hall*: this would have been the governor's official residence (Latin *praetorium*).

band: 'cohort' (NRSV), a body of between 300 and 600 infantry (ten cohorts making up a legion).

28 *scarlet robe*: in Mark (15:17) and John (19:2), the colour is given as purple, the colour of cloaks worn by Roman officers. The soldiers here are using one of their own cloaks (or capes) which were scarlet, in mimicry of the purple robe of the emperor.

29 *crown of thorns*: emperors were shown on coins of this period wearing crowns with radiant spikes, and the soldiers are probably mimicking this.

reed: i.e. in mimicry of the sceptre held by the emperor as a symbol of his authority to rule.

Hail, King: corresponding to the Latin greeting to the emperor, *Ave Caesar*.

32 *came out*: i.e. out of the city.

his cross: i.e. the horizontal cross-beam (*patibulum*), to which the victim would be fastened by the hands before it was hoisted into position on the upright post (which would already be in place); see note to 5:41.

34 *vinegar*: 'wine' (NRSV).

gall: a bitter herb (see Ps. 69:21, to which this verse may be alluding).

would not drink: the purpose of the drink was to dull the pain, but Matthew (as in Mark 15:23) has Jesus refuse it, no doubt to emphasize that he experienced his pain in full measure.

35 *parted his garments, casting lots*: 'divided his clothes among themselves by casting lots' (NRSV). Roman soldiers had the right to the clothing of a dead criminal.

spoken by the prophet: see Ps. 22:18.

36 *watched him*: 'kept watch over him' (NRSV).

37 *his accusation ... KING OF THE JEWS*: the charge for which a criminal was being executed was customarily displayed above his head. The charge

here would have been understood as being sedition, or treason against Roman rule.

38 *thieves*: 'bandits' (NRSV). See Isa. 53:12, 'he was numbered with the transgressors' (quoted in Mark 15:28).

39 *wagging their heads*: shaking of the head was a gesture of derision; see Pss. 22:7, 109:25; Lam. 2:15.

40 *destroyest the Temple . . . in three days*: see 26:61.

   if thou be the Son of God: this repeats the words of the devil in 4:3, 6; see also 26:62.

42 *the King of Israel*: the Jewish form of 'King of the Jews'; see note to 27:11.

43 *He trusted . . . deliver him*: quoting Ps. 22:8.

44 *cast the same in his teeth*: 'taunted him in the same way' (NRSV).

45 *the sixth hour . . . unto the ninth hour*: i.e. from noon till 3 p.m.

   darkness over all the land: see Amos 8:9.

46 *Eli, Eli, lama sabachthani*: Hebrew words from Ps. 22:1.

47 *calleth for Elias*: the bystanders have mistaken (or misheard) Jesus's 'Eli' for 'Elijah', who was taken up to heaven alive (see 2 Kings 2:9–12), and whose return to earth, it was believed, would herald the beginning of the deliverance and restoration of Israel (see Mal. 4:5).

48 *vinegar*: 'sour wine' (NRSV). See Ps. 69:21, 'in my thirst they gave me vinegar to drink'.

49 *The rest said*: in Mark (15:36) this is the same person who proffers the vinegar.

50 *yielded up the ghost*: 'breathed his last' (NRSV). The phrase is perhaps meant to suggest an active, voluntary surrender of Jesus's life.

51 *the veil of the Temple*: the 'veil' was the large tapestry, or curtain, that hung at the entrance to the Holy of Holies, the innermost sanctum of the Temple, where the divine presence was believed to dwell (see Exod. 26:31–4). It having been 'rent in twain' symbolized for early Christians the new form of access to God opened up by Christ through his death (see Heb. 9:1–14, 10:19–22).

   earth did quake . . . rocks rent: earthquakes were traditionally regarded as a sign of God's work; see e.g. 2 Sam. 22:8; 1 Kings 19:11; Ps. 68:8.

52 *saints*: literally 'holy ones'. The term was used by early Christians of themselves, but here it refers to ancient Israelites, whose resurrection was prophesied in Ezek. 37:12.

55 *beholding afar off*: an allusion to Ps. 38:11 (brought out more clearly in Luke 23:49).

56 *Mary the mother of James and Joses*: although, according to Matthew (13:55), two of Jesus's brothers were called James and Joses, it seems unlikely that the Mary referred to here is the mother of Jesus.

56 *mother of Zebedee's children*: see note to 20:20.

57 *When the even was come*: i.e. before sunset, at which time the Sabbath would begin, and no work could be done. The corpses of those executed were required to be buried before nightfall (see Deut. 21:22–3).

    a rich man: Matthew changes Mark's 'honourable counsellor' (15:43) to 'a rich man', probably in allusion to Isa. 53:9.

62 *the day of the Preparation*: i.e. preparation for the Sabbath (see 28:1), not for Passover.

63 *After three days I will rise again*: see 16:21, 17:23, 20:19, and cf. 12:40.

64 *last error shall be worse than the first*: the 'first' error is belief in Jesus as the Messiah; the 'last' is believing that he has risen from the dead.

65 *watch*: i.e. a guard of soldiers, probably the Temple guards, who were under the command of the High Priest.

CHAPTER 28

1 *first day of the week*: i.e. Sunday (the first day of the Jewish week, which was merely numbered because the Jews did not give names to any days other than the Sabbath, the last day of the week).

    Mary . . . Mary: Matthew follows Mark (16:1–8) in having women be the only witnesses to the empty tomb, as does Luke (24:1–3). John presents a different account, in which men are present (20:1–9).

3 *countenance . . . snow*: see note to 17:2.

6 *as he said*: see 16:21.

7 *into Galilee*: see 26:32. Galilee was the homeland of the disciples, and the place where Jesus's ministry had begun.

9 *All hail*: 'Greetings!' (NRSV).

10 *my brethren*: i.e. the disciples.

14 *persuade him, and secure you*: 'satisfy him and keep you out of any trouble' (NRSV).

15 *until this day*: i.e. the story was still circulating at the time when this Gospel was being written.

16 *a mountain where Jesus had appointed them*: 'the mountain to which Jesus had directed them' (NRSV).

18 *All power is given unto me*: this echoes what is said of the Son of Man in Dan. 7:13–14 (see note to 8:20, above). Cf. also Jesus's promise in 26:64.

19 *teach all nations*: earlier, in 10:6 and 15:24, the mission of the disciples was to Israel only.

    baptizing . . . in the name of the Father . . . Son, and . . . Holy Ghost: this is the only occasion in the Gospels in which Jesus gives an explicit command to baptize. The full Trinitarian formula is also rare in the New Testament. According to Acts 2:38, the early Christians baptized 'in the name of Jesus Christ', and not using the threefold formula.

20 *teaching them . . . commanded you*: Matthew once again presents Jesus as a second Moses, the giver of a new set of laws from God (see also 5:17–48).

I am with you always: a reference to the prophecy of Isa. 7:14, quoted in 1:23.

unto the end of the world: i.e. until the time when Jesus as Son of Man would return to earth in judgement (see chapters 24–5).

MARK

CHAPTER I

1 *the gospel of Jesus Christ*: the Greek word *evangelion*, translated as 'gospel', means 'good news', here 'the good news about Jesus Christ'. For 'Jesus Christ', see Introduction, p. xvii.

Son of God: this title for Jesus is used elsewhere in Mark (see e.g. 3:11, 5:7, 15:39). On its significance and meaning, see note to Matt. 4:3.

2–3 *written in the Prophets . . . paths straight*: quoted from Mal. 3:1, and Isa. 40:3.

4 *John*: i.e. John the Baptist.

the baptism of repentance: i.e. immersion in water (baptism) acts as a symbol of spiritual cleansing, following repentance and forgiveness of sins.

5 *all the land of Judea, and they of Jerusalem*: i.e. people from the southern region of Palestine, known as Judea, with its capital, Jerusalem.

6 *camel's hair . . . wild honey*: on John's clothing and diet, see note to Matt. 3:4.

8 *Holy Ghost*: i.e. Holy Spirit (see note to Matt. 1:18).

10 *opened*: for apocalyptic images of the heavens being torn apart, or opened, as a feature of divine intervention in human affairs, see e.g. Isa. 64:1; Ezek. 1:1; John 1:51.

13 *with the wild beasts*: Mark may be alluding here to the belief that when the Messiah came, animals would become tame and live together in harmony; see e.g. Isa. 11:6–8; Hos. 2:18. There may also be an allusion to Ps. 91:11–13, where service by angels is linked with dominion over wild animals.

14 *put in prison*: see 6:17. Jesus begins his ministry in Galilee at a time of ominous political tension and oppression.

the gospel of the kingdom of God: i.e. 'the good news from God about his intention to establish his kingship (or sovereign rule)'.

15 *The time is fulfilled*: the idea that God has determined a specific time for the establishment of his kingdom is common in Jewish apocalyptic writing (see e.g. Ezek. 7:12; Dan. 12:4) and was taken over into early Christian writing (see e.g. Gal. 4:4; Eph. 1:10; Rev. 1:3).

21 *Sabbath day*: i.e. Saturday, the Jewish day of rest, on which only the most essential kinds of activity were permitted, and all work was forbidden.

   synagogue: see note to Matt. 4:23. It was open to any competent Jewish male to expound the Law in the synagogue, as Jesus does here.

22 *authority*: some scholars have suggested that Jesus may have been formally trained and ordained as a rabbi. The Greek word also means 'power'.

23 *a man with an unclean spirit*: i.e. one possessed by a demon ('unclean' meaning 'impure', not 'dirty').

24 *what have we to do with thee*: i.e. 'why are you interfering with us?' (cf. 1 Kings 17:18).

   I know thee who thou art: in Mark, demons always recognize who Jesus is (see v. 34, 3:11, 5:7).

26 *had torn him*: i.e. had left his body with a violent convulsion.

32 *at even, when the sun did set*: the Jewish Sabbath did not come to an end until night had fallen, which was taken to have happened when three stars had appeared. Only then would it have been permissible to carry sick people through the streets.

33 *all the city*: not literally; the phrase is used here and elsewhere in Mark to indicate a large number of people.

34 *suffered not the devils to speak*: see Introduction, p. xxv.

35 *a great while before day*: the practice of praying early in the morning was common among devout Jews; see e.g. Pss 5:3, 88:13, 119:147.

38 *therefore came I forth*: 'that is what I came out to do' (NRSV).

40 *leper*: on leprosy, see note to Matt. 8:2.

41 *touched him*: under the Law, anyone touching a leper became themselves ritually impure (or 'unclean').

43 *straitly charged him*: sternly commanded him (not to tell anyone; see v. 44).

44 *things which Moses commanded*: see Lev. 14.

   for a testimony unto them: i.e. for a proof to the people of his healing.

CHAPTER 2

2 *not so much as about the door*: 'not even in front of the door' (NRSV).

   preached the word: a term often used in the NT for preaching the gospel (see Acts 8:25, 11:19, 15:36).

3 *borne of four*: 'carried by four of them' (NRSV).

4 *uncovered the roof . . . broken it up*: many houses in Palestine had external stairs up to the flat roof, and it would not have been difficult to make a hole in the thatch or mud-plaster (or to remove tiles, as in Luke 5:19, though it is less likely that tiles would have been used outside large towns and cities).

   the bed: i.e. the pallet, or straw mat.

5   *Son*: a term of endearment.

10   *Son of Man*: for the significance of this title, see note to Matt. 8:20.

12   *We never saw it in this fashion*: 'We have never seen anything like this!' (NRSV).

13   *the sea*: i.e. the Sea of Galilee.

15   *publicans*: i.e. tax collectors (see note to Matt. 5:46, above).

     sinners: including not only ordinary 'sinners', but people who did not adhere to the precepts of the Law (as opposed to the 'righteous' of v. 17), and social outcasts. Like 'publicans', they would have been regarded by the Pharisees as 'impure' people with whom it was forbidden to come into contact.

18   *of John*: i.e. of John the Baptist.

     used to fast: i.e. were in the habit of fasting.

19   *children of the bride-chamber*: see note to Matt. 9:15.

21   *taketh away from*: i.e. pulls away from (when the new fabric shrinks).

22   *new wine into old bottles*: see note to Matt. 9:17.

24   *that which is not lawful*: the Pharisees regard the action of the disciples in plucking grains of corn as tantamount to reaping, one of the thirty-nine activities listed as forbidden by rabbinic interpreters of Sabbath legislation (Exod. 20:8–11; Deut. 5:12–15). See *The Talmud: A Selection*, ed. Norman Solomon (London, 2009), 113–17.

25   *what David did*: for the story of how David ate the sacred shewbread, see 1 Sam. 21:1–6. See also note to Matt. 12:4.

26   *Abiathar the High Priest*: in fact it was not Abiathar, but his father, Ahimelech, who was High Priest (see 1 Sam. 22:20, 21:1).

27–8 *The Sabbath . . . of the Sabbath*: the first part of this would have been regarded by Jews as a very radical statement, which would seem to allow rules about the Sabbath to be overridden by human need. It is omitted by Matthew (12:1–8) and Luke (6:1–5).

CHAPTER 3

1   *again*: i.e. on another occasion.

2   *that they might accuse him*: i.e. of performing 'work' on the Sabbath. (To take action to save life was permitted on the Sabbath, but this man's life was not in immediate danger.)

5   *hardness of . . . hearts*: i.e. refusal to recognize the truth; obtuseness.

6   *Herodians*: i.e. political supporters of Herod Antipas, the ruler of Galilee.

7–8 *from Galilee . . . Tyre and Sidon*: the places named here represent the whole of Israel, excluding Samaria (as not Jewish) and the cities of the Decapolis (as mainly Gentile). Tyre and Sidon, while not strictly Jewish territory, had large Jewish populations.

9   *spake to*: i.e. asked, requested.

10 *plagues*: 'diseases' (NRSV).

11 *unclean spirits*: i.e. men possessed by demons (see note to 1:23, above).

13 *into a mountain*: the traditional setting for a divine disclosure, recalling the giving of the Law to Moses on Mount Sinai (Exod. 19–20).

17 *Boanerges*: although said by Mark to mean 'the sons of thunder', the derivation of this term from Hebrew or Aramaic remains obscure.

21 *lay hold on*: 'restrain' (NRSV).

beside himself: 'out of his mind' (NRSV).

22 *scribes . . . from Jerusalem*: see note to Matt. 5:20.

hath Beelzebub: i.e. is possessed by Satan (see notes to Matt. 4:1 and 9:34, above).

23 *parables*: see note to Matt. 13:3, and Introduction, pp. xxix–xxx.

28 *blasphemies*: i.e. not simply bad language, but outright acts of hostility to God.

29 *hath never forgiveness*: 'can never have forgiveness' (NRSV). See note to Matt. 12:32.

30 *Because . . . unclean spirit*: this is probably to be understood as referring back to v. 22: the people who would link the Holy Spirit with demons are guilty of an eternal sin.

31 *brethren*: i.e. his brothers (see 6:3).

CHAPTER 4

1 *the sea side*: i.e. the side of the Sea of Galilee.

8 *thirty . . . sixty . . . an hundred*: i.e. thirtyfold, sixtyfold, a hundredfold. The latter would have represented a bumper harvest (cf. Gen. 26:12).

10 *asked of him the parable*: i.e. asked him the meaning of the parable.

11 *the mystery of the kingdom of God*: i.e. the secret of the fulfilment of God's purposes in the world.

12 *that seeing . . . forgiven them*: adapted from Isa. 6:9–10. The same passage is quoted in Matt. 13:14–15, where it is made clear that in his prophecy Isaiah is being ironical (it is as if, he says, they deliberately *want* not to understand), and Jesus is being equally ironical.

13 *Know ye not*: 'do you not understand' (NRSV).

14 *the word*: i.e. the gospel (see note to 2:2, above).

22 *come abroad*: 'come to light' (NRSV).

25 *For he . . . he hath*: see note to Matt. 13:12.

26 *So is . . . cast seed*: i.e. the kingdom of God may be compared to a man who casts seed. This is the only parable in Mark not found in the other Gospels. What it means is not at all clear. The most likely interpretation is that the disciples must be like the farmer, who sows the seed (the gospel) but then leaves it in the earth (to God) to bring forth the harvest. Another

interpretation is that God is the sower, who, when the hour is come, brings in his harvest (at the final judgement).

29 *putteth in . . . is come*: quoted from Joel 3:13.

31 *less than all the seeds*: the mustard seed was proverbially regarded as the smallest of all seeds (see note to Matt. 13:32, above).

32 *greater than all the herbs*: mustard trees (or bushes) would grow to about 8 or 10 feet in Palestine.

37 *now full*: 'already being swamped' (NRSV).

38 *the hinder part*: 'the stern' (NRSV).

asleep on a pillow: displaying complete faith in God (cf. Ps. 46:1–3; Isa. 43:2). The 'pillow' would have been the cushion on the seat of the helmsman.

39 *Peace, be still*: the ability to subdue the sea is similarly represented as exemplifying divine power in Pss 89:9, 104:6–7, 106:8–11; Isa. 51:10.

CHAPTER 5

1 *other side of the sea*: to the east shore of the Sea of Galilee.

country of the Gadarenes: i.e. the area around Gadara.

2 *the tombs*: traditionally regarded as the haunt of demons.

6 *worshipped*: 'bowed down before' (NRSV).

9 *Legion*: here meaning, simply, a great number. (A legion was a body of between 3,000 and 6,000 troops in the Roman army.)

21 *the other side*: i.e. the western side of the Sea of Galilee.

25 *an issue of blood*: i.e. recurrent haemorrhages, or discharge of blood (see note to Matt. 9:20).

27 *his garment*: i.e. his cloak. (Cf. note to Matt. 9:20.)

34 *be whole of thy plague*: 'be healed of your disease' (NRSV).

38 *them that wept and wailed*: perhaps referring to professional mourners (see note to Matt. 9:23).

41 *Talitha cumi*: the phrase is Aramaic, one of a number of such in Mark (see e.g. 7:34, 14:36, 15:34).

CHAPTER 6

1 *his own country*: i.e. his native town (Nazareth).

3 *son of Mary*: it was customary to describe a Jewish man by reference to his father, not his mother, and this may therefore have been intended as an insult.

4 *A prophet . . . in his own house*: a proverbial saying; see also Matt. 13:57; Luke 4:24; John 4:44.

8 *a staff only*: even this is forbidden in Matthew (10:10) and Luke (9:3).

9 *sandals*: 'shoes' are forbidden in Matthew (10:10) and in Luke (10:4).

coats: here meaning tunics, inner garments worn next to the skin.

11 *verily . . . for that city*: not included in NRSV.

13 *anointed with oil*: healing by unction was widely practised in the early Church; see James 5:14.

14 *King Herod*: i.e. Herod Antipas, who ruled Galilee and Perea as tetrarch (not king, though this may have been the popular designation).

15 *Elias*: i.e. Elijah, who, it was believed, would return as a harbinger of the Messiah (see 9:11–13, and cf. Mal. 4:5–6).

17–18 *Herodias' sake . . . thy brother's wife*: see note to Matt. 14:4.

20 *observed*: 'protected' (NRSV). The AV 'observed' is a mistranslation.

22 *the daughter of . . . Herodias*: see note to Matt. 14:6.

23 *half my kingdom*: Herod's words here recall those of King Ahasuerus in Esther 5:3–6, 7:2.

29 *his disciples*: i.e. John the Baptist's disciples.

33 *outwent them*: 'arrived ahead of them' (NRSV).

34 *came out*: i.e. out of the boat, stepped ashore.

   sheep not having a shepherd: see note to Matt. 9:36.

37 *pennyworth*: 'penny' is the AV translation of denarius, a Roman coin which would represent a day's wage for a labourer. Two hundred denarii would have been a very large sum of money.

39 *by companies*: 'in groups' (NRSV).

45 *go to . . . into Bethsaida*: 'go on ahead to the other side, to Bethsaida' (NRSV).

48 *fourth watch of the night*: between 3 and 6 a.m.

50 *it is I*: the Greek words here mean literally 'I am', which is the name of God in the Hebrew Bible (see Exod. 3:14). See Introduction, pp. xxxiv–xxxv.

56 *the border of his garment*: see note to Matt. 9:20.

CHAPTER 7

2 *defiled . . . hands*: the reference here is to *ritual* uncleanness, i.e. not having performed ritual cleansing (nothing to do with hygiene).

3 *wash their hands oft*: 'thoroughly wash their hands' (NRSV), 'thoroughly' meaning, literally, 'with a fist', i.e. 'up to the elbow'.

   holding the tradition of the elders: i.e. obeying the oral Law (held by Pharisees to be as binding as the written Law; see note to Matt. 3:7).

4 *tables*: the Greek word here should be translated as 'beds' or 'couches'.

5 *Why walk not thy disciples*: 'Why do your disciples not live' (NRSV).

6–7 *Esaias prophesied . . . of men*: see Isa. 29:13.

10 *Moses said*: see Exod. 20:12, 21:17; Lev. 20:9; Deut. 5:16.

11–12 *But ye say . . . his mother*: 'if anyone tells father or mother, "Whatever support you might have had from me is Corban" (that is, an offering to

God)—then you no longer permit doing anything for a father or mother' (NRSV). 'Corban' is the transliteration of an Aramaic word meaning 'an offering', 'a gift dedicated to God'. For the 'vow of Corban', see note to Matt. 15:5.

13 *the word of God*: i.e. the written Law.

17 *from*: i.e. and had left.

parable: here meaning 'riddle'.

19 *purging all meats*: meaning something like 'and thus all foods are clean'.

22 *an evil eye*: i.e. envy. (See note to Matt. 6:23.)

26 *a Greek*: here referring to her religion (i.e. a Gentile) rather than nationality. As the next word indicates, she is a 'Syrophoenician', i.e. a Phoenician from Syria.

27 *the children . . . the dogs*: i.e. the Jews should be 'fed' with the gospel first, before it is offered to the Gentiles ('dogs').

31 *coasts of Tyre and Sidon . . . coasts of Decapolis*: the route described here is a circuitous one; it is hard to see why Jesus should go all the way east to the Decapolis to return to the Sea of Galilee. This verse has been taken to suggest that Mark did not have a very secure grasp of the geography of Palestine.

33 *he spit*: the use of saliva is common in other ancient healing stories (cf. also John 9:6).

34 *Ephphatha*: an Aramaic word (cf. note to 5:41).

35 *string of*: literally, 'fetter on'.

37 *He hath done . . . dumb to speak*: perhaps alluding to Isa. 35:5–6.

CHAPTER 8

1–9 *nothing to eat . . . sent them away*: see notes to Matt. 15:32–8.

11 *a sign from heaven*: i.e. divine confirmation of his authority. Such 'signs' are common in the Hebrew Bible; see e.g. Exod. 4:28–31; Num. 14:11; Deut. 13:1–5, 18:20–2; Isa. 7:10–15.

15 *leaven . . . Pharisees . . . Herod*: on leaven, see note to Matt. 16:6. Quite what this verse means has been much debated. Some scholars regard it as an isolated saying of Jesus, included here out of sequence. The parallel version in Matthew would suggest that the disciples misunderstood Jesus's symbolic reference to leaven, thinking he is referring to the lack of bread in the boat. However, Mark's reference to Herod remains a puzzle. Matthew (16:6) refers to Pharisees and Sadducees, while Luke (12:1) refers only to Pharisees, whose 'leaven' is said to be 'hypocrisy'.

18 *Having eyes . . . not remember*: the wording is reminiscent of Isa. 6:9–10; Jer. 5:21; Ezek. 12:2.

24 *as trees*: 'but they look like trees' (NRSV).

28 *Elias*: i.e. Elijah (see note to Matt. 16:14).

32 *took him*: 'took him aside' (NRSV).

33 *Satan*: see note to Matt. 9:34.

34 *come after me*: 'become my followers' (NRSV).

   take up his cross: see note to Matt. 27:32.

38 *adulterous*: see note to Matt. 12:39.

   cometh in the glory . . . holy angels: see Dan. 7:13–14. For other references to the Son of Man returning in judgement, see 13:24–7, 14:62; Matt. 13:41–3, 19:28, 25:31–3; Luke 12:40, 17:22–30; John 1:51.

CHAPTER 9

 1 *And he said . . . with power*: this verse would be more appropriately placed at the end of the previous chapter. See note to Matt. 16:28.

 2–8 *six days . . . with themselves*: see notes to Matt. 17:1–5.

11 *Elias must first come*: see Mal. 4:5–6, where it is prophesied that Elijah would return to earth as a precursor to the Messiah.

12 *and how it is written*: 'how then is it written' (NRSV).

   set at nought: 'treated with contempt' (NRSV).

13 *Elias is indeed come*: see Matt. 17:13, where it is explained that Jesus is referring to John the Baptist.

17 *a dumb spirit*: 'a spirit that makes him unable to speak' (NRSV). The symptoms described in the following verses suggest epilepsy.

18 *wheresoever he taketh him he teareth him*: 'whenever it seizes him, it dashes him down' (NRSV).

   pineth away: 'becomes rigid' (NRSV); the AV is a mistranslation.

25 *dumb and deaf spirit*: 'spirit that keeps this boy from speaking and hearing' (NRSV).

26 *rent him sore*: 'convulsed him terribly' (NRSV).

38 *followeth not us*: 'was not following us' (NRSV), i.e. was not a disciple. Cases of pagan exorcists using the name of Jesus for the purpose of exorcism were known to early Christians (see Acts 19:11–20).

40 *on our part*: 'for us' (NRSV). Compare Jesus's condemnations of neutrality in Matt. 12:30 and Luke 11:23.

41 *Christ*: used here as a proper name, not as a title (see Introduction, p. xvii), and hence scholars have suggested that the saying may represent the thought of early Christians rather than of Jesus himself.

46 *worm . . . quenched*: cf. Isa. 66:24.

49 *salted with fire*: the meaning seems to be that followers of Jesus will be tested by 'fire', and only the good ones would be preserved. In this sense, 'fire' preserves, like salt.

CHAPTER 10

 1 *Judea . . . Jordan*: Jesus and his disciples are continuing to journey south from Galilee towards Jerusalem (see v. 32).

2 *to put away his wife*: i.e. to divorce his wife. See notes to Matt. 19:1–9.

11 *adultery against her*: under Jewish marriage customs, a woman could commit adultery against her husband, but a man could not commit adultery against his wife, only against another married man.

12 *woman put away her husband*: a woman had no right in Jewish law to initiate divorce. The reference here is probably to Roman law, which did permit the wife to initiate divorce under certain circumstances.

19 *the commandments*: as set out in Exod. 20:12–16 and Deut. 5:16–20, but replacing 'Do not covet' with 'defraud not'.

37 *right hand . . . left hand*: i.e. the places of honour.

38–9 *drink of the cup . . . be baptized*: see notes to Matt. 20:22, 23.

47 *son of David*: see note to Matt. 9:27.

50 *casting away his garment*: 'throwing off his cloak' (NRSV).

CHAPTER 11

4 *without in a place where two ways met*: 'outside in the street' (NRSV).

7–9 *sat upon him . . . Hosanna*: see notes to Matt. 21:8–9.

10 *Blessed be . . . the Lord*: 'Blessed is the coming kingdom of our ancestor David!' (NRSV).

13–14 *nothing but leaves . . . for ever*: what otherwise seems an unreasonable and illogical act on Jesus's part, of cursing the fig tree for not bearing fruit out of season, may be the result of Mark's clumsy syntax here. The clause 'for the time of figs was not yet' seems to be misplaced, and should have come earlier, because it refers back to Jesus having seen a fig tree with leaves, suggesting that it was bearing fruit even though it was early in the season. The cursing of the fig tree is a figure of the denunciation of the Temple by Jesus, within which it is interwoven.

15–17 *the Temple . . . of thieves*: see notes to Matt. 21:12–13.

28 *these things*: probably referring to the cleansing of the Temple on the previous day.

30 *from heaven*: i.e. from God (Jews avoided saying the divine name; see Introduction, p. xxiii).

CHAPTER 12

1–11 *And he began . . . in our eyes*: see notes to Matt. 21:33–42.

13–16 *And they send . . . Caesar's*: see notes to Matt. 22:16–20.

14 *thou art true, and carest for no man*: 'you are sincere, and show deference to no one' (NRSV).

18–26 *Sadducees . . . of Jacob*: see notes to Matt. 22:23–32.

29–31 *The first . . . as thyself*: Jesus quotes Deut. 6:4–5 and Lev. 19:18. See note to Matt. 22:37–9.

32 *none other but he*: see Deut. 4:35; Isa. 45:5–6, 21.

33 *more than . . . sacrifices*: cf. 1 Sam. 15:22; Hos. 6:6.

35–7 *son of David . . . his Son*: see notes to Matt. 22:42–5.

38 *long clothing*: scribes wore a long, flowing robe, the *stole*, which other Jews wore only on special occasions.

40 *devour widows' houses*: i.e. induce poor widows to give money to the Temple.

42 *two mites . . . a farthing*: in English a mite was a copper coin of extremely low value, sometimes used, as here, to denote a half-farthing. (A farthing was worth a quarter of a penny.) The reference is to the Greek *lepton*, the smallest coin in circulation, two of which were equivalent to a *quadrans*, the smallest denomination of Roman coinage.

CHAPTER 13

2 *great buildings . . . thrown down*: see notes to Matt. 24:1–2.

8 *beginnings of sorrows*: see note to Matt. 24:8.

9 *councils*: i.e. local Jewish courts.

11 *lead you*: 'bring you to trial' (NRSV).

14–31 *But when . . . pass away*: see notes to Matt. 24:15–35.

35 *at even . . . morning*: i.e. the four 'watches' into which the Romans divided the night (see note to Matt. 14:25).

CHAPTER 14

See notes to Matt. 26.

1 *After two days was*: 'It was two days before' (NRSV).

Passover . . . Unleavened Bread: by the time of Jesus the festival of Passover (for which, see Introduction, p. xxxvi) was combined with the festival of Unleavened Bread, which lasted for seven days. The combined festival could be called by either name, as it is here. (See 2 Chron. 35:17; Ezek. 45:21–4.)

5 *pence*: i.e. denarii (300 of which would have been nearly a year's wages for a labourer).

12 *first day of Unleavened Bread*: see note to Matt. 26:17.

13 *man bearing a pitcher of water*: normally a woman's work, and so a man doing it would have stood out.

33 *sore amazed, and . . . very heavy*: 'distressed and agitated' (NRSV).

36 *Abba*: the Aramaic word for 'father'.

51–2 *young man . . . naked*: speculation about the identity of this mysterious young man has been fruitless, but it seems likely that he symbolizes in some way the desertion of Jesus by his disciples. There may be an allusion to Amos 2:16.

55 *sought for witness*: 'were looking for testimony' (NRSV).

61 *the Blessed*: a circumlocution used to avoid speaking directly of God.

CHAPTER 15

See notes to Matt. 27:1–2, 15–62.

7 *insurrection*: it is not known which of the numerous Jewish revolts is being referred to here.

34 *Eloi, Eloi*: Mark uses the Aramaic form (rather than the Hebrew, as in Matthew).

43 *an honourable counsellor*: 'a respected member of the council' (NRSV).

44 *any while dead*: 'dead for some time' (NRSV).

CHAPTER 16

4 *for it was very great*: this is another example of a misplaced clause in Mark (see also note to 11:13–14). Instead of following 'rolled away', it should almost certainly come at the end of v. 3, where it would explain the question of the women.

5 *young man . . . white garment*: i.e. an angel (cf. Josephus *Ant.*, 5:277).

9–20 *Now when he rose . . . Amen*: these verses are not included in the earliest Greek manuscripts of Mark, and are regarded by modern scholars as having been added some time in the second century. See Introduction, p. xxvii.

9–13 *Now when . . . they them*: cf. Luke 24:10–53.

17 *these signs . . . new tongues*: cf. Acts 8:7, 2:4–11, 10:46.

19 *into heaven*: cf. Acts 1:9–11.

LUKE

CHAPTER 1

1 *set forth in order a declaration*: 'set down an orderly account' (NRSV).

3 *having had perfect understanding of things*: 'after investigating everything carefully' (NRSV).

5 *Herod*: i.e. Herod the Great.

of the course of Abia: 'who belonged to the priestly order of Abijah' (NRSV). This was the eighth of the twenty-four divisions into which the priesthood was divided (see 1 Chron. 24:10).

of the daughters of Aaron: 'a descendant of Aaron' (NRSV). Aaron was the first priest of Israel (see Exod. 40:12–15).

8 *in the order of his course*: each order of priests served twice a year for a week at a time.

9 *his lot was to burn incense*: priestly duties were allocated by lot, but the privilege of offering incense at the altar immediately before the Holy of Holies was only allowed once.

10 *people were praying without*: i.e. because only the priests could enter the sanctuary.

13 *John*: from the Hebrew 'Jehohanan', meaning 'God's gracious gift' or 'God has shown favour'.

15 *neither wine, nor strong drink*: John is to be a Nazirite, one dedicated to God (see Num. 6:1–4), like Samson (Judg. 13:2–5) and Samuel (1 Sam. 1:11). See note to Matt. 2:23.

17 *Elias*: see 1 Kings 17–19, 21; 2 Kings 1–2; Mal. 4:5–6.

19 *Gabriel*: one of only two angels given names in the Hebrew Bible, the other being Michael (Dan. 8:16, 9:21, 10:13, 12:1).

23 *the days of his ministration were accomplished*: 'his time of service was ended' (NRSV).

25 *my reproach*: childlessness was considered a mark of divine disfavour, and therefore a disgrace (see Gen. 16:2, 30:22–3; 1 Sam. 1: 4–11; Ps. 128:3; Jer. 22:30).

26 *the sixth month*: i.e. after the conception of John.

29 *cast in her mind*: 'pondered' (NRSV).

32 *Son of the Highest*: on the title 'Son of God', see note to Matt. 4:3.

33 *kingdom . . . no end*: the promise made to David (see 2 Sam. 7:12–16; 1 Chron. 17:11–14; cf. Isa. 9:7; Dan. 7:14).

34 *I know not a man*: 'I am a virgin' (NRSV).

46–55 *My soul . . . for ever*: Mary's hymn of praise, known as the Magnificat (from the first word of the Latin version), is based largely on the song of Hannah at the birth of Samuel, in 1 Sam. 2:1–10.

55 *spake to . . . for ever*: see Gen. 17:5–8, 18:18, 22:16–18.

58 *cousins*: 'relatives' (NRSV).

59 *the eighth day*: see note to Matt. 1:25.

68–75 *Blessed . . . our life*: Zacharias's hymn, known as the Benedictus, is, in effect, answering the question asked by the people in v. 66.

68 *hath visited*: 'has looked favourably upon' (NRSV).

69 *an horn of salvation*: 'a mighty saviour' (NRSV). The AV is a literal translation from the Greek. The phrase is one used of God in Ps. 18:2, and elsewhere 'horn' is used as a metaphor for one who will bring salvation; see 1 Sam. 2:10; Pss. 92:10, 132:17.

73 *oath . . . Abraham*: see note to v. 55.

76 *Prophet . . . prepare his ways*: see also 3:4, 7:27, and cf. Mal. 3:1.

80 *in the deserts, till the day of his showing*: 'in the wilderness until the day he appeared publicly' (NRSV).

CHAPTER 2

1 *taxed*: 'registered' (NRSV), i.e. registered for a census, for taxation purposes.

4 *city of David . . . Bethlehem*: under Roman rules for censuses, owners of property were expected to register with the authorities in the chief city

in the district where they resided. For someone from Nazareth, where Joseph lived, this would have been Sepphoris (modern Saffûriyeh). Luke evidently interprets the decree as requiring travel to Bethlehem because of its significance as the birthplace of King David (1 Sam. 16:1–18). See note to Matt. 2:6.

9 *came upon*: 'stood before' (NRSV).

21 *his name was called Jesus*: see note to Matt. 1:25.

22–4 *purification . . . pigeons*: for details of these rites, see Lev. 12; v. 23 quotes Exod. 13:2.

25 *consolation of Israel*: i.e. Israel's deliverance through the arrival of the Messiah (see Isa. 40:1, 49:6).

29–32 *Lord . . . Israel*: Simeon's hymn is known as the Nunc Dimittis (from the opening words, in Latin).

32 *a light . . . Israel*: cf. Isa. 49:6, 46:13, 42:6, 60:1–3.

34 *is set for*: 'is destined for' (NRSV).

36 *tribe of Aser* [Asher]: see Deut. 33:24–5.

38 *redemption in Jerusalem*: equivalent to 'consolation of Israel'; see note to v. 25.

CHAPTER 3

1 *in the fifteenth year*: i.e. in 28/9 CE (Tiberius having become emperor in 14 CE).

2 *Annas and Caiaphas*: strictly speaking, Caiaphas was High Priest at this time, but his father-in-law, Annas, who was High Priest 6–15 CE, continued to wield great influence.

   John the son of Zacharias: i.e. John the Baptist.

4 *as it is written*: in Isa. 40:3–5.

8 *We have Abraham to our father*: 'We have Abraham as our ancestor' (NRSV).

12 *publicans*: i.e. tax collectors. See note to Matt. 5:46.

16–17 *Holy Ghost . . . purge his floor*: see notes to Matt. 3:11–12.

19–20 *Herod . . . prison*: see notes to Matt. 14:1–4.

22 *dove . . . well pleased*: see notes to Matt. 3:16, 17.

23–7 *Heli . . . Rhesa*: no other source is known for these names (which differ from those in Matthew's genealogy, 1:13–16).

27–38 *Zorobabel* [Zerubbabel] *. . . Adam*: some of these names are included in the genealogies presented in 1 Chron. 1:1–27, 2:1–14, 3:1–5.

CHAPTER 4

1–12 *And Jesus . . . thy God*: see notes to Matt. 4:1–10.

13 *for a season*: 'until an opportune time' (NRSV).

17 *the book*: i.e. the scroll. Scrolls were kept in a special place in the synagogue, and were given to readers by the *hazzan*, or attendant.

17–19 *written . . . the Lord*: see Isa. 61:1–2, 58:6.

20 *he sat down*: the Jewish custom was that one stood to read in the synagogue, but sat down to teach (or preach).

25–7 *Elias . . . the Syrian*: for the accounts of Elijah at Zarepath in Sidon, and of Elisha and Naaman, see 1 Kings 17:1–16 and 2 Kings 5:1–14.

35 *in the mids*: 'down before them' (NRSV).

38 *Simon's house*: in Luke's sequence, Jesus comes to Simon (Peter's) house before he becomes a disciple. (Compare Matt. 4:18.)

40 *when the sun was setting*: i.e. when the Sabbath was over. The earlier cures were performed by Jesus on the Sabbath, against Pharisaic interpretation of the Law about working on the Sabbath. (See note to Mark 1:32.)

CHAPTER 5

12–14 *leprosy . . . unto them*: see notes to Matt. 8:2–4.

17 *present to heal them*: 'with him to heal' (a variant manuscript reading adopted by NRSV).

19 *upon the house top*: see note to Mark 2:4.

24 *Son of Man*: for this title, see note to Matt. 8:20.

33–8 *John . . . are preserved*: see notes to Matt. 9:14–17.

39 *No man . . . better*: perhaps meant to explain why some are unwilling to accept the 'new' teaching of Jesus.

CHAPTER 6

2–4 *Why do ye . . . priests alone*: see notes to Matt. 12:2–4.

17–49 *And he came down . . . was great*: Luke's 'Sermon on the Plain' is the counterpart to Matthew's 'Sermon on the Mount'. See notes to Matt. 5:1–12, 39–48.

31 *And as . . likewise*: see note to Matt. 7:12.

38 *shall men give into your bosom*: NRSV has 'will be put into your lap', but 'bosom' here probably means a receptacle like a pocket (which would be formed by pulling out part of the outer garment from above the girdle).

CHAPTER 7

14 *touched the bier*: an action violating Jewish purity laws, which forbade contact with the dead (see Num. 19:16).

16 *a great prophet*: cf. 1 Kings 17:17–24, where Elijah raises from the dead the only son of a widow.

19–27 *he that should come . . . before thee*: see notes to Matt. 11:3–10.

29 *justified*: 'acknowledged the justice of' (NRSV).

30 *the counsel of God against themselves*: 'God's purposes for themselves' (NRSV).

35 *wisdom . . . children*: see note to Matt. 11:19.

36 *sat down to meat*: i.e. reclined at the table. That his feet would have rested on a couch away from the table perhaps explains why the woman anoints his feet rather than his head, which was the more usual practice (see Matt. 26:7).

37 *alabaster box*: see note to Matt. 26:7.

41 *pence*: see note to Matt. 18:28.

50 *go in peace*: (Hebrew *shalom*), the traditional words of parting.

CHAPTER 8

3 *ministered unto him of their substance*: 'provided for him out of their resources' (NRSV).

10 *seeing . . . understand*: this enigmatic remark seems to be alluding to Isa. 6:9–10.

17 *come abroad*: 'come to light' (NRSV).

18 *whosoever . . . seemeth to have*: see note to Matt. 13:12.

19 *his brethren*: for the names of some of them, see Mark 6:3.

22 *the lake*: i.e. the Sea of Galilee.

26–34 *Gadarenes . . . in the country*: see notes to Matt. 8:28, 33 and Mark 5:1–9.

43–4 *issue of blood . . . border of his garment*: see note to Matt. 9:20.

CHAPTER 9

7 *Herod the Tetrarch*: i.e. Herod Antipas.

9 *John . . . beheaded*: see Mark 6:17–29.

28 *an eight days*: a phrase meaning 'a week'. (The last recorded usage in *OED* is 1664.)

29–35 *his countenance . . . hear him*: see notes to Matt. 17:2–5.

42 *threw him down, and tare him*: 'dashed him to the ground in convulsions' (NRSV).

52 *Samaritans*: see Introduction, p. xxx.

53 *as though he would go to*: 'set toward' (NRSV).

54 *fire . . . as Elias did*: see 2 Kings 1:9–14.

60 *Let the dead bury*: see note to Matt. 8:22.

CHAPTER 10

1 *seventy*: a symbolic number, not to be taken literally. The Gentile world was traditionally divided into seventy nations (see Gen. 10), and Moses chose seventy elders from the twelve tribes (Exod. 24:1, 9; Num. 11:16, 24).

6 *turn to you again*: 'return to you' (NRSV).

15 *hell*: i.e. Hades (see note to Matt. 11:23).

18 *Satan*: see note to Matt. 4:1.

lawyer: i.e. an expert in the Law of Moses, probably a scribe (see note to Matt. 5:20).

27 *Thou shalt . . . as thyself*: quoted from Deut. 6:5 and Lev. 19:18.

30 *down from Jerusalem to Jericho*: a journey of about 18 miles. It was a notoriously dangerous road.

31 *priest*: i.e. a religious leader, one who would officiate at Temple ceremonies.

32 *Levite*: one who assisted priests in the Temple (from the priestly tribe of Levi). Both he and the priest in this parable would have been concerned about touching what may have been a corpse (see Num. 19:11–16).

33 *Samaritan*: see Introduction, p. xxx.

34 *oil and wine*: commonly used for medical purposes, the oil as a salve, the wine as an antiseptic.

35 *pence*: i.e. denarii (see note to Matt. 18:28). Two denarii would have paid for a stay of up to two months at an inn.

CHAPTER 11

1 *John*: i.e. John the Baptist.

2–4 *Our Father . . . from evil*: see notes to Matt. 6:9–13.

11 *If a son . . . a stone*: i.e. 'What father among you, if his son asks for bread, will give him a stone?'

15 *Beelzebub*: i.e. Satan (see v. 18). See note to Matt. 9:34.

19 *sons*: 'exorcists' (NRSV).

20 *the finger of God*: representing God's power. See Exod. 8:19.

29 *an evil generation*: see note to Matt. 11:16.

30–2 *Jonas . . . is here*: see notes to Matt. 12:40–2.

38 *washed before dinner*: referring to ritual washing (see Mark 7:1–5).

42 *tithe . . . of God*: i.e. you (the Pharisees) follow the Law in giving to the Temple a tenth part ('tithe') of the harvest, even down to tiny herbs like mint and rue, which are of little value, but you neglect justice and the love of God.

44 *graves which appear not*: 'unmarked graves' (NRSV), which could cause unwitting defilement; see note to Matt. 23:27.

48 *they indeed killed them*: see note to Matt. 5:12.

49 *said the wisdom of God*: not a quotation.

51 *Abel . . . Zacharias*: for Abel (the first martyr), see Gen. 4:8; for Zachariah (the last martyr in the Hebrew Bible), see 2 Chron. 24:20–2.

required of: 'charged against' (NRSV).

53 *began to urge . . . to speak of*: 'began to be very hostile toward him and to cross-examine him about' (NRSV).

CHAPTER 12

1 *leaven*: see note to Matt. 16:6.

5 *hell*: i.e. Gehenna (see note to Matt. 5:22).

6 *two farthings*: the coin here translated as 'farthing' was the as, a tiny bronze coin. Sixteen of them were the equivalent of a denarius, which was approximately a day's pay for a labourer.

10 *blasphemeth . . . be forgiven*: see notes to Matt. 12:31, 32.

13 *divide the inheritance*: for laws on inheritance, see Deut. 21:15–17; elder sons receive double that of younger brothers.

17 *no room where to bestow my fruits*: 'no place to store my crops' (NRSV).

19 *eat, drink, and be merry*: see Eccl. 8:15; cf. 1 Cor. 15:32.

25 *with taking thought*: i.e. by being anxious, or worrying.

27 *Solomon in all his glory*: for Solomon's splendour, see 1 Kings 10.

29 *be ye of doubtful mind*: 'keep worrying' (NRSV).

35 *Let your loins be girded about*: 'Be dressed for action' (NRSV).

38 *second watch . . . third watch*: see note to Matt. 14:25.

45 *But and if*: see note to Matt. 24:48.

46 *appoint him his portion with the unbelievers*: 'put him with the unfaithful' (NRSV).

49 *I am come . . . already kindled*: 'I came to bring fire to the earth, and how I wish it were already kindled!' (NRSV). Fire here symbolizes judgement.

50 *But I have . . . accomplished*: 'I have a baptism with which to be baptized, and what stress I am under until it is completed!' (NRSV). Baptism here refers (figuratively) to Jesus's death.

58 *in the way . . . from him*: 'on the way make an effort to settle the case' (NRSV).

CHAPTER 13

1 *Galileans . . . sacrifices*: Josephus records various brutal reprisals ordered by Pilate (*Ant.*, 18:86–7; *War*, p. 139), but not the incident here.

4 *tower in Siloam*: probably on the Ophel ridge at the south-east corner of Jerusalem, near the Pool of Siloam (see John 9:7). No other account of the fall of the tower is known.

6 *fig tree*: often used as a metaphor for Israel (see e.g. Hos. 9:10).

11 *a spirit of infirmity*: 'a spirit that had crippled her' (NRVS).

14 *not on the Sabbath day*: work was prohibited on the Sabbath; see Exod. 20:9–10; Deut. 5:13–14.

16 *a daughter of Abraham*: i.e. a Jew.

21 *hid in three measures*: see note to Matt. 13:33.

27 *depart . . . iniquity*: cf. Ps. 6:8.

28 *Abraham ... Isaac ... Jacob*: the three patriarchs of Israel.

29 *And they ... the south*: cf. Ps. 107:2–3.

30 *there are*: 'some are' (NRSV).

31 *Herod*: i.e. Herod Antipas.

32 *be perfected*: 'finish my work' (NRSV).

33 *I must walk*: 'I must be on my way' (NRSV).

34–5 *O Jerusalem ... the Lord*: see notes to Matt. 23:37–9.

CHAPTER 14

10 *shalt thou have worship*: 'you will be honoured' (NRSV).

12 *lest they ... be made thee*: 'in case they may invite you in return, and you would be repaid' (NRSV).

14 *the just*: 'the righteous' (NRSV).

18 *with one consent*: 'alike' (NRSV).

26 *hate not*: i.e. 'does not give second place in his affections to'. Cf. Matt. 10:37, and see also Deut. 21:15 for use of 'hated' meaning 'given lower preference'. It is possible, though, that Jesus's word 'hate' is designed as shock-tactics, of the kind he was fond of using.

CHAPTER 15

8 *pieces of silver*: Greek drachmas (each worth about a day's wages for a labourer).

15 *to feed swine*: feeding pigs would be an especially degrading activity for a Jew, because they were classed among the 'unclean' animals.

20 *fell on his neck*: 'put his arms around him' (NRSV).

23 *fatted calf*: a great luxury (cf. Amos 6:4).

31 *all that I have is thine*: i.e. the elder brother's inheritance rights are protected (see note to 12:13).

CHAPTER 16

1 *the same was accused unto him that he*: 'charges were brought to him that this man' (NRSV).

4 *that*: i.e. 'so that'.

6 *write fifty*: 'make it fifty' (NRSV). The implication is that the steward is forgoing his own commission.

8 *unjust*: 'dishonest' (NRSV). This is a difficult parable to interpret, and raises many questions. In what way exactly has the steward been dishonest? Is it in his previous action of 'lending' his master's goods to debtors, or in his transactions with the debtors? One explanation may be that the steward wants to show his master that he is looking after his interests, by making his debtors pay up, and persuades the debtors to do so by suggesting that they get off cheaply by only paying a part of what they owe. This shrewd piece

of minor dishonesty pleases both sides, and the steward deserves praise, as he has acted—in this worldly affair—responsibly and 'faithfully'. This makes him a suitable recipient for other-worldly 'riches'.

children of light: a term often used for the followers of Jesus (see e.g. John 12:36; Eph. 5:8; 1 Thess. 5:5).

9 *make to yourselves . . . habitations*: 'make friends for yourselves by means of dishonest wealth so that when it is gone, they may welcome you into the eternal homes' (NRSV).

14 *covetous*: 'lovers of money' (NRSV).

16 *were until John*: 'were in effect until John [the Baptist] came' (NRSV).

18 *Whosoever . . . adultery*: see note to Matt. 5:32.

19 *rich man*: he has come to be known as Dives (Latin for 'rich man').

22 *into Abraham's bosom*: 'to be with Abraham' (NRSV).

23 *hell*: i.e. Hades (see note to Matt. 11:23).

CHAPTER 17

2 *little ones*: i.e. disciples (not children). Cf. Mark 10:42.

9 *I trow not*: these words are not included in NRSV.

12 *stood afar off*: i.e. keeping their distance, as required under Jewish Law (see Lev. 13:46; Num. 5:2–3).

14 *show yourselves unto the priests*: i.e. for examination (see Lev. 13:2–8, 14:2–20).

20 *demanded of*: 'asked by' (NRSV).

with observation: 'with things that can be observed' (NRSV).

24 *For as . . . under heaven*: 'For as the lightning flashes and lights up the sky from one side to the other' (NRSV).

27 *They did eat . . . them all*: see Gen. 6:5–13, 7:17–23.

28–9 *days of Lot . . . them all*: see Gen. 13:13, 18:16–19:29.

31 *upon the house top*: see note to Matt. 24:17.

32 *Lot's wife*: see Gen. 19:26.

37 *eagles*: 'vultures' (NRSV).

CHAPTER 18

7 *elect*: 'chosen ones' (NRSV).

bear long with them: 'delay long in helping them' (NRSV).

12 *tithes of all that I possess*: 'a tenth of all my income' (NRSV). The AV is misleading, because laws about tithes applied only to earnings.

13 *God be merciful*: cf. Ps. 51:1–3.

14 *justified*: i.e. accepted by God.

19 *good . . . God*: cf. 1 Chron. 16:34; Pss 34:8, 106:1, 118:1, 29.

20 *the commandments*: see Exod. 20:12–16; Deut. 5:16–20.

26 *be saved*: i.e. gain eternal life.

31 *written by the prophets*: alluding to passages such as Ps. 22; Isa. 53.

38 *Son of David*: see note to Matt. 9:27.

CHAPTER 19

8 *taken any thing . . . accusation*: 'defrauded anyone of anything' (NRSV).

   restore him four fold: this was more than required under the Law; see Lev. 6:5; Num. 5:7; cf. Exod. 22:1, 4, 7.

9 *the son of Abraham*: i.e. an Israelite.

12–14 *receive for himself . . . reign over us*: for the possible contemporary resonance of this, see entry on Archelaus in Glossary of Persons, below, p. 265.

13 *pounds*: the coin referred to here is the mina, a golden coin worth 100 drachmas.

28 *he*: i.e. Jesus.

30–9 *colt . . . thy disciples*: see notes to Matt. 21:5–9.

37 *descent of*: 'path down from' (NRSV).

41–4 *wept . . . visitation*: Jesus's lament and prophecy includes allusions to Isa. 29:3; Jer. 6:6–8, 15:5–9.

43 *cast a trench . . . keep thee in*: 'set up ramparts around you and surround you, and hem you in' (NRSV). This corresponds with the kind of siege warfare used by Titus at the siege of Jerusalem, and has been cited as evidence suggesting a date of composition for the Gospel of Luke later than 70 CE. See, however, Isa. 29:3; Ezek. 4:2, for similar imagery.

45–6 *the Temple . . . of thieves*: see notes to Matt. 21:12–13.

CHAPTER 20

6 *But and if*: see note to Matt. 24:48.

9 *let it forth*: 'leased it' (NRSV).

16 *they*: i.e. Jesus's listeners.

17 *that is written*: see Ps. 118:22.

20 *the governor*: i.e. Pilate.

22–44 *give tribute . . . his son*: see notes to Matt. 22:17–45.

CHAPTER 21

5–33 *Temple . . . pass away*: see notes to Matt. 24:1–35.

5 *gifts*: 'gifts dedicated to God' (NRSV).

13 *turn to you for a testimony*: 'give you an opportunity to testify' (NRSV).

14 *Settle it . . . shall answer*: 'make up your minds not to prepare your defence in advance' (NRSV).

19 *In your . . . souls*: 'By your endurance you will gain your souls' (NRSV).

20 *Jerusalem . . . is nigh*: cf. Dan. 9:26–7.

21 *in the countries*: 'out in the country' (NRSV).

22–7 *days of vengeance . . . great glory*: the wording of these apocalyptic prophecies echoes passages in the Hebrew Bible; see e.g. Isa. 63:4; Hos. 9:7; Jer. 21:7; Ezek. 32:9; Dan. 8:13; Zech. 12:1–6; Joel 2:30–2; Isa. 13:10; Zeph. 1:15; Dan. 7:13–14.

CHAPTER 22

1 *Unleavened Bread . . . Passover*: see note to Mark. 14:1.

4 *captains*: 'officers of the temple police' (NRSV).

7–21 *Then came . . . for you*: see notes to Matt. 26:17–23.

15 *With desire I have desired*: 'I have eagerly desired' (NRSV).

25 *benefactors*: a title given to Hellenistic monarchs.

28 *Ye are they . . . temptations*: 'You are those who have stood by me in my trials' (NRSV).

32 *when thou art converted*: i.e. when you have repented [of his imminent denial of Jesus].

35 *When I sent you*: see 10:4 and 9:3.

37 *among the transgressors*: Isa. 53:12.

38 *It is enough*: the disciples have taken literally Jesus's metaphorical instructions to prepare themselves for the coming crisis, and he here dismisses with weary irony their 'two swords'.

40 *Pray . . . temptation*: see note to Matt. 6:13.

43–4 *And there . . . the ground*: these verses do not appear in some ancient manuscripts.

50 *smote . . . ear*: see John 18:10.

51 *Suffer ye thus far*: 'No more of this!' (NRSV).

CHAPTER 23

2 *perverting . . . a King*: the charges against Jesus are framed in political terms, to sound like treason, a matter which would justify taking him before a Roman court.

7 *to Herod*: the trial before Herod Antipas is not mentioned in any of the other Gospels.

11 *set him at naught*: 'treated him with contempt' (NRSV).

15 *is done unto him*: i.e. has been done by him [Jesus].

16 *chastise*: 'have him flogged' (NRSV).

17 *For . . . the feast*: in some ancient manuscripts, this verse is placed after verse 19; in others it is omitted. See note to Matt. 27:15.

18 *Barabbas*: see note to Matt. 27:16.

23 *were instant*: 'kept urgently demanding' (NRSV).

28 *Daughters of Jerusalem*: a term frequently used in the Hebrew Bible; see e.g. Song of Sol. 1:5, 2:7, 5:16, 8:4; Zeph. 3:14; Zech. 9:9.

29 *Blessed are the barren*: see note to 1:25, above.

30 *Then . . . Cover us*: cf. Hos. 10:8.

31 *green tree . . . dry*: the allusion seems to be to Ezek. 20:45–8. Jesus seems to be suggesting that if he, having been pronounced innocent by the Romans, is to be destroyed, what will happen to the guilty?

34–54 *Then said Jesus . . . drew on*: see notes to Matt. 27:34–62.

46 *into thy . . . spirit*: words from Ps. 31:5.

CHAPTER 24

1 *first day of the week*: i.e. Sunday (the first day of the Jewish week).

4 *two men*: identified as angels in v. 23, but recognized as such by their shining clothes.

6 *how he spake unto you*: see 9:22 and 13:32–3.

26 *ought not Christ to have suffered*: 'was it not necessary that the Messiah should suffer' (NRSV).

34 *appeared to Simon*: not recorded (but see 1 Cor. 15:5).

36 *Peace be unto you*: the traditional Jewish greeting.

44 *Moses . . . the Prophets . . . the Psalms*: the three sections into which the Hebrew Bible is divided (the Psalms being the opening and longest book of the third section, the Writings). See Introduction, p. xvi.

46 *it is written*: cf. Hos. 6:2.

47 *preached in his name*: cf. Acts 1:4–8.

49 *the promises . . . power from on high*: i.e. the Holy Spirit. See Acts 1:8, 2:1–21.

51 *carried up into heaven*: a fuller account of Jesus's ascension is given in Acts 1:9–11.

52 *returned to Jerusalem*: see Acts 1:12–14.

JOHN

CHAPTER 1

1 *In the beginning*: echoing the opening words of Genesis.

Word: on John's identification of Jesus as the divine 'Word' (Greek *logos*) of God, see Introduction, pp. xxxii–xxxiii.

6 *John*: i.e. John the Baptist.

8 *sent to bear witness*: see Mal. 3:1.

11 *his own*: i.e. his own people, the Jews.

14 *the Word was made flesh*: this is the most explicit statement in the Gospels of the Christian doctrine of the incarnation (literally 'enfleshment'), the idea that the divine and the human are uniquely brought together in the person of Jesus.

18 *hath declared him*: 'has made him known' (NRSV).

19 *priests and Levites*: see notes to Luke 10:31, 32.

21 *Art thou Elias . . . that prophet*: it was widely believed that Elijah, Moses, or one of the prophets would return to earth to herald the coming of the Messiah (see Mal. 4:5; Deut. 18:15–22); cf. 6:14, 7:40.

23 *I am . . . the Lord*: quoted from Isa. 40:3.

29 *Lamb of God . . . the world*: the use of 'lamb' as a symbol for Jesus is found only in John. The imagery is drawn from the Passover lamb, whose blood saved the Israelites just as the blood of the divine lamb will save all humankind (see Introduction, pp. xxxvi–xxxvii), and also from the depiction of the 'suffering servant' in Isaiah, who is 'brought as a lamb to the slaughter'. See Exod. 12; Isa. 53:7.

39 *about the tenth hour*: 'about four o'clock in the afternoon' (NRSV).

42 *Cephas*: the Aramaic equivalent of the Greek *Petros*, 'Peter' (both meaning 'rock').

46 *any good thing come out of Nazareth*: Nathanael evidently regards Nazareth as too small and insignificant to be the place from which the Messiah would come.

47 *an Israelite . . . no guile*: Jacob had behaved deceitfully before his name was changed to Israel (see Gen. 27:34–6, 32:28).

49 *Son of God . . . King of Israel*: see notes to Matt. 4:3, 27:11, 42. The bringing together of the two titles emphasizes the messianic significance of Nathanael's declaration (cf. Peter's similar declaration in Matt. 16:16).

51 *Son of Man*: see note to Matt. 8:20.

CHAPTER 2

1 *the mother of Jesus*: she is never named in John.

4 *Woman*: a term of respect (see 4:21, 8:10, 19:26, 20:13, 15).

  what . . . with thee: 'what concern is that to you and me?' (NRSV).

6 *purifying of the Jews*: i.e. rites of purification, such as washing of hands and food vessels.

8 *governor of the feast*: 'chief steward' (NRSV); i.e. the master of ceremonies.

14–16 *the Temple . . . merchandise*: see notes to Matt. 21:12–13.

17 *it was written*: in Ps. 69:9.

18 *the Jews*: i.e. the Temple authorities. Most of the references to 'Jews' in this Gospel are to be understood as referring to the religious authorities, or leaders of the Jews, not to the Jewish people in general.

20 *Forty and six years*: this refers to the rebuilding and enlargement of the Temple begun under Herod the Great in 20 BCE. The works were still in progress in Jesus's day (they were completed under Herod Agrippa II in 64 CE).

CHAPTER 3

5 *water . . . Spirit*: i.e. baptism (see 1:33; 1 Cor. 12:13; Titus 3:5).

14 *Moses . . . lifted up*: see Num. 21:8–9.

22 *land of Judea*: i.e. the countryside of Judea.

24 *John . . . prison*: see Matt. 11:2–3 and Mark 6:14–18.

29 *friend of the bridegroom*: i.e. the 'best man', or chief of the bridegroom's party.

33 *set to his seal*: 'certified' (NRSV); i.e. set his seal to.

34 *giveth not . . . unto him*: 'gives the Spirit without measure' (NRSV).

CHAPTER 4

5 *Jacob . . . Joseph*: see Gen. 33:19, 48:22; Josh. 24:32.

6 *the sixth hour*: i.e. noon.

20 *this mountain*: i.e. Mount Gerizim, where the temple of the Samaritans had formerly stood, and which they believed was the only place designated by God for worship (see Deut. 11:26–30, 27:11–13).

24 *God is a Spirit*: the AV here mistranslates the Greek, which should be translated 'God is spirit'.

26 *I . . . am he*: 'I am he; the one who is speaking to you' (NRSV). The literal translation of the Greek phrase translated as 'I am he' is 'I am', which is the name of Yahweh (God) himself in the Hebrew Bible (see Introduction, p. xxxv).

27 *talked with the woman*: more properly, 'a' woman. The disciples are astonished because it was regarded as highly undesirable for a Jewish religious teacher to speak to a woman in public.

38 *I sent . . . their labours*: possibly alluding to Josh. 24:13.

44 *prophet . . . country*: this is said of Nazareth in Matt. 13:57; Mark 6:4; Luke 4:24.

52 *at the seventh hour*: 'at one in the afternoon' (NRSV).

CHAPTER 5

1 *a feast*: it is not clear which of the Jewish festivals is referred to here, if indeed any specific festival is intended.

2 *Sheep Market . . . five porches*: probably referring to the Sheep Gate, in the northern wall of Jerusalem (see Neh. 3:1). Excavations there have uncovered a healing sanctuary and pool with five porticoes (walkways with columns supporting the roof), which may be the pool of Bethesda (or 'Bethzatha', an alternative manuscript reading adopted by NRSV).

4 *For . . . he had*: this verse is not included in NRSV, because not found in the best manuscripts.

10 *The Jews*: see note to 2:18, above.

Sabbath day . . . thy bed: see Exod. 20:8–10. Carrying of burdens on the Sabbath is specifically mentioned in Neh. 13:15–21 and Jer. 17:19–27.

17 *worketh hitherto, and I work*: 'is still working, and I also am working' (NRSV). Cf. Gen. 2:2–3.

31 *bear witness . . . not true*: in Jewish tradition, an individual's testimony about themselves was not accepted as valid.

32 *another*: most commentators regard this as referring to God the Father (see v. 37), but some argue that it refers to John the Baptist.

33 *Ye sent*: 'You sent messengers' (NRSV).

John: i.e. John the Baptist.

34 *But I receive not testimony from man*: 'Not that I accept such human testimony' (NRSV).

43 *another . . . in his own name*: perhaps referring to others claiming to be the Messiah.

45 *Moses, in whom ye trust*: see 9:28.

46 *he wrote of me*: cf. Luke 16:29–31, 24:27.

CHAPTER 6

1 *went over*: i.e. from the western side of the Sea of Galilee to the eastern.

3–15 *And Jesus . . . himself alone*: the Feeding of the Five Thousand is the only miracle recorded in all four Gospels. Cf. Matt. 14:13–21; Mark 6:32–44; Luke 9:10–17 (and see also the Feeding of the Four Thousand, Matt. 15:32–9; Mark 8:1–10).

7 *Two hundred penny-worth*: i.e. 200 denarii, which would be about six months' wages for a labourer.

9 *barley loaves*: cf. 2 Kings 4:42–4.

15 *to make him a king*: i.e. a political messianic figure who would lead a revolt against the Romans.

22 *the other side*: i.e. on the eastern shore.

25 *the other side*: i.e. the western shore.

27 *sealed*: i.e. marked with approval.

31 *it is written*: see Exod. 16:4, but the words here may be quoted from Neh. 9:15.

45 *in the Prophets*: Isa. 54:13; cf. Jer. 31:34.

60 *an hard saying*: what Jesus has been saying is difficult for Jews to accept because eating blood was prohibited under the Mosaic Law (see Gen. 9:4; Lev. 17:13–14).

CHAPTER 7

1 *Jewry*: i.e. Judea.

2 *Feast of Tabernacles*: also known as the Feast of Booths (Hebrew *Sukkot*), this was a seven-day harvest festival beginning on 15 Tishri (the seventh month, equivalent to about mid-September to about mid-October). It was designed to commemorate the wanderings of the Israelites in the wilderness (Lev. 23:33–43; Deut. 16:13–17; Neh. 8:14–18).

3 *His brethren*: i.e. his brothers (see Mark 6:3).

4 *no man . . . openly*: 'no one who wants to be widely known acts in secret' (NRSV).

21 *one work*: i.e. the healing on the Sabbath (5:1–15).

22 *Moses . . . circumcision*: see Gen. 17:9–14; Lev. 12:3. Circumcision had to be performed on the eighth day even if this fell on the Sabbath.

24 *judge righteous judgement*: 'judge with right judgement' (NRSV).

35 *the dispersed*: i.e. the Jews of the 'dispersion' (diaspora), living outside Palestine among the Greeks ('Gentiles').

37 *the last day . . . of the feast*: probably the eighth day, which was kept as a Sabbath at the end of the seven days. For each of the seven days water was ceremonially carried in a golden pitcher from the Pool of Siloam to the Temple, commemorating the water provided from the rock in the desert (Num. 20:2–13).

38 *scripture hath said*: the reference is uncertain, but may be Isa. 44:2–3, or Zech. 14:8 (Zech. 14 is one of the readings at the Feast of Tabernacles).

42 *scripture said*: see 1 Sam. 16:1–13; 2 Sam. 7:12–16; Pss 89:3–4, 132:11–12; Mic. 5:2.

53 *And every . . . own house*: this verse belongs to the start of the next chapter, and is placed there in NRSV, linked by 'while' to v. 1.

CHAPTER 8

1–11 *Jesus went . . . sin no more*: modern scholars generally agree that this passage (with v. 53 from the previous chapter) did not form part of the original text. It is missing in the most authoritative manuscripts.

5 *Moses . . . stoned*: see Lev. 20:10 and Deut. 22:22–4. It may be noted that stoning was the means of death specified for a betrothed virgin (and the offending male).

6 *have to accuse him*: 'have some charge to bring against him' (NRSV).

12 *Then spake . . . light of life*: the 'again' links back to the discourse at the festival of Tabernacles in the previous chapter. Great golden lamps were lit in the Temple court during the festival.

13 *record of thyself*: see note to 5:31, above.

17 *written in your Law*: see Num. 35:30; Deut. 17:6, 19:15.

33 *never in bondage*: i.e. spiritually free (it would not be true in a literal sense, for they had been in bondage in Egypt and in Babylon, and now under the Romans).

40 *this did not Abraham*: i.e. Abraham did not reject messengers from God (see Gen. 18:1–8).

41 *born of fornication*: 'illegitimate children' (NRSV).

44 *Ye are of your father the devil*: the harsh language here reflects the tensions that had developed by the time John was writing between Jewish followers of Jesus and the wider Jewish communities who did not accept claims that Jesus was the Messiah, and who from about 80 CE had begun to expel Jewish Christians from synagogues.

48 *a Samaritan*: see Introduction, p. xxx. Samaritans disputed the claim of Jews to be exclusive descendants of Abraham.

56 *Abraham . . . was glad*: cf. Gen. 17:17 and Heb. 11:17 (referring to Gen. 21:12–13).

58 *I am*: see note to 4:26, above.

CHAPTER 9

6 *he spat*: see note to Mark 7:33.

7 *pool of Siloam*: a famous pool just inside the south-east corner of the old city of Jerusalem, fed by the waters of the Gihon running through a conduit built by Hezekiah (see 2 Kings 20:20; 2 Chron. 32:30).

39 *see not . . . made blind*: perhaps alluding to Isa. 6:9–10.

41 *If ye . . . remaineth*: i.e. the 'blindness' of the Pharisees is not physical, but is spiritual. Because they profess to be able to 'see', their 'blindness' represents a willed refusal to understand the truth, for which they must be held responsible.

CHAPTER 10

1 *I say unto you*: this continues the previous chapter, and Jesus is still addressing the Pharisees.

16 *other sheep*: i.e. Gentiles (cf. 7:35, 11:52, 12:32).

one fold: this is a mistranslation in the AV, and should read 'one flock'. The error probably derives from the Vulgate's *unum ovile* (which should have been *unus grex*, translating the Greek *mia poimnē*).

22 *Feast of the Dedication*: now known as Hanukkah, this feast begins on 25 Kislev (December) each year. It commemorates the rededication of the Temple by Judas Maccabeus in 164 BCE, following its desecration by Antiochus IV Epiphanes (see 1 Maccabees (Apocrypha) 4:36–59).

23 *Solomon's Porch*: a covered walkway (portico) on the eastern side of the Temple.

24 *make us to doubt*: 'keep us in suspense' (NRSV).

31 *again to stone him*: see 8:59. Stoning was the punishment for blasphemy, though only to be carried out after a proper trial (see Lev. 24:16).

34 *written in your Law*: see Ps. 82:6. (Here, and elsewhere in John (12:34, 15:25), 'Law' is used loosely to refer to the Jewish scriptures in general.) Jesus's argument is that if scripture (as in Ps. 82:6) refers to men as 'gods', it should not be grounds for presuming blasphemy when he claims to be one with God.

40 *beyond Jordan*: i.e. across the Jordan, from Judea to Perea.

CHAPTER 11

5 *Now Jesus loved*: 'Accordingly, though Jesus loved' (NRSV). The delay of two days suggests that the raising of Lazarus is meant as a foreshadowing of the death and resurrection of Jesus himself on the third day.

9 *twelve hours in the day*: for Jews at the time of Jesus, the day (which began at dawn and ended at dusk) was divided into twelve hours (which were thus longer in summer and shorter in winter).

17 *four days*: Jewish belief was that the soul lingered near the body of the dead person for three days, so that death only became truly final on the fourth day.

24 *resurrection at the last day*: this had become a common belief among Jews by the time of Jesus (see note to Matt. 22:23).

33 *he groaned . . . was troubled*: 'he was greatly disturbed in spirit and deeply moved' (NRSV).

38 *stone lay upon it*: i.e. the mouth of the cave was sealed by a cylindrical stone (which could be rolled back).

47 *a council*: i.e. a meeting of the Sanhedrin (for which, see note to Matt. 2:4).

   What do we?: 'What are we to do?' (NRSV).

48 *take away both our place and nation*: 'destroy both our holy place [the Temple] and our nation' (NRSV). The great Jewish revolt of 66–70 CE resulted in the destruction of Jerusalem and the Temple.

50 *nor consider that it is expedient for us*: 'You do not understand that it is better for you' (NRSV).

51 *he prophesied*: i.e. unknowingly.

55 *to purify themselves*: i.e. to perform all the necessary purificatory rites (see Num. 9:1–14).

CHAPTER 12

1 *six days before the Passover*: i.e. on the Saturday previous (Passover being on a Friday).

3 *pound*: i.e. a Roman pound (just under 12 ounces, or about 326 grams).

   with her hair: it would have been considered immodest for a woman to undo her hair in the presence of men.

6 *had the bag, and bare what was put therein*: 'kept the common purse and used to steal' (NRSV).

13–15 *branches . . . colt*: see notes to Matt. 21:5–9.

17 *bare record*: 'continued to testify' (NRSV).

20 *Greeks*: these would have been Greek converts to Judaism (cf. Acts 8:27, 17:4).

31 *prince of this world*: i.e. the devil (see 14:30, 16:11).

34 *Christ* [i.e. the Messiah] *abideth for ever*: see e.g. Ps. 89:3–4, 28–9, 35–7; Isa. 9:6–7; Ezek. 37:24–5; Dan. 7:13–14.

38–40 *Esaias . . . heal them*: see Isa. 53:1, 6:10.

CHAPTER 13

1 *before the Feast of the Passover*: see Introduction, p. xxxvi.

2 *supper being ended*: 'during supper' (NRSV). The AV wording seems to conflict with v. 26.

4 *riseth from supper . . . girded himself*: 'got up from the table, took off his outer robe, and tied a towel around himself' (NRSV).

5 *wash the disciples' feet*: a task that would be carried out by slaves for their (Roman) masters.

18 *the scripture*: see Ps. 41:9.

23 *leaning on Jesus's bosom*: 'reclining next to [Jesus]' (NRSV). Diners at special meals would recline on their left sides on couches around a low table. The disciple here would thus be to the right of Jesus, the place reserved for an intimate friend.

   whom Jesus loved: the first appearance of the 'beloved disciple'; see also 19:26–7, 20:1–8, 21:7, 20–3.

27 *Satan*: see note to Matt. 9:34.

33 *said unto the Jews*: see 7:34.

34 *as I . . . ye also*: 'Just as I have loved you, you also should' (NRSV).

CHAPTER 14

2 *I would have told you*: 'would I have told you that' (NRSV).

4 *And whither . . . way ye know*: 'And you know the way to the place where I am going' (NRSV).

16 *Comforter*: 'Advocate' (NRSV), i.e. the Holy Spirit, also known as the Paraclete (from the Greek word here).

18 *comfortless*: 'orphaned' (NRSV).

22 *Judas . . . not Iscariot*: see Luke 6:16; Acts 1:13.

30 *hath nothing in me*: 'has no power over me' (NRSV).

31 *Arise, let us go hence*: some scholars have argued that chapters 15–17 were added later, and that chapter 18 originally followed on from the end of chapter 14 here.

CHAPTER 15

1 *the true vine*: in the Hebrew Bible, the metaphor of the grapevine is often used of the people of Israel (see e.g. Ps. 80:8–13; Isa. 5:1–7; Ezek. 15:1–6, 19:10–14).

20 *the word that I said*: see 13:16.

25 *in their Law*: see Pss 35:19 and 69:4.

CHAPTER 16

8 *reprove the world of sin*: 'prove the world wrong about sin' (NRSV).

32 *to his own*: i.e. to his own home.

CHAPTER 17

5 *with thine own self*: 'in your own presence' (NRSV).

with thee: 'in your presence' (NRSV).

12 *the son of perdition*: 'the one destined to be lost' (NRSV), i.e. Judas.

might be fulfilled: see 13:18 and note; see also Acts 1:16–20.

CHAPTER 18

1 *over the brook Cedron*: 'across the Kidron valley' (NRSV). The 'brook' was a seasonal river, whose wadi (or valley) lies east of Jerusalem, between the city and the Mount of Olives.

a garden: named Gethsemane in Matthew (26:36) and Mark (14:32).

3 *a band of men, and officers*: 'a detachment of soldiers together with police' (NRSV), i.e. Roman soldiers, and members of the Temple guard.

6 *I am he*: or, literally, 'I am', the divine name (see note to 4:26, above).

9 *Of them . . . lost none*: see 6:39, 17:12.

12 *captain*: i.e. tribune, commander of a Roman cohort.

14 *gave counsel . . . the people*: see 11:50.

15 *palace of the High Priest*: i.e. to the house of Annas (here given the title of 'High Priest' because of his eminent position, though he had been dismissed from office in 15 CE).

23 *bear witness of*: i.e. give evidence of, testify to.

24 *Now Annas had sent him*: 'Then Annas sent him' (NRSV).

28 *hall of judgement*: 'Pilate's headquarters' (NRSV). While in Jerusalem, the governor resided at the former palace of Herod the Great in the Upper City (and not, as formerly thought, at the Antonia fortress, the main Roman garrison).

it was early: the last two watches of the night were known as 'cockcrow' and 'early' (or dawn), so the proceedings here are taking place before 6 a.m.

lest they should be defiled: to enter the house of a Gentile would make a Jew ritually 'unclean' and thus unable to eat the Passover meal.

31 *not lawful . . . to death*: scholars are divided on whether the Romans permitted the Sanhedrin to execute criminals, but even if they had the authority they evidently chose not to exercise it in this case.

32 *what death he should die*: i.e. by crucifixion; see 3:14, 12:32–3.

33 *King of the Jews*: see note to Matt. 27:11.

39–40 *a custom . . . a robber*: see notes to Matt. 27:15–16.

CHAPTER 19

1 *scourged him*: this usually only happened after sentencing, as part of the punishment (see note to Matt. 27:26).

2–3 *crown of thorns . . . their hands*: see notes to Matt. 27:28–9.

6 *Take ye him, and crucify him*: only the Romans themselves could carry out crucifixions.

7 *We have a law . . . Son of God*: i.e. Jesus should be stoned to death as a blasphemer (see Lev. 24:16).

12 *whosoever . . . Caesar*: 'Everyone who claims to be a king sets himself against the emperor' (NRSV).

13 *the Pavement . . . Gabbatha*: the Aramaic word *Gabbatha* means 'raised place', and it is now thought to have been a courtyard in the huge palace built by Herod the Great in the Upper City (and not at the Antonia fortress).

14 *Preparation of the Passover*: i.e. when the Passover lambs would begin to be slaughtered in the Temple, in preparation for the meal that evening.

the sixth hour: i.e. noon.

17 *bearing his cross*: see note to Matt. 27:32.

19 *Pilate wrote a title*: i.e. caused an inscription to be written (see note to Matt. 27:37).

23 *made four . . . a part*: 'divided them into four parts, one for each soldier' (NRSV).

24 *cast lots . . . cast lots*: see note to Matt. 27:35.

28–30 *After this . . . the ghost*: see notes to Matt. 27:48–50.

31 *the Preparation . . . taken away*: preparation for the Sabbath would have to happen soon, for it would begin at 6 p.m. It was not permitted under Jewish Law for hanged bodies to remain unburied overnight (see Deut. 21:22–3), but death could be hastened by breaking the legs of victims (so that they could not push up to breathe).

36 *A bone . . . broken*: the reference is to the Passover lamb (see Exod. 12:46); see also Ps. 34:20. See Introduction, p. xxxvii.

37 *They shall . . . pierced*: see Zech. 12:10.

39 *an hundred pound weight*: i.e. Roman pounds, equivalent to about 34 kg (75 lb). This was a large quantity of burial spices, much more than would be needed for one body.

CHAPTER 20

1 *first day*: i.e. Sunday (the Sabbath—Saturday—being regarded by Jews as the last day of the week).

9 *knew not the scripture*: 'did not understand the scripture' (NRSV). 'Scripture' here refers to passages in the Hebrew Bible which were interpreted by early Christians as referring to Jesus's resurrection (cf. Luke 24:45–6; Acts 2:24–32; 1 Cor. 15:4).

16 *Rabboni*: the Aramaic form of 'Rabbi' (teacher); see notes to Matt. 5:20 and 23:7.

17 *Touch me not*: 'Do not hold on to me' (NRSV).

19 *at evening, being the first day*: according to Jewish reckoning, the second day of the week (Monday) would have started at sunset on the Sunday (the Jewish day ran from dawn to dusk).

the Jews: see note to 2:18, above.

Peace be unto you: the traditional Jewish greeting.

22 *he breathed on them*: see Gen. 2:7, where God 'breathed . . . the breath of life' into the nostrils of the first man to make him a 'living soul'.

26 *after eight days*: i.e. at the end of the Passover festival.

CHAPTER 21

1 *After these things*: many scholars believe that this chapter is an 'epilogue' added on to the Gospel of John at some later date.

3–11 *Simon Peter . . . net broken*: cf. the story of the miraculous catch of fish in Luke 5:1–11, where it comes at the beginning of Jesus's ministry.

7 *girt . . . naked*: i.e. he pulled on his fisherman's smock and tucked it into his belt.

8 *two hundred cubits*: 'about a hundred yards' (NRSV).

11 *an hundred and fifty and three*: many attempts have been made to find a symbolic significance in this number. It seems likely that it is meant in some way to represent the universality of the mission of the Church.

12 *dine*: i.e. have breakfast.

15 *more than these?*: i.e. is Peter's love for Jesus greater than that of the other disciples?

18–19 *stretch forth . . . what death*: a prophetic anticipation of Peter's martyrdom on the cross (cf. 13:36–8).

20 *the disciple . . . betrayeth thee*: see 13:22–5.

22 *till I come*: i.e. until I return in glory (referring to the Second Coming).

24 *the disciple . . . wrote these things*: the 'beloved disciple' is here identified as the one on whose witness the Gospel is based. 'Wrote' here is not necessarily to be understood literally (see note to 19:19, above).

GLOSSARY OF PERSONS

Anna a prophetess, or holy woman, who witnessed the presentation of the infant Jesus at the Temple. See Luke 2:36–8.

Andrew one of the disciples, a fisherman from Bethsaida. At the time of the ministry of Jesus he was sharing a house in Capernaum with his brother, Simon Peter. According to John (1:40), he and Peter were disciples of John the Baptist before being called by Jesus. Legend has it that he was crucified on an X-shaped cross at Patras in Achaia in 60 CE. See Matt. 4:18, 10:2; Mark 1:16, 29, 3:18, 13:3; Luke 6:14; John 1:40, 44, 6:8, 12:22; Acts 1:13.

Annas (or Ananus), High Priest of the Jews, 6–15 CE. Though deposed by the Romans, he continued to wield great influence. Five of his sons, and his son-in-law Caiaphas, were High Priests between 16 and 66 CE. According to John (18:13), Jesus was first taken to the house of Annas for interrogation, before being sent to Caiaphas. See Luke 3:2; John 18:13, 24; Acts 4:6; Josephus *Ant.*, 18:26, 95, 19:297, 313.

Antipas Herod Antipas, the second son of Herod the Great, tetrarch ('ruler of a fourth part') of Galilee and Perea, ruling from 4 BCE to 39 CE. He divorced his wife in order to marry his niece, Herodias, and when criticized for this by John the Baptist, had him imprisoned in the fortress of Machaerus, and subsequently executed. According to Luke (23:7–11), Jesus was sent by Pilate to Antipas for sentencing, but when Jesus refused to perform a miracle Antipas returned him to Pilate. See Matt. 14:1–12; Mark 6:14–29; Luke 9:7–9, 23:7–12; Josephus *War*, pp. 138–9; *Ant.*, 18:27, 36–8, 101–29, 240–56.

Archelaus Herod Archelaus, the eldest son of Herod the Great, expected to inherit his title as king, and went to Rome in 4 BCE to press his claim. However, there was much opposition to him (a delegation of Jews went to Rome to protest) and in the end he received only about half of Herod's kingdom, including Idumea, Judea, and Samaria, with the diminished title of ethnarch ('governor of a people or province'). His rule was unpopular, and in 6 CE he was removed by the emperor Augustus, and his domain became an imperial province ruled by Roman governors, of whom Pontius Pilate was the fifth. See Matt. 2:22; Josephus *War*, pp. 118–24, 128–33; *Ant.*, 17:208–9, 299–317, 339–54.

Augustus (formerly Gaius Julius Caesar Octavianus), the first emperor of Rome, reigned from 31 BCE to 14 CE. In general, he maintained a fairly tolerant policy towards the Jews, granting them considerable autonomy and freedom of religion. See Luke 2:1–2; Josephus *Ant.*, 16:162–73.

Bartholomew one of the disciples. He is not mentioned in John, and it has been suggested that he and the Nathanael mentioned by John are the same person (John 1:45–6). According to later Christian tradition, he went to India, and he is supposed to have been martyred at Albanopolis in Armenia. See Matt. 10:3; Mark 3:18; Luke 6:14; Acts 1:13.

Bartimaeus the blind beggar healed by Jesus at or near Jericho on his last journey to Jerusalem. See Mark 10:46–52.

Caiaphas High Priest of the Jews, 18–36 CE. The trial of Jesus took place at his house, and it was at his instigation that Jesus was condemned. See Matt. 26:3–5; Luke 3:2; John 11:47–53, 18:12–14, 24, 28; Josephus *Ant.*, 18:35, 95.

Cleopas one of the two disciples joined by Jesus on the road to Emmaus (Luke 24:18). He is sometimes identified with the Cleophas (or Clopas) referred to as the husband of one of the Marys present at the crucifixion (see John 19:25).

Cyrenius see *Quirinius*

Herod known as 'the Great' was appointed King of the Jews by the Romans in 40 BCE and ruled from 37 to 4 BCE. Jesus was born near the end of his reign, probably in 6/5 BCE. Herod's most famous enterprise was the rebuilding of the Temple at Jerusalem, started in 20 BCE. (The Western or 'Wailing' Wall of this is still standing.) See Matt. 2:1–22; Luke 1:5; Josephus *War*, pp. 73–119; *Ant.*, 15:1–17:192.

Herodias the daughter of Aristobulus, a son of Herod the Great. She was married first to her uncle, also called Herod, a half-brother of Herod Antipas. Antipas fell in love with Herodias, and divorced his first wife in order to marry her. According to Mark and Matthew, she prompted the execution of John the Baptist (because he declared their marriage illegal under Jewish Law, which it was). See Matt. 14:3–12; Mark 6:17–29; Luke 3:19; Josephus *Ant.*, 18:110–19, 240–55.

James brother of Jesus (known as 'the Less' to distinguish him from James, son of Zebedee) became one of the leaders of the Church at Jerusalem. He was reported to have been chosen bishop of Jerusalem and to have been put to death by the Sanhedrin in 62 CE. Various writings were attributed to him. See Matt. 13:55; Mark 6:3, 15:40, 16:1; Luke 24:10; Acts 15:13–21, 21:18–19; Gal. 1:19; Josephus *Ant.*, 20:200.

James son of Zebedee (known as 'the Great' to distinguish him from James, brother of Jesus), a Galilean fisherman when called to be a disciple of Jesus. He and his brother John were named 'Boanerges', or 'sons of thunder', by Jesus, perhaps because of their zeal, and they, with Peter, were a privileged group among the disciples. James was the first of the disciples to be martyred, being beheaded by Herod Agrippa I in 44 CE. See Matt. 4:21, 10:2, 17:1; Mark 1:19, 29, 3:17, 5:37, 9:2, 10:35–41, 13:3, 14:33; Luke 5:10, 8:51, 9:28; Acts 1:13, 12:2; 1 Cor. 15:7.

James one of the disciples, usually identified with the 'son of Alphaeus'. He may have been the brother of the tax collector Levi son of Alphaeus (who is thought to be identical with the disciple Matthew). See Matt. 10:3; Mark 2:14, 3:18, 15:40; Luke 6:15; Acts 1:13.

Joanna wife of Chuza, a steward in the palace of Herod Antipas at Jerusalem, was a follower of Jesus. She was one of the women at the empty tomb. See Luke 8:3, 24:10.

John the Baptist the son of Zachariah and Elizabeth, preached by the banks of the Jordan and practised baptism (immersion in water to symbolize repentance for sins). Luke dates the commencement of his ministry to the fifteenth year of the emperor Tiberius, which would have been 29 CE. He is frequently described as the forerunner of Jesus, and baptized him at the start of his ministry. Josephus describes him as a 'good man' who exhorted the Jews 'to exercise virtue', and recounts his imprisonment and execution by Herod Antipas in the fortress of Machaerus on the east side of the Dead Sea. See Matt. 3, 4:12, 9:14, 11:2–14, 14:1–12, 21:25; Mark 1:4–11, 14, 2:18, 6:14–29, 11:30; Luke 1:5–25, 57–80, 3:1–22, 5:33, 7:18–35, 9:7–9, 20:4; John 1:6–34, 3:23–36, 5:33–6, 10:40–1; Josephus *Ant.*, 18:116–19.

John son of Zebedee, a Galilean fisherman like his brother James ('the Great') and, with Peter one of the inner group of disciples. He comes across as an impetuous character—he and James were described by Jesus as 'sons of thunder' (Mark 3:17)—and he was later a close associate of Peter. In the fourth Gospel he is never mentioned by name (though there is a reference to the sons of Zebedee, John 21:2), but tradition has identified him as the disciple 'whom Jesus loved' (John 13:23, 20:2, 21:20) and to whom Jesus entrusted care of his mother Mary (John 19:26–7). According to tradition, he settled at Ephesus and there wrote the Gospel of John, but the evidence for this is tenuous. See Matt. 4:21, 10:2, 17:1, 26:37; Mark 1:19, 29, 9:2, 10:35–41, 13:3, 14:33; Luke 5:10, 6:14; Acts 1:13, 3:1, 3, 11, 4:13, 19, 8:14.

Joseph the husband of Mary, mother of Jesus, a carpenter at Nazareth. According to the genealogy in Matthew, his descent could be traced back through King David to Abraham, while the one in Luke traces it right back to Adam. He figures largely in the two accounts of the nativity of Jesus, but is hardly mentioned thereafter in the Gospels. See Matt. 1:16, 18–25, 2:13–14, 19–23, 13:55; Luke 1:27, 2:4–5, 16, 33, 43, 3:23, 4:22; John 1:45, 6:42.

Joseph the brother of Jesus is mentioned several times in the Gospels. (The AV uses the Greek form of his name, 'Joses'.) See Matt. 13:55, 27:56; Mark 6:3, 15:40, 47.

Joseph of Arimathea, a wealthy leader of the Jews and member of the Sanhedrin, a secret follower of Jesus. After the crucifixion he requested the body of Jesus, and gave it burial in a tomb he owned. See Matt. 27:57–60; Mark 15:43–6; Luke 23:50–3; John 19:38–42.

Joses see *Joseph the brother of Jesus*

Judas see *Jude the brother of Jesus*

Judas Iscariot the disciple who betrayed Jesus to the Jewish authorities for thirty pieces of silver. The name 'Iscariot' probably means 'man from Kerioth', a village in southern Judea. (Most of the other disciples were Galileans.) According to John, he was the bursar for the disciples (though not a very honest one). He apparently repented of his act of betrayal, and committed suicide. See Matt. 10:4, 26:14–16, 25, 47–9, 27:3–5; Mark 3:19, 14:10–11, 43–5; Luke 6:16, 22:3–6, 47–8; John 6:71, 12:4–6, 13:2, 26–30, 18:2–5; Acts 1:16–20, 25.

Jude the brother of Jesus and one of the disciples. The Epistle of Jude is attributed to him, and he was a prominent leader and missionary of the early Church. In the Gospels he is called 'Judas', the Greek form of his name. See Matt. 13:55; Luke 6:16; John 14:22; Acts 1:13.

Lazarus the brother of Martha and Mary, lived with them at Bethany. He was beloved of Jesus, and was raised by him from the dead. He was much revered in the early Church and through the Middle Ages, and many legends were associated with him. See John 11:1–44, 12:1–10.

Lebbaeus see *Thaddaeus*

Levi son of Alphaeus, a tax collector called by Jesus to follow him (though he does not appear in lists of the Twelve, and is sometimes thought to be identical with Matthew). See Mark 2:14; Luke 5:27–9.

Luke traditionally regarded as the author of the third Gospel and of the Acts of the Apostles. He was apparently a Gentile, a physician by profession, and was from Antioch. He accompanied St Paul on some of his missionary journeys, and stayed with him in Rome. According to legend he was a painter, and is thus the patron saint of artists as well as doctors. See Col. 4:14; 2 Tim. 4:11; Philem. 24.

Lysanias referred to as 'tetrarch of Abilene [Abila]' by Luke, but though Josephus refers to 'Abila of Lysanias' it is not certain that this is the same Lysanias. See Luke 3:1; Josephus *Ant.*, 18:237, 19:275.

Malchus the servant of the High Priest whose ear was cut off by Peter in Gethsemane. See Matt. 26:51; Mark 14:47; Luke 22:50; John 18:10.

Mark a close associate of Peter, and since the second century regarded as the author of the second Gospel, supposedly having based it on the teaching and recollections of Peter. He is often identified with the 'John Mark' (cousin of Barnabas) mentioned several times in Acts and with the 'Mark' (or 'Marcus') mentioned in several of Paul's epistles, and apparently became the first bishop of Alexandria. See Acts 12:12, 25, 15:37–9; Col. 4:10; 2 Tim. 4:11; Philem. 24; 1 Pet. 5:13.

Martha sister of Mary and of Lazarus, lived with them in Bethany, east of Jerusalem. From the description of her, she is often taken as representing the 'active' Christian life. See Luke 10:38–42; John 11:1–40, 12:1–2.

Mary the mother of Jesus and the wife of Joseph, commonly known as the 'Blessed Virgin Mary', lived in Nazareth where she was born. Four more sons (James, Joseph ['Joses'], Jude ['Judas'], and Simon) were born to her, and several unnamed daughters. Following the accounts of the nativity, she is mentioned only a few times in the Gospels. She was formally defined as the 'Mother of God' at the Council of Ephesus in 431 CE, and in the sixth century the doctrine of her corporeal assumption to heaven was given orthodox formulation. See Matt. 1:18–25, 2:11–14, 19–23, 12:46, 13:55, ?27:56, 61, ?28:1; Mark 3:31, 6:3, ?15:40, 47, ?16:1; Luke 1:26–56, 2:4–7, 16–19, 22–4, 33–5, 41–51, 8:19, ?24:10; John 2:1–12, 6:42, 19:25–7; Acts 1:14.

Mary Magdalene (so named because she came from Magdala), a follower of Jesus, who had cast out of her 'seven devils'. Later Christian tradition identified her with the repentant woman who anointed the feet of Jesus (Luke 7:37–8), or with Mary, sister of Martha, but there is no evidence for either. She was present at the crucifixion, and was the chief witness to the resurrection, where the risen Jesus said to her the famous words 'touch me not' (*noli me tangere*). See Matt. 27:56, 61, 28:1; Mark 15:40, 47, 16:1, 9; Luke 8:2, 24:10; John 19:25, 20:1–2, 11–18.

Mary of Bethany, sister of Martha and Lazarus, often taken as representing the 'contemplative' Christian life (by contrast with her sister). According to John, she anointed the feet of Jesus during the last week of his life. See Matt. 26:6–13; Mark 14:3–9; Luke 10:39–42; John 11:1–45, 12:3–8.

Mary known only as 'the wife of Cleophas', one of the women at the cross. She seems to have been the sister of Mary the mother of Jesus. See John 19:25.

Matthew one of the disciples, a 'publican' or tax collector in the service of Herod Antipas when called by Jesus. He may be the person named as 'Levi the son of Alphaeus' in Mark (2:14) and Luke (5:27, 29). Traditionally regarded as the author of the first Gospel, this ancient attribution is now discounted by scholars. See Matt. 9:9, 10:3; Mark 3:18; Luke 6:15; Acts 1:13.

Nathanael one of the disciples, a native of Cana. He is called Nathanael only in John, and is now generally identified with the disciple named Bartholomew in the other Gospels. See John 1:45–50, 21:2; (as Bartholomew) Matt. 10:3:18; Luke 6:14; Acts 1:13.

Nicodemus a Pharisee, learned in the Law and a member of the Sanhedrin. He visited Jesus by night, and became a sympathizer, helping Joseph of Arimathea with his burial. See John 3:1–21, 7:50–2, 19:39.

Peter the most important of the disciples, originally named Simon but given by Jesus the surname Peter (the name by which he is best known). He was a fisherman, the brother of Andrew, and when called by Jesus was living in Capernaum with his wife and mother-in-law. He was often the spokesman among the disciples, and was devoted to Jesus, though he shamefully denied him during his trial. After the resurrection he was a key founder of the early Church in Jerusalem, and subsequently formed a partnership with St Paul. According to tradition, he became the first bishop of Antioch, and then went to Rome, where he was supposedly crucified upside-down during the reign of the emperor Nero (54–68 CE). There is a tradition that his recollections of Jesus lie behind the Gospel of Mark; that he was the author of the two Epistles of Peter is now generally regarded as unlikely. See Matt. 4:18, 10:2, 14:28–31, 16:16–19, 22–3, 17:1–4, 24–6, 19:27, 26:33–5, 37, 58, 69–75; Mark 1:16, 3:16, 8:29–33, 9:2–5, 10:28, 11:21, 14:29–31, 33, 37, 54, 66–72; Luke 5:3–11, 6:14, 8:45, 9:20, 28–33, 12:41, 18:28, 22:8, 31–4, 54–62, 24:12; John 1:40–2, 6:68, 13:6–9, 24, 36–8, 18:10–11, 15–18, 25–7, 20:2–6, 21:2–3, 7, 11, 15–21; Acts 1–5, 8–12.

Philip one of the disciples, a native of Bethsaida, a fishing town. He introduced his friend Nathanael to Jesus. See Matt. 10:3; Mark 3:18; Luke 6:14; John 1:43–8, 6:5–7, 12:21–2, 14:8–9; Acts 1:13.

Philip one of the sons of Herod the Great, ruler from 4 BCE to 33/4 CE of Iturea and the regions north-east and east of Galilee. He rebuilt the old city of Panaias (known as Caesarea Philippi in the NT), and renovated Bethsaida (which he renamed Julias). He married Salome, daughter of his mother-in-law Herodias (and was not the husband of Herodias, as is suggested in Matt. 14:3). See Luke 3:1; Josephus *War*, pp. 138–9; *Ant.*, 18:27–8, 106–8.

Pilate, Pontius the Roman governor (or 'prefect') of the province of Judea from 26 to 36 CE, by whom Jesus was crucified. His official residence was at the coastal town of Caesarea, but he came to Jerusalem at the Passover each year to keep order, and would have stayed at Herod's palace on the western wall, which is where the trial of Jesus probably took place. According to Josephus, Pilate was an insensitive and cruel ruler, who was eventually dismissed from office in 36/7 CE. See Matt. 27:2, 11–26; Mark 15:1–15; Luke 3:1, 23:1–25; John 18:28–19:22, 38; Josephus *War*, pp. 138–9; *Ant.*, 18:35, 55–63, 85–9.

Quirinius, Publius Sulpicius ('Cyrenius' in the Gospels), appointed Roman governor of Syria with authority over Judea in 6 CE. In 6/7 CE he conducted a local census in Judea (which was much resented by Jews, and led to a major rebellion). Luke's dating of the nativity by reference to this census under Quirinius is very hard to reconcile with the information in Matthew (2:1) that Jesus was born in the lifetime of Herod the Great, who died in 4 BCE. See Luke 2:2; Josephus *Ant.*, 18:1–2, 26.

Salome the daughter of Herodias by her first husband, became the wife of Philip the Tetrarch. She danced for her stepfather Herod Antipas, who was so pleased he said he would give her whatever she asked. On the instruction of Herodias she asked for the head of John the Baptist. Her name is not given in the Gospels account, but is recorded in Josephus. See Matt. 14:6–11; Mark 6:21–8; Josephus *Ant.*, 18:136–7.

Salome a woman who followed Jesus to Jerusalem and was present at the crucifixion, sometimes identified as the wife of Zebedee and the mother of James and John. See Mark 15:40–1, 16:1.

Simeon the aged Jew who took the baby Jesus in his arms at the Temple and spoke the words known as the 'Nunc Dimittis'. See Luke 2:25–35.

Simon the brother of Jesus, known only by the references to him in Matt. 13:55 and Mark 6:3.

Simon the Canaanite see *Simon the Zealot*

Simon a Pharisee see *Simon the leper*

Simon of Cyrene a passer-by who was compelled by the Romans to carry the cross-beam of the cross for Jesus on the way to the crucifixion. He was the father of Alexander and Rufus, who seem to have been prominent in the early Church. See Matt. 27:32; Mark 15:21; Luke 23:26.

Simon the leper entertained Jesus in his home in Bethany, and it was here that a woman anointed Jesus's head with precious oil. In Luke's version of the story Simon is a Pharisee, not a leper, and in John's account the woman is named as Mary, the sister of Martha and Lazarus. See Matt. 26:6–13; Mark 14:3–9; Luke 7:36–50; John 11:2, 12:1–8.

Simon the Zealot (or 'Zelotes'), one of the disciples, sometimes referred to as 'the Canaanite'. His surname may indicate that he was associated with a Jewish insurrectionary movement known as the Zealots. See Matt. 10:4; Mark 3:18; Luke 6:15; Acts 1:13.

Susanna a follower of Jesus who gave of her means to support him and the disciples. See Luke 8:3.

Thaddeus one of the disciples, also named Lebbaeus. He has been assumed to be identical with 'Judas the brother of James' (i.e. Jude, the brother of Jesus) in the lists of disciples in Luke and Acts. See Matt. 10:3; Mark 3:18; Luke 6:16; Acts 1:13.

Theophilus a friend of Luke, to whom the third Gospel is addressed (as is Acts). He was apparently a Roman of high social standing, who had become a Christian (his name means 'lover of God'). See Luke 1:3; Acts 1:1.

Thomas one of the disciples, who has become famous as 'doubting Thomas' because he would not believe in the resurrection unless he could touch the wounds of the risen Jesus. In John his name is given as 'Didymus' (or 'Twin'). He is supposed to have brought Christianity to India and been martyred there, and various apocryphal writings circulated under his name, including the gnostic 'Gospel of Thomas' and the 'Acts of Thomas'. See Matt. 10:3; Mark 3:18; Luke 6:15; John 11:16, 14:5, 20:24–9, 21:2; Acts 1:13.

Tiberius (Tiberius Claudius Nero Caesar) succeeded Augustus as emperor of Rome and ruled from 14 to 37 CE. He appointed Pontius Pilate as governor of Judea in 26 CE. Herod Antipas honoured Tiberius by giving the name Tiberias to the new capital he built between 17 and 20 CE, but he is remembered by Jews for expelling the Jewish community from Rome in 19 CE. He is the 'Caesar' referred to in the Gospels everywhere except in Luke 2:1. See Matt. 22:17; Mark 12:14; Luke 3:1, 20:22, 23:2; John 19:12, 15; Josephus *War*, pp. 138–9; *Ant.*, 18.

Zacchaeus a rich tax collector who, being 'little of stature', climbed a sycamore tree to see Jesus. He subsequently entertained Jesus at his house, and made restitution to those he had wronged. See Luke 19:1–8.

Zacharias a priest at the Temple, the husband of Elizabeth and father of John the Baptist. He celebrated the birth of the child to his aged wife and the coming redemption of Israel in the 'Benedictus'. See Luke 1:5–24, 57–80, 3:2.

Zebedee the husband of Salome and the father of the disciples James and John. See Matt. 4:21, 10:2, 26:37; Mark 1:19, 3:17, 10:35; Luke 5:10; John 21:2.

GLOSSARY OF PLACES

Note: the two main types of settlement in Palestine at the time of Jesus were the 'town' or 'city' (Greek *polis*) and the 'village' (*kome*). The main distinguishing feature was that a village was usually unwalled, while a town or city was walled.

Aenon a place 'near Salim' where John the Baptist carried out baptisms (see John 3:23). It is located about 5 miles south of a city known as Scythopolis at the time of Jesus, on the west bank of the Jordan.

Arimathea has been identified with Ramathaim-zophim (or Ramah) in Ephraim (1 Sam. 1:1) and with Rathamin (1 Maccabees (Apocrypha) 11:34) in north-west Judea. Its location remains uncertain.

Bethany a village about 2 miles south-east of Jerusalem, on the slopes of the Mount of Olives. It was where Martha, Mary, and Lazarus lived, and its Arabic name, Al-'Ayzariyyah, is derived from the name Lazarus.

Bethabara (given as 'Bethany' in many ancient manuscripts, but not to be confused with the other Bethany, near Jerusalem), the place 'beyond Jordan' where John the Baptist baptized (John 1:28), and so, perhaps, the scene of Christ's baptism. It is generally thought to have been on the east side of the Jordan, across from Jericho.

Bethlehem a town in Judea about 6 miles south of Jerusalem. It was the birthplace of King David, and it was believed that it would therefore also be the birthplace of the Messiah. In Matthew's Gospel (2:5–6) he refers to Micah's prophecy that out of Bethlehem would come one who would be a 'ruler in Israel' (Mic. 5:2), and he regards the birth of Jesus in Bethlehem as a fulfilment of this prophecy. Luke (2:4) also gives Bethlehem as the birthplace of Jesus. Christian tradition from as early as the second century CE identified a specific cave in Bethlehem as the place where Jesus was born, and in about 338 CE Helena, the mother of the emperor Constantine, had a church built over the site. It was rebuilt in the sixth century CE by the emperor Justinian, and parts of this structure still remain. The Church of the Nativity, as it is known, has always been a major site of pilgrimage, not only for Christians but for Muslims also, who revere Jesus as an important prophet.

Bethphage a village on the Mount of Olives near Bethany, on the east side of Jerusalem.

Bethsaida a small fishing-town on the north shore of the Sea of Galilee, and according to John's Gospel (1:44) the birthplace of the disciples Philip, Andrew, and Peter. It was largely rebuilt by Herod Philip the Tetrarch, who renamed it 'Julias' in honour of Livia Julia, the mother of the emperor Tiberius.

Calvary see *Golgotha*

Caesarea Philippi a major city (modern Banias) at the foot of Mount Hermon in the far north of Palestine, about 20 miles from the Sea of Galilee.

Cana a village about 9 miles north of Nazareth, in central Galilee.

Capernaum a town on the north-west shore of the Sea of Galilee, the site of which has been identified at Tell Hûm. It was an important centre of the ministry of Jesus. Five of the twelve disciples lived there (Simon Peter, Andrew, James, John, and Matthew), and excavations have uncovered what may be the house of Peter, and a synagogue dating from the fourth century CE, which stands on first-century foundations and may be on the site where Jesus preached.

Cedron see *Kidron*

Chorazin a town lying north of the Sea of Galilee, about 2.5 miles north of Capernaum.

Cyrene the capital of the Roman province of Cyrenaica (present-day Libya).

Dalmanutha see *Magdala*

Decapolis a federation of ten allied cities, all but one situated east of the Jordan in northern Palestine, including Damascus, Gadara, and Gerasa. The term refers both to the cities and to the region in which they were situated.

Emmaus a village said to be 'about threescore furlongs' (6 or 7 miles) from Jerusalem (Luke 24:13). The site is uncertain, particularly because a variant reading in some manuscripts of Luke has it as 160 furlongs from Jerusalem. Suggestions include Kuloniyeh to the west, Khamasah to the south-west, and Amwas, about 19 miles north-west.

Ephraim a town of uncertain location, said in John 11:54 to be 'in the region near the wilderness', which may mean east of the Jordan. It is possibly the Ephraim mentioned in 2 Sam. 13:23.

Gadara one of the cities of the Decapolis, situated about 6 miles from the Sea of Galilee. It was near here, according to the accounts in Mark (5:1) and Luke (8:26, 37), that the episode of the 'Gaderene swine' took place. (In Matt. 8:28 in the AV the location of this incident is given as near Gergasa (modern Kursi, on the east coast of the Sea of Galilee), following a variant reading in the manuscripts.)

Galilee in the time of Jesus a Roman province in northern Palestine extending from the Mediterranean to the Jordan. It was ruled for the Romans by Herod Antipas, the Tetrarch. Its position between Egypt and Syria made it an important trade route, and it had a mixed population of Jews and Gentiles.

Galilee, Sea of a large inland lake, about 12 miles long and 7 miles broad at its widest. At the time of Jesus it formed a natural boundary between Jewish Galilee on the west and the largely Gentile territories of the Decapolis and Gaulanitis on the east. It was an important natural resource, particularly for fishing. Although usually called the Sea of Galilee in the Gospels, it is also referred to as the Lake of Gennesaret, and the Lake of Tiberias.

Gennesaret a district on the north-western shore of the Sea of Galilee. (The Sea of Galilee was hence also sometimes called the Lake of Gennesaret.)

Gergasa see *Gadara*

Gethsemane a garden (or olive grove) somewhere on the side, or at the foot, of the Mount of Olives (see Luke 22:39). The Hebrew word means 'oil-presses'.

Golgotha an Aramaic word meaning 'Place of a Skull'. Also known as Calvary (from the Latin *calvaria*, meaning skull), it was the place of Jesus's crucifixion, just outside the walls of Jerusalem. Its location is uncertain, but the traditional site is marked by the ancient Church of the Holy Sepulchre in Jerusalem.

Gomorrah see *Sodom and Gomorrah*

Idumea known as Edom in the Hebrew Bible (see Gen. 32:3), the region to the south-east of Judea.

Jericho an important city about 8 miles north of the Dead Sea, near the Jordan. It was granted to Herod the Great by Augustus *c*.30 BCE, and he built splendid palaces there. Jesus passed through it on his final journey south to Jerusalem.

Jerusalem the religious and political capital of Judea, and the most important city in Palestine. Its population in the time of Jesus has been estimated at about 30,000. It had been massively reconstructed by Herod the Great, who built a theatre, amphitheatre, a fortress (named Antonia, in homage to Mark Antony), and a magnificent royal palace in the Upper City. Most importantly of all, in 20 BCE Herod began rebuilding the Temple on a lavish scale, many parts of the sanctuary being overlaid with gold and silver.

Judea the territory roughly equivalent to the ancient kingdom of Judah. In the time of Jesus it was the most southerly of the three provinces

(Galilee, Samaria, and Judea) into which Palestine, west of the Jordan, was divided. Following the deposition of Herod Archelaus in 6 CE, it became a sub-province of the Roman province of Syria, and was thereafter ruled by a succession of Roman prefects (of whom the fifth was Pontius Pilate).

Kidron (or Cedron), the valley or gorge on the east of Jerusalem, separating the city from the Mount of Olives. A seasonal brook (of the same name) runs through it, but the wadi (riverbed) is dry for many months of the year.

Magdala a town on the western shore of the Sea of Galilee (the precise location is unknown). Mark (8:10) gives the name as Dalmanutha, but nothing is known of such a place.

Nain a small town in central Galilee, about 6 miles south-east of Nazareth.

Nazareth where Jesus was brought up, a small town in Galilee on a hill overlooking the Plain of Esdraelon, about 15 miles south-west of the Sea of Galilee.

Olives, Mount of a hill just outside Jerusalem, separated from the city by the Kidron valley. It was spoken of in the Hebrew Bible as the place where the Messiah would appear (see Zech. 14:1–10).

Perea the name of the region north-east of Judea and south-east of Galilee. It is the place referred to in Mark 3:8 as 'beyond Jordan'.

Salim see *Aenon*

Samaria the name of a city and territory in the centre of Palestine, between Galilee and Judea. The city was the capital of the ancient kingdom of Israel (i.e. the Northern Kingdom, in contrast to Judah), but its inhabitants at some point around the fourth century BCE became a separate religious sect, with their own temple on Mount Gerizim.

Sodom and Gomorrah ancient cities, probably located somewhere along the southern shore of the Dead Sea, whose wickedness was said to have attracted divine wrath and led to their destruction by brimstone and fire from heaven (Gen. 18:20–19:29). They became proverbial for their sinfulness, and as examples of divine retribution (see e.g. Jer. 23:14; Ezek. 16:44–58; Amos 4:11; Matt. 10:15).

Sychar a village in Samaria, near the ancient Canaanite city of Shechem, the ruins of which lie at Tell al-Balatah, just east of modern Nablus in the West Bank.

Syria in the time of Jesus a Roman province north-west of Galilee, two of whose main centres were Damascus and Antioch.

Temple of Jerusalem the centre of Jewish religious worship and practice, the only place where sacrifices could be offered. The 'First Temple' was built by King Solomon, but was destroyed by the Babylonians *c.*587 BCE. It was rebuilt following the return of the Jews from exile in Babylon in 538 BCE, and this 'Second Temple' was subsequently lavishly refurbished by Herod the Great, starting in 20 BCE. It was destroyed by the Romans following the capture of Jerusalem in 70 CE, and was never rebuilt. The Western or 'Wailing' Wall still remains.

Tiberias, Lake of an alternative name for the Sea of Galilee, after the establishment by Herod Antipas in about 25 CE of the city of Tiberias on the western shore.

Tyre and Sidon cities on the Mediterranean coast, in the ancient land of Phoenicia (roughly equivalent to modern Lebanon), which was part of the Roman province of Syria. At a distance of about 40 miles from the Sea of Galilee, they were the furthest north that Jesus is said to have travelled. They were frequently denounced by the prophets for wickedness (see e.g. Joel 3:4), and Jesus also refers to them in apocalyptic terms (Matt. 11:21–2).

GLOSSARY OF WORDS AND TERMS

abide remain, stay, continue

accompt account

adjure solemnly charge

a-dying dying

aforehand beforehand

aforetime formerly

after following behind (Luke 23:26)

against to (Matt. 10:18)

a-hungered, an hungered hungry

allow approve of

aloes fragrant resin from the Aquilaria shrub

ambassage deputation to or from a sovereign

Amen 'may it be so', used as a response in the Hebrew Bible and carried over into Christian liturgy; used as a concluding formula, the equivalent of 'Finis'

amend recover

and if (Matt. 26:15)

anon at once, instantly

apostle (in Christian usage) a special emissary or representative of Christ (from Greek word meaning 'one sent')

athirst suffering from thirst

audience hearing

aught anything

avouch affirm, assert, avow

bag purse

baptism immersion in water as a sign of repentance

beam plank of wood

bestow store

bewray betray

brasen brazen (made of brass)

brethren brothers

brimstone sulphur

bushel vessel used as a bushel measure

by and by at once

call invite (John 2:2)

careful worried, full of care (Luke 10:41)

catch snatch (Matt. 13:19)

cattle sheep (Luke 17:7)

centurion the commander of a company of 100 infantry in the Roman army

changer *see* exchanger

charge exhort

charger large plate

closet small inner room in a house

clothes cloths (John 19:40)

coat tunic (long undergarment) (John 19:23)

coasts district, neighbourhood, region

commit entrust (John 2:24)

commune confer

comprehend overcome (John 1:5)

confess acknowledge

corrupt *v.* spoil, destroy; *adj.* bad, unwholesome, inedible

couch bed

covenant *n.* contract; *v.* agree

cubit unit of measurement (derived from the forearm) of 17.4 inches

cumber obstruct, take up space (Luke 13:7); trouble (Luke 10:40)

cup frequently used as a metaphor for 'that which God allots'

day-spring early dawn

dehort dissuade by exhortation

deny disown, break every link with

despitefully contemptuously, insolently, shamefully

disciple follower; one taught (as opposed to an apostle, who is 'sent')

discreetly wisely

divers a number of, various

doctor teacher

draught sewer, cesspool; catch (of fish)

dresser gardener, vine-dresser

dropsy medical condition marked by swelling caused by fluid retention

dung put manure on

durst darest

either or (Luke 15:8)

Elias Greek form of Elijah

Eliseus Greek form of Elisha

entreat treat

Esaias Greek form of Isaiah

espoused betrothed, contracted to be married

estate (short for) person of estate

exchanger banker, dealer in money

faint lose heart

fan a wooden shovel or fork, used for separating chaff from corn by throwing it into the air

fare feast

fat vat (Mark 12:1)

fatling young animal (such as a calf or lamb) fatted for slaughter (Matt. 22:4)

fear (often in sense of) awe, wonderment

firkin a (variable) measure of capacity, half a barrel

forasmuch as in consideration that

forsomuch forasmuch

frankincense aromatic gum resin used for burning as incense

fuller one who fulls cloth (cleansing and thickening it by beating and washing)

furlong an eighth of a mile (Roman *stadium*)

garment cloak

garner granary, storehouse for corn

garnished decorated, embellished, put in order

generation offspring (esp. in phrase 'generation of vipers')

Gentile Jewish designation for a non-Jew

gird tuck the lower edge of the outer robe into the belt to allow freedom of movement (hence the phrase 'gird up [one's] loins', i.e. prepare for strenuous exertion)

glorify (in theological sense) to advance the glory of God by faithful action or suffering

goodman male head of a household or other establishment

grave tomb

grave-clothes strips of cloth (John 11:44)

gross dull, stupid (Matt. 13:15)

hale drag, haul

hallowed blessed, honoured as holy

halt *adj.* lame, crippled

haply by chance, perhaps

hardly violently, forcibly

heart desire, inclination, centre of will (Matt. 6:21)

heavy weighed down with grief (Matt. 26:37)

hide mix

hire wages

hireling hired hand

his its (e.g. Matt. 5:13, 24:32, 26:52)

hither here

holden held

holpen helped

Hosanna 'Save us!'

howbeit however

husbandman farmer

hyssop shrub (used in Jewish purification rites)

impotent invalid, sick person

inherit receive, obtain

instant importunate, pressing (Luke 23:23)

instantly earnestly (Luke 7:4)

intreat entreat; treat

Jeremias Greek form of Jeremiah

jot smallest letter (in Greek the iota i)

lade load

latchet thong for fastening a sandal

learn study

leaven yeast, fermenting dough

lift lifted

light lamp (Matt. 6:22; Luke 11:34)

list wish, desire

lo look!, see!

lowering louring, dark and threatening

madness fury (Luke 6:11)

maimed lacking a limb

mammon wealth, possessions

manners conduct, behaviour (Luke 7, heading)

mansions rooms, dwelling-places

master teacher

meat food; fish (John 21:5)

meet suitable, proper

merchandise business

mete measure

members limbs, bodily organs

mids midst

millstone large stone for grinding corn in a mill

minister *n.* servant; *v.* serve, wait at table

misdeeming suspicious, misjudging

mite coin of the lowest value

moe more

mote speck, particle of dust

moved stirred, in turmoil (Matt. 21:10)

murmer grumble, complain; mutter (John 7:32)

myrrh aromatic gum resin used in perfumery and as an ingredient in incense

nation people (not nation-state)

Noe Noah

noised rumoured, reported, spread abroad

occupy trade with, invest

offend cause to stumble morally

ordain appoint

ought aught, anything; owed

over all through (Matt. 10:23)

overcharge overfill

palsy paralysis

paps breasts

penny, pence denarius, denarii

porter gatekeeper

presently immediately, without delay

press crowding

prevent speak before, anticipate (Matt. 17:25)

privily secretly

prove try out, test

proverb mysterious saying, parable (John 16:25)

publican tax collector

publish proclaim

purge prune (John 15:2)

purifying ceremonial washing

quicken give life to

raiment clothing

ravening greed

record witness, testimony

reckon settle accounts with

remit, remission forgive, forgiveness

resemble compare

room seat; place

salute, salutation greet, greeting

sanctify make holy

savour *v.* relish, like, care for; *n.* taste

scourge *v.* flog with a whip of cords; *n.* whip

scrip small bag or wallet, especially as carried by a pilgrim, shepherd, or beggar

season time

seed offspring, children

set seated

shewbread the twelve loaves that were placed by the altar of incense in the Temple, and which were eaten only by the priests

show tell, declare

single honest, sincere, free from deceit

sop morsel of bread

sorrow pain (John 16:20–3)

sore greatly, to a grievous extent

spikenard (or nard) a fragrant ointment made from a north Indian plant

spoil plunder

stall manger (Luke 13:15)

stanch stop, staunch

stave staff, club

stay restrain (Luke 4:42)

strait narrow

straitly strictly

strawed strewn, scattered

stricken advanced (esp. in years)

strove disputed (John 6:52)

stuff belongings, household goods

subtlety treachery

suffer allow, permit; bear with

sunder pieces

sup eat

surfeiting over-eating, gluttony

sycamine mulberry

synagogue Jewish place of worship and prayer

tare tore (Mark 9:20)

tarry wait, stay

tempt test

testament covenant

testify declare solemnly (John 13:21)

thereabout about it (Luke 24:4)

throng v. crush

through into (Luke 12:39)

tidings news

tithe tenth part

tittle the mark or dot over the letter i

token sign

touching concerning

travail labour pains, birth-pangs

treasury the thirteen bronze chests in the Court of the Women where Temple offerings were placed

trespasses transgressions, sins, faults

tribulation persecution (a term frequently found in apocalyptic writing)

trim put (a lamp) in order for burning

trode trod, trampled

trow believe

unpossible impossible

unprofitable unworthy

unwashen unwashed

usury interest

verily truly

vessel container (usually for liquid)

virtue healing power

wallow roll about on the ground

want lack, run out of (John 2:3)

ware aware; v. wore

watch remain awake, keep vigil

wax grow, become

wellbeloved dearly loved one

whereunto to what

whether which

whiles whilst

whit bit, least portion or amount

white bleach, whiten; ripe (John 4:35)

wise way (esp. as 'in no wise')

wist knew

withered wasted, paralysed (John 5:3)

wrought worked

yoke pair (Luke 14:19)

Bhagavad Gita

The Bible Authorized King James Version
With Apocrypha

Dhammapada

Dharmasūtras

The Koran

The Pañcatantra

**The Sauptikaparvan (from the
Mahabharata)**

**The Tale of Sinuhe and Other Ancient
Egyptian Poems**

The Qur'an

Upaniṣads

ANSELM OF CANTERBURY   **The Major Works**

THOMAS AQUINAS   **Selected Philosophical Writings**

AUGUSTINE   **The Confessions
On Christian Teaching**

BEDE   **The Ecclesiastical History**

HEMACANDRA   **The Lives of the Jain Elders**

KĀLIDĀSA   **The Recognition of Śakuntalā**

MANJHAN   **Madhumalati**

ŚĀNTIDEVA   **The Bodhicaryàvatàra**

	Travel Writing 1700–1830
	Women's Writing 1778–1838
WILLIAM BECKFORD	**Vathek**
JAMES BOSWELL	**Life of Johnson**
FRANCES BURNEY	**Camilla**
	Cecilia
	Evelina
	The Wanderer
LORD CHESTERFIELD	**Lord Chesterfield's Letters**
JOHN CLELAND	**Memoirs of a Woman of Pleasure**
DANIEL DEFOE	**A Journal of the Plague Year**
	Moll Flanders
	Robinson Crusoe
	Roxana
HENRY FIELDING	**Jonathan Wild**
	Joseph Andrews and **Shamela**
	Tom Jones
WILLIAM GODWIN	**Caleb Williams**
OLIVER GOLDSMITH	**The Vicar of Wakefield**
MARY HAYS	**Memoirs of Emma Courtney**
ELIZABETH INCHBALD	**A Simple Story**
SAMUEL JOHNSON	**The History of Rasselas**
	The Major Works
CHARLOTTE LENNOX	**The Female Quixote**
MATTHEW LEWIS	**Journal of a West India Proprietor**
	The Monk
HENRY MACKENZIE	**The Man of Feeling**

The Oxford World's Classics Website

www.oup.com/uk/worldsclassics

- Information about new titles
- Explore the full range of Oxford World's Classics
- Links to other literary sites and the main OUP webpage
- Imaginative competitions, with bookish prizes
- Articles by editors
- Extracts from Introductions
- Special information for teachers and lecturers

www.oup.com/uk/worldsclassics

American Literature

Authors in Context

British and Irish Literature

Children's Literature

Classics and Ancient Literature

Colonial Literature

Eastern Literature

European Literature

History

Medieval Literature

Oxford English Drama

Poetry

Philosophy

Politics

Religion

The Oxford Shakespeare

A complete list of Oxford World's Classics, including Authors in Context, Oxford English Drama, and the Oxford Shakespeare, is available in the UK from the Marketing Services Department, Oxford University Press, Great Clarendon Street, Oxford OX2 6DP, or visit the website at www.oup.com/uk/worldsclassics.

In the USA, visit www.oup.com/us/owc for a complete title list.

Oxford World's Classics are available from all good bookshops. In case of difficulty, customers in the UK should contact Oxford University Press Bookshop, 116 High Street, Oxford OX1 4BR.